FORGOTTEN VOICES
DESERT VICTORY

IN ASSOCIATION WITH THE
IMPERIAL WAR MUSEUM

JULIAN THOMPSON

EBURY
PRESS

D1574967

1 3 5 7 9 10 8 6 4 2

Published in 2011 by Ebury Press, an imprint of Ebury Publishing
A Random House Group Company

The Random House Group Limited supports The Forest Stewardship Council
(FSC), the leading international forest certification organisation. All our titles that
are printed on Greenpeace approved FSC certified paper carry the FSC logo. Our
paper procurement policy can be found at www.rbooks.co.uk/environment

Mixed Sources
Product group from well-managed
forests and other controlled sources
www.fsc.org Cert no. TT-COC-2139
© 1996 Forest Stewardship Council

FSC

Printed and bound in Great Britain by Clays Ltd, St Ives PLC

ISBN 9780091938574 (Hardback)
9780091940980 (Trade Paperback)

To buy books by your favourite authors and register for offers visit
http://www.rbooks.co.uk

Contents

Acknowledgements

The indispensable ingredient of this book is the oral testimony of those who took part in the campaigns that eventually led to Allied victory in the Desert. The recording of the accounts by the witnesses was the work of the Sound Archive of the Imperial War Museum. Thanks to the meticulous attention to detail of the staff of the Archive, the narratives are accessible and there for all time. Over many years in my writing career I have had occasion to be grateful to Margaret Brooks, the Keeper of the Sound Archive. Once again her department has supported and advised me in my work. She leaves the Imperial War Museum before this book is published, and I thank her for all that her department has done to help me in my work. I am also grateful to Terry Charman, Elizabeth Bowers, Peter Taylor and Madeleine James. Richard McDonough of the Sound Archive has been especially helpful in guiding my research.

I must also thank the Photographic Archive at the Imperial War Museum, especially Hilary Roberts and David Parry, for their assistance and advice. Barbara Levy, the Imperial War Museum's literary agent, was instrumental in suggesting that this book be written. Jane Gregory, my own agent, has encouraged me in my literary efforts for over quarter of a century, and I am grateful to her for her advice and support.

Liz Marvin and Charlotte Cole, my editors at Ebury, have both patiently and good-humouredly kept me on track; to them both many thanks. The maps are the expert work of Peter Wilkinson.

Jane Thompson has been my abiding supporter and confidante; to her my love and gratitude.

Julian Thompson, December 2010

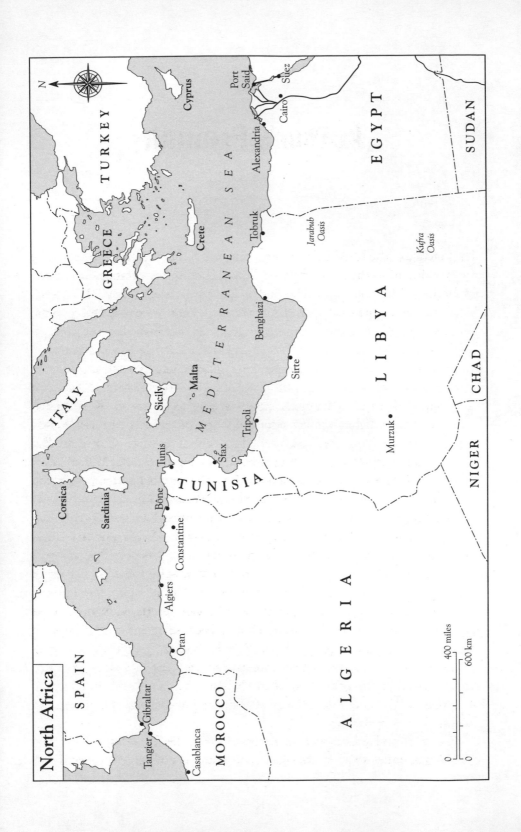

North Africa

SPAIN

MOROCCO

ALGERIA

TUNISIA

ITALY

GREECE

TURKEY

Cyprus

Crete

LIBYA

EGYPT

SUDAN

CHAD

NIGER

MEDITERRANEAN SEA

Corsica

Sardinia

Sicily

Malta

Tangier
Gibraltar
Casablanca
Oran
Algiers
Constantine
Bône
Tunis
Sfax
Tripoli
Sirte
Benghazi
Tobruk
Alexandria
Cairo
Port
Said
Suez

Jarabub
Oasis

Kufra
Oasis

Murzuk

N

400 miles
600 km

0
0

Author's Preface

The defence of the Middle East against the Axis powers of Italy and Germany was, for Britain in the Second World War, second in importance only to the protection of the homeland. The Middle East was strategically vital as a staging post to India, the Far East and Australia and, later, as an alternative to the Barents Sea route to Russia. The Suez Canal was an invaluable waterway on the India and Far East routes, though access through the Mediterranean to the canal was, for protracted periods, prevented by enemy action, and at times convoys had to be routed round the Cape of Good Hope in South Africa. Far outweighing these considerations, however, was access to oil. Without oil, Britain could not fight. Britain's principal source of fuel to power its aircraft, ships and vehicles lay at the head of the Persian Gulf in what is now Iran. But there was an alternative way to the oilfields and India – via the North Africa deserts. This was the route by which the Axis powers would attempt to reach the great prize of the oilfields at the head of the Persian Gulf. The British held the key access point of the route, Egypt. The British had to stop the Axis forces from gaining ground in North Africa, and taking Egypt, and thus Suez.

Initially the threat came from a large Italian army based in the country's colony, Libya, and later from German divisions sent there by Hitler in February 1941 to assist his ally. For over two and a half years, the fighting ebbed and flowed across the Egyptian and Libyan deserts, known by those who fought there as the Western Desert, because it lay to the west of the great British base in Egypt. As the British efforts to push the Axis forces out of Egypt for the last time gained momentum, British and American troops landed at the other end of the North African littoral, in Morocco and Algeria. The two Allied forces, one advancing east and the other west, eventually met in Tunisia.

The Western Desert covers more than 1,000 miles from east to west, and extends 800 miles south at its widest point, and is only sparsely populated.

Some tracks cross the desert at a few points, but the only road capable of taking heavy wheeled trucks ran along the coast, with an occasional parallel track a few miles inland. Both sides in the Western Desert campaign relied on the main road, and feeder tracks, for every item of supply, including water. Although tracked vehicles, and some wheeled vehicles, could roam at will over the empty spaces rather like fleets at sea, any force needing large quantities of ammunition, fuel, water and food was tied by the umbilical cord of logistics to the road. This was why almost all the fighting took place within sixty miles from the coast. The Germans and the British took advantage of the open flank offered by the desert inland to outflank their opponents. Both sides found that as they advanced, their line of communication became stretched, making supply difficult. Conversely, as they retreated, supply became easier. The terrain in much of the northern part of the Western Desert, except for the salty dunes on the coast, consists of a plateau mostly covered by a gravel plain, over which vehicles can drive quite fast. Access to the plateau from the coast is guarded by a five hundred-foot escarpment which, except in a few places, cannot be climbed by vehicles, even tanks; hence the tactical importance of the passes, such as the Halfaya, or 'Hellfire', Pass. A railway ran along the Egyptian coast from Alexandria to Mersa Matruh, about 150 miles west, and later a light railway extension was constructed as far as Sallum, a further 135 miles west, near the Libyan border.

South of the plateau, the massive dunes of the Egyptian, Libyan, Rabiana and Murzuq Sand Seas extend down to Sudan, and what was then French Equatorial Africa and French West Africa. These sand seas are impassable to all but a handful of desert experts. A few oases, hundreds of miles apart, provide the only splash of green amid the dust and glare. The oases, however, were too far inland to be of much value to anyone other than special forces who used them as bases.

In summer the Western Desert is blazing hot during the day, but surprisingly cool at night away from the coast. There is very little rain, but sudden stinging sandstorms can blot out visibility and bring all activity to a stop for hours. Winter can be cold enough for soldiers to need greatcoats, scarves and jerseys.

The terrain in Algeria and Tunisia, where the Allied campaigns were fought after landing at various points on the western end of the North African littoral, is mostly mountainous desert, which is very different in texture to the Western Desert. But, just as in the Western Desert, the Allied advance was made with one flank against the sea. The single main west–east road ran parallel to the coast, about fifty miles inland, with feeder roads to the main ports. This coast road was unusable by heavy military vehicles. The Allies in Algeria and Tunisia had the use of a railway system as a backup to the road for logistic supply, but this was in a poor state of repair, and required frequent changes of gauge along its length. Both the main road and railway climbed from sea level at Algiers to over four thousand feet. There were more centres of population in this part of North Africa than in the Western Desert. Many of the valleys were heavily cultivated, with abundant scrub and cork forest in northern Tunisia. Algeria and Tunisia are hot in the summer, but in winter have a far higher rainfall than the Western Desert; flash floods and mud added to the discomforts of campaigning.

Throughout the war in the Western Desert the Italians outnumbered the Germans, but the reverse was true in Algeria and Tunisia. The Italians generally get a 'bad press' for their fighting qualities, or rather lack of them, but like many soldiers of whatever nationality, they fought well when properly led. On the whole the Italian troops were let down by their senior officers. The Germans were uniformly formidable throughout; with highly professional leaders at all levels, well trained to seize the initiative.

The British troops based in Egypt at the outbreak of war were, in the main, well-trained regulars. They were soon joined by the hardy, and enthusiastic, all-volunteer Australian and New Zealand Divisions. The 4th Indian Division, a first class, all-volunteer formation was added to the order of battle early in the campaign. The British and Commonwealth equipment was generally better than the Italian equivalent, but German armour and anti-tank guns were superior until about mid-1942. As the campaign progressed, other divisions arrived. Some like the 50th, a Territorial division, had fought in France in 1940; others like the 44th needed a great deal of training before they were ready to face the German army.

Introduction
by John Simpson

Most of us get our ideas of the deserts of North Africa from a few grainy photographs, from black-and-white war films mostly filmed in studios rather than on location, and from our imaginations. Deserts, we feel, are vast featureless stretches of open sand, piled up in drifts and dunes.

The Western and Libyan Deserts, where most of the fighting described in this compelling book took place, are not necessarily like that at all. There are indeed great areas of open, drifting sand; but there are also immense rocky defiles and low mountain ranges, harsh and surprisingly colourful, sometimes covered with the toughest plant-life on earth, low, grey-blue tufts of desert bush.

Only the summer heat matches our expectation. Once, in the Libyan Desert, my thermometer registered a temperature of 61 degrees centigrade: 136 degrees Fahrenheit. By nine o'clock that night it had fallen to nine centigrade, 48 Fahrenheit. Merely to exist in a climate like this, let alone fight, work or even think efficiently, is extraordinarily difficult. The North African desert wasn't just, in the familiar phrase, a quartermaster's nightmare; it could also be a nightmare for every individual officer, NCO and private soldier who fought there.

And yet, in this excellently researched book, another view of the desert occasionally drifts through: the sheer grandeur of the landscape, the freedom it offered from army regulation, the opportunity for individual enterprise of the most stimulating kind. In what other theatre of the Second World War could adventurous and significant experiments like David Stirling's Special Air Service and Ralph Bagnold's Long Range Desert Group have thrived, or the smaller and more eccentric units like Popski's Private Army been permitted?

The desert represented a liberation of tactics and thought, of the kind T. E. Lawrence had developed a quarter of a century earlier. And, as with

Lawrence and his men, the grandeur and loneliness of the desert, and the closeness of death by heat and deprivation as well as by bullets and shells, sometimes built up a sense of existential fear and wonder. A man who fought both at Tobruk and Alamein once told me, 'I have never dreamed such dreams, or thought such thoughts as when I lay out under the stars there, night after night.'

From 1940 to 1943 the course of the Western Desert campaign fluctuated remarkably. At first, in the late summer of 1940, Italian forces based in Libya attacked the British and Commonwealth forces based in Egypt, which was notionally neutral. Once in Egyptian territory the Italian advance came to a halt, and three months later, in December 1940, the British staged a counter-attack which resulted in serious defeat for the Italians. Alarmed by the possibility that Italy might start to collapse altogether, Hitler sent German ground and air detachments to North Africa to stiffen the Axis resistance in early 1941.

On two major occasions during the next eighteen months the German-led forces pushed the British right back into Egypt. Yet both times the Axis supply-lines were so far extended that they could not continue. The British and their allies – Australians, New Zealanders, South Africans, Indians, Poles, Free French – staged powerful counter-attacks which hurled the Axis troops back into Libya. On 27 November 1941, when the 240-day siege of Tobruk was broken, it was the first time in the Second World War that German armour and superior tactics had effectively been stopped in their tracks.

But the story wasn't over. The British had to thin out their forces to meet attacks elsewhere in the Mediterranean and the world. In June 1942 General Rommel, in command of the Afrika Korps, defeated the Allies at Gazala, captured Tobruk at the second attempt, and drove his enemies back into Egypt once again. General Auchinleck, C-in-C Middle East Command, took personal charge of Eighth Army, and only managed to stop Rommel little more than sixty miles west of Alexandria. Allied civilians, as well as Egyptians, blocked the road to Cairo in their panic. There was a run on the banks, and the British embassy in Cairo burned its sensitive documents. Despite his success Auchinleck was sacked, and Alexander took his place. Montgomery took over Eighth Army.

The tide had already turned against Rommel. Montgomery was able to build up his strength until it far exceeded that of the Axis forces, and his victory at Alam el-Halfa in August 1942 was followed by a comprehensive defeat of the Axis forces at el-Alamein three months later. It was the start of an advance which took the Allies into Tunis by February 1943 and brought a complete German and Italian surrender in North Africa three months later.

This was Britain's first significant success on land against the Germans since the comprehensive defeat of its forces in France in 1940. It enabled Churchill to look both Roosevelt and Stalin in the eye at their future meetings, even though Stalin felt able to dismiss el-Alamein as small beer compared with the immense tank battle of Kursk. Max Hastings has asserted that, as compared with the First World War, British troops almost invariably came off worse when they fought the Germans on a basis of equality. On page 280 of this book Major Bill Miskin agrees: 'The Germans as soldiers were much better than we were.' It took very careful planning to beat them.

This is a beautiful and valuable book, built up with immense skill from the words of dozens upon dozens of survivors, by a man who is himself a soldier of outstanding ability, who understands military success. In the Falklands War Julian Thompson commanded 3 Commando Brigade, which yomped from San Carlos Water to capture Port Stanley: as complete and sharp a victory, on its far smaller scale, as Alam el-Halfa and Alamein.

Reading this book reminded me of nothing so much as a beautifully crafted, first-class radio documentary. Its minimal commentary allows the people who were there to tell the story in their own words. Such documentaries remain in the mind for years afterwards. This book will do the same.

John Simpson
February 2011

Forgotten Victory

How green we were. There was no fear, exhilaration – at last we were going into action – we were going to show these Italians what was what. The South Notts Hussars were coming.

From late 1939 onwards, the British Commander-in-Chief Middle East, the brilliant and perceptive General Sir Archibald Wavell, had been making preparations to fight the Italians whose army of over 250,000 was stationed in Libya. Wavell was responsible for more than just Egypt: his command included Sudan, Palestine, Jordan, British Somaliland, Aden, Iraq and the shores of the Persian Gulf. His resources to defend this vast area were slim. His scheme for defending Egypt included ordering Lieutenant General Sir Henry Maitland Wilson, Commanding British Troops in Egypt, to make plans to invade Libya, on the basis that attack is the best form of defence. By April 1940, Wilson had formed at Mersa Matruh what became known as Western Desert Force consisting of all that Wavell could spare: the understrength 7th Armoured Division, two regiments of artillery and some motorised patrols. Lieutenant General Richard O'Connor, a bold and unorthodox soldier, commanded the force.

On 10 June 1940, with the defeat of France imminent, Italy declared war on the United Kingdom. O'Connor's immediate reaction was to cross into Libya and harass the Italians. This included the temporary capture of Forts Capuzzo and Maddelena, and seizing the chief engineer of the Italian army from a convoy of vehicles deep inside Libya. For several weeks skirmishes with the Italians established the tactical superiority of Western Desert Force, as well as providing an opportunity for valuable reconnaissance and practice for future operations. The newly formed Long Range Desert Group also carried out missions into Libya.

Finally, on 13 September, and only after being prodded by Mussolini, Marshal Rodolfo Graziani, Commander-in-Chief Libya, invaded Egypt with four divisions of the Tenth Italian Army, accompanied by a large logistic tail, including a mobile brothel. After a leisurely advance, he halted sixty miles inside Egypt at Sidi Barrani, some eighty miles from Mersa Matruh. Here he had a large monument erected to mark his magnificent achievement.

Except for aggressive patrolling by the British, all went quiet until December. By now O'Connor's force had been strengthened by the addition of the 4th Indian Division, and 7th Royal Tank Regiment (Matilda tanks), with a brigade of the 4th New Zealand Division and the 6th Australian Division in reserve. The Italian Tenth Army occupied a line of camps between Maktila on the coast to Sofafi fifty miles inland. Behind these lay the main Italian force at Sidi Barrani and back to the Libyan frontier; in all, some ten divisions with tanks. The Italian artillery outnumbered the British by two to one; air force comparisons were similar.

Wavell told O'Connor to mount a five-day raid on the Italians. In fact, it was the start of the campaign in the desert.

Captain Brian Wyldbore-Smith
Adjutant, 4th Royal Horse Artillery, 7th Armoured Division
We did a lot of exercises in the desert with the units being mechanised. The 7th Armoured Division was under command of Major General Hobart. When we were training for movement across the desert, particularly in soft sand, I used to go to Siwa oasis in trucks, and once found some Italians there from Libya. They seemed to be nice chaps. We weren't at war, but obviously they were out of bounds.

Major Ralph Bagnold
Staff Officer, GHQ British Army in Cairo
[Some years before,] I met an Italian party in the desert that had travelled from Kufra. We found them in Sudan, where they should not have been. They were very matey, gave us a wonderful dinner with lots of wine. I reported to the Foreign Office, and they were not concerned. I thought a lot of one Italian officer called Lorenzini; like me, he liked the desert.

When the war broke out my feelings were, 'Oh dear here we go again.' Having left the army, I was recalled as a reservist, and found myself in Egypt. Because of a collision at sea, the ship taking me to East Africa limped into Port Said for repairs, and I took the opportunity of taking a train to Cairo to look up old friends. I was met by Colonel Miller, who said, 'Wavell wants to see you.'

So I went to see him; a short stocky man with one eye. He had a very strong personality. He asked me where I was going, and when I told him, East Africa, he asked if I would rather be in Egypt. I said, 'Yes.'

He said he would fix it.

Private John Stokes
2nd Battalion, The Queen's Royal Regiment
I got married during embarkation leave. Being married affected my outlook on the war. After leave we sailed for the Middle East. It was very emotional, leaving my new wife and my family. We had no briefing about what we were to face. The worst aspect of overseas service was lack of contact with family and home.

Lieutenant General Richard O'Connor
Commander, Western Desert Force
I was military governor of Jerusalem, and never expected to move from there. I suddenly got instructions to report to General Wilson, commanding in Cairo. He said, 'I want you to go down and command the Western Desert Force – a force we are just preparing.'

I asked him a few questions about it and he said, 'War will probably be declared within the next two or three days, so I want you to go down this afternoon and get on with it.' And so I did. I went and found a completely untried staff. We all had to get to know each other and to understand the making of a corps headquarters immediately. The next morning, war was declared.

Private Mario Cassandro
35th Anti-Aircraft Battery, Italian Tenth Army
I heard about the outbreak of war when tied to a pole in the desert on the Tunisian frontier with Tripolitania. I had done something that didn't please the sergeant in charge of my unit. I saw a lot of traffic going up and down the road nearby, asked what it was, and was told that Italy was in the war against France and England. I didn't know why. I was surprised, but felt there was more reason to fight the French than the English. In September I was taken from the Tunisian frontier to Cyrenaica; I was told we were to invade Egypt. Morale was not very high among the few people that I worked

Lieutenant General Richard O'Connor (left), Commander Western Desert Force with General Sir Archibald Wavell, Commander-in-Chief Middle East, before the attack on Bardia.

with and knew. I had a very jovial officer, but not a great leader; he was not very inspiring.

Lieutenant Paolo Colacicchi
Platoon Commander, Machine Gun Battalion, Italian Tenth Army
I was surprised and despondent when I heard about the outbreak of war. I was commanding a platoon in a machine-gun battalion on the Tunisian border, and I was told to call my men and tell them that we were at war with France and Britain; this was a few days before France gave up. The main reaction among the men was 'What about our mail? Aren't we going to hear from home any more?' Which is symptomatic of the type of man we had there. These were not all young, a few were, but they were tired and wanted to go home; they were thinking of their fields left unattended. They had no aggressive feelings. We had all been told that supplies and weapons would be produced in the event of war. In fact, they were never produced; they didn't exist. We realised that the British Army we were facing in Egypt, even though considerably smaller than ours, was better trained and better equipped especially in transport, tanks and armoured cars.

The armour on our tanks was paper-thin. The heaviest tank we had at the beginning was the M11, which had a 47-mm gun in the turret, but it could not swing all the way round, it had about a ninety-degree arc. This meant that five Italian tanks confronted by ten enemy tanks could not fire as they retreated. Our anti-tank guns were very poor. The rifle was the 1891 model, and our machine guns were smaller versions of the British Bren. If you didn't oil them they didn't work and if you did oil them, the sand jammed them.

Our supply system was chaotic. Our rations were enormous biscuits, so hard you had to bang them on the side of a lorry to break them, and Italian bully beef, which we didn't think was as good as the British bully beef. The officers ate well; the difference between our food and the men was too marked.

There were brothels in Libya, and the women could not buy food in the market, so they were taken on the strength of units. So you would find yourself with six NCOs, fifty men and twelve prostitutes. They gradually left.

Bombardier Stephen Dawson
339 Battery, 104th (Essex Yeomanry) Field Regiment,
Royal Horse Artillery
We were told about the fall of France while at Nablus in Palestine. Our CO made a speech saying that the French had lost, and our 'own dear island is in

danger, who knows what the future will be'. We wondered what was going to happen. He should not have talked like that. It upset us. We left the parade feeling that we might end up wandering the world like the Foreign Legion, with nowhere to go.

Captain Charles Laborde
426 Battery, 107th (South Notts Hussars) Field Regiment,
Royal Horse Artillery
Suddenly we got seven days' notice that we were moving. Then, of course, things began to happen. First of all the horses were to go, which was very sad, and the day before the colonel had organised a so-called 'hunt'. There were no hounds and no quarry but all the officers went out and we had a tremendous gallop about. Then, of course, the equipment started to arrive. The poor 104th, the Essex Yeomanry and the Lancashire 106th – they were completely denuded of everything. Suddenly we were absolutely smothered with equipment. It was a fairly hectic seven days.

Gunner Ray Ellis
425 Battery, 107th (South Notts Hussars) Field Regiment,
Royal Horse Artillery
We knew we were going into action and we got some chalk and wrote on the side of the train taking us to Egypt, 'Mussolini, here we come!' How green we were. There was no fear, exhilaration – at last we were going into action – we were going to show these Italians what was what. The South Notts Hussars were coming.

Major Ralph Bagnold
Staff Officer, GHQ British Army in Cairo
When the 'hot' war broke out in 1940, the Italians declared war, and France collapsed, I took my courage in both hands and sent a note to Wavell. Within half an hour I was sent for and Wavell was alone. He sat me in an armchair and said, 'Tell me about this.'

So I told him that we ought to have a mobile ground scouting force to penetrate the desert to the west of Egypt to see what the Italians were up to. He said, 'If you find that the Italians are doing nothing, what then?'

Without thinking, I replied, 'How about some piracy on the high desert?'

His rather stern face broke into a broad grin, and he said, 'Can you be ready in six weeks?'

'Yes, provided…'

'Yes', he replied, ' I know there will be opposition.'

He rang his bell. A lieutenant general came in, the chief of staff [Arthur Smith]. Wavell said, 'Arthur, Bagnold seeks a talisman. Get this typed out and I will sign it straight away.'

It read, 'I wish that any request made by Major Bagnold in person shall be met instantly and without question.'

It was typed and Wavell signed it. I had in mind a reconnaissance force. With the expertise I had, I could take a self-contained force across the desert for thousands of miles.

Sergeant Armourer/Air Gunner/Navigator Ian Blair
113 Squadron, RAF

I didn't know which aircraft I was to fly in, but knew I would be flying. We were told the squadron would be briefed at 0600 hours for an 0800 hours take-off to attack El Adem, an Italian airfield. I normally flew as an air gunner with Flight Sergeant Tommy Knott. When I looked on the battle order, I saw I wasn't flying with my skipper: all the crews had been mixed up. I said to Tommy, 'We have been flying as a crew for nearly three years, and now when they need us they are breaking us up.' Tommy Knott complained, and all the crews reverted to normal. I was to fly as an air gunner, although I was also a navigator. We had to bomb up the aircraft and fuel them. The intelligence officer got up and said we could expect opposition from the Italians with their biplane fighter, not dissimilar to the Gladiator, he said they are armed with .5-cal guns. He said the metal on the back of the Blenheim will deflect the shot – we believed him. We were green as cabbages.

I wore blue overalls and a scarf; if was hot, the aircraft was like an oven. When you got airborne you froze in your own sweat. Off we went, it was a lovely day. I felt a bit twitchy, with gut ache, not uncommon. I felt confident in my own ability to shoot. I was in the turret, which was a Bristol turret, hydraulic with a single gun. The gunner sits on a little seat and has handlebars about eight inches wide with the triggers underneath. You twisted the handlebars to rotate the turret, or move the gun up or down.

We climbed, set course, it was cloudless, and I was constantly looking upwards; I wore dark glasses. The sun was the obvious direction from which attacks would come. We didn't have any fighter cover. We got over the border, and with the turret abeam you could look out and see the other aircraft. We were number eight. I kept looking for hostile aircraft. We got down low, rushed across the perimeter of the airfield, and I gave some Italian soldiers standing on the airfield a quick burst. Next to them was a long line of Breda 65 aircraft, and I fired down the line of them. I don't know if I hit anything. We dropped two bombs, and then turned and made a second pass. I changed the magazine and then we saw the fighters. The guy behind us was hit by small-arms fire from the ground and had to make a forced landing and was taken POW. We were so low we were creating dust storms.

The enemy fighter, a CR.42, came in and attacked another of our chaps. I opened fire on him and he peeled off, and I thought 'this air fighting is a piece of piss'. Then another came and attacked us, he knew what he was doing, he closed right in. He was about thirty yards away, and in our blind spot, we were pursued at low level and we really had to sweat. I said to the skipper 'turn port'. The Italian was firing, but his deflection was not all that good, and as I was about to fire, he broke off. We flew back on the deck. The Italian fighters had no endurance, so couldn't stay with us.

When we got back I looked at the wing and we had no hits. But the skipper said, 'If that's our fighting, we've had it.' We thought we were doomed. The Blenheim was a beautiful aircraft but not fast enough. It wasn't any good against opposition, even the Italians, let alone the Germans.

Private Robert Hawksworth
Bandsman and Stretcher-Bearer, 1st Battalion, Durham Light Infantry
We were moved up to Mersa Matruh in July 1940, an Egyptian barracks near the sea, and we were soon attended to by the Italian air force from a great height. They dropped a lot. On the second or third day there we had been posted out to companies as stretcher-bearers, two per company, and I was kept in the RAP as an assistant to the MO. I went into the barracks on an errand, the hand-worked klaxon started to sound, and in no time bombs started to drop. The Italians were flying high, so how the hell they found us I don't know. We didn't seem to have much ack-ack protection. We were bothered about twice a day by the Italians, and only essential people were allowed in the barrack buildings.

But our worst enemy at the time was the desert sore. If you cut yourself, septicaemia set in and it was difficult to treat, until a new drug arrived: M&B tablets. Our MO invented a way of treating the wounds with ground-up M&B tablets and Vaseline and soldiers were told to keep the bandage on for as long as possible. From then on we made our own ointment for desert sores.

Bombardier Stephen Dawson.

When a soldier became injured on the battlefield immediate action would be taken by the stretcher-bearer, if available. The wounded man would be evacuated in an ambulance to RAP. The RMO would carry out minor surgical repairs to allow the casualty to be evacuated further back to a Casualty Clearing Station and thence to a field hospital. From there he would be taken to a military hospital. The most immediate danger is shock, which sets in as soon as a man is wounded, and arterial bleeding must be stopped. The first thing is to get him breathing again, and then stop the bleeding. Then treat him for shock. Give him tea to drink and give him a cigarette, I've never seen so many non-smokers start smoking. The onset of fright is usual, so reassurance is necessary.

Gunner Ray Ellis
425 Battery, 107th (South Notts Hussars) Field Regiment, Royal Horse Artillery

I heard a screaming sound and the next thing there was this vicious explosion and I hurled myself to the ground. It was a stick of bombs falling but I didn't know it at the time. I hadn't heard any aircraft and there had been no air-raid warning. There was this devastating flashing, crashing and blast – it went quiet. Then there was another scream and a soldier came out into the street. He was holding his guts in and all his stomach had been torn open and his entrails were trickling through his fingers. He was screaming. He sank to his knees, his screaming changed to a gurgle and he just dropped, almost at my feet. He was the first man I saw die.

Sergeant Armourer/Air Gunner/Navigator Ian Blair
113 Squadron, RAF

One occasion I flew as an observer/bomb aimer with the CO, Squadron Leader Barney Kiely, attacking El Adem. We were carrying fragmentation and incendiary bombs. This was the only time I flew with the CO on an operation. We had trouble turning off the downward-pointing identity light, which you flash from the cockpit using a switch, and also the blue station-keeping light. The other aircraft with us told us that we had managed to turn them off. We used to carry a tin hat with us in those days. We were bombing from five hundred feet, and as we approached the targets, light ack-ack started coming up – what we called 'flaming onions', a stream of ack-ack rounds that looked as if they were all tied together. I had never seen them before. I instinctively ducked, which made the skipper laugh. We batted along, missed the hangar with our bombs, and when we got back we found the station-keeping lights still on; no wonder the ack-ack was so accurate.

Private Robert Hawksworth
Bandsman and Stretcher-Bearer, 1st Battalion, Durham Light Infantry
In September news reached us that the Italians had reached Sidi Barrani, about seventy miles from us. We had no idea what the plan for the future was.

Sergeant Emilio Ponti
Tank Gunner, Italian Tenth Army
We took Sidi Barrani and I was one of the first to enter with my tank. My major was the CO of the battalion, and I was his gunner. There were three of us, a driver, the gunner – me – and the major, with his binoculars, looking out of the top of the turret. A general came up, I was told that he was General Bergonzoli, a famous Italian general. We called him General '*Barba Elettrica*' – 'Electric Whiskers'.

He said, 'Lads, you have conquered Sidi Barrani, but we won't allow you to put your flag up.'

I replied, 'Why? The Arabs and British have left. We didn't kill anybody. They just went. And this is our first town in Egypt, and we are entitled to it.'

'No, you are not', he said, 'you are not entitled to it. The blackshirts have got to come in.'

The first night in Sidi Barrani, the British navy came close to the beach and put a few shells in, and damaged quite a few of the lorries belonging to the blackshirts, and killed some of them. The day after, we said, 'That could have been us. But as they get much more pay than us, it serves them right.' You become really cruel when you are in the army.

Flight Sergeant Frank Waddington
Navigator, 37 Squadron, RAF
We landed at Kabrit by the Great Bitter Lake, on 25 November 1940, having flown from England. We did some operations from there, pasting the Italians, in support of our army. To bomb Benghazi we would fly forward to Landing Ground 9, it didn't have a name. There would be some poor erks there, living in tents with petrol and bombs. We would refuel there and bomb up. Sometimes we would hang around until dark. The thing I remember about the Western Desert was that it was the only time in my life that I have known absolute silence.

When we left Landing Ground 9, we would bomb places like Derna, Tobruk and Benghazi. It was quite enjoyable. When we got to the target I think all the Italians must have gonein to the shelters because the anti-aircraft fire just stopped. We used to bomb at low level, at about two thousand feet, just bombing the buildings or aircraft, and go round again, which you would never, never, do over Germany; there you just wanted to get rid of them as quickly as you could. So from that point of view, life was enjoyable. I couldn't get over the fact that I was a long way from home and missing my mother and my brother. The mail used to take many weeks to arrive in Egypt. We continued operations until after Christmas, then we were sent to Greece.

Major Ralph Bagnold
Commanding, Long Range Desert Group (LRDG)
Within six weeks we got together a volunteer force of New Zealanders whose equipment had been in a ship sunk by a submarine and so they were at a loose end. The New Zealanders were wonderful people who were used to using trucks and maintaining them.

The first trip into enemy territory was in September 1940, and the object was to see if the Italians were preparing for a raid or offensive against south-ern Egypt. We could read the tracks and see if their outpost at Uweinat in southern Libya, near the Egyptian/Sudan border, was being reinforced. They could have raided Aswan, seized the dam and flooded Egypt. When we met that Italian party in the desert ten years before, we had discussed the idea as a joke. I thought if Lorenzini was still in Libya that he would be capable of carrying out that sort of raid.

We discovered that the Italians were not planning a raid. We captured a small Italian convoy; took about half a dozen men without a shot being fired. This trip was so successful that for the next patrol we doubled our size. When the group was increased in strength it had to have an official name, so we chose the Long Range Desert Group.

Clothing was important, there is a tremendous contrast in temperature between night and day in the desert. The sand radiates the heat, and it can get up to fifty degrees Celsius by day, and below freezing at night. So you need enough clothing and blankets for the night, yet in daytime just enough clothing to stop the sun burning your skin. All we wore was a shirt and shorts. The Arab head-dress was good as it flapped in the wind and kept one cool, and in a sandstorm you could wrap a piece of cloth round your face. We got the head-dress from the Palestine police, because we didn't want to risk breaking secrecy by putting out a contract in Cairo for Arab head-dress. I had sandals made, the Indian North-West Frontier *chapli*, a very tough sandal with an open toe, so that if sand got into it you could shoot it out with a kick. There were no flies in the deep desert, no animals, nothing for a fly to live on. You had them in the oases. There were snakes and scorpions in the oases too. No diseases in the desert either. We had one man who fell through the windscreen of a truck and cut himself very badly. We sewed him up with needle and thread from the first-aid kit, and it never went septic. It was so dry, you would sometimes come across a camel that had wandered off and died, perhaps fifty years before. The skin was dry and cracked, but you could look inside, see the organs intact, shrivelled up but otherwise complete.

Sergeant Armourer/Air Gunner/Navigator Ian Blair
113 *Squadron, RAF*

We departed base at 0820 hours to bomb the Derna airfield, 350 miles west of Maaten Baggush, with fragmentation bombs. The pilot was Pilot Officer Reynolds. We arrived over the target at fifteen thousand feet. It was a cloudless day, an enemy aircraft had been firing at us, and as it broke off .50-cal bullets came in with a bang. The aircraft was diving and it suddenly came to me that the pilot was bent forward over the controls and we were diving at a rate of knots. The Blenheim was accelerating rapidly. I had been kneeling by the bomber aimer's seat. I stood up and pulled the control column back a bit, although it was difficult with the weight of the dead pilot. But I could turn the aircraft with the 'spectacles' on the control column. I turned it north out to sea, hoping that the fighter would not follow us out to sea. I got on the intercom and told the gunner to crawl up and join me and help me pull the pilot out of his seat. We dragged him out, got the aircraft straight and level, turned east, then steered a bit south of east, and hoped we would get back to base. The air gunner sent a message on WT saying that the navigator was flying the aircraft back. I had not had any flying experience at all. I had flown with Tommy Knott for a long time and had watched him. I found that the controls worked. I knew where the switches and controls were located.

I said to the air gunner, 'Hank, we have two options: we can either get over base and you hop out and I'll try and land the thing, or you stay and take a chance.' He said he would take a chance. I never thought of baling out.

It took an hour and three-quarters to get back. My plan was to make a very wide circuit and approach from a long way out, and drag it in low over the desert. We had telegraph wires down the eastern end of the airfield. I had to get over the wires, and then put it down. Things started going pear-shaped. I was prepared for the vibration when I put the wheels down, and that when I changed pitch the revs would go up and I would have to throttle back. But what I didn't bargain for was that the design of the ailerons on the Blenheim was such that it turned the aircraft the wrong way momentarily, that took me by surprise. I could see a great conglomeration of people on the ground, ambulances and tenders. I knew the speed to bring it in at, about 85 knots, I trimmed it tail-heavy, but overdid it and had to hold the stick forward. As soon as I crossed the threshold I cut the throttle, and the aircraft bounced, I tried to open the throttle, and I only opened up the port engine by mistake. The aircraft slewed round ninety degrees, and stopped. The first person on board was the doc, and he said, 'Sick quarters.' I had a lovely hot sweet cup of tea. Then I went to my tent. I was OK. The AOC said if this man can fly an aeroplane without a course it is high time he went on a course.

Lieutenant General Richard O'Connor
Commander, Western Desert Force

After the Italians had made their offensive, and we had fallen back to Mersa Matruh in our own time and the way we wanted to, we hoped very much that they would follow us up, as we had a plan to annihilate them. Unfortunately they stayed about seventy miles short of Mersa Matruh. As they wouldn't come to us, I felt that we should do something about them, and wrote to General Wavell suggesting it. He had had the same idea, and written to General Wilson, copy to me, and our letters crossed. He had in mind a five-day raid against the Italians whose positions were faulty, because their troops were so disposed as to be out of supporting distance of each other.

My resources were very limited: two divisions, the 4th Indian Division and 7th Armoured, both excellent and well-trained divisions, and one very valuable asset – one battalion of infantry tanks. The enemy had a vast superiority in numbers, about eight to one. In spite of that, their morale was poor and they had no enthusiasm for the war. It was essential that we made a plan that would throw them off balance, and stop them from taking advantage of their large numbers. We were helped in this by the form of defence that they adopted which consisted of a number of camps strongly fortified, but – and here was the weakness – they were out of supporting distance of each other. We therefore decided to take advantage of that and deal with them individually. We decided that we would attack one camp, and to make that attack more effective we would move troops between the camps and attack them from the rear; in fact, the way that their rations would come.

Brigadier John Harding
Brigadier General Staff, Western Desert Force
The Italians in their ring of static camps did no patrolling. The 7th Armoured Division patrolled extensively. Dick O'Connor planned a night approach march and an attack on the camps from the rear. The 7th Armoured Division moved out to prevent any interference from the Italians from the west, while the 4th Indian Division with heavy tanks attacked from the west, the unexpected direction.

Lieutenant General Richard O'Connor
Commander, Western Desert Force
The simple part of the operation was the actual attack. The difficult bit was getting the troops into the position from which to carry out the attack. This included an advance by day to within about twenty miles of the objective. The no-man's-land was about seventy miles, so that needed an advance during the day of fifty miles, followed by a rest for some hours during the evening and night, then an advance further through the gap between the two camps, and attacking them from the west.

During the day we enlisted the help of the RAF to keep the enemy right out of the sky because of the enormous amount of dust we produced in moving to our forming-up places.

The battle lasted about four days, the first stage was the attack on the first camp, and then we went northward, attacking each one separately. Each fort held about a division. By being behind their front we would be protecting ourselves against air attack. They would be afraid to attack us because they would be damaging their own people. Each attack was preceded by a heavy bombardment which came as a complete surprise, immediately followed up by the I tanks who blasted their way into the camps, closely followed by the infantry.

Private John Stokes
2nd Battalion, The Queen's Royal Regiment
In December we marched for about nine days and attacked the first Italian defensive position. This was my first experience of going into action. I wondered about my reaction to fixing bayonets and going in, but was more bothered about my sore feet and aching legs. Of course we were all very scared. We were shelled, all spread out across the desert. I lay down and the shells fell among us. I felt a ping on my steel helmet, and thought 'Oh dear!' I saw a piece of metal lying in front of me and went to pick it up and it was red hot. It was an interesting experience and strange and new. My main feelings were that I was hungry and my legs were aching.

Captain Philip Tower
Adjutant, 25th Field Regiment, Royal Artillery
We supported the attack on Sidi Barrani. I was amazed that we could move two divisions through the desert and the Italians never spotted us. My regiment fired in support of the attack on Nebeiwa by the 11th Indian Infantry Brigade, at dawn, a complete success, our infantry tanks penetrated the Italian defences. Then we supported the attack on Tummar East at midday, after which we supported the attack on Sidi Barrani itself. It was a complete walkover. I saw thousands of Italian prisoners, delighted that the war was over.

Captain Bob Hingston
F Troop, 426 Battery, 107th (South Notts Hussars) Field Regiment,
Royal Horse Artillery
The Italians were utterly lamentable. We were pretty green, but they were appalling soldiers. The first thing I saw was four of their guns perched right out in the open, not dug in. Why they'd put them there when there was quite a bit of cover around I cannot imagine. They started firing and so I managed to range on to them and gave them a good plastering; that was the end of them – they weren't manned for the rest of the day.

Major Robert Daniell
3rd Royal Horse Artillery attached 107th (South Notts Hussars) Field
Regiment, Royal Horse Artillery
My job was to sit on the main road at night and when the battleship *Warspite* opened fire on Maktila camp, I had to fire different kinds of Very

lights to show the battleship – standing several miles out to sea – whether their rounds were falling plus or minus. The first round was an armour-piercing 15-inch shell. It passed a very short distance from me, and went on two or three miles before it exploded. I carried on and got several of their shells into Maktila camp. It had a devastating effect on the camp, all the Senussi soldiers ran away after the first shell hit. Several lorries were set on fire, which made the shooting easier. The Italians did not reply. They were bent on loading up their lorries and getting out of the place.

Private Mario Cassandro
35th Anti-Aircraft Battery, Italian Tenth Army
The first time I saw an Englishman I was lying in a hole; I had an Italian sergeant on top of me. I heard a lot of noise, people shouting and people running. We jumped out and started running, and as we were going we saw all these Italians sitting down and realised they were prisoners, and joined them.

Signaller Ted Whittaker
425 Battery, 107th (South Notts Hussars) Field Regiment,
Royal Horse Artillery
We were marched to a place where there were piles of Italian kit, which we could take. I got a dagger. There was a large store of tinned food and condensed milk. My mother had always stopped me from eating condensed milk with a spoon, and there was no one to stop me there. We found a gramophone and a pile of opera records. So for some time we sat and ate tinned food with Nestlé's condensed milk and listening to opera. I found a nice silk black shirt. There were pullovers, black woolly hats with pom-poms, small Beretta pistols and huge revolvers. After this we went back to Mersa in triumph wearing black woolly hats, and black shirts. We were soon told to 'take that bloody stuff off and look like soldiers; and have a wash and shave'.

Lieutenant General Richard O'Connor
Commander, Western Desert Force
We had a great disappointment after the capture of Sidi Barrani: the 4th Indian Division was withdrawn for service in Eritrea. The new division, the 6th Australian, a very good one, wouldn't be ready for action for nearly a month. That meant that the whole impetus of our pursuit would vanish, the enemy would be alerted, and we would no longer be able to surprise him.

Major Ralph Bagnold
Commanding, Long Range Desert Group (LRDG)
The increased size of the LRDG enabled us to raid two Italian posts several hundred miles apart on the same day. Having done this, I had the idea of raiding Murzuq oasis in the extreme west of Libya, near the Tibesti Mountains, astride the Libyan and French Equatorial African border. It meant trying to get help from the French in Chad. We didn't know if they were on the Vichy side or the Free French side. I took an aircraft and flew to Chad, where I found that the army commander was on the Vichy side, but all other officers were on the Free French side. I told them I was going to raid Murzuq, and wanted help with rations and petrol.

The second-in-command, Lieutenant Colonel d'Ornano, spoke to the governor, and said that this was their chance, and turned to me and said, 'I'll give you everything you want, on one condition, you take me and two other officers with you, and we'll fly the French flag alongside yours.'

The raid on Murzuq was very successful, but unfortunately d'Ornano was killed by an Italian machine gun. The result was that de Gaulle appointed Colonel Leclerc in his place as commander of the Free French in Chad. Leclerc was a great leader, and, without any previous desert experience, formed a column to capture Kufra – fifteen hundred miles from Cairo – which was too strong for our little force to take on.

He was short of navigators for the desert, so I lent him a navigating truck complete with sun compass. He captured Kufra.

Some time after this patrol, which covered 4,300 miles in all, I went to do another job at GHQ as my health was beginning to suffer. Major Prendergast, the second-in-command, took over.

Private John Stokes
2nd Battalion, The Queen's Royal Regiment
The next objective was Bardia. We spent Christmas 1940 in defensive positions and patrolling to locate enemy positions. Our Christmas dinner was corned beef and biscuits.

Captain William Boulton
339 Battery, 104th (Essex Yeomanry) Field Regiment,
Royal Horse Artillery
Our first advance was to Bardia. Close to the border between Egypt and Libya at Sallum, there was a rough track that climbed the six hundred-foot

escarpment in bends all the way up. The Italians had a long-range gun at Bardia that fired at you as you climbed the escarpment.

I was a troop commander, up at the OP directing fire. The battery commander might select the OP, or leave it to the troop commander. The OP party consisted of an officer, a signaller, and an OP assistant, or OP Ack for short. The first thing you did on arrival was to lay a telephone line to the guns. You had a radio, but it often failed. At the gun end the radio might not work either. Line was reliable but could be easily cut by shellfire, or torn up by vehicles.

Bombardier Stephen Dawson
339 Battery, 104th (Essex Yeomanry) Field Regiment,
Royal Horse Artillery
We were to shell Bardia, and our guns opened fire for the first time that afternoon. One of our officers said, 'We can reach them, but their guns can't reach us.' The next day I was sitting on the step of my lorry eating a bully beef and biscuit sandwich and Italian shells started falling round me. After that shells began to come over fairly regularly. Our first casualties came that day, two men wounded. That afternoon, to our horror, Italian bombers appeared, twenty-seven of them, and bombed us. Only four killed. The first man to be killed was screaming, 'Finish me finish me.' A sergeant took out his .38 pistol and shot him in the head. After this people started digging their slit trenches properly. Being under fire for the first time, we asked ourselves, 'Is it like this every day?'At a minute to twelve on Christmas Eve I rang up a friend on the gun position and said, 'Happy Christmas.' He replied, 'You will hear a happy Christmas in a minute,' and the guns fired about eighteen shells into Bardia.

Captain William Boulton
339 Battery, 104th (Essex Yeomanry) Field Regiment,
Royal Horse Artillery
We were positioned round the perimeter and positioned so that we could engage enemy. We moved a number of times. The gun crews lived and slept close to the guns. But as we were spread out it was easy to get lost at night if you had to go off to Battery HQ or RHQ and wander about for ages. It was cold at night. After two nights at Bardia, I gave up sleeping above ground on my camp bed, instead I used to dig a hole and sleep with all my clothes on. But vehicles driving about couldn't see these holes, and we had at least one fellow killed by being run over at night.

Eventually we moved so that we could engage targets well within the enemy perimeter, the final move being at night just before the battle for Bardia. We would fire at the enemy gun flashes or movement. The enemy made no attempt to attack us while we were waiting outside Bardia, nor did they seem to have any reconnaissance out. It was here that we were bombed for the first time of many. It was rather unnerving, but we had only a couple of casualties.

Brigadier John Harding
Brigadier General Staff, Western Desert Force, renamed XIII Corps
January 1941
The Italians were entirely defensive and sat tight behind their defences. One of the Australian brigade commanders reported that a bunch of Italians came in to surrender, and were told they hadn't got time to deal with them, and to go away and come back in the morning.

Gunner Robert Taunt
Field Artillery, 6th Australian Division
We crossed the desert in box formation, and you could see the whole 6th Division on the move. We moved at night and laid telephone lines and surrounded Bardia. The 7th Armoured Division cut Bardia off. The first couple of days we had no infantry in front of us. We came under fire from Italian artillery. The Italian ammunition didn't seem to be all that effective, their shells seemed to go into the ground a long way before exploding. You could hear the shells coming, but you didn't hear the one that landed close. We had a British medium regiment behind us, perhaps they were too far away for the Italians to reach, so they shelled us.

Bombardier Stephen Dawson
339 Battery, 104th (Essex Yeomanry) Field Regiment,
Royal Horse Artillery
The attack on Bardia was made by the 6th Australian Division. We moved to a new position at night and we didn't get fired on and I suppose the Italians didn't realise we had moved. We admired the Australians very much. They were tall men, bronzed and casual, with a laconic way of talking.

Captain William Boulton
339 Battery, 104th (Essex Yeomanry) Field Regiment, Royal Artillery
The plan for the battle of Bardia included a barrage by the artillery, which lasted for an hour or so, followed by a creeping barrage once the infantry

started going in. The navy had a monitor with 15-inch guns, and two gunboats offshore which did a lot of damage.

Bombardier Stephen Dawson
339 Battery, 104th (Essex Yeomanry) Field Regiment,
Royal Horse Artillery
At dawn after a night march we opened fire on Bardia, and to our surprise there was no return fire, and the Aussies went in. They went in groups of about six, with their long bayonets. We fired a barrage in their support. We called our forward OP 'Coventry', after the city which had been bombed. It was nice to hear OP Coventry calling for eight rounds gunfire.

Anonymous Australian Officer
6th Australian Division
The attack began on Friday 3 January. Infantry and tanks had moved to their assembly positions in darkness. Some time earlier artillery batteries had moved to new positions where the enemy could not find them. The success of the attack depended on getting the heavy tanks within the perimeter and this meant that crossings had to be made for them over a ditch many feet wide and several feet deep. Also, tracks had to be cut through the barbed wire and mines removed – all tasks for the engineers. To accomplish this, the rapid fire of seventy guns fell at 5.30 am on a selected strip of fifteen hundred yards of the enemy position. At the same time the 2nd/1st Battalion, accompanied by engineers, crossed the Start Line and advanced as close to the barrage as they could get. As soon as the barrage lifted to more distant targets the 2nd/1st cut its way through the wire and rushed the enemy posts. A curtain of fire was put round the enemy by artillery, and the engineers took up their task at once. Altogether they made four tracks twenty feet wide across the ditch, reached the barbed wire and removed some hundreds of mines so that, with the arrival of the tanks at 6.50 am, the way was prepared for them, and they entered the perimeter with the 2nd/2nd Battalion. These tanks, with the infantry running to keep up, attacked the series of enemy posts on the perimeter and some of the nearer batteries. When the Italians saw shot and shell merely bouncing off the tanks and the Australian infantry upon them they realised the hopelessness of the position, and surrendered freely.

Soon long columns of green-clad troops could be seen streaming out of the position. By 8.30 am the 2nd/2nd Battalion with its tanks had advanced three miles and a halt was called upon a pre-arranged line to allow the tanks to refuel and replenish their ammunition. Meantime the 2nd/1st Battalion had moved to a commanding feature in the north, and the 2nd/3rd Battalion, with part of the cavalry, had come into the perimeter to fill the gap between the other two battalions, and this ended phase one of the attack.

During this interval our artillery moved forward while the 2nd/5th Battalion and part of the 2nd/6th came in ready to renew the advance. When phase two commenced at 11.30 am, the enemy guns were prepared. Fewer tanks were available and the attack had lost its impetus. Good headway was, however, made and many prisoners taken. The day ended with two of our brigades deep in the enemy positions and twenty thousand prisoners in our hands.

On the morning of 4 January the attack was resumed. From their advantageous positions, all three battalions of the 16th Brigade, with artillery support and accompanied by a few tanks, moved forward to objectives dominating the town of Bardia itself. Immediate success accompanied this thrust and a large number of prisoners and guns were captured. Another battalion, the 2nd/4th, was put in to continue this move and by late afternoon some of our troops were in Bardia and the engineers had seized the waterworks and other vital points. During this fighting a group of seven Italian medium tanks made a serious thrust against HQ 2nd/3rd Battalion, till two of the brigade anti-tank guns intervened. A duel then ensued in which all the tanks were knocked out and one of our guns put out of action. Throughout the whole of 4 January, the south-east section of the defence continued to hold out and strenuously resisted the efforts of the 17th Brigade, who however made some headway. As this area still contained a number of enemy batteries it was decided during the night to launch an organised attack against it next day. Accordingly on the morning of 5 January, the 2nd/8th and 2nd/11th Battalions, supported by artillery and a few tanks, moved forward. The attack proved successful, many guns were captured, and the enemy surrendered freely. At the same time, the pressure was relieved on the 17th Brigade who quickly took advantage of the situation, and shortly after midday the position was in our hands. The prisoners totalled two thousand officers and 42,000 other ranks. Enormous quantities of materiel were taken including 260 field and medium guns, 130 light and medium tanks, scores of anti-aircraft and anti-tank guns, hundreds of machine guns and anti-tank rifles, and at least seven hundred motor vehicles.

Australian troops assault Bardia at dawn.

A column of Italian soldiers captured at Bardia being marched into captivity.

Bombardier Stephen Dawson
339 Battery, 104th (Essex Yeomanry) Field Regiment,
Royal Horse Artillery
The next morning thousands and thousands of prisoners came out. They looked pathetic, calling 'Aqua, *aqua*'. We couldn't spare any water to give them. In the afternoon we drove through an area we had been shelling, and there were lots of Italian bodies lying there. I laughed, more hysteria than anything. You got used to the sight of the dead.

Sergeant Emilio Ponti
Tank Gunner, Italian Tenth Army
We withdrew to Tobruk. Our regiment made a gap in the border wire for the infantry, who had no trucks and had to walk. They had very little water. We were lucky in the tanks. The infantry were cannon fodder. The desert is a horrible place. I hope I don't have to go there again. We worried about how to survive.

We were told to defend Tobruk. Our tanks were overhauled there, and the Italian air force were at El Adem. The engineers dug ditches, and we went into defence in the holes and ditches. Now and again the British used to attack us from the air. Things were getting nasty, and we knew that the British had reached Bardia. Then we saw the Italian Air Force evacuating El Adem, but we were left to defend Tobruk.

Captain William Boulton
339 Battery, 104th (Essex Yeomanry) Field Regiment,
Royal Horse Artillery
The moment it was over we went on to Tobruk. Within a couple of days we were outside the Tobruk perimeter, and it was rather the same routine as at Bardia. At Tobruk the Italians had built concrete defences all round the place. As soon as they were shelled or bombed they went underground, and the attacking infantry would throw in grenades. For about three nights before the battle for Tobruk began it was my job as battery captain to bring up ammunition, most of which was from several miles away, from El Adem. I had no sleep for three nights. Halfway through the battle I went to sleep on the gun line, despite the noise.

Sergeant Emilio Ponti
Tank Gunner, Italian Tenth Army
The British bombardment started and turned searchlights on us. On 21 January 1941, at six o'clock in the morning, the artillery fire intensified.

The major got off our tank and would not come with us. The order came telling us to move towards the anti-tank ditch because the British were advancing. The firing was terrific. I stayed inside the tank, I wasn't going to be killed. We ran out of ammunition, and went back to get some more. We couldn't find the major anywhere. When we returned, the British artillery fire had stopped and the infantry came in. I said, 'We have lost. Why kill people? Let's go back and wait for them to come. I am not going to fire.'

We had no enthusiasm. We didn't believe we were doing the right thing. To get killed for some madman seemed stupid. I said to the driver, 'We don't want to get killed.' 'Thank you sergeant,' he said.

So we went back, and some anti-tank shells nearly hit us; they could penetrate our armour. We went back about a mile. There was pandemonium, no one knew what they were doing. The officers were all hidden. We got to where my tent was, jumped out, leaving the tank engine running. We got in a ditch, which had been dug to take water pipes up to a distilling plant. It wasn't finished. But the ditch was handy because bullets were flying about. My mate got hit. But I was all right. I took my pistol out and threw it away. I started crawling towards the medical centre, which was underground. I listened carefully to ensure that no bullets were flying about, because I would have to get out of the ditch. There seemed to be a bit of a lull. I jumped up and ran in and it was packed with officers, not with sick. It was deeply dug in underground. The CO was there, and he asked, 'Sergeant Ponti, how's things outside?'

I said, 'Fantastic, within a couple of seconds you'll have the British here.'

This Australian came in with his bayonet on his rifle, and said, 'Hands up!', but he said it in Italian, '*Mani su*'.

I pulled out my white handkerchief and went out first. As I went out, the Australian asked, 'Whose is that tank out there?'

'Mine,' says I.

'Why isn't it stopped?'

'You can get in it and use it; very, very new, *nuovo nuovo*,' I replied. So we surrendered.

Brigadier John Harding
Brigadier General Staff, XIII Corps
The battle for Tobruk followed the same pattern as Bardia, with extensive patrolling and a break in by infantry followed by tanks, and a clearing-up of the defensive area by infantry assault. The bulk of the Italian forces did not put up much resistance, although there were pockets of stiff resistance.

General 'Electric Whiskers' Bergonzoli, Commander Italian Tenth Army, after his capture.

Lieutenant General Richard O'Connor
Commander, XIII Corps
We then advanced to Derna and Mechili and had to decide whether we were going to follow the enemy along the Benghazi road, or across the unre-connoitred desert and cut right across the communications of the Italian Tenth Army and hope to stop them escaping. I had been thinking about this for some time. We had maps. We didn't want to recce it because we didn't want to give the show away. We sent aircraft, which were told to fly low, but did not want to send patrols. As I drove along behind the 7th Armoured Division, I saw nothing but broken-down vehicles in the desert and I wondered if we would get any there at all.

Brigadier John Harding
Brigadier General Staff, XIII Corps
Telling 7th Armoured Division to cut across the desert was a very brave decision, nobody knew just what the going was like, and we were short of petrol and ammunition. The 7th Armoured Division stopped about half-way across, they were concerned that they would run out of fuel, so Bingo Brown, the air liaison officer in Western Desert Force, flew me down to the armoured division HQ in a light aircraft, and we discussed the situation, and Creagh, commanding the division, agreed to press on. It is a very difficult piece of desert. Communications were difficult at night. It was entirely successful. The Italians were cut off at Beda Fomm. The 11 Hussars – with some artillery, tanks and infantry of the support group of the 7th Armoured Division – routed the Italians.

O'Connor's two divisions had destroyed ten Italian ones, capturing 130,000 prisoners, 180 medium and over 200 light tanks, and 845 guns, for a total loss to themselves of 500 men killed, 1,373 wounded and 55 missing.

Bombardier Stephen Dawson
339 Battery, 104th (Essex Yeomanry) Field Regiment,
Royal Horse Artillery
We didn't get to the Battle of Beda Fomm. We were stopped in the desert when a brigadier came past and said to Sergeant Pond, 'Oh sergeant, I thought you'd like to know, we've taken Beda Fomm, and Bergonzoli's in the bag.'

'Thank you, sir,' replied Pond, 'I'll tell the men that, sir, they will be delighted.'

'Jolly good show,' said the brigadier and drove off.

After he had gone, Sergeant Pond said, 'Who the fuck's Bergonzoli?'

Rommel Takes the Stage

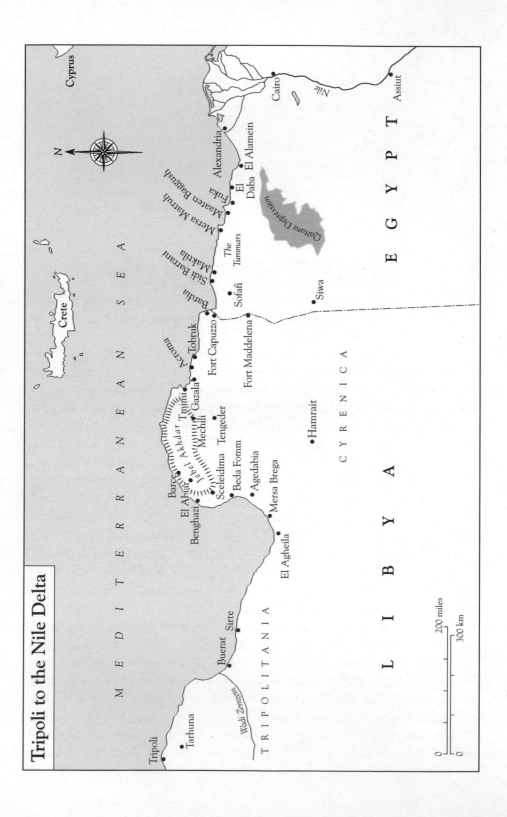

Tripoli to the Nile Delta

Morale was high. As long as you are going
the right way, it is bound to be.

Wavell did not exploit the utter defeat of the Italian Army in Libya –
culminating in the Battle of Beda Fomm, south of Benghazi – by
advancing on Tripoli.

O'Connor's swift advance had alarmed the German government, which
suddenly realised that the British might overrun Tripolitania, and hold
North Africa right up to the French colony of Tunisia. This might
encourage the French, in their extensive North African colonies, to defy
the Vichy government in France, and once more take up arms against the
Germans. With the whole coast of North Africa in Allied hands, the
balance of advantage in the Mediterranean would swing against the Axis.
Accordingly, the Germans despatched a force to assist the Italians. Five
days after the Battle of Beda Fomm, Lieutenant General Erwin Rommel
arrived in Tripoli with the advance party of the 5th Light Division, tasked
with assisting the Italians to defend Tripolitania. Later to become the 21st
Panzer Division, this formation, with the 15th Panzer Division, would
become the nucleus of the Deutsches Afrika Korps (DAK) and Panzer
Armee Afrika. Rommel had made a name for himself commanding a
panzer division in the invasion of France in May 1940.

While the Germans were preparing to reinforce the poorly equipped
Italians, the British – at Churchill's insistence – transferred troops and
equipment away from North Africa in what transpired as a hopeless
attempt to defeat the German invasion of Greece and Crete. Richard
O'Connor replaced Wilson as Commander British Troops in Egypt, Wilson
having been sent to Greece. The XIII Corps reverted to its original title,
Western Desert Force, and was put under command of Lieutenant General
Philip Neame, without a proper headquarters or staff. Neame was made

responsible for the defence of the whole of the Libyan region of Cyrenaica with the 9th Australian Division, the 3rd Indian Motor Brigade and the 2nd Armoured Division (the 7th having been sent back to Egypt).

The 9th Australian Division, which had replaced the experienced 6th Australian Division, had one of its brigades in Tobruk, and the other two dispersed to hold the roads on the north-east side of the Jebel Akhdar in the Cyrenaican bulge. The 2nd Armoured Division was an armoured division in name only; it was badly equipped and under strength.

On arrival Rommel ignored orders from both the German High Command and the Italians to remain on the defensive, and instead his forces overwhelmed the small British force at Mersa Brega, in the south-east bend of the Gulf of Sirte. His success there led him to exploit forward and mount a full-blooded offensive. This led to the lengthy siege of Tobruk and the first British attempt to relieve the garrison: Operation Battleaxe.

Lieutenant General Richard O'Connor
Commander, XIII Corps
I ought to have pressed straight on, on the afternoon of Beda Fomm. It would not have been a matter of disobeying orders: at the time I had no orders. I blame myself. I was so engaged in the battle itself, and didn't use the Australian brigade, which I kept as a reserve for the Battle of Beda Fomm, and could have used it to press on to Tripoli.

Brigadier John Harding
Brigadier General Staff, XIII Corps
Morale was high. As long as you are going the right way, it is bound to be. Then reports came in of German troops arriving in Tripoli. I didn't know enough about Rommel at the time, I ought to have known more. Our calculation was that they wouldn't be in a position to start an offensive for some time. I was wrong. We underestimated Rommel's drive and energy. I personally did not credit him with the qualities that I would have done had I known how he had performed in the German offensive in France in 1940.

Captain Hans-Otto Behrendt
Adjutant to Lieutenant General Rommel
I and three other officers travelled with General Rommel from Munich to Tripoli. I was very close to him in Tripoli because I was the only officer on his personal staff at the time who spoke a bit of Italian. I accompanied him

General Irwin Rommel with his aides.

daily in the desert. I liked the desert, it is not a lonely place: you are closer to the creator, God.

In the port of Tripoli Rommel told my friend, an engineer lieutenant, 'Build me 150 tanks.'

The engineer looked stupefied, and Rommel asked, 'Don't you have timber here in the harbour, and canvas covers for vehicles?'

'Yes sir'.

'So you can give me 150 tanks,' replied Rommel.

These were left in Tripoli and fooled the British in our first campaign.

Captain Vernon Northwood
Officer Commanding, A Company, 2/28th Battalion, 9th Australian Division

We were a Western Australian battalion. Many of our men had worked in the gold fields and were tough and resourceful. Others had come from tight family communities. Having formed in Australia in July 1940, we arrived in Palestine in February 1941. We settled in thinking that we would get down to some training; we had not done much. But within a matter of weeks we were sent to Tobruk. The 6th Australian Division had gone through so quickly that there was stuff everywhere left by the Italians. We weren't fully equipped and so we went out into the wadis and found abandoned Italian equipment, such as mortars and Breda light machine guns, and vehicles; I had a beautiful Fiat.

Corporal Ray Middleton
HQ Company, 2/28th Battalion, 9th Australian Division

We were told that our job was to garrison North Africa and carry out training. We learned that the Germans had landed in Tripolitania and thought 'so what, that's five hundred miles away. We've got the new 2nd Armoured Division with us. Two brigades of our division are ahead of us'. We didn't think we would be attacked.

Tobruk was very good port along a long desert coast, with few other ports. The Italian defence line was built in a semi-circle about eight miles out from the port. When we arrived in Tobruk, we were dumped in a piece of desert and told to make shelters; we had nothing, so people scrounged bits of corrugated tin. We weren't near the Italian-built concrete sangars then. We were told that Rommel's forces had reached Agedabia and might come on.

I had about an hour's instruction on the Italian 47-mm Breda anti-tank gun. The gun had no sights on it, and I was told point it straight at the target and don't fire until the tank is two hundred yards away.

Company Sergeant Major Alan Potter
D Company, 2/28th Battalion, 9th Australian Division
We were going to Tobruk for training. We got there on 26 March, and bedded down to await transport to take us forward. We were still in training mode. We had a clip of five rounds of ammunition for every rifle. For our Boys anti-tank rifles we had two rounds. We got our training all right, but in a different way.

The Tobruk perimeter defences constructed by the Italian engineers – and they were good – consisted of barbed wire and concrete positions, about 170 of them. Each position would hold about thirty men, each had a machine gun or heavier weapon; and underneath, oblong concrete rooms, where the troops lived and slept. The first dust storm we had was our first day. You couldn't open your mouth without it filling with sand.

Captain William Boulton
339 Battery, 104th (Essex Yeomanry) Field Regiment,
Royal Horse Artillery
I was sent to Cairo HQ to find out what the regiment was to do next. During this time we had never changed our clothes and only bathed in the sea once. I had in my bag a rather crumpled set of khaki drill uniform and I put it on. At HQ there was an immaculate Guards officer who looked at me as if I was a drowned rat and asked where I had come from. He said, 'You've got to go straight back to Mersa Matruh,' which was a bit of a blow. We thought we might be sent to Greece.

We went from there to Mersa Brega; it was quite pleasant. We were between a marsh and the sea on the main road. We were pretty relaxed as we were told that the Germans had practically nothing in Africa. We had no decent maps, and one of our first tasks was to make a proper map of the area. Otherwise we didn't move about much. The other people there was a TA regiment, the Tower Hamlets Rifles, part of the Rifle Brigade, a battalion of Free French, and some Northumberland Fusiliers who were machine-gunners.

Rifleman Albert Handscombe
Wireless Operator, HQ Company, 9th Battalion, The Rifle Brigade
(Tower Hamlets Rifles)
We were in 2nd Armoured Division, my brigade was sent up to take over from 7th Armoured Division. We had no news about Germans being in North Africa, but we soon found out when they hit us early in the morning,

and in twenty-four hours we were non-existent. We lost the entire B Company, except for the company commander. They came through us like a dose of salts. We weren't expecting anything: suddenly there were shells, bullets, aircraft. The attack went on for the whole of that day and the following day.

Captain William Boulton
339 Battery, 104th (Essex Yeomanry) Field Regiment,
Royal Horse Artillery
We had an OP on higher ground with a good view over the road. Our resupply ammunition was about ten miles away. We had been in position for about a fortnight when the German attacks started on 31 March. We had no warning of the attack. I was on my way with some trucks to collect ammunition. Then began some of the most stressful time I had in the war. I was told to get back to the regiment as soon as possible. It took me about half an hour to return to the gun line. There was a tremendous amount of gunfire. We had to evacuate our forward OP. Late in the afternoon we were ordered to withdraw. By now the Germans were about three hundred yards away. We withdrew in short stages, which meant by the time we got dug in we had to withdraw again. We needed more petrol. Some NCOs were sent off to get petrol and were taken prisoner.

Bombardier Stephen Dawson
339 Battery, 104th (Essex Yeomanry) Field Regiment,
Royal Horse Artillery
Suddenly the road was full of vehicles going westwards, with infantry riding on them. In no time at all we were racing down the road, and were about the last troops out. It was a farce. On one occasion we stopped to answer a call of nature, and an aircraft came over high up, and everyone scattered in panic. We came across an RAF lorry with four or five bods sitting in it. And one of our chaps went up to them and said, 'Hey youse, what does RAF stand for? Never seen that before, tell me what it stands for?'

They didn't answer. We said, 'Come on Scouse, come back.'

He was quite menacing; we had seen nothing of the RAF. Any plane we saw was German, it gets on your nerves after a bit. It became instinctive to fire on any plane that came over.

That night we laagered up near some armour, and thought we'll be all right with this armour. And in the morning we saw they were all wrecks from the Battle of Beda Fomm.

William Boulton.

Captain William Boulton
339 Battery, 104th (Essex Yeomanry) Field Regiment,
Royal Horse Artillery
There came an order to get up on the escarpment and go back on the same route that we had followed from Mechili. It was difficult to get up, but in one place there was a deep wadi. We got the whole regiment in there, and learned that the rest of the force had already got on the escarpment and left us on our own.

Bombardier Stephen Dawson
339 Battery, 104th (Essex Yeomanry) Field Regiment,
Royal Horse Artillery
We came to the escarpment at Sceleidima. There was an air of tension. We lost touch with the regiment, and our battery was on our own. Then we saw some armoured cars from the King's Dragoon Guards. We were short of water, and we peed into the radiators, which were drying out. We lay quiet as a large number of troops passed us in the night: it was the Germans on the coast road below the escarpment. They didn't see us.

Brigadier John Harding
Brigadier General Staff, Western Desert Force
I was surprised at the speed at which Rommel advanced from Tripoli in a full-scale offensive, driving us back; and at their opportunist tactics, their excellent recce, the performance of their battle groups. Our HQ was at Barce. Wavell came up to speak to Neame and I was his chief of staff. When Wavell came out of the discussion he talked to me and said, 'I suppose I could have sent less to Greece.' I begged Wavell to send Dick O'Connor back, I didn't have much faith in Philip Neame; he was a stranger to the desert. Dick had stomach trouble and was commanding BTE [British Troops in Egypt], while Jumbo Wilson went to Greece. Wavell sent him [O'Connor] back to hold Neame's hand. This was a mistake. Dick O'Connor wasn't in command.

Captain William Boulton
339 Battery, 104th (Essex Yeomanry) Field Regiment,
Royal Horse Artillery
The 2IC, Arthur Howell, was in charge: the CO was away. A small party reconnoitred the route brilliantly for forty-five miles. The going was rough with scrub and some wadis. It wasn't possible to spread out and we moved

head to tail; thank God there was no air interference. When we got to Er Regima we were suddenly told that the Germans were close and we must move to the right and join the road at El Abiar, which we did. From there we decided to filter back to the delta, unless we were told to do something else in the meantime. We had got back to somewhere west of Derna by late in the afternoon, and were suddenly told that one battery and Arthur Howell was to turn south and go to Mechili at once. This was a bit of a blow, because we had had a long journey and it was getting dark. About halfway to Mechili we stopped for a brew-up, and a huge staff car came up and the chap inside asked where we were going. When we told him, he said 'You had, better hurry because Mechili is under attack or you will not get there in time.' In that car there were Generals Neame and O'Connor. Not long afterwards they went into the bag. We were the last to see them before that happened.

Captain Hans-Otto Behrendt
Adjutant to Lieutenant General Rommel
During the advance from Mechili to Derna, Rommel told me to go ahead. We reached Derna picking up on our way British soldiers and generals, amongst them the famous General O'Connor who had defeated the Italians at Sidi Barrani, and General Neame and other officers and men until we reached the airport at Derna.

Lieutenant General Richard O'Connor
Commander, British Troops Egypt
It was a great shock. It was miles behind our own front, and by sheer bad luck we drove into the one bit of desert into which the Germans had sent a reconnaissance group.

Captain Hans-Otto Behrendt
Adjutant to Lieutenant General Rommel
On the way to Derna we encountered a British soldier with a broken-down motorbike and when we drove up, he asked us if we were going to the 3rd Armoured Brigade, and I said 'Yes'.

He got into my car, and after a while he said 'strange car'.

'Yes, you are right, this is a German car, and we are Germans,' I replied. All he said was 'Oh'.

I admired him for his coolness.

Captain William Boulton
339 Battery, 104th (Essex Yeomanry) Field Regiment,
Royal Horse Artillery
We got to within five miles of Mechili and there were abandoned rifles lying in the track so it was decided that Arthur Howell and our battery commander Bob Puckle should go forward to see what had happened. They found shot-up trucks and dead bodies, and decided that Mechili had fallen. So we turned round.

Bombardier Stephen Dawson
339 Battery, 104th (Essex Yeomanry) Field Regiment,
Royal Horse Artillery
At the end of the day we reached El Abiar. As we approached we heard an explosion, and discovered that it was the water supply being destroyed because the inhabitants thought we were the enemy. We were now back on the main route east. We still couldn't find our RHQ or the rest of the regiment. We had also lost a gun. We decided to make for Tobruk. We didn't know what was going on.

I saw three planes diving in over us, and everybody was screaming and shouting and we drove off the road, although we knew we couldn't get far off the road, and they flew past us. When we got back on the road, one of the chaps shouted, 'Breaks the monotony, boys!'

When we reached the Tmimi crossroads, where the Mechili track crosses the main road, there were about fifty Australians waiting, they'd been told we were coming. They raised a thumb, fags hanging out of the side of their mouths, and shouted, 'Good on you, cobber.'

I loved the Australians. And about fifty yards further on, our A Troop dropped trails to provide cover for these men to fall back. Then we came across a mass of trucks waiting to go into the perimeter. A little later a German bomber came over, and we were all fed up, cold and tired, and about two thousand men seized their rifles and fired, the plane dipped and went straight down and crashed in flame. We all cheered. No one thought about the men inside the plane at the time. We were fed up and resentful at running away all the time.

Rifleman Albert Handscombe
Wireless Operator, HQ Company, 9th Battalion The Rifle Brigade
(Tower Hamlets Rifles)
I got as far as a hill overlooking Derna and was sitting in my truck next to the driver. Suddenly I saw a German tank in the distance, there was a

tremendous crash, and a shell came whistling straight through the cab. I opened the door, whipped off my headset, out the door, rolled on the ground, and ran across the road off to the far side. I got myself together and looked across the road to see if I could do anything for my pal, but he was beyond recognition. The cab was demolished and the wireless set with it. I didn't even have a rifle. It was hopeless to go back there. I could see troops withdrawing all round me. I fell in with other chaps from all regiments. So we made for the nearest town, which was Tobruk. We got to the coast and walked along. In Tobruk I met one of the officers from the battalion. He got together all the Rifle Brigade chaps, about thirty of us. Here we met the Australians holding Tobruk. We were put to work in the docks.

Brigadier John Harding
Brigadier General Staff, Western Desert Force
After I lost my two generals, O'Connor and Neame, captured, I got back to Tmimi and there was just one staff officer. I went into Tobruk and found General Morshead commanding the 9th Australian Division and between us we organised the defence of Tobruk. I set up a headquarters at Tobruk. At this stage I got a message to say that the C-in-C was coming up. I was very busy trying to sort out the mess. The 9th Australians were very good organising the defence of Tobruk. In walked the C-in-C with an Australian general, Lavarack, and Freddie de Guingand and Charles Gardner. I had set up a blackboard and maps in the first floor of the Municipia, where the HQ was. I told him my assessment of the situation. He said, 'If you think you can hold it, you'd better hold it.'

I said, 'I think we can hold it provided the navy can keep us supplied, and Rommel doesn't wheel up a mass of heavy tanks and attack us.'

So he said, 'Hold it.'

With that he said he had to get back to his HQ, adding, 'I am leaving General Lavarack to take command. Give me your millboard.'

Which I did, and in his own hand he wrote out a directive, to General Lavarack to hold Tobruk, on one side of a sheet of foolscap paper.

Then he handed it to me and asked if it was all right. I replied that it was. He then told me to show it to General Lavarack and asked him if it was all right. He said it was.

Off Wavell went.

General Lavarack and I talked about how we would organise things, and later the telephone from Cairo rang. A staff officer the other end said, 'Where is the C-in-C?'

I replied that he had left hours before, and was told that he hadn't arrived. I said that it was dark but would send out search parties in the morning. A little later the telephone rang again and it was the C-in-C ringing from Sollum and telling me that he had had a forced landing, and to send another 'Lizzie', a Lysander, in the morning. He sounded completely unperturbed.

Battery Quartermaster Sergeant Fred Brookes
425 Battery, 107th (South Notts Hussars) Field Regiment,
Royal Horse Artillery
I was back in camp, having a quiet sip of ale and smoking a cigarette with one or two mates around. This staff car came tearing across the camp, pulled up, and out jumped a brigadier who said, 'Your regiment will be back here in about an hour, and you will be moving out at first light tomorrow morning. Draw ammunition, stores, anything you're short of, rob who you like within the area, get fully equipped and be ready to move out.'

I said, 'Yes sir!', saluted smartly and went on a predatory mission with two or three trucks.

We set off on our six-hundred-mile journey to Tobruk at 0730 hours on 5 April. We were escorted through Cairo with sirens sounding. We went through like a dose of salts, shouting, 'Pull the traffic over to one side, and make way.'

Bombardier Ray Ellis
425 Battery, 107th (South Notts Hussars) Field Regiment,
Royal Horse Artillery
Once past Mersa Matruh, there were signs of panic: troops coming back at great speed, everything going east. We passed rear aerodromes of the RAF where we could see crates being set on fire, which we knew contained aero engines. We met convoys of ambulances coming back. It all grew a bit sombre. It seemed that everyone in the Army of the Nile was doing their level best to put the greatest distance between themselves and the enemy – everybody was rushing headlong back into Egypt. The only troops moving westwards were the South Notts Hussars.

Captain Bob Hingston
F Troop, 426 Battery, 107th (South Notts Hussars) Field Regiment,
Royal Horse Artillery
We got to Sollum, near the escarpment, when suddenly everybody pressed the panic button. We were to get to Tobruk as fast as we possibly could. We

had to get up that sensational road zigzagging up the steep escarpment. I stood up in the front of my truck, looking back, and there was my troop – beautifully spaced out, all driving skilfully. We got to the top and there was this huge notice held up in front of us 'CLOSE UP'. We at the back of the convoy had to sprint a hell of a way to close up all the gaps.

Sergeant George Pearson
425 Battery, 107th (South Notts Hussars) Field Regiment,
Royal Horse Artillery
My gun tower was tail-end Charlie of the regiment. My battery commander, Major Birkin, who stuttered a little, came up and said, 'N..n..now, w..w..when we get on top, if we get attacked by t..t..tanks, your truck, ammunition trailer and gun tower will hold them off as long as you c..c..can.'

I was praying that there would be no German tanks anywhere. By the middle of the afternoon, a few tanks appeared on the escarpment side. I was watching them, and they were German tanks, and they kept pace with us, following along. I was shaking in my shoes, thinking, 'Oh my God, please, please don't make me have to drop off.' Luckily they didn't attack, but I had distinct looseness of the bowels.

Captain William Boulton
339 Battery, 104th (Essex Yeomanry) Field Regiment,
Royal Horse Artillery
The 9th Australian Division had just arrived in Egypt and had been told to get into Tobruk, and hadn't fired a shot yet. We were then parcelled out around Tobruk. The Australians looked at us with the expression on their faces that said, 'I wonder what those bloody Pommies are going to do?' We looked at them and thought, 'They haven't even got their knees brown.'

Captain Vernon Northwood
Officer Commanding, A Company, 2/28th Battalion,
9th Australian Division
I did not think of there being a danger of a German offensive, until A Company was put out on the Derna Road side of the perimeter. The battalion had a very wide frontage. Vehicles were coming back with British troops, in what we called the 'Benghazi Handicap'; things had gone very wrong. There didn't seem to be any organisation, they said, 'Better get out of here, Rommel's coming,' and things like that. We said, 'We're not going to get out of here. We have been told to stay.'

All of a sudden the perimeter closed. The first intimation I had of trouble was on 10 April when this Royal Horse Artillery major came looking for me, and said, 'Are you going to stay here?'

'Where else have we got to go?' I replied.

I realised he was dead serious, when I saw him bringing his guns up.

THE SIEGE OF TOBRUK

Driver Bill Hutton
425 Battery, 107th (South Notts Hussars) Field Regiment,
Royal Horse Artillery
They said 'dig in'. Well I got a pick and shovel and it was just like rock. I hit the ground and sparks flew up from my pick. I thought 'to hell with it', made up my bed and went to sleep. I woke up next morning and some cocky chap came along and said, 'We're the last in, Rommel's out there with his Panzers.'

'Who's Rommel, and what's a Panzer?' I asked.

Captain Bob Hingston
F Troop, 426 Battery, 107th (South Notts Hussars) Field Regiment,
Royal Horse Artillery
On Friday 11 April, a number of German tanks appeared on my right heading very rapidly towards the perimeter. Then they stopped and ran across our front and we had a fairly good shoot at them – there were several left behind, damaged. I claimed that I'd hit them but the 1st RHA claimed them too.

Lance Sergeant Harold Harper
426 Battery, 107th (South Notts Hussars) Field Regiment,
Royal Horse Artillery
The tanks came over the ridge probably about six thousand yards away, which rather shook us as on exercise we were used to firing at eight, nine or ten thousand yards. They didn't attack in strength. The firing was almost incessant. It was rather like a cup tie – when you knocked a tank out, everybody cheered. I think we managed to knock out three or four before they retired.

Australian infantry await a German attack at Tobruk.

German artillery in action during the siege of Tobruk.

Anonymous Australian NCO
2/17th Battalion, 9th Australian Division
When we got back to Tobruk we were told that our posts must be held at all costs. Even if tanks broke through, we in the posts were to hang on and wait for the enemy infantry. We had the chance of testing out these tactics. On 13 April, after dark, enemy infantry got through our wire about a hundred yards to the left of the post I was in. They opened up on us and we couldn't shift them by fire.

Bombardier Ray Ellis
OP Assistant, 425 Battery 107th, (South Notts Hussars) Field Regiment, Royal Horse Artillery
First there was a lot of shellfire landing upon us. Looking through the binoculars I could see these men creeping towards our OP, running from cover to cover, diving into holes in the ground as they approached. I realised I was watching German troops advancing towards me in the front line.

Anonymous Australian NCO
2/17th Battalion, 9th Australian Division
So Lieutenant Mackell led a fighting patrol, which drove them back with the bayonet. He took with him Corporal Edmondson and five others. They charged the enemy in the face of heavy machine-gun fire and Edmondson was mortally wounded. But he kept on, then saved Lieutenant Mackell's life by bayoneting two more Germans. They had Lieutenant Mackell at their mercy. Then Edmondson died. That bayonet charge demoralised the enemy, and those who escaped were driven back through the wire. But for this they would have probably surrounded our post with their superior numbers, and made a wide gap in our defences. As it was they didn't make another push for several hours. We kept firing on them all through the night, until about half-past five, when the tanks appeared. We sat tight and watched them go by, for we had been told not to attract attention by firing on them. But you can imagine it wasn't a very encouraging sight. We had no communications with our other posts and we didn't know if any others had been overrun. But we had been told to stick there, and we did.

Bombardier Ray Ellis
OP Assistant, 425 Battery, 107th (South Notts Hussars) Field Regiment, Royal Horse Artillery
There was mortar, machine-gun and shellfire. You had to stick your head

over to observe – that was our job – and it wasn't a very pleasant sensation watching this lot come towards you. Captain Bennett gave the orders; I was just helping him, really. We were two men in a very tight situation, passing information to each other. The signaller was on the telephone and you're passing the orders. As the tanks advanced we were reducing the range of the guns, so our own shells fell nearer and nearer. The tanks made short work of the anti-tank ditch and no problem coming through the barbed wire. Eventually they actually passed through us so that gunfire was falling on our own position, they were either side a matter of a few yards away. Following the tanks were German infantry with their bayonets fixed.

Gunner David Tickle
Gun position, 425 Battery, 107th (South Notts Hussars) Field Regiment, Royal Horse Artillery
Captain Bennett was at the OP and he'd been overrun. The call came down the telephone line, 'Target me.' We thought, 'Crikey what's happening?' He kept shouting, 'Target me.' Then it dawned on us what had happened.

Anonymous Australian NCO
2/17th Battalion, 9th Australian Division
About forty tanks went through and then we came up again, and engaged the infantry and gunners who were trying to bring field guns and anti-tank guns through the gap. These were easy meat. We shot up their crews before they could get into action. And every time the infantry tried to get through the gap, we drove them back with Bren guns and rifles. After the tanks went through no guns and no infantry got past us. In the meantime the British gunners behind us had broken the tank attack and soon tanks and infantry were scrambling back through the gap. Into this traffic jam we fired everything we had.

Bombardier Ray Ellis
OP Assistant, 425 Battery, 107th (South Notts Hussars) Field Regiment, Royal Horse Artillery
The Australian infantry went into action against them – bayonet fighting. Men paired off and fought individual battles. I was absolutely petrified. I hadn't even got a bayonet and, if I had, it wouldn't have done the slightest bit of good to me because I wasn't trained, and to take on a German infantryman would have been suicide. All I could do was pray. No German

came towards me and fortunately the Australians overcame the German infantry who started to retire and took cover in the anti-tank ditch. We switched our fire to the ditch and did great carnage there, dropping our shells right into the trench, and there were hundreds of them there – and I mean hundreds.

Between Friday and Monday we never slept at all. Everyone's face was one mass of sand. Their eyes were little red slits. The guns were so hot, all the yellow paint had gone. At the end of that battle, whisky bottles were passed, and we drank it from the bottle, gulping and passing it on. Things gradually quietened down, and it was obvious the battle was over. Everyone fell on the desert where they were, anywhere, rolled themselves in their blankets, and went into a dead sleep.

Major Robert Daniell
Regimental Headquarters, 107th (South Notts Hussars) Field Regiment, Royal Horse Artillery
After the attack had ceased, in the evening, the Reverend Parry, myself and Doctor Finnegan and a couple of men for carrying water went up to the gap in the wire where the German tanks had come through. We found that the anti-tank ditch, which was about nine feet deep, was absolutely crammed with German wounded who had crawled in there from the vehicles that our shells had set on fire. We started giving them water, but, while the doctor was attending one of the badly wounded soldiers, I saw a German rise up on his feet and have a shot at him with a revolver. I shouted to the doctor and the Reverend Parry to withdraw. I left the water with the wounded and I said to them – a lot could speak English, 'If you shoot at my efforts to alleviate your wounded, you can fend for yourselves.'

Sergeant Bob Faulds
425 Battery, 107th (South Notts Hussars) Field Regiment, Royal Horse Artillery
We realised that the Germans were a totally different cup of tea from the Italians that we'd known all about from the previous campaign. In May we heard all about German paratroops taking Crete, and we said, 'Well if they can take a great Greek island, what about Tobruk?' We felt very isolated, very cut off. We began to wonder whether in fact we were going to be able to hold out in Tobruk.

Captain Vernon Northwood
Officer Commanding, A Company, 2/28th Battalion,
9th Australian Division

Tobruk was a thorn in Rommel's side. He couldn't go too far into Egypt without taking Tobruk first, or his line of communication would be threatened. That was why we held it; to deny it to Rommel. Everybody was aware why it was important. On patrol, a thousand yards out from the perimeter, you could hear the German supply convoys on the road to the east, supplying Rommel's troops. We knew what they were trying to do.

Night was the most active time. We patrolled into the enemy areas every night. We didn't call it no-man's-land; General Morshead, commanding the division and the Tobruk garrison, said it was our land. The Italians were frightened of being close to the perimeter at night and used to withdraw well back. We had posts manned a thousand yards out from the perimeter. They were left out even by day. We owned the ground a thousand yards out from the perimeter.

Company Sergeant Major Alan Potter
D Company, 2/28th Battalion, 9th Australian Division

On patrols you would go out through the wire and walk so many paces, everything by paces. You would go roughly a hundred paces, stop, look and listen. Then walk on again a hundred paces, stop, look and listen; and on again. If you came to an enemy sangar, or something that had to be investigated, you'd move forward and have a look at it. A commander should not do this often; I did it to show the troops, or out of bravado. Invariably I was the one to go. But when you are going forward at night on a sangar, and you don't know whether it's occupied or not, and you are getting pretty close to it, and any moment you expect somebody to suddenly jump out and shoot you in the belly – that gets the adrenalin running.

Captain Vernon Northwood
Officer Commanding, A Company, 2/28th Battalion,
9th Australian Division

The flies were the worst feature. The dugouts left by the Italians were very dirty, and full of fleas. We threw out the rubbish left by them. The water situation was pretty grim. Tea was made centrally and brought up at night with the main meal. You had a water bottle a day for drinking. I used to shave in a tobacco tin, after cleaning my teeth I would spit the water back into the tin and shaved in it. I had a little piece of sponge. We shaved every day, to avoid sores.

First thing in the morning you stood-to. Then perhaps there would be some mortaring or shelling. At midday a heat haze settled over Tobruk, and in places you could move around in the haze; you could walk about and talk to the men. The men took their boots off and walked about in the sand to clean their feet. You took your shirt off and the sun baked off any sweat. We weren't hungry. We had bully beef made into a stew by the cooks with macaroni and spaghetti left by the Italians. It filled bellies. In the daytime you had your own bully beef and biscuits.

Private Kev Robinson
9th Australian Division
Our range of vision in a heavy sandstorm would be reduced to below fifty yards and so although you could hear enemy activity in front of you, you couldn't see anything. That wasn't our greatest problem in a sandstorm: the worst was the living conditions. When a sandstorm was blowing, the fine dust used to clog up everything, for instance the intakes on the carburettors on our trucks. The sand got under the glass in your watch and it would stop. You couldn't shave or wash because the sand got into your skin, unless you had lots of water your skin got torn by the razor. A heavy one could blow for two days, and you might get them once a week. For me personally, the worst aspect was the effect it had on food. We got a hot meal once a day, after dark. If there was a sandstorm blowing, you couldn't eat the whole of the mess tin, because the last spoonfuls were sand. We used to eat down to the last cupful, and throw it out.

Trooper Harry Lupton
Tank Gunner, C Squadron, 2nd Royal Tank Regiment
We had one fellow who had been a chef at the Savoy, called D'eath, known as 'Death' to us. Then we had some wonderful grub. He had ideas about what to do with the horrible things we were issued with. To see him slicing up an onion was something to watch. He wasn't there long, unfortunately. We tried making puddings out of the biscuits and tinned milk. It wasn't our favourite. You got a ration of water each day, and it was kept in a canvas bag and if you hung it outside the tank in the sun it cooled the water. Tea was brewed as often as possible.

Peter Salmon as a Lieutenant after the war.

Company Sergeant Major Alan Potter
D Company, 2/28th Battalion, 9th Australian Division
Lord Haw Haw broadcast that we were rats living in the ground in holes. We thought it was funny. We had our own sense of humour, for example imagining that we were eating a wonderful meal.

There were enormous blue flies. In one place there was an Italian machine gun on fixed lines across our sangar. To defecate you had to get out of your hole, and go to a nearby anti-tank trap which had wire mesh over it to prevent the Germans using it as an approach route, but it had a hole in the mesh on our side to allow us in. We had a hole dug in the anti-tank ditch, to which you could nip across quickly, but sometimes 'Spandau Joe', as we called him, used to open up as you were halfway across. By taking a flying leap you could get through the hole, and bullets would hit the top lip of the anti-tank ditch behind you.

Private Peter Salmon
C Company, 2/28th Battalion, 9th Australian Division
We were so short of water, and got desperately thirsty, particularly if you had to do anything in the heat. Dust, flies, lack of water and boredom is what I remember about Tobruk. I read my New Testament about ten times. In the day you pulled a groundsheet over your head to keep the flies out, and tried to sleep.

Company Sergeant Major Alan Potter
D Company, 2/28th Battalion, 9th Australian Division
When we went back to the Blue Line it was more restful. I had my nineteenth birthday in the Blue Line and my mother had sent out a cake. I had the three platoon sergeants in to share the cake. We would go to unload the destroyers at night. My brother was on one, the *Vampire*. One night we went out in a flat barge. In raced the destroyer, put down wooden planks to the barge, unloaded all reinforcements, food, ammunition, and on the other side they were loading wounded. Then we found wounded people coming down as well, having been caught up with the reinforcements by mistake and being slid down the plank on our side. After this, back we came and as we were leaving the lighter, I saw a sack, I felt it and it obviously had food in it, so risking court martial, I sneaked it out and back to our lines. It was three very large tins of almost rancid margarine.

Taking troops for a swim in the harbour was really wonderful. One day, coming back in the truck, somebody passed round a bottle of Italian cognac found by the water's edge. I had some. We finally got back and there were a couple of fellows I had to take for extra drill. As they passed me they became four, then back to two. I gave them 'about turn', and they became four. I can't remember dismissing them. During the night I was violently sick and it was quite messy. Next day we were having manoeuvres with tanks: unfortunately I couldn't go, I was very, very sick. I learned later that none of the others drank that cognac, they kept passing it back to me and I was the only one drinking it. I wasn't a drinker and under those dehydrated desert conditions, straight cognac had an effect on me.

Private Peter Salmon
C Company, 2/28th Battalion, 9th Australian Division
One day we were unloading a ship, and having trouble getting a gun barrel off. All of a sudden from up on the bridge, we heard this very English voice: 'Can't you great big Aussies get that itsy bitsy gun barrel off?' We had a tremendous respect for the navy; they were our lifeline… It was very difficult navigating in Tobruk harbour, with no lights, and lots of wrecks.

Sergeant Eric Watts
1/12th Regiment, Royal Australian Artillery
We embarked in the destroyer HMAS *Waterhen*. Until we embarked we did not know where we were going; the sailors told us, Tobruk. We left Alexandria about two o'clock in the afternoon; we couldn't get too close to Tobruk in daylight, because the German Stukas would be looking for us. After three or four hours, when it got dark, the destroyer went along the coast and into Tobruk harbour. The destroyers had to unload everything as quickly as possible – ammunition, food, spare parts for guns and trucks, and troops. A sailor grabbed me by the arm and almost threw me off the gangplank. They had to unload us and then load the wounded, and all this done in about an hour.

The pier had been bombed, and they used a bombed ship as a walkway on to the harbour side. We were a bit anxious, we wondered what would happen. We could hear the artillery and small arms firing. It was about midnight and we got on trucks and were driven on terrible rough roads.

The following morning we were organised in one of the wadis running down to the sea. Here we got our vehicles and collected our guns. We dug our gun pits for our 60-pounders, they were big with sandbag walls around them because the guns were pretty big. This took two days and nights, including slit trenches for the gun crews. I was a sergeant in charge of a 60-pounder. We were limited to ten rounds per day. The shells were so heavy, the destroyers could bring in only a limited number each night.

Captain Brian Wyldbore-Smith
Staff Captain, 9th Australian Division

The circumference of the Tobruk garrison was about twenty miles, and they probed, trying to break in and the artillery was used to break up attacks. We also used the 4.5s for counter-battery fire. The OPs were up observation ladders because the desert was so flat. At the top of the ladder was a steel shield because they used to shoot at us with small arms. You climbed up the ladder in the dark, and then spent the day there. They used to shell the ladders; we had lots of ladders, so they wouldn't know which one you were up. Some of them were twenty feet high. If you were lucky you were above the blast. I only did it occasionally, when my staff duties allowed. You talked to the guns by telephone. The maps were quite good by then. You could see the German positions, dug in with minefields and wire.

You got shelled and bombed almost every night, so you spent the night in a dugout. Everything of any value was dug in, so we didn't lose much. Except when a ship came in, usually a destroyer, and they shelled like mad and sometimes hit unloading parties and stores.

Company Sergeant Major Alan Potter
D Company, 2/28th Battalion, 9th Australian Division

The company was going out on a raid from the blue line area and the platoon sergeants went up to establish the start line, and had to stay there for when their troops were brought up for the start of the attack. There was a tragedy within the company while they were waiting to embus in trucks to come up to the Start Line. One fellow with a Bren gun, fiddling with the mechanism, loosed off a shot. It hit one fellow in the head and killed him straight off and hit another, who was sitting on the top of a high rocky wall. The bullet went in by the knee, out of his groin and knocked his testicles about. So we had two casualties before we even started. That was quite a successful attack and a fellow who had previously been referred to as 'Moonshine' won himself a Military Medal, not the one who shot the other two. How? Because as we were moving in on the enemy, he got a bit excited and started firing. For that he was given the credit for opening the attack and got a Military Medal.

The next casualty we had was a young lieutenant returning with a patrol. A sentry called out to him, 'Halt.' Then the lieutenant should have given the password. But at the identical time the sentry called out 'Halt', a shell exploded, the lieutenant went to ground. The sentry saw a man going to ground, and as he rose again the sentry shot him through the forehead.

Then a lieutenant who had been the sergeant major before me was killed through the inadequacy of another officer who had been sent to recce a minefield. This officer didn't progress far enough to find out that there was an extension in the shape of a 'hook' at the end of the minefield. The other lieutenant took a patrol out later and went down the line of the minefield to find the end of it. He didn't know about the 'hook' and blew himself up.

That is what happens in war. You regret that a good man has been lost, but it is a part of war itself.

Sergeant Eric Watts
1/12th Regiment, Royal Australian Artillery
The Italian infantry had no heart for the war, but their artillery was pretty good. Our troop took 60-pounders of First World War vintage to Tobruk. But each troop in the regiment had different guns: Italian guns and 18-pounder British guns from the First World War. There was tons of Italian ammunition left in the caves dug in the sides of the wadis running down to the sea. The trouble was that some of it didn't go off, it had been sabotaged in Czechoslovakia we were told. When they fired it at us you could hear the shell screaming over and thud into the sand. The same thing happened when we fired: about fifty per cent of the shells went off.

We were told that Lavarack had appointed Morshead to hold Tobruk for two months. Morshead was around the troops a lot. He showed an interest in us and what we were doing. We were told that Tobruk was a good port, and out at El Adem there was a good airfield. It was good enough for the Stukas to use. Being attacked by a Stuka is frightening because they make a scream as they dive; they didn't attack us directly, maybe they couldn't find us. They attacked some of the chaps firing the Italian guns. Also we were closer to some ack-ack guns. The enemy shelling was worse than the bombing; it was more accurate. But after a while we became a bit blasé. They had to order us to wear our tin hats. There were air raids every day.

Company Sergeant Major Alan Potter
D Company, 2/28th Battalion, 9th Australian Division
There is quite a lot of luck involved in patrolling. On one occasion three of us went out to establish if there were mines on the Derna Road. Having found a couple of Italian mines on the actual road, we went forward, and found a vehicle that had been destroyed. The door facing the enemy was open, there were a lot of enemy cigarette butts around it; they were obviously using it as an Observation Post. We went on through their front line – you

could do this in the desert, where they did not have a continuous line of trenches. That is when I heard an Italian singing, a beautiful voice. I thought how crazy the world was. We were doing the usual thing of going to ground at regular intervals. Just as we were about to return after taking cover in a little scrape in the sand, the Italian artillery opened up right in front of us – we had penetrated as far as the artillery. Had it not been the sheer luck of going to ground at the time that they opened up, we would have been totally exposed by the flash of the guns.

On one reconnaissance patrol on a place we called White Cairn, I took out a reinforcement officer with a section. We thought that there was no one there, but we advanced quietly. One person, thinking he saw a landmine in front of him, bent down to examine it. It turned out to be a clump of spinifex grass, but as he bent down a Bren gun magazine fell out of his top pocket and clattered on the ground. Two machine guns opened up from that position. That saved us, because had we got closer we would have been in trouble.

Private Peter Salmon
2/28th Battalion, 9th Australian Division
We had faith in the people commanding us, and faith in one another that we would pull through – in a good unit. We were all volunteers. You don't think about killing the enemy: it's kill or be killed. You get a feeling that you are invincible. Like a lot of young people, you think nothing is going to happen to you. Timing is important. Many of the tragedies were caused by bad timing: the tanks didn't come up on time, the position wasn't taken on time and so on.

Company Sergeant Major Alan Potter
D Company, 2/28th Battalion, 9th Australian Division
Two nights later we went out again. The platoon commander could not come out: while showing his troops an anti-personnel booby trap he managed to put it through his hand. The new company commander, Captain Johnson, came out and took the patrol. It was a platoon patrol; you don't usually get a captain taking out a platoon patrol, with me the CSM, and a platoon sergeant. Captain Johnson took two sections to come in on one side and I took one section to come into the White Cairn from the other side. Before long, firing started. We moved in. Near my objective, I suddenly saw a strange figure in front of me in Australian equipment. It was Captain Johnson. He had come through the line of trenches on the other side, discovered nothing, and come across to the White Cairn expecting it to be unoccupied, getting there just as

our section was moving in. It was a wonder he wasn't shot. He was facing me. Then an Italian threw a grenade, I pushed Captain Johnson down, tripped and ended up lying on top of him. Shrapnel hit him on the left side of his head and me on the right side of my head. I found that my tommy gun had run out of ammunition. I got down behind the wall of the sangar and saw the enemy just round the corner of this little oblong wall; so what do you do? I had a grenade in each pocket of my shorts, in my haste to get one out, it got caught up in the lining of the pocket. Finally I got it out, and, with my finger in the pin and yelling, I ran round the corner to this poor Italian who had a rifle, not pointing at me, but holding it as protection against me. I could not pull the pin without blowing myself up. If he had been a German all he would have to have done was to shoot me. I took his rifle from him and, thinking that there was a bayonet on it, I tried to stick him with it, but there wasn't a bayonet and all I did was prod him, and take him prisoner. The show finished and we moved back to our carriers, which had brought us part of the way. On the way I was walking with this fellow, I was losing a bit of blood, enough to drench me. Only a few minutes before I had been trying to kill him, and I asked him if he had any children in sign language, and he told me he had four, and described their heights. I thought again; how crazy.

Corporal Ray Middleton
HQ Company, 2/28th Battalion, 9th Australian Division

We had lots of Red Devil grenades around the HQ, which had been dropped by aircraft. With Private Armstrong I was sent to pick them up. I had a ten-foot pole, and poked the grenade first, and if it was all right, I would put it in a sandbag. Armstrong carried the sandbag like Father Christmas. I came to one, it was damaged, but I wasn't sure, so I picked it up and threw it; it didn't go off. I poked at it with the stick, and it still didn't go off. I said 'it's a dud'. So I hit it, it exploded, and all the shrapnel went straight at me. I had twenty or so shrapnel wounds. I was taken to the hospital in Tobruk, which was marked with a Red Cross, and right by was a battery of ack-ack guns. They were a justifiable target, so a lot of bombs dropped nearby. The doctor said that I must still have some shrapnel in my left eye, which they couldn't get out, so I had to be evacuated to Egypt.

Company Sergeant Major Alan Potter
D Company, 2/28th Battalion, 9th Australian Division

My head wound wasn't all that serious, but I was evacuated from Tobruk. Waiting in the hospital there, the Stukas came over at night dropping bombs quite close. I was this cocky young fellow who had been in the front line and wasn't going to be worried by a few bombs dropping round the hospital until one landed right outside and the explosion and flash came through the window. Most of the fellows, once the alarm went, hopped out of their beds, even those who couldn't walk, and went down to the shelter. I didn't, feeling very confident, but when this bomb went off I found myself under the bed very quickly.

I was evacuated by ship. In the captain's cabin there was an Italian officer, immaculate, shaved and perfumed. He was an Italian OP officer we had caught a few nights previously, preparing to move their OP nearer to our line. He had an enormous amount of information on him.

I did not have feelings of great elation at getting out; I was glad to be alive. Earlier, when I felt I wanted to get out of Tobruk, I was sitting on the toilet in the Blue Line, and an insect landed on my hand. We had been told if this insect bit you, and you brushed it off, it left its head behind, and the result was enough to get you evacuated. I said to it, 'Bite you little bugger, bite.' It didn't.

Brigadier John Harding
Brigadier General Staff, Western Desert Force
The Germans occupied Halfaya, and Sollum. We were told we were getting a lot of new tanks. We were told to drive Rommel back from Tobruk. The offensive, Operation Battleaxe, was very rushed.

Lieutenant Colonel George Richards
GSO1, 7th Armoured Brigade
I was GSO1 of 7th Armoured Division for Battleaxe. It was a political battle fought because Churchill wanted it and we were not ready. We got some Honey tanks the day before the battle and there was no chance to train in them.

Captain Peter Vaux
Officer Commanding, Reconnaissance Troop, 4th Royal Tank Regiment
We were part of 7th Armoured Division. Before Operation Battleaxe we assembled near Sidi Barrani. In my troop I had four light tanks and two carriers. You lived in crews. You had two packs each. The big pack we left behind in the A1 echelon and the small pack was carried on the tank. We did all our own cooking. In May/June, dawn might be about four-thirty and by then you had to be packed up and out and about; as far as my troop was concerned, out in a line of observation. So reveille would be 3.30 am. You

would be out all day. You wouldn't necessarily be fighting or moving all that time, but you had to stay alert so it was quite difficult to get any food. And we always joked that as soon as the dixie came to the boil, you were ordered to move. But you brewed up whenever you could. You seldom got a chance to cook breakfast, but if you did, it would be a porridge made out of biscuits, called burgoo, and sometimes the dreadful tinned bacon. During the day we ate biscuits, tinned cheese, margarine and jam. In the evening you hoped to get a meal, but first the tank would have to be refuelled, re-ammunitioned, and then any repairs attended to – the tracks might need tightening. You might get a bit of a wash. You probably didn't get to bed until about 11 pm. There would probably be O Groups in the evening. At night you had to have at least one man awake, sometimes more, but at least one in the turret manning the wireless and looking out. You got more and more tired, which resulted in a slowing down of your mental processes, taking more time to decode messages, taking longer to read a map, for example. We ate a lot of bully beef, and occasionally sardines or pilchards. The amount of water varied. Until we got jerrycans, petrol was brought up in four-gallon flimsy cans which leaked. The Quartermaster in the echelon had a supply of soap, toothpaste and razor blades.

The temperature in the tank was high, especially when the engine was running. Our light tanks were petrol engined, the Matildas had two London bus diesel engines. We didn't wear overalls, just shorts and shirts. There was controversy: some people said overalls would protect you against fire. Others said you would be worse off if the overalls caught fire. We were all issued with topees, as were the Italians and the Germans. We all threw them away. On our feet we wore ammunition boots, but officers had desert boots made of suede.

Trooper Harry Lupton
Tank Gunner, C Squadron, 2nd Royal Tank Regiment
When we moved back to Mersa Matruh from Alexandria, the Germans had got near the frontier wire. In June it was decided to make an attack on the Germans and relieve Tobruk.

I was a gunner on an A13 Cruiser tank. When we moved up to the 'wire', by night we were generally parked closer together in laagers, whereas in daytime the tanks were usually more spread out, and if stopped, covered by a camouflage net to conceal them from aircraft. We could see the German tanks but too far off for our two-pounders. So we waited almost hull-down until they got nearer, but unfortunately they had bigger guns and fired first. A solid shot went through the front of our turret, just above the gunner's position, badly wounding the tank commander. After going through the tank commander, the shell clanked around in the back of the tank where the wireless would have been, and sent bits of metal flying about the tank. I was fortunate because we had a little bloke in our tank, Charlie Gibbs, the wireless operator and loader, who was half Chinese; we called him Charlie Chan. We had no wireless on our tank, and Charlie sometimes liked to sit in the gunner's position, while I squatted on the floor in the loader's position. Because he was so short, he only got a cut on his head, and I got a scratch on my neck. So we pulled back and took the tank commander for treatment at the MO's place, between us we got him out of the turret and laid him on groundsheet alongside the tank. The MO came and looked at him. He died soon after we got there.

Captain Peter Vaux
Officer Commanding, Reconnaissance Troop, 4th Royal Tank Regiment
The brigade commander talked about the relief of Tobruk. We were tasked with retaking the Halfaya Pass. C Squadron was given the task of capturing the pass. B Squadron moved south of Halfaya with A Squadron in reserve. C Squadron was annihilated. The squadron commander sent a message before he was killed, saying that his tanks were being torn to pieces by heavy guns.

I came across a stack of anti-tank mines that were awaiting being laid. I picked up about six and put them in a sandbag on my tank. When we withdrew we left a number of broken-down tanks behind, either because they had failed mechanically or were damaged by fire. The colonel told me to go out and do what I could to make these tanks unusable. Most of them were burnt, but there were about four or five that hadn't been. I looked into all of them and I found there were no crews in them. We smashed the wirelesses, took the breeches out of the guns. I threw into each tank one of the anti-tank mines which I had picked up, then splashed petrol in, fired a Very cartridge in and ran. Most satisfactory – they all burnt and blew their turrets off. While I was doing this I was aware that there were some German tanks on the horizon and that there was a man standing on the turret of one. It was getting towards evening. He was looking at me through binoculars, about two thousand yards away. I could see him through my own binoculars. Then shells started falling round me; probably from Mark IV tanks, which had 75-mm guns. I then motored off, and I couldn't go very fast because the ground was rough, and as I did so I became aware that there was a tank following me and catching me up. Soon he was alongside me, moving parallel to me, and I didn't fire at him as I thought there was a chance that he didn't know I was enemy. He then turned and left.

'Hellfire Pass', Halfaya Pass.

Trooper Harry Lupton
Tank Gunner, C Squadron, 2nd Royal Tank Regiment
We were told to stay back and wait for a new commander. We kept the same tank, it had a hole in it but could still move. There were no replacements available. We went back into the battle the next day. We found the answer against German Mk IIIs, with 50-mm guns, and Mk IVs, with 75-mm, was to keep moving and shoot on the move with our two-pounder, and try to get round the back or the side and do some damage to them.

The Germans didn't seem to be able to fire effectively on the move. It was a case of jinking and moving quickly, and firing when you could see a tank in a position where you could get a hit. As the gunner, I decided when to fire. The gunner could see out only through his telescope or through a small hole covered by a flap just above the telescope. Inside the turret there is considerable engine noise, the occasional sound of your two-pounder firing or the machine gun, depending on the type of target. You don't think about whether something is going to hit you as you are zooming around.

On one occasion our wireless operator had been cooking a rice pudding outside the tank, and somebody shouted get moving and he had to jump up and back into the tank still holding the dixie, and it wasn't quite cooked. He stuck his boot in the tin and was clattering around the turret loading my gun with this big dixie on his foot. We did on that occasion manage to hole a couple of German tanks.

Corporal William Bateman
Signals Platoon, 1st Battalion, Durham Light Infantry
We detrained at Mersa Matruh and we hadn't been told what for. We were then told we were to attack Fort Capuzzo. We got briefed and that we would be supported by a squadron of I tanks. We were to carry out the initial attack into Fort Capuzzo and one of the battalions of the Guards Brigade would go on our right up the coast and take Sollum. The other battalion, Scots Guards, were in reserve and to support us.

Lance Corporal Joseph 'Chelsea' Lamb
Section Commander, A Company, 1st Battalion, Durham Light Infantry
Before the attack the battalion padre held a church service and said 'a lot of you won't be coming back'. I thought you should be bloody well going in yourself. We went up at dawn, as far as we could in trucks, right up to their positions, got out and dashed forward. We went in and they knew we were coming. One company attacked the fort, another company attacked another

area nearby, we tackled the aerodrome area, it was all flat. This was the first do for the whole battalion. 'Crackers' May was my company commander in A Company.

Private Robert Hawksworth
Bandsman and Stretcher-Bearer, 1st Battalion, Durham Light Infantry
The Capuzzo operation was like something out of a *Beau Geste* film. The fort was occupied by the Italians. The idea was to cut off their retreat from the rear. I was the MO's batman, and we were in rear of the attacking companies; no smoke, few tanks and not a lot of artillery.

Corporal William Bateman
Signals Platoon, 1st Battalion, Durham Light Infantry
Everything went lovely to begin with. We set off at about four o'clock in the morning, moving in open formation in trucks. We had no wireless communication between trucks. Everything was done with hand signals. I was in the signal platoon stores truck. There we were, belting away. We go nicely through the wire outside Fort Capuzzo and all of a sudden there was a big bang and an anti-tank shell had come right through between me and the driver. He dived out. It was a good job it didn't explode, it would have blown us to bits.

Major Peter 'Crackers' May
Officer Commanding, A Company, 1st Battalion, Durham Light Infantry
We started in a dust storm, advanced in trucks. We got fired on and baled out and we advanced fifteen hundred yards across open desert. I can only assume they didn't put their sights down because all the bullets were going over our heads until we got close. Then they started hitting. These were Italian gunners. I was very surprised because a gunner with whom I crossed bayonets parried my point. Having done bayonet fighting, which was useful, I forced him down, and turned to one of my soldiers and said, 'Fix this bloody wop.' He plunged his bayonet in and said, 'Got him, sir.'

Lance Sergeant Thomas Wilson
Section Commander, A Company, 1st Battalion, Durham Light Infantry
We got the order to get out and form up and fix bayonets. I felt 'I'm going to get it or come out of it alive'. I just kissed my bayonet. The spirit keeps you going. The whole company was lined up. There was no wireless in the company. The order to advance was given. I commanded a section. We

shouted and screamed as we charged. In peacetime you are told to use aggressive words in a bayonet charge. Now when it comes to the actual charge, the shouting and screaming all comes out, it relieves your mind. I was aware of men going down around me. As the line went forward, some got ahead of the others. Young Woodall was ahead of me wrestling with an Italian, I bayoneted him and because I had one up the spout I shot him. Another big Italian, about six foot, had hold of young Woodall, I am small, and he made a grab for my rifle. I didn't hesitate for one second, or even quarter of a second. I dropped him.

Private Robert Hawksworth
Bandsman and Stretcher-Bearer, 1st Battalion, Durham Light Infantry
We had a grandstand view. We had a lot of casualties. The carrier platoon suffered heavily. The noise was tremendous, even where we were. Colonel Adherne led the attack standing up in a Morris pickup truck. We were about a mile away. We were very busy. As the battle developed, we were inundated by casualties. I was helping the MO, along with the other two stretcher-bearers, applying dressings, releasing tourniquets. We had inadvertently occupied an old Italian cookhouse area, and near us was a small dump of garlic powder. This smelt strongly when hit by a shell. Despite the fact that we were in our first battle, and initially were shaken, our training took over instinctively. The wounded were all lying in the open. We were ready to move on because we were told that after the battle we would advance. Some chaps were lying screaming; some made no noise at all. One corporal was trying to crawl back and rejoin the action.

Lance Corporal Joseph 'Chelsea' Lamb
Section Commander, A Company, 1st Battalion, Durham Light Infantry
We took the first positions, there was a bit of hand-to-hand fighting, but we came under heavy fire, and we had to get down. We were pinned down. This was about three or four hours after we went in. It was all dead level, no cover anywhere; there was a sangar here and there. When we went in there was a Bren carrier about a hundred yards in front of me, and I shouted at our lads, 'Keep away from the carrier. Keep in the open. They'll go for that carrier.' No sooner had I shouted this than the carrier went up in flames.

There was machine-gun fire and mortar fire, and shelling. Just then, I saw some wire on my right, two hundred yards away, and I saw six of our Matilda tanks coming. I said, 'Right lads, put your bayonets on your rifles.' I waved at the tanks, hoping they would pepper the enemy positions to our front. No way, they went straight on into the 88s, anti-tank guns, and they were all wiped out. Then about an hour after, I looks and all of a sudden there were about six Jerry tanks coming for us, and I shouted, 'Right lads, every man for himself. Live to fight another day or else you've had it. Follow me.' And we dashed away. We didn't stand a chance against those tanks. We ran like hell. One of our carriers came up and ten of us jumped in, all on top of each other.

Major Peter 'Crackers' May
Officer Commanding, A Company, 1st Battalion, Durham Light Infantry
Then the Germans arrived in tanks, and we found it really very difficult. We had only the Boys anti-tank rifles, and no anti-tank guns. All our tanks had been knocked out. Then, at last light, the enemy tanks withdrew; we were able to pull back to the top of Halfaya. My CSM had a bullet through both shoulder blades, and we had suffered severe losses. It was quite ridiculous we were supposed to take Capuzzo from the Italians. Then the Germans arrived in tanks. I lay for some hours between two tanks not daring to move. Then they withdrew and I was able to get out.

Corporal William Bateman
Signals Platoon, 1st Battalion, Durham Light Infantry
We both left the truck, and everybody had gone through. We laid low and couldn't see anybody for a bit, but met up with two others. It was getting near dusk and we heard this rumble. We dived into a big hole, and this Jerry light tank came up and swerved right round and went away.

Private Robert Hawksworth
Bandsman and Stretcher-Bearer, 1st Battalion, Durham Light Infantry
We were given orders to withdraw. We wondered what would happen if the enemy had broken through. We would have had to stay with the wounded. The RMO said, 'I might send you back. But I must stay with the wounded.'

We left in late afternoon, after the wounded had been taken away by ambulance. The battalion withdrew to the start position and transport was brought up to take them away. It was the first hand-to-hand action the battalion had taken part in. We were outnumbered and defeated. We withdrew through a battalion of our brigade. As we withdrew, a sergeant major of the Guards shouted, 'You silly sods. What have you been up to?'

The following day we realised what we had been through, and God knows what the chaps who had done the fighting had been through. As the wounded came back, there would be a well-known footballer who had lost a leg, or an excellent shot who had been blinded in one eye. We knew them well.

Lance Corporal Joseph 'Chelsea' Lamb
Section Commander, A Company, 1st Battalion, Durham Light Infantry
When we got back and congregated with the rest of the company that is where the reaction set in. One of the lads started crying. I started laughing like hell. We lost half our battalion, and we lost half the company, out of about ninety men only forty-six got out. That was one of the worst dos we were ever in. If we'd only had the right kit.

Corporal William Bateman
Signals Platoon, 1st Battalion, Durham Light Infantry
We laid low all night; we could hear firing and just about dawn we saw in the distance trucks and men marching back and it was the battalion assembling. They looked at us and said, 'You've been reported missing.' We couldn't get no grub from the cooks. So when we pitched in we put all the bully beef and biscuits in this dixie and cooked it ourselves.

They were bringing the wounded in and checking up on who was and who wasn't there. The signals officer, Lieutenant Blakeley, had lost an arm and part of a leg; he died. The others were only bullet and shrapnel wounds. The CO, Lieutenant Colonel Arderne, was still out trying to find people. D Company had the worst casualties. The two signallers with them were both killed. 'Popeye' Davis, who was sent back with a message, had his head blown off, and 'Tiddly' Binks, who also tried to get back, was shot. There were a lot missing. We pulled down Halfaya Pass and back to Buq Buq.

Brigadier John Harding
Brigadier General Staff, Western Desert Force
The offensive was very rushed, and the GHQ assessment of German armoured strength was too optimistic. It petered out; this was the only time I saw Archie Wavell in tears when he came to visit us. Our own tanks were under-gunned and under-armoured. The Germans handled their armour and infantry better than us. That was Battleaxe.

Crusader

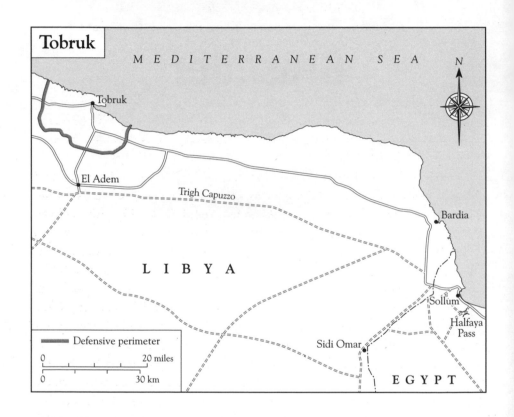

I said, 'Geoffrey, where's the regiment?'
'What do you mean, the regiment?' he replied.
'I have got some orders for you.'
He said, 'You'd better give them to me. This is the regiment, all that's left.'
They had had twenty-two officers killed in a day.

T he failure of Operation Battleaxe left Tobruk still under siege and Western Desert Force back in Egypt. Five months elapsed before the British attacked again. During this time there was considerable reorganisation by both sides.

General Sir Archibald Wavell was replaced as Commander-in-Chief Middle East, and sent to take over as Commander-in-Chief India, swapping places with General Sir Claude Auchinleck. On his arrival, Auchinleck immediately ordered that planning be put in train for an offensive to relieve Tobruk, and clear Rommel out of Cyrenaica. The Western Desert Force became XIII Corps once more, a new Corps, XXX, was formed, and on 26 September 1941, the Eighth Army was born. General Sir Alan Cunningham was sent to command it, arriving fresh from victories over the Italians in Somaliland and Abyssinia (modern-day Ethiopia). In August, September and October 1941 the Australians were relieved in Tobruk by the British 70th Division reinforced by the 4th Royal Tank Regiment. The German Panzer Group Africa was formed, with Rommel in command. Under him he had two corps: the Deutsches Afrika Korps consisting of 15th and 21st Panzer Divisions, the 90th Light Division, and the Italian Savona Division; and XXI Italian Corps of four divisions. The Italian X Corps remained under Italian command.

The concept for the forthcoming British offensive, Operation Crusader, was that Lieutenant General Alfred Godwin-Austen's XIII Corps would distract the Savona Division, which was defending the frontier from Sidi Omar to the crucial Halfaya Pass. Meanwhile, led by 491 tanks, Major General Willoughby Norrie's XXX Corps would cross the frontier wire well to the south, curve up towards Tobruk, locate and destroy the enemy armour. With the enemy tanks defeated, XXX Corps would be able to take the vital ground of Sidi Rezegh ridge, and push north to link up with the Tobruk garrison, who at the right moment would have sortied south towards them. Eventually, the two corps would meet with the Tobruk garrison.

In essence, Crusader was a left-hook punch by the bulk of the British armour, to destroy Rommel's armour, followed by a right-cross punch when the enemy was reeling. The trick would be to locate Rommel's tanks, without being surprised by him first. This caused some disagreement between Cunningham and his corps commanders. He decreed that the XXX Corps's first objective should be Gabr Saleh, some thirty miles south-east of Sidi Rezegh, hoping this would lure Rommel out into the open. Cunningham also insisted that one of 7th Armoured's brigades – 4th Armoured – be detached to protect XIII Corps, weakening the left hook. Norrie did not like this at all, preferring to drive all his armour, including 4th Armoured Brigade, straight for Sidi Rezegh and El Adem, the latter having a key German airfield, which would force Rommel out into the open. Godwin-Austen, on the other hand, despite already having 130 tanks of his own, favoured the idea of the 4th Armoured Brigade being detached from the left hook in order to protect him, asking for it to be directly under his command. Norrie protested, and Cunningham compromised. The 4th Armoured Brigade would keep close to the New Zealanders of Godwin-Austen's XIII Corps, but would remain under command of Norrie's XXX Corps; a muddled command set-up.

While all this planning was taking place, a flood of new equipment had been arriving in Egypt for the Eighth Army. In preparation for the offensive a new force, the Special Air Service (SAS), took part in its first operation. Raised by Lieutenant David Stirling of the Scots Guards, the SAS originally consisted of a mere sixty-five men directly under command of the Commander-in-Chief Middle East. To deceive the enemy, this force was called L Detachment Special Air Service Brigade, a brigade that did not exist. It eventually expanded to become the Special Air Service Regiment. Its first forays were unsuccessful, but once the SAS soldiers had learned the art of operating in the desert from the Long Range Desert Group (LRDG), their operations to destroy enemy aircraft on their airfields were highly effective.

Meanwhile the whole of the LRDG came under command of the Eighth Army, and was kept busy gathering information.

Captain David Lloyd Owen
Officer Commanding, Yeomanry Patrol, Long Range Desert Group

I joined the Long Range Desert Group in July 1941. I was instructing at the officer cadet training unit in Cairo, not enjoying what I was doing, and very keen to get back into the desert. I happened to run across a friend of mine who was in the Coldstream Guards, had joined the Guards Patrol of the LRDG, and had been on the early raid into the Fezzan. He told me a little bit of what he had been up to. I was terribly excited by the whole thing. They had been operating independently and miles away from base. The original role of the LRDG was deep reconnaissance, but Bagnold realised that they must have an offensive role as well: they had the equipment and the ability to move vast distances over the desert.

I had my first interview with Bagnold. I had taken part in the first campaign against the Italians at Sidi Barrani. I knew very little about the desert, or indeed anything else. He asked me a lot of questions to which I could hardly give a coherent answer. The LRDG had expanded and now consisted of one New Zealand patrol, two from the Guards Brigade, one from Rhodesians who were serving in the British Army, and another from the Yeomanry. It so happened that at the time I applied to join there was a vacancy for an officer in the Yeomanry patrol: the man commanding had been wounded. But I was not a Yeomanry officer, I was in the Queen's Royal Regiment, and thought my chances of acceptance were very remote indeed. After satisfying Bagnold, I suppose, he agreed to take me on; I expect because they wanted someone urgently. My next problem was persuading my CO to release me from the officer cadet training unit, but I succeeded. When I got away from Cairo, I found myself commanding about twenty-five men from the Yeomanry, and a few men from the Scottish Commando, out from Britain, for whom there was no proper role in the Middle East at the time, so they had volunteered for the LRDG.

All the five patrols – one New Zealand, two Guards, one Rhodesian and one Yeomanry – carried out the same tasks but, of course, being formed of such different kinds of men (a guardsman acts in a different way to a Rhodesian, and a Yeomanry soldier, who is a part-time cavalryman) probably differently too. The CO therefore had different instruments to play in the orchestra of operations. The Yeomanry were from a whole division that had come out to Palestine with horses: how futile. They were high-class chaps, good at reconnaissance – their role in the cavalry – mostly countrymen, not scared of being on their own in the dark, which some townsmen were. They were very different from the soldiers in a regular infantry regiment, not needing to be told what to do all the time.

Trooper Roderick Matthews
Yeomanry Patrol, Long Range Desert Group
Before the war, in order to get free riding, I joined the North Somerset Yeomanry. We were sent out to Palestine, which after a time became very tedious. A friend of mine joined the Yeomanry Patrol of the LRDG. He came back with Lloyd Owen looking for more volunteers. Out of four hundred volunteers, twelve were taken. I was a gunner, and later became a driver. Discipline in the LRDG was on the basis that everyone had to rely on each other. The biggest punishment was 'Return to unit'. You joined someone's truck and the old hands told you what to do.

Captain David Lloyd Owen
Officer Commanding, Yeomanry Patrol, Long Range Desert Group
We went straight to Kufra, then the main base of the LRDG, about six hundred miles south of Tobruk. When I joined we had ten vehicles in the patrol, 30-hundredweight Chevrolets, able to carry up to three tons of load, and each having two or three men on the vehicle. They were capable of travelling a distance of up to 1,800 miles and existing for up to six weeks with the rations, water and petrol each carried. Water was unobtainable anywhere, except in the main oases and in the odd well which we knew of; but most of them had been poisoned by the Germans, or by ourselves, or were rancid with camel dung. We hardly ever drew water from anywhere other than the main oases. Once in the desert you had no trouble with illness, except for desert sores. You didn't have a doctor, just a medical orderly. You could sometimes get on the wireless back to base and ask for advice from the MO. On at least one occasion we had teeth extracted by the medical orderly acting on instructions from the MO over the wireless, with a good deal of rum as an anaesthetic.

The desert was a marvellous place to be, acting independently. Having been told what I was required to do, nobody told me how to do it, or interfered. I had to keep in touch by wireless at scheduled times of the day. We were working with excellent men, in a free atmosphere with complete

74

Captain David Lloyd Owen at Siwa Oasis outside the Farouk Hotel, standing in front of a 30-hundred-weight truck.

mastery of the terrain. I never thought for one minute that we would get lost. We never relied on maps – they were useless. We used a piece of paper, worked out our longitude and latitude within a mile or two, and fixed it exactly at night by star sights, using a theodolite. There was intense boredom sometimes, and intense anxiety at others. It was fascinating country to travel over; there was always something new. The Great Sand Sea, which we crossed many times, was a wonderful challenge. As we got more experienced we began to know exactly what each sort of sand would do to us, whether it was good going, whether we would get stuck, whether we would have a difficult time. Sometimes we went for miles through rocky country where you couldn't move more than ten miles in a day. At other times, on beautiful flat desert, you could drive for two hundred miles at forty miles an hour.

We had some narrow escapes, but the enemy was usually pretty easy to avoid; we were so well trained and alert. You could see the dust of moving vehicles miles away. You could even see vehicles standing still from a long way off. On every vehicle there was somebody looking forward, another looking to the side, and another behind. What we were more frightened of were enemy aircraft. We hated them. With a patrol of five vehicles, we cut down from the original ten, it was quite easy for two or three aircraft to take on each vehicle one by one and knock them out. If you were lucky enough to escape being killed or wounded, and your vehicle was destroyed, you had a long walk home without much, or any, water. If spotted by aircraft we used to disperse to the four winds as fast as we possibly could and then go flat out in any direction to make it as hard as you could for the aircraft to hit us. You would then all rendezvous at the last place where you had spent an appreciable amount of time – spent the night, or had lunch, depending on the time of day at which you were attacked. This worked well and, with luck, you might get away with only one vehicle destroyed, and you could go back and pick up the crew after you had rendezvoused with the others. Normally you could salvage something from the vehicle. Although attacked several times by aircraft, I never had my vehicle destroyed.

Private Alexander Stewart
Fitter, Long Range Desert Group
On one occasion we were chased by German armoured cars and the whole patrol split up. While being chased we had a puncture. Everybody on the truck thought we were going to be captured, but we were well ahead of the Germans, got out, frantically jacked up the truck, and changed the wheel. We got away just as the Germans appeared over the dune.

Captain David Lloyd Owen
Officer Commanding, Yeomanry Patrol, Long Range Desert Group
We were kept very busy, with about only three days between patrols. We had many tasks, such as taking an SOE agent into the desert, or some Libyans to take a wireless set into a town held by the enemy; going to see if tanks could cross a particular piece of desert, or on road watch. The road watch was probably the greatest contribution to the intelligence-gathering. This was a watch on the only tarmac road from Tripoli to Alexandria, the main lifeline of both opposing armies. We set up watch and reported on the movement of every vehicle that went in either direction for months on end.

On road watch we might be in the same place for two weeks, and each of you was only on watch every few days; the rest of the time you were sitting in a wadi four or five hundred yards back from the road. You sat, trying to avoid the flies, trying not to think how thirsty you were, because you had such a limited amount of water, trying not to think when you could next have something to eat, because it was quite impossible to brew up during the hours of daylight because of the flies. When it got dark the flies disappeared.

Private Alexander Stewart
Fitter, Long Range Desert Group
On one occasion, on road watch miles behind enemy lines, as close to the road as we could get, a German convoy pulled off the road about a hundred yards from us. Our hearts stopped as they walked towards us. Some dropped their trousers, others had leak, before returning to their trucks.

Lieutenant David Stirling
Officer Commanding, L Detachment, Special Air Service Brigade
The German airfields were strung out along the coast of North Africa, and I had the idea of attacking them by small groups of men parachuted in. I wrote a paper on the subject and, avoiding the military police security guards, managed to get into GHQ in Cairo, and to see the deputy chief of the General Staff, Major General Ritchie. As a result, the Commander-in-Chief, Auchinleck, allowed me to recruit and train sixty-five men from the Middle East commandos.

Guardsman Bob Bennett
L Detachment, Special Air Service Brigade
I started in the Grenadiers, and volunteered for the commandos. I was in 8 Guards Commando. We had been sent to the Middle East to carry out

David Stirling.

raids. We did nothing; almost every operation was either cancelled, or a waste of time. Following the disbandment of the Commandos in the Middle East in June 1941, I went back to the infantry reinforcement depot. Fortunately, Lieutenant Stirling of the Scots Guards troop of 8 Commando visited and asked for volunteers to operate in small numbers behind enemy lines in the desert. David Stirling's idea was to destroy aircraft, using a few men. We were taken to Kabrit. There was nothing there. Someone asked, 'Where's the camp?'

Stirling said, 'That's the first operation, you steal it.'

We went in the night to the New Zealand Division camp; most of the division were out in the desert. We stole tents, a marquee, even a piano. The next day we had a perfect camp at Kabrit.

Lieutenant Carol Mather
GHQ Liaison Squadron, Phantom

The commando I was in was disbanded. The option was returning to England and rejoining my regiment. I had no intention of doing that and being stuck back there. David Stirling had an idea to form a special unit. At that stage we hadn't much confidence that he could actually get anything off the ground. We officers in the commando were so jaundiced with schemes that never came off that we shied away from the idea of joining Stirling. He only took one officer from our commando, Jock Lewes, Welsh Guards. I had the option of joining David Stirling and I turned it down. Eventually my troop commander, Major Dermot Daly, told me that he had been given command of the GHQ Liaison Squadron (Phantom), and asked me to join him, which I did. I had to learn about living and driving in the desert, navigation by night using the stars, and the sun compass, invented by Bagnold. We were formed into patrols of three vehicles each, and each patrol had a fitter and wireless operator. We used high-graded cipher to code and decode our messages. We sent short messages by Morse. We used 15-hundredweight [trucks], not four-wheel drive, but quite sturdy. We didn't have tents, we slept out.

Guardsman Bob Bennett
L Detachment, Special Air Service Brigade

No one in the Middle East knew anything about parachuting. Stirling asked for instructors to come out from Ringway in England to teach us, and they wouldn't send anybody. Jock Lewes was the training officer; he and Stirling had jumped before, from Lysanders. We started practising parachuting, jumping from a small truck mounted on rails. Two people pushed it as we jumped off. This was followed by us jumping off 15-hundredweight trucks at twenty miles an hour. That caused so many accidents that we all said 'We have had enough of this', so Lewes stopped it. Then came the day the first parachute jump was to be done, from Bristol Bombays. The first lot went up, I was in the second lot. We were standing watching, and I thought I saw something come out, and said to Dave Kershaw, my mate, 'I'm sure I saw something come out'. He said, 'If it had, it would have had a parachute on'. Soon afterwards the plane landed. The first two had jumped, and the static line hadn't been fastened correctly, they were killed instantly. People said, 'This is a right unit, the first two out are bumped off!'

Jock Lewes got everybody on parade, and explained that the two, Duffy and Ward, had been killed because the RAF had allowed the attachments for the static lines to be fitted incorrectly, so the hook from the strop had twisted out of the fastening. He said it would be put right, and we would all be jumping in the morning. He added that anyone who wanted to could leave. Not one man did. We sat up all night smoking.

The next day every man jumped. Jock Lewes was first out, followed by the other officers. We all gave the static lines a good tug when we got into the aircraft. I blacked out until the parachute opened, we were jumping from two thousand feet, long enough for me to get my mouth organ out and play a quick tune. I never liked parachuting after that. The first jump was wonderful, but not any others I did.

Jock Lewes was a slim, good-looking chap, and had been stroke for the Oxford boat before the war. Paddy Mayne had been recruited from 11 Commando. Jock Lewes invented the Lewes bomb, mixing thermite from incendiary bombs with 808 plastic explosive to make a bomb that would ignite as well as explode on being detonated. Into the plastic you inserted a primer, a detonator, fuse and a time pencil. We used two-hour time pencil. On a fighter you put it in the cockpit; on bombers you had to throw them up on the wing in little canvas bags.

We were raring to go on our first operation against two airfields, one at Gazala and one at Tmimi, on the coast about 150 to two hundred miles behind the enemy lines. Before that we did five daylight and one night jumps. We had a big exercise marching from Kabrit to Cairo before our first operation. We marched by night and lay up by day, each man covered himself with a piece of hessian to conceal him from aircraft. The object was to get into Heliopolis airport and stick labels on the planes to represent bombs. We got in quite easily, despite the RAF having been warned.

For the first operation we flew up to Baggush and had a terrific meal laid on by the RAF; it reminded us of the Last Supper. The weather deteriorated, the wind started blowing hard, they asked David Stirling if he wanted to cancel or delay; he said that we had to go.

Lieutenant David Stirling
Officer Commanding, L Detachment, Special Air Service Brigade
I didn't want to postpone the operation for two reasons. First, we had come from the Middle East commandos, whose operations were postponed or abandoned time after time. Not only did this affect morale, but the Middle East HQ lost confidence in us. So when I started the SAS, I swore that if we undertook to take on a target on a particular night we would do so regardless. Second, in this case especially, there was no question of postponement because our operation was linked to zero hour for the coming offensive: Crusader. We were to land two and a half days before the start of it, because I needed at least one and a half days to carry out observation from the escarpment, which overlooked the airfields and allowed us to see where the guards were, and the way in. We would go in on the third night and destroy most of the German aircraft in that area; this would have been done by 65 men.

Guardsman David Kershaw
L Detachment, Special Air Service Brigade
We were pleased to be going on our first operation. As we crossed the coast, I looked out and my stomach turned over, you could see the white waves. When we got the green light to go, Paddy was out first, followed by the others. I hit the deck, and couldn't get out of my harness as I was being dragged along, trying to spill the air out of the canopy. Eventually the canopy collided with a big boulder. It collapsed, and I got out of the harness. The idea was to bury the chutes, but doing so in those conditions was impossible.

Guardsman Bob Bennett
L Detachment, Special Air Service Brigade
I was in Paddy Mayne's stick. We had containers on separate parachutes for our explosives, water and heavier kit. I hit the deck and was dragged for about half a mile by my chute. We were dropped about thirty miles from the coast. It was pitch black, and took a long time to get people together; every-body was shouting. Two of our chaps had broken ankles. We had to leave

them, and what happened to them I don't know. We found only two containers, so we were short of everything: water, explosives.

Lieutenant David Stirling
Officer Commanding, L Detachment, Special Air Service Brigade
There was very high wind, and flying sand, which meant that the aircraft could not see where they were. My stick came down twelve miles from where we should have been. We were badly scattered, and our containers were miles away, we could not find them. The wind was so strong we were dropped from about three thousand feet, not five hundred, as arranged. As you descended on the parachute, you couldn't see the ground because of the flying sand. Quite a few of us were knocked out, and it was a struggle to get out of the parachute harness. The high wind scattered the container parachutes all over the place, and we were reduced to two containers, none of which contained explosive, so we could not attack the German airfield, which was our target. It was much the same with the other sticks.

Guardsman David Kershaw
L Detachment, Special Air Service Brigade
After a few moments I met Paddy. We consulted about what to do, we shouted, and eventually we saw the others. Keith had hurt himself and we left one other with him. I had pain in both my arms. We salvaged a couple of containers, but not with anything we could use. After lying up for the rest of the night, Paddy decided to make for the RV. Unfortunately we could not find Keith and Arnold who we had left behind, and I don't know what happened to them.

We were told to look for a beacon light, and after the second day, Bennett said, 'There's a light over there.' It could have been miles away.

I said, 'That's Mars.'

'No,' he replied, 'it's a light.'

Anyway it was still there, stationary, for a long time, and we agreed it was a light. At dawn we saw a plume of smoke, and a truck shot out and picked us up. We contacted Stirling at the RV, he having made it somehow.

Captain David Lloyd Owen
Officer Commanding, Yeomanry Patrol, Long Range Desert Group
My task was to go to Bir Tengeder and drive on to watch a track and report any movement, while waiting for the SAS to come in. We had a red lantern hanging from one of our vehicles, and in the early dawn Paddy Mayne was

LRDG Chevrolet trucks moving through a pass in the Western Desert.

Two men of the LRDG on road watch.

seen walking across the desert with about nine men. About two hours later David Stirling and a couple more came walking in. David Stirling told me how the operation had gone and that it was an abject failure. He was one of those remarkable men who never gave in to failure. He was even more determined than ever to make the next operation a success. I was turning over in my mind why they wanted to do this absurd parachuting. Why didn't they let us take them to where they wanted to go, to destroy aircraft on the ground, or attack HQs? We could take them almost like a taxi to within a mile or so of where they wanted to go, drop them, push off ourselves for a day or so, meet them at an agreed RV and take them home. I threw this idea at David Stirling while we were sitting having a mug of tea – heavily laced with rum – in the early dawn. I think he was a little doubtful: he had never worked with us. Anyhow, we took him to the next RV to meet up with Jake Easonsmith, one of our finest patrol commanders. He was detailed to take Stirling and his force back home to Siwa, whence they would go back to Cairo. It wasn't until a week or two later that Stirling told me that he had been so impressed by the way that Jake and his patrol operated that he decided that, from then on, he would like to work with the LRDG, and they did work with us until the end of 1942, when they got their own transport.

TOBRUK

Sergeant Harold Atkins
Platoon Sergeant, 14 Platoon, C Company, 2nd Battalion,
Queen's Royal Regiment (West Surrey)
We were in a base camp in the delta. Suddenly we were told everyone was to pack, just equipment and big pack, nothing more, including twenty-four-hour rations. In the early hours of September 1941 we were told we would be moving out that night. We were to wear plimsolls and we would be embarking in destroyers. We all thought we were in for a long sea journey, even going home. I was in HMS *Kingston*. We sailed in the late evening and after clearing Alexandria harbour it was announced over the tannoy that we were heading for Tobruk. We were to relieve the Australians so that they could be rested.

The voyage went without incident. On the night of the second day we approached Tobruk harbour. Although Tobruk was under air raids most nights, the night we went in there was no raid. The destroyer pulled in alongside a hulk in the harbour; we were told, 'Pick up your kit, away you go'. It was all done quietly and very efficiently by the Royal Navy.

We were marched out to the defensive perimeter of Tobruk. An advance party was sent up to learn what was required of us. I was in the advance party and went to a post called R65, which was on the south-east corner of the perimeter. The platoon sergeant said, 'OK, Pommy,' they made us welcome, and started to familiarise us with the routine. The main activity was patrolling. Each post had to send out patrols deep into no-man's-land to get information about the German and Italian positions.

Private Elisha Roberts
C Company, 1st Battalion, Durham Light Infantry
I went to join the 1st Battalion in Tobruk as a reinforcement from the 8th Battalion. I had dysentery and sat with my backside over the tailboard of the truck all the way from leaving the destroyer at Tobruk harbour to arriving with the battalion. I didn't dare pull my trousers up.

Private Tony Temple
Stretcher-Bearer, 1st Battalion, Durham Light Infantry
We arrived at Tobruk at night-time. You could see the flashes of guns, but we were not shelled or bombed. An Australian guide led us to our positions, to relieve their battalion. I took over from an Australian stretcher-bearer who told me that in the position we were in the salient, you rarely took out a casualty by day, the enemy was too close. Nearly everything was done at night, even going to the toilet. The only thing I knew that was agreed between the two sides, not verbally, was the cooking in the morning. We used to take it in turns: we would light up first one morning, and they would light up first the next morning and there wasn't a shot fired during break-fast. Then we started hammering each other again.

Bombardier Stephen Dawson
339 Battery, 104th (Essex Yeomanry) Field Regiment,
Royal Horse Artillery
I got jaundice and was evacuated to Egypt by destroyer at night. There the base hospital had malarial swamps near, so I got malaria. I spent about two months out of Tobruk. While waiting to go back I was held in a terrible artillery regimental depot. One day they called out a list of names, and we guessed that it was for men to go back to Tobruk because all the men on

the list had been there before. We were all lined up, about thirty of us, and the sergeant major said, 'You're all on draft, you're going back to Tobruk. Tonight.'

Talk about glum heroes. A voice said, 'I can't go sir, I'm going to hospital today.'

'You're back to Tobruk tonight just the same.'

There was roar of laughter in the ranks.

It was exactly the same as when I left. As if I had never been away. It was like coming home. I hated the army in base areas, it gave me the creeps. It was quite different out in the field, you could wear what you like; there is an element of excitement.

Sergeant Harold Atkins
Platoon Sergeant, 14 Platoon, C Company, 2nd Battalion,
The Queen's Royal Regiment (West Surrey)
I went out one night with the Australians and, quite honestly, everything I had been taught about patrolling went out of the window. The British go into great detail briefing and the instructions are precise. The Australian briefing consisted of saying, 'OK, Pommy, we're going out tonight. Coming with us? We'll show you around.'

I would say 'OK'. There was no briefing. The platoon sergeant would say, 'Dick, Harry. You are coming with me tonight. I want four pairs.' We made our way out of the wire through our own minefields. To get out of the wire there was a little gap, and then an anti-tank ditch. Leading from the wire to the anti-tank ditch there was a minefield. To get over the anti-tank ditch was a little wooden bridge. Then there was an outer minefield stretching for several yards. To negotiate that you picked up a piece of telephone wire secured to a stake, and the patrol commander put this under his arm, kept it taut and he followed the wire with the patrol all in single file behind him. Once he had marched the required number of paces he reached the end of the wire where it disappeared into the ground. When we took over we did the same. There was no record of where the minefields were and several people had been lost until someone discovered the way through using the telephone cable.

Once we got clear of the minefield, the sergeant sent off his men in different directions and told them to return at a certain time. I didn't know what they were supposed to do. I must not criticise them, they defended Tobruk brilliantly.

We did it differently. We had a briefing. After we relieved the Australians, only one Australian battalion remained. For most of our time in Tobruk I commanded 14 Platoon, because young officers were in such demand for other jobs and we were short. I went on patrol every other night, or more. I acquired a lot of experience.

Captain Vernon Northwood
Officer Commanding, A Company, 2/28th Battalion,
9th Australian Division
We were brought out at the end of September, when British units were brought in to relieve us. We had problems with desert sores. The men were very tired. When we came off the ships and arrived at Alexandria General Blamey was on the jetty and sent one of his staff officers to find out why the men were so quiet. He thought they were going to wave and cheer with relief of being out of Tobruk. He asked me, and I replied that they were so tired. They were very thin, burnt as brown as dark wood, and very alert, from all the patrolling. But they were on edge.

We were taken back to Palestine. We were badly dressed, a few wore German caps; there is always a clown in any military organisation. Everyone was ragged. Every man was given a bottle of beer during the night at a stop on the journey by train from Alexandria to Palestine. The effect was disastrous, it went straight to their heads. They wandered off the train into the desert. I wondered how we would find them. In the end we had to put out a cordon and usher them back to the train. We were proud of what we had done: the 9th Division was the first force to stop Rommel.

Private Thomas Thornthwaite
Carrier Platoon, 1st Battalion, Durham Light Infantry
On arrival in Tobruk we had Australian guides and were taken into a wadi. There were lots of caves, and we spent the night there. I had an overcoat on and I was tired and I couldn't care less, and it rained during the night and I got soaked. Next morning there were four Australians outside cooking in a forty-gallon drum. They said get in line. They were digging a scoop into a mixture of bully beef, biscuits and custard. When someone mentioned that the custard was in with the stew, the Australian says, 'It's all going down the same way.' Our officers, as is normal, were on one side, and the Australians shouted, 'If you want some, come over here.' The officers had china plates, the Aussie with his big ladle hit the plate and broke it. They had no respect for officers. They had to like the officer before they would obey him.

We were taken up to the line in old Italian trucks, about six miles from the port area. It was about eight o'clock at night. It seemed to take hours.

Eventually, we got out of the trucks and followed the Australian guides; we couldn't see where we were walking. Suddenly they said, 'Right, this is it.' To begin with you couldn't see anything, it was all underground; there was a room about six foot wide, six foot high and twenty foot long, illuminated by lamps burning oil, so the ceiling was black. There were trenches to the firing-position slit trenches. There were wooden bunks with wire, no mattresses. For latrines you had a four-gallon petrol tin with the top cut off, and a piece of wood with a hole cut in on top. You kept this in one of the gun pits. At night one person used to climb out of the gun pit and stand on top, and another would lift the tin full up to him. He would go and empty it into the anti-tank ditch nearby. This had been going on for months. One night the chap on top was just reaching down to take it from the chap below when he heard the sound of a mortar bomb coming in. He flung himself down and the tin just dropped and emptied itself all over the chap below.

We had a petrol cooker to cook the food. We were on the salient position. At night, trucks used to bring up hot food and tea in dixies from battalion headquarters to the companies. You could see over on the Jerry side the lights of trucks bringing up their rations at exactly the same time. And nobody did anything about it on either side.

Sergeant Bolzano
Deutsches Afrika Korps
Sometimes it was a gentlemanly war; when we besieged Tobruk, we were laying mines outside Tobruk, and in the darkness a voice said, 'What are you doing here?'

To our surprise one of our soldiers answered, 'We are laying mines.' The British answered calmly, 'That's exactly what we are doing.'

Both sides went on laying mines, not shooting at each other; and left at the end.

Private Thomas Thornthwaite
Carrier Platoon, 1st Battalion, Durham Light Infantry
One of the enemy mines was shaped like a plant pot full of ball bearings, and it had stem on it with three wires on top, and it would be buried with just the three wires sticking out of the ground. When you stood on it, it would ignite, shoot up out of the ground, and explode just about knee height. They caused a lot of injuries. The anti-tank Teller mine had a screw on top to set it, and you could use a coin to turn it red to red to arm it, and green to red to make it safe. And under the supervision of the engineers, we

would brush the sand off, and turn the screw to safe and lift the mines. The Germans were aware of this, and changed the settings.

Private Tony Temple
Stretcher-Bearer, 1st Battalion, Durham Light Infantry
I was on a company-strength night patrol to take prisoners, to identify who was opposite us. To begin with everything went well. We were given covering fire from machine guns of the Northumberlands, which eventually stopped to allow us to go in towards the German defences. When we came to the wire we found it was knee-high; it was hard to get under, and picking your way over it took time, and you were very vulnerable. As we were making our way through it a ball of light shot across our front, and the Germans opened up with machine guns and mortars. We got over the wire. Just then, one soldier came and said, 'I've lost three fingers of my hand.' We looked at it and it wasn't bleeding badly, and he didn't seem to be in pain. We bandaged him and told him to make his way back to our trenches. He jibbed at this and said he wasn't going anywhere, and wanted us to take him out. So I and my mate, Sharpie, got him back to the other side of the wire. About halfway through the wire there was flash of green light near his belt buckle. I took this to be tracer ammunition; when I looked at it there was very little bleeding, and it looked just like a scratch. He was still moaning on, he said he was not in pain, just that we had to take him out. I think he was frightened to be on his own. We were frightened too; shit scared. We put another field dressing on, got him clear of the wire, told him to stay there, and we would come back for him. We then heard shouts from the left and right, found another wounded man, and put a field dressing on him; and then on another. At that moment we came across the company second-in-command. He told us that we were withdrawing. We went to the two wounded, and then found some more, we must have dressed about six. The only one who didn't make it was the one who had lost three fingers, the one we thought had a minor stomach wound. He died in the carrier being taken back. We found that sometimes there wasn't a large flow of blood externally, like the man with the stomach wound. Most men were quiet when wounded, probably shock. Not many screamed and shouted.

When we got back to company HQ I was asked what had happened; afterwards, I was awarded a mention in despatches.

Sergeant Harold Atkins
*Platoon Sergeant, 14 Platoon, C Company, 2nd Battalion, The Queen's
Royal Regiment (West Surrey)*

On one patrol I made a bit of a pig's ear of it. I had been briefed to take out
a reconnaissance patrol of about ten men, go to an enemy position, and
identify what was there. It was night without a moon. One could see a bit,
but not well. The CSM had been rather generous with the rum issue, and
one or two of the men had hiccups. Silence on a patrol is very important.
Halfway out, some men started hiccuping. I decided to send the patrol back
under the corporal, and go on by myself. I gave them the compass, and told
them to tell the company what I was trying to do, but told them to wait for
an hour before starting off.

I went forward and identified what I thought was going on in the enemy
position. But I was worried at being alone. I headed back to Tobruk, navigating by the North Star, which we had been given a brief lesson on how to
do. I arrived at a main track running parallel with the perimeter. I wasn't
sure whether to go left or right. I chose the wrong way and went left and
into a minefield. I set off a mine. But fortunately it didn't do me any
damage, just gave me a fright. So I lay down for the night, with my head in
my steel helmet until daylight. I said to myself, if I stand up I will attract
the attention of someone in the perimeter. There was a danger of being
caught in the early-morning bombardment, with which the Germans
greeted each day.

I stood up and it turned out that I was near A Company. Sergeant
Booker heard me, told me to stand still, and he would send out a party to
guide me in. I was severely told off by the CO for leaving the patrol. The
information I was able to supply turned out to be accurate it was discovered
later, although they didn't believe me at the time.

Private Thomas Thornthwaite
Carrier Platoon, 1st Battalion, Durham Light Infantry

To count distance on patrol, you would transfer a pebble from one pocket
to another. One night we had to go out and get a prisoner from the German
lines. Their wire was only about eighteen inches high, but twenty feet
wide. Suddenly, a man told the officer in charge that he could see a
German sentry, smoking. He suggested that the patrol stopped, but the officer said 'No'. So the patrol went on, and suddenly all hell broke loose. The
sentry had thrown the cigarette away and fired. Suddenly the men from the
front of the patrol ran back through us. We ran off too. I got separated from

the others, and found myself trapped inside the German wire. I lay there trying to compose myself, eventually I got up and started moving again, and got my bearings by the searchlights in Tobruk being turned on during an air raid. I came to our wire, and wondered whose position this was. I lay there and saw a couple of chaps coming and wondered if they were German or British. I couldn't make out what language they were speaking. I let them go past. At dawn I stood up and shouted, 'How do I get in here?' The chaps in there, I think it was the Essex, just shouted instructions to help me get in. When I got back, the lieutenant in charge of the position gave me a drink of rum, and they got on the telephone to my own battalion. I found my belongings being bundled up ready to be taken away. I was missing. The officer had come back and reported that we had all run away and left him. He was on the next ship out of Tobruk and court-martialled.

Brigadier John Harding
Brigadier General Staff, XIII Corps
I had been BGS Western Desert Force, and on reorganisation I went to BGS XIII Corps. I admired Wavell, he had a wonderful way of inspiring confidence. But I didn't have any strong feelings about his going at the time. I didn't know Auchinleck, Godwin-Austen or Cunningham. The next operation was to launch a major offensive and drive the Germans out of Egypt and Libya, planned at Eighth Army HQ. I knew Sandy Galloway, who was BGS Eighth Army, so I knew quite a bit about it. The plan was to employ XXX Corps with the bulk of the armour to drive Rommel back out of Libya. As far as XIII Corps was concerned, we were on the coast to hold the enemy there, while XXX Corps operated to our south.

Private Thomas Thornthwaite
Carrier Platoon, 1st Battalion, Durham Light Infantry
We didn't know when we going to be relieved. I used to think if I ever get out of this, I will go to a pub and have a pint of beer, I'll never complain about food again. I will never waste food. You felt as if you would never get out. But you found true friends there, you were all the same; there was no selfishness.

Lieutenant Carol Mather
GHQ Liaison Squadron, Phantom
Before Crusader, which had two objects – one, to relieve Tobruk and second, to destroy the enemy armour – my patrol was sent off to the Jarabub oasis, miles to the south of our battle line, and simulate the signal traffic of

Lieutenant General Sir Alan Cunningham when commanding the 8th Army in the Western Desert.

an armoured division as part of the deception plan. It was pretty amateur. We spent about a week there. There was no one about; it was quite eerie.

Sergeant Ernest Cheeseman
Fitter, 5th Royal Tank Regiment
We had been re-equipped with the Honey M3 light tank back in Egypt. Everybody picked up the nickname the 'Honey' tank; it was originally called the Stuart. It was very small compared with the Cruiser tank we had been equipped with up to now. It had a 37-mm handy little gun, and a seven-cylinder aircraft radial engine at the back. The seventh cylinder was vertical, at the bottom. The bottom cylinder was in effect the sump. The tank had been standing all night, the cylinder was full of oil that had drained down. If the piston in that cylinder was a bit worn, the oil would have trickled past the cylinder on to the cylinder head which was upside down. If you pressed the starter button, you risked blowing the cylinder head off. So before you could start up, you had to crank the engine round twice. This was a ten-minute job – not good, especially if the Jerries were after you. The tank was a real bungled job. It must have been built by a committee. I cursed British tanks, but this was the limit. We had been taught the hard way: if hit, a quick exit was paramount, because the tank will brew up. The driver had a roomy driving position, but to get out he had to get out of his seat and past his controls, and lift the visor in front up with his shoulder and clamber out. By which time he would be burnt to the bone. So we had to put in a quick-release action on the visor in front of the driver.

Captain John Pringle
8th King's Royal Irish Hussars
We were lined up on the border ready to make a sweeping attack from the south to relieve Tobruk. I was in charge of the 'thin skins', a small collection of vehicles organised to carry petrol and ammunition and keep close to the battle. We had to stay on the edge of the fighting so, if in the middle of the fighting the tanks needed replenishment, we were ready to do so. It was quite dangerous. We had no armour, and were within gun range of the enemy. The battle raged fiercely. I saw our tanks, Honeys, in battle for five days. The German Mk IV could hit the Honey tank at sixteen hundred yards and put them out of action. The Honey had to get within six hundred yards before the Honey gun could make any impression on the Mk IV. We were hopelessly outgunned. We were led to believe that our protection was the speed of the Honey tank. It didn't work out that way at all.

Sergeant Ernest Cheeseman
Fitter, 5th Royal Tank Regiment
We went on tracks up into the desert through the Egyptian border, rather than on rail or transporters. The fitters had nothing to do, just fill the tanks up with petrol and oil and carry on. These 'mangles', as I called them, did well in the rough and tumble in the desert; they were air-cooled, so you did not need water for the engine.

The main work on tanks was at night-time and if near the battle area, we went into a close-order laager. The tanks on the outside with guns facing out, and one member of each crew awake all night. Soft-skinned vehicles were inside, like a wagon train in the wild west. So we fitters got very little sleep, working on vehicles for twenty-four hours at a stretch.

About once every other night a tank would catch fire. The tanks would have just come in, everything was red hot, and you had to fill up with petrol as quickly as possible. We were using high-octane aircraft petrol. You just need to blink and it catches fire. So the man filling up using four-gallon cans would put on every bit of clothing he could, with gloves and a mask. The can would be punctured ready, handed up, and everybody else would retreat, while two fellows with fire extinguishers stood each side. The petrol would slop over on to a red-hot exhaust and 'whooooooooof', he was a column of flame. Dowse him down with the fire extinguisher, and keep filling. That happened certainly every three nights; we used a lot of fire extinguishers. We sometimes were told 'no noise' – how do you use a sledgehammer without making noise, for changing a track? The recce would tell us the Jerries are close, no noise; or far away, you can make a noise. The tank crews slept alongside, when they went to sleep, they 'died', they were so tired. One night I swung a sledgehammer within a foot of a sleeping tank crew's head and it never disturbed the rhythm of his snoring.

Another night, I was changing batteries and there was heavy dew, I let go and slid off the turret and bumped on the ground where the tank crew was lying asleep, I landed between the bed rolls. They did not stir.

The fitter's lorry was the only one that was blacked out, so light did not shine out from inside, and was used by the colonel, Drew, for his briefings. I have been working on a vice in the lorry overhearing what they were discussing for the following day. Once they were organising code names for the next day. They'd all finished when one of the majors said, 'Oh bloody hell, we haven't got a codename for the close laager map reference for the next night.' Another said, 'Bloody arseholes!' – he was tired and wanted to go to bed. The colonel said, 'Good idea, the codename for the next night's close laager will be arseholes.' He was a good man; known as 'Detention Drew', we would follow him anywhere. He was a stickler for discipline, but fair.

Driver Ted Clemence
Attached 3rd Transvaal Scottish, 5th South African Brigade,
1st South African Division

I was driving a Bedford four-wheel drive three-ton truck. The Transvaal Scottish were a great bunch; good soldiers. I drove supplies and troops. The brigade was moving forward to the Sidi Rezegh airfield. The situation was confused. We knew that sooner or later we would be involved. We were aware of tank battles going on around us. We dropped the troops off and were told to pick up wounded and take them to the field ambulance. There were two of us, and an African driver. The action got closer and closer to the field ambulance. Tanks passed us, and an RHA battery moved in near us. Our people were pushed back.

We got the odd spent anti-tank shell bouncing past us. We never had any orders to move our soft-skinned vehicles away; we couldn't move the field ambulance. We would drive forward and find a medic with a collection of wounded; he would shout to us, and we would pick up the wounded. We had stretchers fitted in the truck, and walking wounded sat on the floor; they were very brave and uncomplaining. Some died on the way back. Some because their tourniquets were not released, as you should do. We were under fire some of the time. Eventually the field ambulance was so full of wounded that we found it difficult to find anywhere to put them. We had to put them on the ground because we couldn't leave them on our stretchers, as there weren't enough. We went on all night and into the early morning.

Trooper Harry Lupton
Tank Gunner, C Squadron, 2nd Royal Tank Regiment

We had to take the Sidi Rezegh area, which had an airfield on it. When you were on the feature you could see a long way around. It was on the way to Tobruk. We were laagered up, and you could hear a lot of movement of tanks, both German and British. There was a big storm with torrential rain in the middle of the night. Next morning some of the tanks were stuck in water where they were parked in a small hollow. All the flowers came out, it was an amazing sight. The desert wasn't exactly boggy but it slowed down our movements. It slowed down the Germans too, but they still had the advantage over us in the quality of their tanks. We had had a wonderful position on the edge of the escarpment looking down on the Germans and I don't know how many shots I fired on that occasion at the Mk IIIs coming up the hill, but you could see them bouncing off. One of the Mk IIIs blew off one of our tracks. It destroyed the sprocket, so you couldn't replace the track unless a fitter put on a new sprocket. We weren't any use, you can't steer the tank with no track on one side. We backed away from the edge of the escarpment, took out the two-pounder gun breechblock and the machine gun, and walked away. It was odd, we just walked about as if we were on Blackpool front until someone drove up in a tank and said 'Hop on here', and took us out of action, about a mile further back where A Echelon were. We were given another tank, which had been hit and all the crew killed, so it was in a bit of a state, but we joined another troop for a while. The aircraft on the airfield were in flames.

If I had been in a tank that had brewed up after being hit, I might have been more scared than I was. If you are knocked out in some other way, you don't have time to think about it, or opportunity to be scared. But brewed up is a very different thing. A fire is horrific in a tank: there is all the petrol in the engine, and the ammunition all round you in the turret. I saw some tanks brew up. Even if the crew got out they were usually maimed in some way by the fire.

Going into battle got easier as you gained experience, as you had some idea of what was going to happen. It didn't mean that you did better next time, you just knew what would happen, for instance if you were hit, you knew what it would be like. You never knew when your luck might run out. The main thing you were concerned with in a battle was getting through it and doing as much damage to the enemy as you could. You sometimes thought about it before going to sleep, but often you were so tired that you went to sleep. We didn't talk about the war between ourselves much. When you lost a friend you did not talk about it much, perhaps for a few days you might say 'poor old Max, pity, I miss him'. Then it seemed to go out of mind, and out of the conversation, because it was liable to happen to anyone at any time, and you didn't want to dwell on it too much. Generally all of our tank crews, as long as they were in crews, didn't crack up. New replacement people seemed to bed in all right. When we were in the battle area, people carried on and perhaps looked forward to a spell of leave.

Trooper Victor Woodliffe
Tank Gunner, 10th Royal Hussars
We set off as the battle of Sidi Rezegh continued. We went round to a flank, and suddenly we were attacked by some German Mk IV tanks; they were huge. We fired, moved, and fired and moved, and our tank was hit on the

E6918

Infantry of the 2nd New Zealand Division link up with Matilda tanks of the Tobruk garrison. The New Zealanders had fought along the coast road to relieve Tobruk and end the eight-month siege.

turret with a mighty clang. I was knocked unconscious. When I came to the tank was on fire, with flames whizzing round the turret. The heat was tremendous. I was gulping for air. My trousers were alight. I managed with difficulty to climb up and out through the top and threw myself to the ground, rolling over and over to extinguish the flames. The skin was hanging off my right leg. Bullets and shells were still flying around. Another tank from the regiment picked me up and put me behind the turret, and withdrew. In the meantime they attempted to inject me with morphine; what was left of my trousers were covered in sand and I was in agony. The tank took me to a first-aid post. I don't have much recollection of what happened after that.

Trooper John Bolan
Tank Driver, 1 Troop, A Squadron, 6th Royal Tank Regiment
At Sidi Rezegh, part of the battle to relieve Tobruk, I was in 1 Troop, driving Captain Longworth's tank. It was a huge battle. By the time we set off from the start line, which we had approached in the dark, it was daylight. We were moving and the German tanks were hull-down. During the course of the battle the squadron leader, Major Mills, got killed so Captain Longworth took over. So Sergeant O'Hara took command of my tank, called Fearnaught. While we were attacking, some German tanks came round the back of us, by the end we had only twelve tanks left in the regiment. That was when Brigadier Campbell told us to attack them, he took charge of us twelve, I was driving one of them, and Brigadier Campbell led us and gave the order to charge. He was in an open touring car. When we were moving up to a ridge, there were a couple of burnt-out vehicles, he stopped by one, and he waved his arm. It stopped an attack by the Germans. He got the VC.

It was chaos. We lost a lot in that charge. After it was over, we picked up crews, some of them badly wounded. I went back to pick up a crew that was knocked out, and on the way back a German armoured car appeared moving parallel with us. He didn't fire at us, and we couldn't move the turret because of all the blokes clinging on to the tank, so we couldn't fire at him. During the charge we got hit and it blew off the suspension, but we could still keep moving. No one in our tank was injured. We had lost a lot of men.

Lieutenant Carol Mather
GHQ Liaison Squadron, Phantom
At the Sidi Rezegh battle I was with 4th Armoured Brigade HQ, under Brigadier Alec Gatehouse. The garrison was going to breakout and meet us as we broke in. It was a very confused day; I had no idea what was happening.

A big tank battle took place that day; towards evening we were sitting on the Sidi Rezegh position, and were suddenly overrun by German tanks. Our armoured screen had been broken into and we were surrounded. We all scarpered, every man for himself. The HQ was two tanks and one armoured command vehicle (ACV); they left. I had my three vehicles some distance away; two disappeared, and I had one left, luckily with a wireless. We were joined by one 25-pounder gun, one Honey tank, and the CRA [Commander Royal Artillery] of 7th Armoured Division. We didn't know where we were going, just looking for friendly faces. There were masses of little groups all over the desert, all lost; so were the Germans. Groups of vehicles attached themselves to other groups in the dark, sometimes the enemy by mistake. We used our wireless that evening, but communicating to Eighth Army HQ. We really didn't know what was going on. We spent a whole day driving round the desert occasionally bumping into German groups, they didn't engage us and we didn't engage them. The next day we found the Brigade HQ, consisting of just one tank. The brigadier, while all this had been happening, was at HQ 7th Armoured Division, and wasn't caught.

Driver Ted Clemence
Attached 3rd Transvaal Scottish, 5th South African Brigade,
1st South African Division
We could see the German tanks approaching and they overran the field ambulance. The 25-pounders were firing at the tanks, as were some South African anti-tank guns. Our CO had been killed the night before. We should have been ordered to withdraw; it was chaos. How we weren't hit I don't know. We stood there doing what we could for the wounded, we weren't going to pick people up any more. There were tanks fighting where we had been picking up people.

We didn't have slit trenches dug. The German infantry came in behind their armour. We stood there. The Germans brought in their own medics; we were encircled. We didn't know what to do. The infantry started rounding people up, though the medics kept working. I didn't feel at all happy. It was so frustrating to be doing nothing; I said to my friend, 'We must not get stuck here.' By now it was almost nightfall, and as it got dark the Germans were still rounding people up. Two of us ducked off past burning vehicles. We had no plan, just get away. We walked off into the open desert. There were German Very lights going off. We walked and walked and did not encounter any German patrols. We hadn't eaten all day, and were short of water, but were elated that we had got away.

We came across a Dodge four-by-four recce car. One tyre was flat, but nothing else wrong. The ignition was OK, and we managed to start it. No keys required in that type of vehicle, just press a button. We ambled along for at least two or three kilometres and then it gave up the ghost, and we started walking until, not long after that, we were picked up by a patrol from the Indian Division. They were good to us, gave us water. We had lost our greatcoats, and were given greatcoats, questioned by their intelligence officer. We slept the night on the ground. They decided to send us to a New Zealand brigade nearby. The NZ were the finest troops I have ever met. They were friendly, they didn't mess about, and different from the way we carried on in the South African army, where you didn't attempt to talk to the officers. The NCOs were in between. The officers never spoke to you. In our unit you didn't get promotion unless you spoke Afrikaans. The NZ asked us what we had been doing, they sent a message through to our people. They told us that they had spare vehicles with them and put us to work collecting wounded. The officers all seemed to know what was going on, as did everybody, however low in rank.

Sergeant Ernest Cheeseman
Fitter, 5th Royal Tank Regiment
We did get among the tank battle at Sidi Rezegh; you had to be as close to the tanks as possible, you moved from wadi to wadi. If Jerry was firing at our tanks, sending armour-piercing over, if it misses it misses, but if you are far back you get the 'overs'. Once a shell hit the ridge, bounced and landed on the lap of a chap lying on top of the truck; he died in the ambulance on the way back. Sometimes a tank in a hull-down position would send for the fitters to repair a slipping track, or something else that could be fixed quickly. We were the AA road scouts, getting damaged tanks out of the battlefield. If a tank was not repairable on the battlefield or in the laager, it had to be taken back to workshops. We had a big six-wheeled Scammel that could tow a tank off the battlefield. If there had been fatalities in the tank, a shell had come in and mangled whoever was in the way, it was like getting into a steel butcher's shop. Once a shell had gone through the gunner's body and gone on to hit the traversing gear on the gun. I had to repair it, and I was vomiting with the smell. I never got used to it, I accepted it.

Trooper Victor Woodliffe
Tank Gunner, 10th Royal Hussars
When I came to, the doctor was examining my eyes, and saying, 'Eyes should be all right.' I don't know how long I was there, and it seemed as if I

was covered in cod liver oil all over. I came to again in a small vehicle with two soldiers who were talking about a battle that was going on. I was unable to see anything because my face was covered by a mask, and I was coming in and out of consciousness.

Captain John Pringle
8th King's Royal Irish Hussars

I was captured on 27 November 1941. I had gone up to the Sidi Rezegh landing ground with the commanding officer and was watching the battle, and we were not involved at the time. He was making an assessment of what he was going to do with the regiment. The Germans put down a smoke screen and moved up anti-tank guns behind the smoke and so were able to fire on the regiment over open sights. We started to retreat and went back as fast as we could to get out of range of these guns. I went back in my little wireless truck with the CO. After going for about five or six miles, we pulled up out of range of the anti-tank guns, and formed a laager, with the object of bringing in brigade HQ, which we had left on the landing ground. The men got out of their tanks ready to show the brigade HQ into their proper position. We were getting this organised, when we heard the noise of the tanks approaching; we thought this was brigade HQ. Shortly after, we heard German being shouted from the tanks. Fighting took place, in places hand-to-hand. We weren't in tanks, they were. It was very nasty. My wireless truck was unarmoured, and I had no soldiers with me whom I was responsible for, so I made a bolt for it in my truck to find my 'thin skins' and get away. After a while, it was dark and I heard tanks nearby. I couldn't tell whether they were friend or foe because it was so dark. So I thought in case it's Germans, I'd better get out of my wireless truck and approach on foot, so that I could lie down or keep out of the way somehow, which I wouldn't have been able to do in a truck. In a while I heard tanks around me and lay down in some scrub. Shortly after a spotlight shone on me, a burst of machine gun was fired over my head, and there were about three tanks within fifty yards of me. I put up my hands and that was that. It was, in fact, Rommel's HQ that had captured me. He was sitting on a tank smoking a cigar. I speak German, and I asked him, 'I am alone. I can't do any harm, why not let me go?' He said, 'No, we've made a big hole in your armoured forces and tomorrow and the next day we're going to finish them off. But anyway, good luck.'

Captain Peter Vaux
Intelligence Officer, HQ 7th Armoured Division
When Rommel did his dash for the wire with about a division and darted towards the east, his garrison was still holding the Halfaya Pass. Our main maintenance area full of petrol and ammunition was down that way, but he missed that, and also missed us by a whisker. But we had to move in the night, and drove right through a German laager. And at the back of our group were the fitters, and as we went through, the fitters leant out of their half-track, scooped up a German soldier, and took him with us. When we stopped, the fitters came up and said, 'We have got a prisoner for you.' He was an infantryman. He was a good chap, although plainly scared stiff. Inside the ACV we had a German speaker, and this soldier wouldn't say a word, except 'I am a German soldier, and this my name, rank and number'. So we sent for the MPs to take him into custody. He came out of the vehicle with me, and I stood there with my revolver, he was looking furtive and I thought he was about to make a run for it, so I pointed my pistol at him and said, 'Stand still.' He thought I was going to shoot him. He fell on his knees and said, '*Nich pistollen.*' I was very embarrassed and soldiers came running asking me what I was doing to the prisoner. I ordered them to put him back into the ACV and start interrogating him at once. He still would not give any more information, and we congratulated him and gave him a cup of tea, and then the MPs came and took him away.

Brigadier John Harding
Brigadier General Staff, XIII Corps
XXX Corps started off and then got into difficulties, largely because the Germans were better equipped, their armour was better and they had better guns. The offensive gradually petered out. XXX Corps got split up and defeated in detail. It failed.

At XIII Corps HQ we had very little detailed information about the operations of XXX Corps. We knew there was a big battle at Sidi Rezegh. My general, Godwin-Austen of XIII Corps, was told to take up the running with the New Zealand division and some other troops and drive his way to relieve Tobruk. So we set off on that. The Omars were still held by the Germans and we had to mount a holding operation against them and advance the New Zealand division astride the Trigh Capuzzo to Tobruk. At the start of that operation, Godwin-Austen set off to meet Willoughby Norrie of XXX Corps, somewhere along the Trigh, to discuss the position with him. I was to follow with the rest of the HQ and meet him at an agreed rendezvous west of the Omars, along the Trigh. We were tidying up, and I was about to start off with the rest of the HQ, when the army commander telephoned me and asked me what I was doing, so I said I was just off to meet my general who had gone to meet Willoughby Norrie. He said, 'You must not go, because the situation is very uncertain.'

I replied, 'Oh sir, but I must go, otherwise the general has no communications, he is expecting me'.

'Oh no, you must stay where you are.'

The telephone wire led outside from the caravan, and a young staff officer was standing nearby, so I put my hand over the mouthpiece and shouted out to the officer, 'Cut the bloody wire.'

He did.

So I shouted, 'I can't hear you sir.'

We set off. I met my general, and advanced with the New Zealand Division to Tobruk. We couldn't get in touch with the people inside Tobruk. So we decided that the only thing to do was to fly me into Tobruk; the Germans were between us and the garrison. A Lysander was sent up from GHQ, and we cleared a strip, which was under desultory shellfire when the Lysander landed, as was our HQ. We flew into Tobruk, hedge-hopping over the Germans; I have never been so frightened in my life, as the Germans shot at us.

Captain Ronald Perkin
Intelligence Officer, 4th/16th Punjab Regiment, 7th Brigade, 4th Indian Division

I was given the job of navigating the lorried brigade into the attack. Moving through the desert as a brigade involves a huge number of vehicles, all three battalions together, the sappers, masses of gunners, and the medical people. We started off with about fifty yards between each vehicle because of the threat of air attack. We were to attack an Italian defended box in the Omars. I was in a 15-hundredweight truck. As it started to get dark, everybody closed in. I had a light shining backwards. We kept going. We moved through a gap in the wire. I used a prismatic compass and had good maps. There was no one there and there were no mines.

We got into the rear of the enemy positions. The battle of the Omars started with an attack by the Royal Sussex. They attacked with tank support at daylight. Unknown to us the German 88 mm had been brought forward to that position, which knocked out most of our tanks. The Royal Sussex took very heavy casualties. My battalion followed up on foot and joined the attackers in the position. I could hear the bullets cracking past.

Next day, the CO told me that the mortars were running out of ammunition, and I was told to take a carrier and load it with mortar ammunition and take it to the mortars. Just as we passed one of our tanks, we were fired on by German guns. We jumped out and took cover by the tank. I got on top of the tank and looked inside and there were two bodies burned badly, they were dead. We took cover by running like hell to some nearby Italian trenches. We were now pinned down in an isolated place. At dark we pulled out and got back to the battalion.

The next night we put in an attack on the remaining enemy positions, mostly Italians. The attack failed; the positions were too strong. Eventually the position was taken. One of our companies went in with about a hundred men and came out with twenty-seven. I wouldn't say that I was a callous person, but once they are dead they are dead, even friends.

Sergeant Harold Atkins
Platoon Sergeant, 14 Platoon, C Company, 2nd Battalion,
The Queen's Royal Regiment (West Surrey)
The Eighth Army put in a major attack to relieve Tobruk, and at the same time the garrison was to breakout. It was a night attack and ended in utter failure. We advanced towards the place, but we walked into a hail of machine-gun and mortar fire. While we were advancing, there was almost no cover, just open desert. All you could do was listen to the stuff whistling overhead, and mortar bombs thumping down. I told my platoon to move out to the right flank, about fifty yards. A runner came and told me the company commander was to hold an O Group, but I didn't know where. I never got to the O Group, I just lay there. Some got to the O Group, and an officer – Captain Armstrong, newly joined, just married – a mortar bomb landed by the O group and blew off Captain Armstrong's head. Things quietened down and the company commander decided to withdraw. Then I discovered that I had lost two or three of my own platoon. The CO wasn't very pleased by our performance. He told us, 'We will take it and we'll do it in daylight.' He sent us in two platoons forward, and my platoon in reserve. Fortunately the enemy had gone that night and we walked in unopposed.

Private Thomas Thornthwaite
Carrier Platoon, 1st Battalion, Durham Light Infantry
We had to attack and take positions on the way to El Adem airfield. On our way we passed a wadi where the Northumberland Fusiliers were dug in. The

Soldiers of the 4th Indian Division with a captured enemy flag at Sidi Omar.

Durhams in the middle of the desert, we stopped and talked to them, and the officers had to get us moving again. We took the position from the Italians; as we were approaching we could hear vehicles starting up to take them away. And as we got to the guns, there were the gunners with their cases all packed, ready to be taken POW. Lieutenant Keith, the signals officer of the battalion, carrying a satchel of Very cartridges, was hit by an Italian phosphorus smoke grenade which set light to his satchel. He was burnt to death.

I and another chap were collared by an officer, it was still pitch dark, and he led us over to a small Italian vehicle rather like a Jeep. He sat in the front with an Italian driver. We drove off in the direction of El Adem, but didn't encounter any Jerries. We got back and reported that there were no enemy in the vicinity.

Private Robert Hawksworth
Bandsman and Stretcher-Bearer, 1st Battalion, Durham Light Infantry
We attacked to coincide with the New Zealanders breaking into the garrison. The battalion went in A Company left, C Company right and B and D companies held back in reserve, ready to make a bayonet charge, which they did. The objective was secured, but one of the company commanders was fatally wounded. We were mobile with the MO and the padre. We had our stretchers and transport and followed behind the advancing companies and had a good view of the action. As a battalion we went through well. There were not a lot of casualties. The following morning going round the companies, morale was very high. They were digging slit trenches against the possibility of a counter-attack.

Brigadier John Harding
Brigadier General Staff, XIII Corps
We got to Tobruk, and, by the grace of God, during that night the New Zealand division broke through the Germans encircling Tobruk. Godwin-Austen sent a signal to GHQ saying, 'Tobruk is relieved but not half as much as I am.'

Sergeant Harold Atkins
Platoon Sergeant, 14 Platoon, C Company, 2nd Battalion,
The Queen's Royal Regiment (West Surrey)
Meanwhile the main force had been fighting hard at Sidi Rezegh to get to us. We could hear and see some of the tank battles that eventually forced Rommel back.

Because we had no transport and being part of the Tobruk garrison, we were to be sent back to the delta to rest and re-equip. But before that we were sent to the Sidi Rezegh area to pick up the British dead and bury them; one of the most unpleasant tasks that anyone has to perform. You are aware that there, for the grace of God, go I. The sights were horrible. Some of those bodies had been lying out there for several days: no heads, limbs hanging off, green corpses, half a body. We set about this. You would come across a chap who had been killed and it was impossible to pick him up in one piece, legs and arms hanging by a shred, one had to use a shovel, and just chop off the limb; lay the main corpse in a blanket, put in the head or arm, or leg, and roll up the blanket and take it to the cemetery. If there was an identity disc, fair enough; if not, you couldn't identify them. While doing that job, a general came driving across the desert, I saluted him. He said, 'Some of my boys are lying out there dead in a tank. Could you bring them in?' I said 'Yes, sir.'

So off we go. We found a crew of three, the driver, gunner and commander. The turret was shut down. An armour-piercing shot had penetrated the tank. All I could see when I opened the lid of the turret was a bit of a head, the gunner with no head, and the whole of the tank commander's insides and legs intertwined with the crew below him. They had been there for a week and the stench was so bad we had to wrap field dressings round our noses and pull them out. They had identification on them, and we learned that the tank commander had just been married, he had his photographs on him. Just long enough to travel from England and then – 'bang'. They were gruesome sights and they live with you for the rest of your life. I don't talk about it very much. I don't think it is something that the fighting soldier should be asked to do. It should be done by lines of communication troops.

The general went to the CO of my battalion and said, 'I want to congratulate you on a well-disciplined battalion, I have just been saluted for the first time for many many weeks.'

Captain Brian Dillon
Motor Contact Officer, Staff of XXX Corps
After Sidi Rezegh, I went forward to give the Gloucester Hussars orders. I found a small group of tanks and trucks; they were sitting round a fire drinking tea and with a bottle of whisky. The only face I recognised was Geoffrey Gordon-Creagh. I said, 'Geoffrey, where's the regiment?'

'What you mean, the regiment?', he replied.

'I have got some orders for you.'

He said, 'You'd better give them to me. This is the regiment, all that's left.'

They had had twenty-two officers killed in a day.

Geoffrey Gordon-Creagh had seven tanks shot under him.

Captain John Pringle
8th King's Royal Irish Hussars
I was not kept by the Germans for long; they handed us over to the Italians in Derna. We were carted off to Benghazi where we spent about five days, before I, with half a dozen others, was put in a submarine. We were told we were being taken to Italy. We weren't pleased, we didn't think we were well placed, and might be sunk. I don't know why I was singled out. It might have been that I spoke Italian. The others weren't in my regiment; I didn't know any of them. In fact I slept on the floor the whole way to Taranto, my first sleep for about four days. Most prisoners went in ships.

Trooper Victor Woodliffe
Tank Gunner, 10th Royal Hussars
Eventually I was taken to Fort Maddelena and there was conversation going on around me, and hearing someone saying 'poor sod'. The next thing I was being lifted in my stretcher into an airplane ambulance. I was trying to be sick. It seemed that we landed near Mersa Matruh and was taken to an underground hospital run by the South Africans. I was immediately taken to the operating theatre and cleaned up. I do not know how long I spent in that hospital. I then went to a hospital at Tel el-Kebir. My face wounds began to heal, although I couldn't walk. I was visited by some technicians who wanted to know if I had any suggestions about what tank crews should wear in action. I was there for several months and bedridden. I couldn't close my eyes as I had no eyelids. After another operation I was taken to South Africa in a hospital ship. In a hospital in Johannesburg I had plastic surgery on my eyelids with skin taken from my arms, and plastic surgery on my leg, with skin from my stomach.

Brigadier John Harding
Brigadier General Staff, XIII Corps
The command set up at that time was far from satisfactory. Orders formed a basis for discussion rather than for something that had to be done. Cunningham collapsed with a nervous breakdown soon after the telephone call I had with him, and was replaced by Neil Ritchie, who had been on the GHQ staff. He was pretty junior, and had two corps commanders who were senior to him and pretty strong-minded.

Gazala Gallop

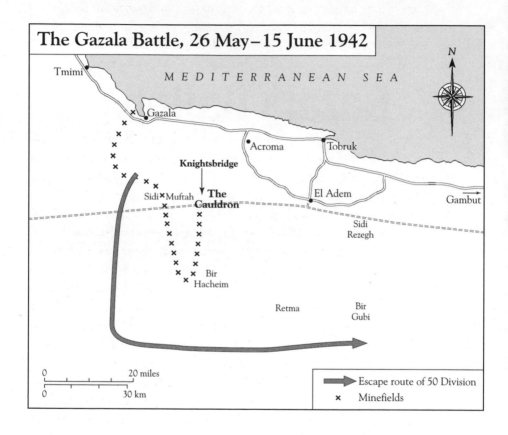

The Gazala Battle, 26 May–15 June 1942

N

MEDITERRANEAN SEA

Tmimi

× Gazala

Acroma

Tobruk

Knightsbridge

Sidi × Muftah

The Cauldron

El Adem

Gambut

Sidi
Rezegh

Bir
Hacheim

Retma

Bir
Gubi

0   20 miles

0   30 km

Escape route of 50 Division

×   Minefields

I have never seen anything like it. In the distance there was a
big arc of little tongues of fire. I realised, to my horror, that this was
practically the whole of the Afrika Korps waiting for us. Soon after the
first flashes, everything fell on us. The fire was absolute murder.
We were on this down slope and they were sitting on the
edge of this shallow bowl. Absolute chaos.

By his appointment to command the Eighth Army, Neil Ritchie had risen five ranks from major to acting lieutenant general in four years. For about ten days while the Crusader battle was unresolved, the Commander-in-Chief Middle East, General Sir Claude Auchinleck, remained at army headquarters to hold Ritchie's hand. For the battle was in a state of flux, with German and British units strewn across the desert, interspersed with each other in a confusing mix. Rommel had over-reached himself by his dash into Egypt. Behind him, the New Zealanders had broken through to Tobruk and on to the high ground overlooking it. Eventually, on the night of 7–8 December 1941, after more confused fighting, Rommel reluctantly recognised that he must retire: first to Gazala and, ultimately, to El Agheila, where he had started his offensive ten months before. He arrived there on 5 January 1942.

A year earlier, hopes of a further advance by the British to Tripol-itania had been derailed by the order to divert troops to Greece. This time the distraction was provided by events in the Far East, where, on 9 December 1941, the British went to war with Japan. Auchinleck was ordered to send aircraft and troops to take part in this new war. Ritchie, meanwhile, was advised that he should prepare a defensive position in the vicinity of Gazala, in case Rommel should strike back. Instead, assured by the intelligence staff at GHQ that this was not in the offing, Ritchie prepared for an offensive into Tripolitania, bringing forward supplies and improving his line of communication.

On 21 January 1942, Rommel, his battered armoured formations re-equipped with new tanks, began to advance. By 4 February the Eighth

Army was back at Gazala. Rommel halted, having outrun his supplies. A pause now ensued.

Ritchie, still thinking in terms of taking the offensive, continued to stock Tobruk and nearby locations with supplies in readiness for a push west. After some months, realising that Rommel might strike first, Ritchie prepared his army for a defensive battle. He opted for a linear defensive layout. Behind a thick belt of mines stretching from Gazala on the coast inland to Bir Hacheim, guns and infantry were positioned in a string of defensive 'boxes'. Some of the boxes had nicknames like Knightsbridge. In the rear, Ritchie positioned his armoured reserve: on the right flank, the 1st South African Division, and British 50th Division extended as far as the Sidi Muftah box held by the 150th Brigade of the 50th Division. Tobruk, now stripped of many of its minefields – the mines having been lifted and relaid south of Gazala – was held by the 2nd South African Division. All three divisions were under the command of Lieutenant General W. H. E. ('Strafer') Gott's XIII Corps. At the extreme left of the line of minefields, the Free French Brigade held Bir Hacheim. The two armoured divisions, 1st and 7th, under Lieutenant General Willoughby Norrie's XXX Corps, were some fifteen to twenty miles back; not concentrated, but dispersed in brigade locations. A second line of boxes at Acroma, Knightsbridge and El Adem were intended to provide depth to the defensive layout. Some five miles beyond Bir Hacheim sat the 3rd Indian Motor Brigade in lonely isolation.

The disadvantage of Ritchie's defensive deployment was that Rommel might overcome each isolated box (or 'cowpat' as more cynical British officers called them) in turn, or drive through the gaps between them, rather as O'Connor had done to the Italian 'camps' in his offensive at Sidi Barrani. Furthermore, between Sidi Muftah and Bir Hacheim, the minefields were not defended by boxes or artillery, flouting the basic military precept that an obstacle is not an impediment to enemy movement unless it is covered by fire.

On 26 May 1942, Rommel's Panzerarmee Afrika attacked (it had assumed this title when the Italian XX Mobile Corps came under his command). Before long it became apparent that the whole of Rommel's Panzerarmee was going to swing well south of the minefield line before turning and heading north-east, behind the foremost British boxes, and through the second line, in the direction of El Adem. What ensued was a confused battle, especially in the area that became known as 'the cauldron', right in the heart of the British positions. Hoping to destroy Rommel, the British armour was itself destroyed.

Lieutenant General Ritchie (smoking pipe), Commander 8th Army, with his Corps Commanders, Generals Norrie (on Ritchie's right) and Gott (on his left), during the Battle of Gazala.

Lieutenant Peter Lewis
Officer Commanding, 15 Platoon, C Company, 8th Battalion,
Durham Light Infantry

We were in the officers' mess of the infantry base depot early in 1942 when eight officers were posted to a brigade of the DLI at Gazala. We did not particularly like the idea of being posted to a regiment other than our own. But we were soon to find out that we couldn't have been posted to a finer brigade than the one consisting of three Durham battalions. After the first day of our journey we stayed the night at Mersa Matruh. We were surprised to find a group of officers, who had left the infantry base depot the day before, whose train had been machine-gunned and the engine driver killed. They had been brought back to Mersa Matruh and told they would move up with us the next day. We swam in the Mersa Matruh lagoon, which was very dirty. After dinner, drinking in the mess, where someone had done some drawings of very attractive blondes and brunettes, an old hand said to me, 'This is the last luxury you will see going up, and the first you'll see coming back – if ever you get back.'

While in the mess, I heard someone say that we should watch out for milestone 105, which was where the German fighters regularly strafed the cattle trucks taking troops forward. We got up early next morning and climbed into the metal cattle trucks. We had to shovel wood and straw out of the wagon before we could get in. It was Spike Galloway who was being posted to one of the other Durham battalions who was first to notice the freshly patched cannon-shell holes in the sides of the metal wagon; one just above my head. Our stop that night was Capuzzo. We watched very carefully for milestone 105 and as it came closer we got jittery, and got our things together in case we had to jump for it – except Spike, who spent his time brewing tea. Other than some rowdy members of a Scottish reinforcement draft who opened fire on an RASC truck convoy, which was running level with the train, there were no incidents.

Captain Harry Sell
Staff Captain, 151st Brigade, 50th Division

We took over part of the Gazala line from the South Africans. We developed the positions with the 150th Brigade on our left and South Africans on our right. We were in boxes. In the box were the three battalions with artillery, sappers and so on, in all-round defence and in depth. Every night the supplies would come up from Tobruk. In rocky ground you had to build up stone sangars, but mostly at Gazala we could dig down. We made

114

dugouts, with roofs on them, and sandbags over them. The positions were connected by string or wire, which you tugged to alert the next position in the event of an enemy approaching. We stood-to at dusk and dawn. At midday it was so hot that it caused mirages.

The perimeter consisted of 'mattress' wire, flattened barbed wire, about three hundred yards deep. You hung booby traps on it. Beyond that there was a minefield. Beyond again there were outposts, and beyond that, listening posts. There were gaps in the mattress wire marked with white tape so patrols could go out; every night we sent out patrols. Every gap was covered by a gap-covering party, and as the patrol came up they would take the mines out and the patrol would pass through. They wouldn't put the mines back in until after the patrol had come back.

A platoon would be out in an outpost and the platoon would send out a listening post, consisting of a corporal and two privates; he would report back by landline what he had heard, these soldiers were out by themselves half a mile from any friendly troops, dug into a trench in the desert. The platoon outpost was properly dug in as a miniature fortress.

Lieutenant Peter Lewis
Officer Commanding, 15 Platoon, C Company, 8th Battalion, Durham Light Infantry

On arrival at the box, George Chambers, the adjutant, wheeled me in to see the CO, Tim Beart. The DLI was very much a county battalion, and I don't think they were keen to have people from other regiments joining them. Colonel Beart looked through my details, glanced up at George Chambers and said, 'Good God, George, they are sending us journalists now.' I then met my company commander, who showed me where I was to bed down. 'That's your home.' he said. I found myself looking down at a slit trench about seven foot long by three feet wide.

I met my platoon after seeing the company commander. I had twenty-eight men, all dubious about someone coming in who wasn't a Durham. I had never been north of Watford in my life. Not until I took out my first night patrol, about two days after I arrived, and got to the right place and back – in this case a truck in the middle of the desert at night – did they have confidence in me. I was terrified. You had to navigate by compass. We travelled several miles, worried that when it came to going back I would miss the box. It happened to other people several times. I could hear these Durham blokes muttering behind me, 'He's a bloody Londoner, aye, he'll get us lost.'

Captain Harry Sell
Staff Captain, 151st Brigade, 50th Division

Food in the box was hard tack and bully beef. We got half a gallon of water a day, of which a quart went into your water bottle, and the rest went to the cookhouse. Nothing was fresh; you might get a tin of pineapple as a treat. Sometimes in a battalion, cooking was done by sections and platoons, rather than centrally as a battalion or company. Bulletins were issued telling you the various ways you could cook bully beef. To prevent scurvy, every day officers went round, put an ascorbic acid tablet on each man's tongue, and watched him swallow it.

You kept a two-gallon tin for washing. You took Italian gas-mask filters and put them on top of the tin. After cleaning your teeth you spat the water into the filter, and it went through to the tin. Eventually you built up about half a can of water. You washed your face, poured it back through the filter, washed your socks, and filtered it again. Water came either from wells or from Tobruk; it was brackish and salty.

If it was soft you could dig latrines. If it was rock you had to use thunderboxes and carry them to a place where you could dig a pit. The sanitary squad would go round with a tin of petrol, pour it into the latrine pit and light it, to burn every thing up. There was a urinal called the 'desert rose', consisting of a tube made of tins joined together and stuck in the sand, with a big tin on the top. Most people out there had an attack of gippy tummy at some time or other, but the doctors had a medicine that 'sealed' you up. We made a joke of everything that was irksome. Someone wrote a poem about the life of the staff in Cairo, and how they wasted water, every verse ended, 'Every time they pull the chain, three days' ration goes down the drain.'

Lieutenant Peter Lewis
Officer Commanding, 15 Platoon, C Company, 8th Battalion, Durham Light Infantry

The Germans were thirty miles away when I arrived. To begin with, we were not shelled in the box. At night a listening patrol might go out to locate a minefield that the intelligence office had heard might be being constructed, or perhaps to a wrecked enemy armoured vehicle to retrieve documents, maps, and information on what unit it belonged to. We went on what the CO called 'commerce raiding', to a set of tracks far to the south: the main supply route for the Germans and Italians, used by soft-skinned vehicles, but very rarely armour of any sort. We went out in carriers, infantry in trucks, with perhaps a couple of guns, and machine gunners. We would go out and lie up until you saw a nice convoy, and shell it, and then break cover with the carriers to shoot up as many of the lorries as we could, turn and race back, leaving some of the enemy trucks blazing. It did not always go smoothly. On one occasion we unintentionally raided a column which had an ambulance with it. I was standing near the ambulance, when one of the carrier platoon who had acquired a German sub-machine gun earlier that morning, fired it by mistake, and drilled a neat pattern of holes through the sump of the ambulance. All the oil drained out, and the ambulance was immobilised. There was a lot of shouting and screaming, and while we were busy apologising to the Italians, a couple of German armoured cars appeared on the horizon. We said we were jolly sorry, and tore off as fast as we could back behind the little escarpment we had come from.

Captain Ian English
Officer Commanding Carrier Platoon, 8th Battalion,
Durham Light Infantry
In the 8th Battalion we had a post about three miles out in front called Strickland's Post, named after the first platoon commander to establish the post. It consisted of a platoon, a section of machine guns from the 2nd Cheshires, and two anti-tank guns. It was dug in with some wire but not mined. It was an early warning post.

Day patrols were normally commanded by a captain with a section of three carriers, a section of 25-pounder field guns and a forward observation officer, and a section of machine guns; all mobile. The task was to go out, may be fifteen or twenty miles, in daylight and keep observation of what was happening. They weren't offensive, they were recce patrols, and the captain reported to brigade HQ every two hours on a number 19 wireless set. We used to go through country that had been fought over at the end of the Crusader operation and there were German tanks lying there and 25-pounders. We would see the German tanks and half-tracks moving about. The heat haze was a problem, and it was difficult to make out exactly what one was seeing. It got very hot; at midday you couldn't put your hand on the metal sides of the carriers.

There were also columns, called 'Jock' columns, initiated in the early days by Brigadier Jock Campbell. These consisted of a force of infantry, sometimes up to a battalion, and a battery of 25-pounders, anti-tank, and anti-aircraft guns, a lot of vehicles that would move in desert formation – fifty or sixty yards between vehicles, and quarter of a mile between columns – covering a lot of ground. These were sent for a specific purpose, normally to shoot up an enemy position or column, perhaps to try to draw the Germans out.

Sergeant Ray Ellis
425 Battery, 107th (South Notts Hussars) Field Regiment,
Royal Horse Artillery
Moving in desert box formation, the soft vehicles were in the middle. The guns were on the outside, with the armoured units coming up in rear in their own box formation. These huge dispositions moved about the desert like ships at sea. It was rather like that in effect, because as the vehicles moved along through the sand they left a trail of dust behind them just as ships leave a wake in the water.

Captain Michael Ferens
Officer Commanding, C Company, 6th Battalion,
Durham Light Infantry
I was detailed to command a Jock column. One of the objects was to get the 25-pounders into action; the column would move forward and spread out, so it didn't provide a good target for bombers, while the OP officer would move forward to a point from where he could observe the country, and if he spotted a target, such as vehicles, he engaged it with his guns. In the evening the column would move back about five miles into a laager. I would pick a map reference and tell the OP officer where this would be.

On one occasion we went back into laager; the OP officer, Captain Pickering, was to join us there. He got on the blower, told us he was lost, couldn't find us, and would I put up a red Very light? I thought this was a stupid request and said, 'No.' Some time later he came on the blower again, he still couldn't find us, and would I put up a Very light? Eventually I decided I would, and eventually he came in. I tore him off a strip for jeopardising the safety of the column by asking for a Very light to be put up. He asked, 'What would you do?' He showed me his compass, and all the fluorescent bits from the card were floating about – they had all become detached.

One night we observed a working party of Germans and we decided to attack them. We mounted 3-inch mortars on sandbags in the back of 15-hundredweight trucks, at dusk got down to within possible range, turned the trucks round so the back was facing the enemy and, at the given signal, bombs were put in as fast as we could. When the first bomb burst the other end, we stopped putting in bombs, and drove as fast as we could back to the laager.

Captain Harry Sell
Officer Commanding, D Company, 8th Battalion, Durham Light Infantry
I went out on a number of patrols. They were recce patrols, as we had news of enemy activity: armour moving down the Trigh Capuzzo. We had to go and confirm it and, if necessary, take prisoners. We went out and captured some enemy as they went to the latrines in the night. We learned that Rommel was about to make a push, supported by the Ariete Division [an Italian armoured division]. The aim of another patrol was to destroy some armoured cars. We found them unawares. We sent some Bren gunners out to a flank, they opened up on the two or three armoured cars, while this attracted the attention of the armoured cars, we motored up with our two-pounder anti-tank guns portee, got within range, and finished them off. We knew Rommel was gathering strength, but did not know where he would strike.

Captain Ian English
Officer Commanding, Carrier Platoon, 8th Battalion,
Durham Light Infantry
On 26 May the Germans launched their attack and the first night drove round Bir Hacheim and got behind the main Gazala line. Their supplies were situated in an area about ten miles in front of our position in a place marked on our maps as 'many tracks'; we suddenly realised that this place was being used a lot. To begin with we had an easy time, most of the transport were Italians, we disrupted their convoys; they didn't put up much of a fight. We captured their water lorries and took lots of prisoners. Then they started to defend these places. On one patrol I was leading we saw all this transport and were shooting at it. Suddenly, on the right, I saw an Italian tank. We got the anti-tank rifles off the carrier, and stood looking at each other. One of my section commanders, Sergeant Hill, got fed up with this, got into his carrier, and went flat out for this tank. Sergeant Hill was standing up in the front of the carrier with his tommy gun, and the commander of this tank had his head and shoulders out and surrendered. Unbelievable! We couldn't bring the tank in, but took the crew prisoner. For several days we had easy pickings, which put the men's tails right up.

Lieutenant Peter Lewis
Officer Commanding, 15 Platoon, C Company, 8th Battalion,
Durham Light Infantry
At Gazala as a prelude to the German attack, the Italians moved two companies towards Strickland's Post. We were in the vicinity on a

commerce raiding patrol. A machine-gunner tipped off Ian English and he thought the enemy was just a patrol. When he went to look, he realised it was much more.

Captain Ian English
Officer Commanding, Carrier Platoon, 8th Battalion,
Durham Light Infantry
Taking a section of carriers, two anti-tank guns, a section of mortars, and an infantry platoon we went out to Strickland's Post, then south-west from there towards 'many tracks'. We hadn't gone far when we were fired on by machine guns and it was obvious that an Italian position had been established. I thought this will be another easy day, we'll clear these people out, and we got the Bren guns going. I exposed myself unduly, got shot through the neck, and taken back to Strickland's Post and that was the end of the action for me that day. But the second in command of the battalion, Major Clark, was at Strickland's Post at the time, and he organised an attack with what we had there. Very soon the position was pretty well covered, and while I was lying there in the ambulance, my batman came in and said we have taken 150 prisoners.

Lieutenant Peter Lewis
Officer Commanding, 15 Platoon, C Company, 8th Battalion,
Durham Light Infantry
I took part in the attack. They were dug in. We were shelled by mistake by our own guns; one of my chaps in a carrier was killed by shrapnel. At one point we saw an anti-tank gun, which we charged in our carrier, with one chap firing a tommy gun over the driver's head while I was firing a rifle. We got there in the nick of time, ran over the gun pit, threw in some grenades, and shot up the crew. We took over a hundred Italian prisoners. The Germans shelled them as we marched them off.

Captain Michael Forrester
GSO 3, HQ XIII Corps
On 26 May, Rommel struck. Instead of attacking in the centre, which we expected, he feinted in the centre using the Italians and brought the bulk of Panzerarmee Afrika round the flank and both sides of Bir Hacheim. I remember the reports coming in from our forward troops, but not until mid-morning on 27 May was it clear to us that the main thrust was coming round the southern flank, and not in the centre. Advance HQ XIII Corps moved

into one of the smaller boxes in rear, at Acroma, so we didn't have to think about the security of the HQ and could devote ourselves to the battle. For much of the time the situation was extremely confused. The general visited General Pienaar commanding the South Africans on the 27th and this seemed to go well. We left at dark and on our way back we encountered a troop of armoured cars; it took us some time to recognise that they weren't ours. They must have come to the same conclusion at about the same time, opened fire and gave chase. It was only due to the superb driving by General Gott's driver that we got away.

Second Lieutenant Herbert Bonello
520 Battery, 107th (South Notts Hussars) Field Regiment,
Royal Horse Artillery
We were well to the south, in front of a gap in the minefield at Bir-el Harmat, guns pointing westwards over the minefield. All the supporting trucks were in line, dispersed at the back. I noticed, as I got ready to get down in the old sleeping bag, there was a tremendous amount of activity by flares on the other side of the minefield. No one realised the import of those flares. Nobody had the slightest idea of what was coming. We kicked a football about that night.

Trooper David Brown
Tank Driver, 1st Royal Tank Regiment
We were down south just in front of Bir Hacheim and during the morning we saw this dust cloud going up where Jerry was, he was moving round the left to make a hook and come in where the 7 Armoured Division were. At the time it was like a fox in a hen coop, everybody dashing about all over the place.

Driver Bobby Feakins
520 Battery, 107th (South Notts Hussars) Field Regiment,
Royal Horse Artillery
The battery commander, Major Gerry Birkin, went out in an armoured car used as a mobile OP to investigate reports of German armour moving down in the south. He was up in the turret and sighted a lot of dust, and said, 'Would you just check this?' I went up and a shell landed a bit behind us. He said, 'Whoops.' Then I said, 'Oh sir! Quick!' I thought I'd seen a vehicle moving in direct line towards us. I came down and sat in my seat, and he went up. The next round came straight inside the armoured car. I didn't realise it had hit us, and I turned and there were two radio operators without

heads – absolutely nothing from the shoulders. I had blood and muck all over me. Major Birkin slumped into my arms and he was actually dead at that point, hit right in the tummy. I was wounded in the legs. On the inter-battery wireless, I said, 'We've been hit. We've been hit.'

Sergeant Harold Harper
520 Battery, 107th (South Notts Hussars) Field Regiment,
Royal Horse Artillery
We had only gone about six or seven hundred yards when we heard gabbling on the battery commander's radio which immediately told us that something was wrong, Captain Ivor Birkin, the battery commander's brother, jumped out and dashed across. When we reached the armoured car – I'd never seen anything like it in my life. Major Birkin lay flat on the floor, obviously dead. I opened up the two doors at the back. Apparently the armour-piercing shell had gone clear through the middle of the battery commander as he was standing up and chopped off the heads of the two wireless operators. All you could see was those two lads, their hands still holding their mouthpieces, although their heads were lying on the floor. The third wireless operator was the one who was gabbling out the message.

Captain Birkin ordered me back to our armoured car, I was moving to pick up Captain Birkin when just out of a cloud of sand came a Royal Gloucestershire Hussars' Grant tank. We hit it head on, and bounced back about five yards. The engine was on fire so we all jumped out and dashed across to tell Captain Birkin. There we were, stranded.

Driver Bobby Feakins
520 Battery, 107th (South Notts Hussars) Field Regiment,
Royal Horse Artillery
A tank came past, Captain Birkin's driver lifted me on and hung on to me; from my waist down I couldn't feel a thing. I was on the back with Captain Birkin's driver, Harold Harper, Captain Birkin and Wright, the signaller, with a broken leg. There was stuff flying around, we were under shellfire.

Sergeant Harold Harper
520 Battery, 107th (South Notts Hussars) Field Regiment,
Royal Horse Artillery
The tank commander had no idea we were there and kept firing. We had to keep dodging as best we could when the turret and barrel came swinging round. One of our fellows fell off and we thought he'd been crushed to

death. Most of us received wounds from the German shelling, although at the time we weren't aware of their extent: there was too much happening.

Driver Bobby Feakins
520 Battery, 107th (South Notts Hussars) Field Regiment,
Royal Horse Artillery

I fell off the tank. It continued on its way and I was left out in the open miles from anywhere in no-man's-land. Where tanks turn, their tracks throw up a ridge and that looked like a haven for me; I hid there. The pain had started to come and I just couldn't use my legs. I had a great gaping hole in my right leg and my left leg and knee were full of shrapnel. I must still have been in shock, but I knew what was going on around me and my one concern was to keep safe. After a while a tank came by, saw me out in the open, and came over. The commander said, 'What the hell are you doing here?'

'Having an afternoon cup of tea, you silly bugger.'

He replied, 'Well I'm sorry old chap, I'm going into action now, but on my way back I'll pick you up.'

Away he went. An hour and a half, two hours: watching shells drop round me, none too close, just wondering about the things you've done and you'd like to do. Fear, because you didn't know what was going to happen. But he did come back, and I felt that heaven had opened up. One of the crew lifted me on, and they drove me back.

Driver Ernie Hurry
520 Battery, 107th (South Notts Hussars) Field Regiment,
Royal Horse Artillery

I had a load of NAAFI stuff dropped off to my truck and had to give it out to the men: cigarettes, tins of fruit. I'd left my vehicle and walked across to another. All of a sudden I heard the shemozzle on the other side of the hill. I said to a chap, 'Somebody's having it pretty rough over the other side.' We sat there talking and I saw a German tank pull over the hill.

Second Lieutenant Herbert Bonello
520 Battery, 107th (South Notts Hussars) Field Regiment,
Royal Horse Artillery

It seemed to happen so quickly that we were more flabbergasted than panicked. B Troop had to turn round and face the other direction. D Troop were able to get their gun tower's limber up, and push off. We were in the middle, in a slit trench under fire. Clearly the attack was coming from the south, it was too late to go east, you had to go north. We should have gone much sooner. When do you scarper? When do you go into action?

Driver Ernie Hurry
520 Battery, 107th (South Notts Hussars) Field Regiment,
Royal Horse Artillery
While we were making our minds up, six or seven more tanks appeared over the hill. I ran back to my truck and drove it to the rear of the guns. The guns opened up as I waited there. The Germans were very close. Captain Bennett stood up in his vehicle, with a blue flag, which meant that everybody had to withdraw. I went to the gun position and picked up three or four signallers, got them on the running boards. I was fired at and chased by one of the tanks; I could see the bullets spurting up sand in front of me. I put on speed and kept going.

Driver Bill Hutton
520 Battery, 107th (South Notts Hussars) Field Regiment,
Royal Horse Artillery
MacNamara was Sergeant Taylor's gun layer and the tank was coming straight for the gun. Fred Taylor was telling him to fire, and he said, 'I can't see a fucking thing.' Taylor said, 'Pull the trigger, man.' He pulled the trigger just as the tank was going to climb over the gun. It blew the turret off, killed everybody in the tank, which carried on and climbed right over the gun.

There I was all by myself. I could hear the squeaking, creaking noise that tanks make. I bobbed my head up, and soon put it down again – three German tanks all within spitting distance. There is a hell of a difference from being in action with one of your pals, you can make silly jokes about it, but when you're on your own it's a different cup of tea. I saw chaps walking about with their hands up, so I came out with my hands up. It wasn't long before your arms begin to ache.

Captain Peter Vaux
GSO 3 Intelligence, HQ 7th Armoured Division
In HQ 7 Armoured Division we had a fire-maker, in order to burn our maps immediately in the event of capture. It happened at Gazala, on 27 May; we were planning to carry out an attack, and Rommel pre-empted us. We were surprised: there was a failure in communication between the King's Dragoon

Guards and people further up the chain of command. The King's Dragoon Guards reported the enemy advance, but the reports did not get to divisional HQ. At about 5.30 am the duty officer who shared the bivvy with me alongside the ACV – the armoured command vehicle – came running to me and said, 'There are five hundred vehicles south of Hacheim moving north-east and we are going to move.' We packed up quickly, but not quickly enough because almost immediately there was a lot of gunfire and British tanks of 4th Armoured Brigade came through us, retreating fast, with their guns pointing behind them. Shortly after, as we were pulling out and on the move, we were overrun by German armoured cars. They shot up ACV 1, killed the driver, but the people inside managed to set fire to their maps and jumped out. We kept going in ACV 2 and we had a hatch in the top, and I looked out straight into the eyes of a German armoured car commander, about ten yards away, who called out, 'Put your hands up, captain.' I hadn't been introduced to him so I took no notice! We kept going, and although they fired at us, and bullets bounced off our relatively thin armour, we got away, and gathered together what was left of the HQ. We had lost the main ops vehicle, and with it the general, the G1, the G2 and the G3, the whole of the ops staff. The G office vehicle, which was soft-skinned, was up there too because we hadn't expected to be attacked, and the chief clerk failed to use his fire-maker, but fortuitously the Germans set the vehicle on fire. In that truck there were previous op orders, copies of war diaries and intelligence summaries.

Once we stopped we got in touch with corps HQ on the wireless. They were totally unaware of what was going on. They began to ask us for information. We tried to get information from the brigades and passed it to corps. We were commanding the division, for two or three hours. I was in charge. We tried to tell everybody what was happening, and eventually we transferred command of the brigades to corps. We then moved to a safer place.

Captain Hans-Otto Behrendt
Adjutant to General Rommel
Rommel took a risk; concerned about his supply situation, he personally led his supply trucks from Bir-el Harmat through a British minefield.

Captain Peter Vaux
GSO 3 Intelligence, HQ 7th Armoured Division
The G staff and the general escaped and joined the HQ the next day. Our ACVs were disguised to look like ten-ton trucks, to try and fool the enemy that they were logistic vehicles, not command vehicles. [When captured,]

General Messervy tore off his badges of rank and pretended to be a private soldier. The G3 spoke German, and I heard one say to another, 'They came out of one of those big lorries' – the implication being that they were logistic personnel. After a while the Germans moved. The British prisoners were put in a truck, and moved along with the German column. The general managed to find a hammer, and thought he might hammer the back of the driver's head, through the canvas, but he didn't. Eventually they stopped and they laagered, a group of armoured cars and half-tracks. At dusk they were shelled by the British, the Germans got very excited, and ran about taking casualties, while the British soldiers ran off and got into some slit trenches and hid. The Germans shouted and called for them to come out, but they didn't. Then the Germans gave up and drove away. The general and staff started walking, and came across a British unit. By the following evening we had a G Staff and a general and were back in business again.

Lieutenant Martyn Highfield
Troop Leader, C Troop, 452 Battery, 74 Field Regiment,
Royal Horse Artillery
We were in the 151 Brigade box. After his initial attacks Rommel was held up behind 150 Brigade, quite a way south of us. He attacked the 150 Brigade box and destroyed it over a period of three days. A small column was formed up in the rear of our box, to go down, but it was dive-bombed by Stukas and destroyed. We were not allowed to go to the rescue of the 150 Brigade box.

Private George Iceton
Driver, 6th Battalion, Durham Light Infantry
Apple column was commanded by Major Watson and D Company with anti-tank guns, mortars and artillery, some Cheshire machine-gunners, and some three-ton troop carriers to carry the infantry. We stood to attack on either side of the box. On the morning of 30 May we were told to move out and head for a point north-east of Knightsbridge. We were on the ridge, and held as the divisional commander's reserve. We had been there only a few hours when we heard that 150 Brigade was in serious trouble. We were told to move to a position in rear of 150 Brigade box. But we were stopped on a ridge. We could see the battle going on. It was like being in a grandstand, watching these tanks going for each other. I sat there with a colour sergeant, talking about mining; we were both miners.

Lieutenant Peter Lewis wearing a German helmet in his dugout at Gazala.

Private James Kilby
Medical Orderly, 150 Field Ambulance

I was a conscientious objector and joined the RAMC. I was an orderly on an ambulance with an RASC driver. In the Gazala line, I was in the 150 Brigade box. I worked in the operating theatre, in a tent. One day we began to hear the sounds of battle. Suddenly some tanks appeared, they had black crosses, they had cut in behind our box. They started herding everybody up on to a nearby bank of sand. But I and the surgeon were operating on a wounded man; a German officer came through and seemed satisfied. But eventually I was ordered out, and joined the others on the sandbank.

They took all our vehicles and moved on to Tobruk, and sent most prisoners back. The medical personnel were allowed to stay with some wounded, both British and German. We were completely surrounded by Germans. In the morning we saw a Fieseler Storch [light aircraft] landing, some officers got out and walked around the camp. I speak German, and one of the German wounded I was attending to on a stretcher said, 'That is Rommel.' He walked through the camp.

We stayed and worked for the wounded. There was fighting going on around us. The next day the Germans came in, in force with masses of vehicles. We were working flat out with German doctors. We did amputations. The Germans had no enmity towards us. We worked together. One German officer asked for his revolver to shoot himself with, as he thought they were losing, which at that stage they were. But they destroyed the 150 Brigade box, and eventually headed for Tobruk.

We were left behind and had little supplies or water. It was decided that we would move back. To begin with, a khamsin [a hot, dust-filled wind] blew up, which stopped us going. We sent out the wounded in ambulances. We walked out towards the Guards box at Knightsbridge. We had to hitchhike or march, and eventually got into Tobruk.

Sergeant Ray Ellis
425 Battery, 107th (South Notts Hussars) Field Regiment,
Royal Horse Artillery

We were to rendezvous with the tank regiments we were supporting near Bir-el Harmet, fire a barrage at 0300 hours, and at 0600 hours advance west into 'the cauldron' to engage what we were told was a weak German rearguard. The worst part of a battle is before the battle, waiting for it to open; that is when you have fear. I was tired, physically tired, and tired of battles, fighting, deserts and killing – sick of the whole thing. My gun crew were new and this was their first experience of warfare. I felt sorry for them because they were obviously all frightened. I don't say this in any way to belittle them – everybody's frightened – but by that time I'd got past that stage. I was only twenty-two, but as far as warfare went, I was an old man. They were also homesick. It was only a matter of months since they'd been at home with their wives and sweethearts. Again, we'd passed that – by this time it was two or three years since we'd been home. So I felt sorry for these men who were homesick, frightened and cold. I knew what it would be like when the barrage started, the first FLASH and CRASH; all the noise and the screaming of shells. Then you knew the enemy guns would reply, and back into the old carnage. I wished no gun would ever fire again. I was war-weary. Then you got 'Take post'. You get on the gun, just tensing yourself. Everything is very still and quiet, then the shout through the megaphone, 'Zero, minus five...four...three...two...one... FIRE!' A screaming crash as every gun along the front opens up and the battle is started. There is no longer time to think about being wounded or killed, or lonely, or tired – you're involved, the gun is firing, leaping about and you're firing the programme.

Captain William Pringle
425 Battery, 107th (South Notts Hussars) Field Regiment,
Royal Horse Artillery
I was a FOO in a Honey tank with the 3rd County of London Yeomanry, who charged a battery of German 88s, led by their colonel. He waved his flag, 'Yoiks, tally ho, tally ho.' A bit childish, we were there to win the war as far as I was concerned. When I eventually got him on the wireless, he told me he knew where he was going, what he intended to do and that it was my job to do what I was told. We went straight at them. The first gun was on him in seconds and BWHUUFF – he'd gone and the whole lot came to a screaming halt, there was total chaos everywhere. The tank I was in had a burst petrol tank so they had tied a hundred gallons in five-gallon tins on the back with string. I tried to bring down gunfire on the positions, but there was so much smoke and dust you couldn't see it. I thought, 'There's only one place for you, Pringle, and that's out of here.' I said to the driver, 'Turn round, and get on back.'

'I can't,' he said.

'Why not?'

'Can't get it into gear,' he replied.

'Stop your engine and start it.'

'I've tried that, sir, it doesn't work.'

I told him to rev it up, put the gear in reverse position, let me get my feet in, and I would try pushing it with my feet. The first time it didn't go in. There was a right old battle going on outside the tank, but I was more interested in getting the bloody engine started. There was no use going out on foot because you'd be shot to bits. I said, 'Keep the revs on whatever you do, and if we go, don't stop.'

I straightened my legs, the tank gave a hell of a bunny jump and kept going backwards. We reversed seven miles. I told the driver, 'Don't you stop, I'll murder you if you stop.'

Sergeant Ray Ellis
425 Battery, 107th (South Notts Hussars) Field Regiment,
Royal Horse Artillery
After the barrage was fired, it was, 'Cease firing, rear limber up.' We closed down, clamped the gun, hooked it on to the limber, the gun towers came up and we moved into the advance as the whole front moved forwards. It was just before dawn when we came up to the crest and everything opened up around us. He was waiting for us – he must have had it all ranged and ready, because the first shells landed right among us. It was appalling. The sky ahead was a sea of flames as all their guns opened up. It was carnage, but we just kept going because what the hell else could we do?

Lance Sergeant Ted Whittaker
425 Battery, 107th (South Notts Hussars) Field Regiment,
Royal Horse Artillery
I have never seen anything like it. In the distance there was a big arc of little tongues of fire. I realised to my horror, that this was practically the whole of the Afrika Korps waiting for us. Soon after the first flashes, everything fell on us. The fire was absolute murder. We were on this down slope and they were sitting on the edge of this shallow bowl. Absolute chaos.

Sergeant John Walker
425 Battery, 107th (South Notts Hussars) Field Regiment,
Royal Horse Artillery
It was a little bit like a saucer, sloping upwards from the centre. We were put in position on a very exposed piece of ground with the enemy in front of us, where they could see us better than we could see them. They had the opportunity of coming round both our flanks underneath the lips of the saucer.

Although they didn't overrun us, they were able to stay where they were, finding protected positions for their tanks. It was a very unpleasant sensation having a rest in the evening, knowing they were going to start an attack. I don't think anybody had more than an hour's sleep. It wasn't until about eleven at night when things went quiet, and we were ready at our posts by three in the morning.

Captain William Pringle
425 Battery, 107th (South Notts Hussars) Field Regiment,
Royal Horse Artillery
The tanks kept creeping closer and more of them seemed to be around. We couldn't see our tanks anywhere until that night – we saw them behind us, trailing away up to the north which was the last place they should have gone. The British high command said that all the German tanks were up north and the ones opposite us were wooden ones. Well I nearly exploded because we had been in the desert three years, and had seen every German tank that ever came into the desert, and if we didn't know, then who the devil did? I went and saw Peter Birkin and played hell, and said if we didn't get out of here that night, we'd had it. He agreed and we both went to the colonel. He said he'd put it to the divisional commander. I said we'd got to have more ammunition and a lot of it. He said, 'Don't worry, Bill, don't worry, there's lots of ammunition on the way.'

'I hope it gets here before daylight,' I replied.

'Why?'

'The German tanks are round behind and they'll shoot it up,' I said.

'How do you know?'

'I can hear them.' You can't move tanks around without making a horrible squawking of tracks. I was annoyed, probably wrongly, with his lack of ability to convince higher command that they'd got it wrong.

Major Robert Daniell
Regimental Headquarters, 107th (South Notts Hussars) Field Regiment,
Royal Horse Artillery
I got through to our brigadier, Carr, he said, 'Bob, you are to stand and fight in the position where you are now, you are not to move. Do you understand me? You are not to move at all.' I told him that if I obeyed I would lose every single man I had. He replied, 'You are a Horse Artillery officer, you have been properly brought up and you know that in battle you will obey orders or take the consequence.'

Sergeant Ray Ellis
425 Battery, 107th (South Notts Hussars) Field Regiment,
Royal Horse Artillery
It was dark and cold and I was standing by the gun when two figures approached, Captain Slinn and Lieutenant Timms. They stopped for a chat and I asked, 'What's the situation, sir?' Captain Slinn said, 'We're being left to fight a rearguard, sergeant. We're going to stop and it's one of those "fights to the last man and the last round" jobs. It's going to be a bloody awful day. I think there will be very few of us left at the end of this day.'

Lance Sergeant Ted Whittaker
425 Battery, 107th (South Notts Hussars) Field Regiment,
Royal Horse Artillery
During the night they told us not to be alarmed: the British tanks were going out to refuel and rearm. On 6 June we stood-to from before first light. As it got light we looked up the ridge and there were the tanks in position – we could just see the tops of them silhouetted. As it got a bit lighter we knew we were for it – they were German tanks, hull-down.

Bombardier Albert Parker
425 Battery, 107th (South Notts Hussars) Field Regiment,
Royal Horse Artillery
Then you knew that was it. I felt shattered. How does a young man feel when he thinks his life's going to finish there and then? You'd made a picture in your mind of the Germans, about nine feet tall, big, strong and swarthy, invincible.

Sergeant John Walker
425 Battery, 107th (South Notts Hussars) Field Regiment,
Royal Horse Artillery
The tanks didn't come forward so fast on the immediate front. But there was a roar of tank engines coming up the sides. It was very confused, fast, we were shooting like mad. We shot at both lorried infantry and tanks. We still didn't get hit ourselves, not even by a machine-gun bullet, yet they were spurting along near us all the time.

Gunner Dennis Mayoh
426 Battery, 107th (South Notts Hussars) Field Regiment, Royal Horse Artillery

If a tank was going sideways from right to left, or left to right, we had to hit him in the tracks. If the tank was coming for you, as it moved up and down, we had to try and aim for the belly; if not the belly then the top of the gun, which should knock his turret off. Sergeant Faulkner was at the trail giving orders and at the same time looking for any danger to the left or right. I was laying the gun. On the telescope you've got a cross. You would wait for the tank to come across, and as it got there, you would say, 'On. On. On. Fire.' You would fire just as the tank's nose reached the cross, allowing for the distance.

Sergeant Ray Ellis
425 Battery, 107th (South Notts Hussars) Field Regiment, Royal Horse Artillery

They brought in their artillery. Shells started to fall among us. That's when you get in your slit trench and you hide behind any little rock you can find. They called in their air force as well, it was absolutely devastating. The bombs crashing down, shells at the same time, all on to the area round the guns.

In the middle of the morning they came again with their tanks and got very close. Their artillery was still firing, the Stuka raids were coming over regularly and when the tanks attacked you had to get out of your slit trench and go and sit on the gun amidst all the shellfire, machine-gun fire and cannon fire from the tanks. The air was alive with red-hot steel. I hit a tank and it slewed round and burst into flames. The next thing I remember I was in the air as if someone had picked me up and thrown me up – spinning in the air. We'd had a direct hit on the gun. I dropped, 'WHHOOMPH', on to the ground. I lay there a second or two dazed, and then before I picked myself up again, I went spinning in the air again and dropped again. This time I think I was unconscious for a short time. When I came round I was dazed, and I knelt and heard the battle going on in a dazed sort of way. I stayed like that for quite a long time. Then it went quiet again, and I realised the tanks had been fought off. I looked round my gun, it was upside down, the crew were draped on the floor all round. I thought I must be wounded, but couldn't feel anything. My shirt and body were all black, my clothes were bloodstained, and I was in a hell of a state. The whole crew had been killed, and my next thought was for self-preservation. I found a little hole and lay in it, and started to try to build rocks round it. The shelling started again, and they changed to air burst, spraying down red-hot splinters.

Slit trench at Gazala.

Lance Sergeant Ted Whittaker
425 Battery, 107th (South Notts Hussars) Field Regiment,
Royal Horse Artillery

What use is a forward observation expert when the enemy is on your position – it's like the proverbial spare at a wedding. I've never felt so helpless. I told my mates what the colonel had said, 'We've only got to hang on twelve hours.' The reply to that was, 'A fat lot of fucking use that's going to be.'

Medical Orderly Harry Day
Regimental Headquarters, 107th (South Notts Hussars) Field Regiment,
Royal Horse Artillery

Captain Slinn and Lieutenant Timms were taken by stretcher back to the RAP. The men's wounds were beyond talking about. The actual decision about giving these men a lethal dose of morphine rested entirely with the doctor, who was completely justified. That included Captain Slinn and Lieutenant Timms; they would never have been normal human beings again. It was a relief for them and it was my duty to do it by hypodermic syringe, under the instructions of the doctor.

Signal Sergeant Jack Sykes
426 Battery, 107th (South Notts Hussars) Field Regiment,
Royal Horse Artillery

I was sitting in the vehicle passing messages; there was a bloody big bang. I was half unconscious because the shell had hit underneath my seat. I was wounded in my arms, back and knee. Walter dragged me out and put me in a slit trench. After that I took no part.

Lance Sergeant Ted Whittaker
425 Battery, 107th (South Notts Hussars) Field Regiment,
Royal Horse Artillery

I heard Major Daniell shouting, 'Are there some gunners? I've got a 25-pounder here – somebody man it.' I thought, 'I can't sit here.' I jumped up and said, 'Here, sir,' and there were two other fellows. He said, 'There's a few rounds in there, you might as well fire them.' Then off he drove. There was a German tank a few hundred yards away. I guessed the range. There were three rounds, no armour-piercing. We loaded this HE and fired, it went over the top of the tank. The turret turned and WHHUMP. To my horror I was the only one standing. The machine-gun bullets had gone straight through the shield.

Sergeant Ray Ellis
425 Battery, 107th (South Notts Hussars) Field Regiment,
Royal Horse Artillery
A shell burst right over Number One gun and the crew just fell to the ground and nobody moved. It occurred to me that with two guns out of action, that was half the strength of the troop gone and the next time they put in an attack this could mean they would get through. With a great deal of reluctance I got out of my hole and went over to Number One gun. It was in a parlous state, the shield was all riddled, at least one of the tyres was flat, but it was workable. From somewhere men started to appear – they were signallers, drivers, specialists, but they helped to man the gun.

As one was mown down, somebody else appeared. It eventually got to the point where they were not just South Notts Hussars, they were strangers. A man from the Royal Signals came on to the gun position. He caught a burst of machine-gun fire in the bottom part of his body. He was terrified. I crouched down trying to console him, 'You're all right lad, you're all right. Don't worry, you're not badly wounded, we'll soon have you away, I reckon you've got a Blighty.' Trying to ease his fear, I noticed sand settling on his eyes. He died in my arms.

Sergeant John Walker
425 Battery, 107th (South Notts Hussars) Field Regiment,
Royal Horse Artillery
Our second in command, Major Daniell, drove on the position in a staff car and told us to pull our guns out and form a 'hollow British square'. He immediately pushed off – he didn't stay to organise it. I was able to pull my gun out, my driver came up with the vehicle, I hitched it in, and we started to climb into the truck, when a shell came right through my driver and the front of the vehicle. It was wrecked and the driver killed. We decided that that was enough. There was nothing we could do. The German tank was about fifteen yards away. Other guns on the same site had already surrendered, they were just driving through us.

Sergeant Ray Ellis
425 Battery, 107th (South Notts Hussars) Field Regiment,
Royal Horse Artillery
Eventually I was left with just one man, a complete stranger, he wasn't even a South Notts Hussar. He was standing on the right of the gun, I was pulling the gun round and aiming at the tank, then getting on the seat, aiming and

firing. He was opening and closing the breach, and I was loading. It was a bit chaotic. I'd just fired a shell and got hold of the trail arm, when I heard a machine gun which sounded as if it was a few inches behind me. This man was just splattered as he was flung, spinning, against the inside of the gun shield. I looked behind and could see a tank within twenty or thirty yards behind me with gun still smoking. I tensed, waiting for the burst of fire, which never came. I shall never know if the gunner had compassion, or had run out of ammunition, or something distracted him. I like to think he had compassion, realising it was the end. Every gun was out of action, and as far as I know, mine was the last shot fired by the regiment.

I was very, very thirsty and I walked over to Peter Birkin's armoured vehicle. In it were the bodies of the driver and Jim Hardy. He had been cut in two, but his water bottle was hanging there. I got my knife, cut his webbing, took the water bottle, and drank the lukewarm water from old Jim's water bottle. I looked down on his lifeless face and burst into tears, seeing an old pal from the day I joined the regiment.

A tank rolled up and there was German with his head poking out the top, he just beckoned me up on to the tank. I jumped up there and I could see he was a sergeant. We looked at one another, we'd been fighting each other all day. We both shrugged our shoulders and looked up to heaven – what a bloody silly thing it was. It was a matter of two enemies who had no enmity.

Rifleman Douglas Waller
Anti-Tank Gunner, 9th Battalion, Rifle Brigade

As an anti-tank gunner you would be rushed off rather like the fire brigade; drive off with the gun on the portee to where the enemy were attacking. There were three on the gun: I was the loader; Rifleman Bill Ash; Corporal Alf Reeves was in charge. We had a Bren gunner Sid, and the driver of the portee, Magridge. We lived on the truck. We had the six-pounder anti-tank gun issued just as the Knightsbridge battle started. The two-pounder had a six-inch piece of concertina rubber on the telescopic sight, and you put your eye up against it. When it fired it rocked back and the rubber cushioned the effect. The six-pounder was different. The size of the charge made it rear up until the spades on the end of the trail had dug in. But you didn't put your eye up to the sight. You had to keep your eye well away when you fired. Unfortunately one or two people put their eye too close and when they fired it chopped their eyes. We lost two gun layers like that. Sometimes I would take over from Bill as layer. Squinting down the telescopic sight in the heat and dust haze got quite tiring. Once I thought the layer had fired the gun before I had got out of the way, but it was an enemy shell exploding. It cut my head right across and a flap of skin fell over my eyes. Bill got a couple of safety pins and pinned it up and put on a field dressing. I didn't feel anything when he put in the pins. My head throbbed after that, bang – bang – bang.

Trooper David Brown
Tank Driver, 1st Royal Tank Regiment
At Knightsbridge, the Germans had screens of tanks out in front of 88-mm guns. In the morning we watched what we thought were Mk IIIs and Mk IVs in the distance shimmering in the heat haze, looking like black beetles. You weren't always sure whether you were watching German tanks or ours; because of the heat haze, tanks were just black objects. You would move forward slowly, the tracks would go clank, clank, clank. You'd stop and look, and there would be some chat going on over the air, 'I think they're our friends. They might be our South African friends, and things like that.

It was our job to find out where the 88-mms were. I was in a Honey, and went in quickly as far as we dared to draw their fire. They opened up and we saw flashing lights in the distance and big gouts of sand going up near the tank. They were firing solid shot. You could always tell, if it was HE there would be a whizz – bang – black smoke, and that would be it. We reversed out of it. We had done our job, and left them to the Grants and the 25-pounders.

You could hear the enemy shells going by, making a noise like an express train, especially the 88-mm – the tank would rock a bit – or a 105-mm coming down with a crash and a bang. If you got a near one, the lights would go out. It got a bit hectic at times. The tank commander would shout, making himself understood with a few choice words what he wanted done. You did it. You didn't worry about what was said to you. I could watch the bit in front of me. But my vision was a bit limited. I was directed by the commander, 'Left a bit, right a bit, you see that bir, make for that.'

We were sitting there observing these German tanks in the distance shimmering in the heat haze. We were getting shelled and the accepted thing to do under shellfire specially heavy shellfire, was to move your tank about a bit, not far: left stick, right stick, move about under it. The shelling got heavy and we thought the Germans might be moving in our direction. The tank commander said to me, 'You'd better ease her back a bit, about a hundred yards.' Over on the left I saw some infantry in slit trenches, and near them was one of our two-pounder anti-tank guns, a pop-gun compared with what was firing at us. They were just firing away as if they were on a range at home. Eventually there was an air burst above them, and when the black smoke cleared, I could see them: there was one lying near the gun; another shell burst; it was like watching a film. It knocked another out, he was obviously wounded, and the other two were lying round the gun. The wounded man still fought the gun; his movements were so slow. He got the last shot off, it was like an act of defiance. Then he slumped forward on the gun. Then we moved back, I don't know what happened to him. He was extraordinarily brave.

Guardsman Jack Holness
Anti-tank Gunner, 3rd Battalion, Coldstream Guards

On two or three occasions we were told we were to pull out, only to have it cancelled. We were told on 13 June we were going to evacuate the box that night, before we were overrun. We were under such heavy shellfire that we were not manning the gun. We were in a dugout about four feet deep with overhead protection of sandbags on top of minefield pickets and an armoured plate. I was in there at about midday, with my section sergeant, when a shell hit the dugout. I came to out of the blur of unconsciousness, buried, as was my section sergeant. My left arm was free from the elbow down. I felt for him and felt his hair. He was gasping. I held his head above the sand. But I was trapped by the end of a minefield picket and was supporting the whole weight of the armoured plate, which had come down on my arm. In my state of consciousness I thought I had lost my legs. I passed out, and came to again, and my pals in my section were trying to pull us out. They put us into a pit full of mortar ammunition, and I thought if this gets hit, we are all gone. Eventually Corporal Burke went off to get help. An ambulance came, and picked us up, with the MO and the padre. We were taken to the RAP. I had shrapnel in the back and in the neck, and one arm was useless. I was fixed up with dressings. My section sergeant was still unconscious. The RAP had been given the order to pack up, and we were told to crawl under an ambulance that had been dug in. We lay under this vehicle for hours until it was dark. At about eleven o'clock at night we were taken out by medical orderlies from under the vehicle. We walked with orderlies to an ambulance, there were three of us walking wounded, and four on stretchers. I sat with my back to the cab. We were told that we were getting out through the gap in the mine-field. The battalion would march out. There was very little transport in the box. I went out in the ambulance; it was shelled, and shot at, but although it was a painful bumpy ride we arrived the next morning at Sidi Barrani, where there was a CCS. Next morning we were taken to Tobruk. From there we were taken to Mersa Matruh.

Lance Corporal Ernie Gallantree
Carrier Platoon, 3rd Battalion, Coldstream Guards
It came to the time to evacuate the Knightsbridge box. We had a conference and were told we were surrounded and there was no way out and efforts would be made by our tanks to get us out. There was the usual shelling and dive-bombing going on, so it was impossible that day. So we were told that we were to try that night, and leave most of the stuff behind. It struck me as a Dunkirk thing. We had to do a tactical withdrawal. There were vehicles that we couldn't take, and most marched out. We went out with our carriers, at night. It took the enemy by surprise. The enemy just got the tail end of the column moving out. As we were going along, there were Very lights going up all over the place. Then we went through Gazala, the following morning.

After the withdrawal from the box we took part in what we called the 'Gazala gallop' towards Tobruk. We came to a halt in a wadi, waiting for orders. We had just brewed up, we couldn't see anything, it was getting towards afternoon, when Corporal Brooks asked, 'What's over there?' There were seven or eight tanks in the distance, we couldn't make out who they were. And I said, 'I think we'd better get our heads down.' We dropped into the trenches we had dug when we first stopped. I sat there with a mug of tea. The enemy tanks opened up on our carriers. An armour-piercing shell went straight through the engine of my carrier. Tins of water were blown up. The Germans left, then came back again just before dusk. They opened up, and I saw the tracer coming over the top of mc as I lay in my shallow. I was terrified. There seemed to be a battle going on between our tanks and theirs. We stayed in that position all night. The next morning it had quietened down. We got orders to move. We all had to ride on one carrier towards Tobruk.

Josephine Pearce
Nurse, Hadfield-Spears Front Line Surgical Unit, attached to Free French
After a while we were transferred from Tobruk to Tmimi. We arrived at night and pitched camp and made up the beds in one tented ward. We had sheets stitched together to make a red cross, which we pegged down in the

desert. On our way there we kept passing British columns going in the opposite direction, and we were going in the wrong way. While it was quiet we decided to have a wash. It was difficult in Tobruk because of the water situation: you had to decide whether you were going to wash your hair, your clothes, or yourself, and keep enough to drink. In Tmimi there was plenty of water. So we stripped and were having a wash, when a British orderly put his head through the flap; we all yelled. He said, 'You've got to get away; Rommel's on his way. There's going to be a battle here.'

Captain Harry Sell
Officer Commanding, D Company, 8th Battalion,
Durham Light Infantry
After the 150 Brigade box was overrun, and Rommel attacked Knightsbridge behind us, we were contained by the enemy. We found that opposite to us was a junction between the Italian Pavia and Ariete Divisions. Although there was a weak spot there, the Germans had put in some strongpoints in the gap. I was sent for by the brigade commander and the divisional commander, who told me that we were surrounded and the only hope of getting out was to burst our way through the Germans and Italians, make our way out into the desert and reorganise back near Mersa Matruh. It was explained to me that this breakout must be done quickly, before the enemy had time to probe our defences in greater strength. I was told that I had to eliminate the German strongpoint, and hold a bridgehead between the two Italian divisions so that the brigade could get through. After they had got through I could withdraw. They said this attack must take place at dusk. First, all the divisional artillery would be turned on the enemy. After that I would attack. I was given some sketches and air photos, and given half an hour to think it over and make any comments.

I went back and requested that no artillery be fired before my attack. I said that if we attacked at a time before the enemy evening stand-to, they would still be in their dugouts, and if my attack was put in without any preliminary gunfire, surprise would be achieved. I might be able to get into their positions without being fired at. Then it was in the lap of the gods. They agreed. I went back and got my company ready. I was given the carriers. I was given three South African armoured cars, some sappers, and some mortars. After our brigade saw my success signal, they would come through the gap. I had to wait for the 9th DLI to come through; they would fire Very lights when they were through.

Captain Michael Ferens
Officer Commanding, HQ Company, 6th Battalion,
Durham Light Infantry

It was decided that 50 Division, who were surrounded, would retire by attacking west through the Germans and Italians. At this time, Major Watson, commanding HQ Company, went sick; Captain Proud took over C Company, my company, and I was put in command of HQ Company. My next orders, from my CO, were to command the rearguard to 151 Brigade when they left the box. I didn't feel too good about being rearguard. The plan was to leave the box through the minefield gaps – the 8th Battalion first, the 6th second, the 9th third – to proceed west and then south through the line of communication of the Germans and Italians until clear of them, and then swing east, and go back to the wire between Libya and Egypt at Fort Maddelena. The 8th were to move off at dusk, followed by the 6th and then the 9th. Colonel Percy commanding the 9th was told that if he considered the passage following the 6th was too dangerous, he was given the option of returning back through the box and proceeding along the coast to Tobruk.

Lieutenant Martyn Highfield
Troop Leader, C Troop, 452 Battery, 74 Field Regiment,
Royal Horse Artillery

We knew that severe battles were taking place in the cauldron, and we were all called together by the battery commander, Bill Cheeseman. He told us that we had lost a big armoured battle and we were going to have to retreat, starting at night. We would breakout through the enemy lines opposite us, drive south, and round Bir Hacheim and drive north-east to Fort Maddelena. 8 DLI were to go first, and a section of guns would go with each party. I went back to my troop, and briefed the section of guns.

Private George Iceton
Driver, 6th Battalion, Durham Light Infantry

When we were told we were to breakout and withdraw, the first reaction was disgust as we thought we were doing a good job. We didn't realise how serious it was. Suddenly, out of the blue, we are told we have got to get back to the Egyptian frontier. We were told that the situation behind us was desperate, and Tobruk cut off. We were given compass bearings to march on. We felt confident; we hadn't been touched, really. Those of us who had been in France tried to convince the others that it always looks worse than it is. Going west first made sense because the Germans had gone past and

Michael Ferens as a Major.

one would hit only their supply lines if we went that way first, and then swung round, before turning north-east. The trouble was that the RASC troop carriers had been taken elsewhere, so we had to pack the infantry on the battalion vehicles. We buried stores that weren't needed to make room for the troops on the trucks, and also, if we had to go back into the box, there would be supplies there for us. The ammunition dumps had explosive charges fixed on them timed to go off in twenty-four hours, to catch the enemy if they came into the box after we had left. Everyone was warned about it.

The battalion was organised into two groups, one under the CO, and one under the 2IC. There had been a duststorm all day. It cleared up before dark, but it allowed us to move our vehicles into position under cover of the dust.

Captain Harry Sell
Officer Commanding, D Company, 8th Battalion,
Durham Light Infantry

During the day we lifted the mines in front of us, and just at the right time we drove forward in our vehicles as fast as we could and we got almost right up on to the enemy positions before they realised what had happened. I was lucky – my truck was hit by an anti-tank shell and blown to pieces, but I and my driver got out. We went right through the dugouts with bayonets, tommy guns and grenades and cleared them out. We then took up defensive positions to keep counter-attacks from coming in. Our armoured cars shot all the German machine-gunners. Our battalions went through. The Italians on each flank tried to stop them, but there was no concentrated effort on their part.

Lieutenant Peter Lewis
Officer Commanding, 15 Platoon, C Company, 8th Battalion,
Durham Light Infantry

My platoon were glad to be leaving the Gazala position, but apprehensive about driving through the enemy positions, and they made some rude remarks about the idea. I pointed out that if we didn't do this we would be in the bag, like 150 Brigade. We formed up at Strickland's Post in single file in the dark; when we got there the vehicles opened out into a vast square, at least a mile square, of soft-skinned vehicles, protected by carriers. We just kept going. My column was commanded by the CO, Jake Jackson, who led; the other column from our battalion was commanded by the 2IC. It worked. It was like ships at sea in a convoy. We fired over the side of the trucks with rifles, Brens, tossing grenades out: it was like the Wild West. Their positions were dug in, and difficult to see, but the enemy were taken completely by surprise.

Lieutenant Martyn Highfield
Troop Leader, C Troop, 452 Battery, 74 Field Regiment,
Royal Horse Artillery

At dusk we moved forward; there was lot of firing and some vehicles were hit. Some vehicles had stopped and after ten minutes I thought, 'This isn't right,' and walked to the head of the column to find out what was happening. There was an ambulance on fire on one side. The driver said he had lost sight of the vehicle in front when the firing started and didn't know what to do. I went back and called forward my guns and vehicles and formed up into two columns and set off on foot with a compass to lead them out. Beyond Strickland's Post there was a track used by the Germans to move up and down out of range of our artillery in the box. This we called 'many tracks', and we took about two or three hours leading this column with an infantry section with me as protection, to get to 'many tracks'. When we arrived it was a moonlit night and we could see a strand of barbed wire. I sent the infantry to see if there was a way round it, and they couldn't find one. So I decided to take the column through. We closed the vehicles up and took them through in their two parallel lines. After we had gone about four hundred paces, I found another barbed-wire fence. There was an explosion behind where a vehicle had struck a mine. I arranged for that column to follow the tracks of the one that had successfully got through, but three more vehicles blew up doing this. I asked, 'Is everyone through?' and was told that there was a vehicle still stuck, the driver had frozen stiff with fright. So I went back and got up on the running board, and told him that I would go ahead, and he was to follow me on to the safe tracks. I ran in front of him, there was a nasty explosion, and fell on my face, but didn't lose consciousness. My driver and signaller came and put shell dressings on me, and I was able to walk. I thought that it was not sensible to lead the column and went back and found an infantry captain and asked him to take over the lead. I think that I had tripped a wire setting off a light Italian mine that had sprayed me with pebbles and shrapnel, from the top of my head to my heels. The worst holes were on my waistline, but my web belt had reduced the velocity of the fragments.

Private George Iceton
Driver, 6th Battalion, Durham Light Infantry
The 8th did a good job and made a good gap, and apart from a bit of trouble with mines, we did all right. We started at 8 pm and we were supposed to be through the gap by 2 am. Once the 8th started their attack, everybody on the enemy side started shooting. We had four killed while we were waiting. Eventually we set off and it was a relief to get going with shells falling all round. We collected the outpost platoons as we passed.

The navigators did well, but the one in the CO's column hit a mine dropped by the Italians. Our minefields were always marked with wire, as were the German ones. The Italians didn't mark them, they just dropped them anywhere. I was at the tail with just two carriers behind me. Just as the battalion got going, I had to swap trucks with one of the battalion trucks, which looked as if it would break down. It had a slipping clutch, which I could manage. After going through the gap we kept going all night, driving without lights.

Lieutenant Martyn Highfield
Troop Leader, C Troop, 452 Battery, 74 Field Regiment,
Royal Horse Artillery
The column went on during the night. I was in shock and didn't feel the pain too badly. At first light we saw vehicles, and these turned out to be from divisional HQ. We drove all day and reached Fort Maddelena in the evening. Whole groups of vehicles were there. I handed over the vehicles to Bill Cheeseman. We had lost one gun in the night, when the column had gone too fast. I walked across to the CCS and into the medical chain. I was one of the lighter casualties. After four days the ambulances reached Mersa Matruh. It was pleasant to be dressed in hospital and be attended to.

Captain Michael Ferens
Officer Commanding, HQ Company, 6th Battalion,
Durham Light Infantry
Moving at night the 8th Battalion surprised the Germans and Italians and got through reasonably easily. By the time the 6th Battalion drove south, the enemy was awake and there was more opposition. Colonel Percy decided that he would exercise his option and instead of following the 6th he would lead the 9th back towards Tobruk. My duty, as rearguard, was to follow the 9th Battalion. Colonel Percy sent me a message and told me that when his troops went back into the box, I had to follow him. We were at the time out in the

area of the outpost, west of the box, with a troop of 25-pounders, some two-pounder anti-tank guns. By the time the 9th Battalion had gone back into the box and out again the other side, dawn was just breaking. We followed the 9th back through the box, there was no opposition, and set off in a rough column of vehicles towards the coast. When we go to the escarpment there were some South African engineers on the top, and they told us that they had just mined the track down the escarpment. They agreed to remove the mines, and we went down the track to the coastal road. My instructions were to cross the coastal road near the sea, at the water point near El Mrassas, and proceed along tracks by the coast towards Tobruk. We were bombed as we went down the escarpment but to no ill effect, crossed the coastal road, and got to the water point, turned along the coast. Here we had our first action. We were attacked by German tanks, about seven of them, the two-pounders fired from their portees, the 25-pounders got into action immediately, the column stopped, we debussed, took up positions. The 25-pounders and the two-pounders had a rare old battle with these tanks.

Captain Harry Sell
Officer Commanding, D Company, 8th Battalion,
Durham Light Infantry
We held the hundred-yard gap for five hours. The trouble started when the CO of 9 DLI, who was watching the fighting, came to the conclusion that we had been destroyed. He turned the battalion round and headed for Tobruk. I was sitting with my officers wondering what to do. Our wirelesses had broken down, and by daybreak the Germans had rallied and we were being pretty heavily pounded. Peter Barr, one of my platoon commanders, was killed. I said that we would get out. We broke out south into the desert and swept round positions occupied by the Free French, near Bir Hacheim. I got back as far as the wire between Egypt and Libya. But we were shot up all the way and by the time I arrived I had three armoured cars, myself and two other blokes. The rest of the company were wiped out; either in the fight for the enemy strongpoint or on the drive out.

Captain Michael Ferens
Officer Commanding, HQ Company, 6th Battalion,
Durham Light Infantry
We ultimately arrived in Tobruk in the late afternoon, not knowing anything, other than the division was retiring to Fort Maddelena. We were running short of petrol. I went into some HQ and asked where I could refill.

E12790

25-pounder field guns in action at night, 2 June 1942.

E12919

A Grant tank stops alongside the burning wreck of a German PzKpfw I, 6 June 1942.

An officer told me that I now came under Tobruk garrison command and had to report to the camp commandant. I wasn't having any of this. I found a petrol point, refilled and moved off to rejoin the division. We set off and up the road to El Adem. There was wire across the road with some Indian troops; it was getting towards dusk by now. I suppose I had thirty or forty vehicles, plus the guns. I told the Indian troops that this was a column going out on reconnaissance, and they pulled aside the wire and let us through. We drove down the coast road towards Bardia. It was dark, and I pulled the column off the road and we had a few hours' rest. I realised this was a stupid thing to do, because we didn't know where the enemy was, and before dawn we set off again. We were turned off the coast road at Bardia, because it had been blown, and we set off across the desert. But ultimately we rejoined the division at Fort Maddelena, for which I was very thankful. We got back to the battalion. We got a great reception. Everybody had their story to tell about the withdrawal from Gazala. Within forty-eight hours the Germans attacked Tobruk and it fell soon after. If I had followed the officer's orders I would have spent the rest of the war in the bag.

Lance Corporal Ernie Gallantree
Carrier Platoon, 3rd Battalion, Coldstream Guards
We got to a rallying point just outside Tobruk, but inside the perimeter. An officer came along in a 15-hundredweight truck and said, 'Follow me.' We drove in the carrier along the El Adem airstrip and he told us that we had to take up defensive positions where we could. We had no time to dig in, but fortunately there were some dummy anti-aircraft guns around the strip dug in, we pulled one down and got into the sangar into which it had been positioned. We left our carrier a little way behind us. I had the Bren gun and someone else had one of the two two-pounder anti-tank guns, and another guardsman the other. There were five of us in the sangar. And we were to defend this place against these bloody great tanks. We fired at them but were fighting a losing battle. One of the lads was going to make a run for it as we saw these tanks coming for us. I stopped him. We fired at the tanks, and had little impression. One tank came towards our little sangar. They say that in situations like this things go through your mind: thinking of home, your loved ones, and it was certainly true and that was one of the most scaring times I had. It went through my mind: 'Is he going to crush us, or machine-gun us, or blast us with a shell? Shall I roll that way? Shall I jump over the sangar wall that way?' Anyhow, fortunately it came quite close – about five yards off – and stopped. It came round the edge of our sangar and

there was a young German in the turret, and he beckoned us over, '*Raus.*' We jumped up. He was my age, we were all young. He said, in English, 'Get your coats, it's very cold at night.' We were just in shorts, no shirt, and a tin hat. I grabbed my greatcoat, and I grabbed also my side pack from the carrier, it was full of cigarettes, issue cigarettes, called Victory Vs, and a jerrycan of water. He put a shell through our carrier. They put our weapons in front of the tracks and drove over them, crushing them. He said, 'Go, follow your comrades.' There were Very lights going off all over the place, Germans marking their positions. We were all collected up in a barbed-wire area. On the way I picked up a cardigan from a dead British soldier, I was glad of that.

Gunner Gordon Fry
Signaller, 12th Battery, 4th Field Regiment, South African Artillery, 2nd South African Brigade
I was in the OP as the wireless operator. When we first got there the Germans were out in the perimeter. Then we heard that they had broken through, the chaps in the 'Gazala Gallop' came through but didn't stop. We had the truck all packed up. An order came: if anyone goes now they will be treated as deserters. So we stayed. We could have got out, but we stayed. There was a gap we could have got out of. That was it. Orders came to spike the guns. You break the sights, and put two shells in the gun and that blows up the barrel. We felt that they should have said 'Every man for himself'. They didn't give us a fair chance to get out. You are bewildered when you are taken prisoner. The Germans said that they were going to hand us over to the Italians and we should look out because they will steal everything of value.

Back to Alamein

*The offensive by Rommel ended with the Eighth Army
being driven back to the Alamein position.*

Tobruk finally fell to the Germans on 21 June and the Eighth Army retreated east in a state of disarray. Lieutenant General Ritchie decided to deploy part of the Eighth Army in a defensive position at Mersa Matruh while some of XXX Corps were sent straight on to Alamein, ninety miles further east. Lieutenant General Holmes's X Corps Headquarters, sent from Palestine, defended Mersa Matruh itself, with the 10th Indian Division and the 50th Division, the latter still reorganising after its narrow escape from the boxes at Gazala. Here Ritchie hoped to stop Rommel, or at worst gain time to improve the positions at Alamein. In the meanwhile, Norrie was busily strengthening the defences at Alamein, the last defendable position west of Alexandria and the delta. There was a great deal of work to be done.

At this stage General Auchinleck came forward and took over command of the Eighth Army from Ritchie. He now had the onerous task of commanding an army in the field, and bearing responsibility for the whole Middle East theatre. He brought with him Major General Dorman-Smith, the Deputy Chief of the General Staff (Operations) at GHQ Middle East, who also acted as Auchinleck's unofficial chief of staff while he commanded Eighth Army. Opinions on Dorman-Smith were, and still are, widely diverse. All agree that he had a fertile and agile brain, and could formulate plans at amazing speed. But many who encountered him thought him too clever by half, and that he had too much influence on Auchinleck. After the fall of Tobruk, Rommel kept going. The first line of defence was General Gott's XIII Corps, dug in south of Mersa Matruh. Rommel drove them back just six days after taking Tobruk and soon surrounded X Corps at Mersa Matruh. Most escaped, and a jumble of both corps hurtled back to the Alamein line, on occasions moving on parallel tracks to Rommel, and in some cases even behind him.

The existing Alamein positions were reinforced and extended in the nick of time. Reinforcements included the 9th Australian Division, which had been training in Syria after its epic defence of Tobruk the previous year. Throughout July, in what has come to be called the First Battle of Alamein, confused fighting took place at various points along the Alamein line, and ended in stalemate. Rommel was stopped – for a while.

At this juncture, the top command in the Middle East was changed. Auchinleck was replaced as C-in-C Middle East by General Harold Alexander. Gott was originally selected to command Eighth Army, but was killed in an aircraft crash before he could take over, and the post went instead to Lieutenant General Bernard Montgomery. Although little known to the public at the time, Montgomery was highly regarded by General Sir Alan Brooke, the Chief of the Imperial General Staff, the head of the British Army, under whom Montgomery had served during the retreat to Dunkirk. Montgomery was originally selected to command the First Army for the landings in North Africa, which would be known as Operation Torch. On his arrival in North Africa in August 1942, Montgomery immediately galvanised Eighth Army by making it clear that there would be no more retreats, and impressing all the troops with his confidence in a successful outcome. At the Battle of Alam Halfa, on the Alamein position, he soundly defeated Rommel's attempt to break through to the delta; it was to be the German commander's last throw.

As part of the preparations for Montgomery's next battle, Alamein, Special Forces were active behind the enemy lines. On the whole the LRDG information-gathering operations were successful, but some of the major raids by the SAS, notably that at Benghazi, were too ambitious, or had been compromised by bad security, and ran into trouble.

Captain Harry Sell
Officer Commanding, D Company, 8th Battalion,
Durham Light Infantry
We were all on the escarpment near Mersa Matruh and we occupied a position next to the 9th DLI. We then continued the same drill in defence as before, getting ready for another attack. We had no mines or wire. We were

General Sir Claude Auchinleck, Commander-in-Chief Middle East, June 1941–August 1942.

Standing in the back of the car: left, Major General John Harding; right, General Sir Harold Alexander, Commander-in-Chief Middle East.

attacked by enemy aircraft. It was not clear what we were supposed to be doing. Apart from getting our daily sitreps we had no information on the future. It became apparent that we would have to stop running. We heard that a position was being built at Alamein. The nearest minefield was at Fuka, which was behind us. We got continual exhortations to harass the Germans and impose losses on them until the line could be stabilised.

As I had the weakest company, I was in the rear. I had C Company in front of me, and A Company on my right. Running between the two was a line of telegraph poles running south from Mersa Matruh, and there were huge gaps between companies. We used to carry out nightly patrols. One night my lookouts came in and said there were German tanks on the line of the telegraph poles. I didn't believe them, as I had heard nothing. They were insistent, so I got up, went to have a look, and sure enough they were all talking German and there were a lot of tanks. I came back and tried to contact the CO, he was at brigade, I tried to tell brigade about the approaching enemy, but they said it was impossible. Not long afterwards the tanks started moving. On our left were the 9th DLI and 25-pounders of 274 Field Regiment. A huge parachute flare was put up by the Germans, and I thought it must be a signal. At dawn the 25-pounders started firing. I saw a body of tanks going for the 25-pounders and they wrote them off. Then I saw the anti-tank guns of the 9th DLI firing. I frantically called for support from the artillery. I could see lorried infantry debussing and asked for the mediums to be brought down on them. I could see some tanks being knocked out; the anti-tank gunners went on firing right to the last, but eventually the tanks overran them. One gun went on firing after the others, and very slowly, which meant to me that the crew was probably wiped out except for one man or so. The lorried infantry attacked and finished off the 9th DLI. We were then sitting at Mersa Matruh like ducks on the escarpment, waiting for the next onslaught on ourselves.

Lieutenant Peter Lewis
Officer Commanding, 15 Platoon, C Company, 8th Battalion,
Durham Light Infantry
The first enemy attack on us came in the late afternoon. Our anti-tank guns did a good job, knocking out enemy tanks.

Because of the success of breaking out at Gazala the brigadier decided we would do it again in the same way. But having done that we would come back in again, a massive raid on wheels, to do enough damage as we could, and reoccupy our positions. We did exactly that. But we had more casualties this time. We got right through to their lines of communication. We had a Vickers mounted on the back of a 15-hundredweight truck and in one place we backed the truck up against a tent full of Germans and let rip. We got right to their rear areas. When we came back they were ready for us and caused quite a few casualties. On the way back I got behind a gunner truck, and there was a hand hanging over the back of the truck under a tarpaulin, and I wondered whose it was.

As we were breaking back in, we were bombed by the RAF. The return journey took the whole battalion through the middle of an Italian laager. We fired into the laager and tossed in the odd grenade. The battalion reached its original positions at daybreak. Although the attack was successful, there were many of us who thought that the attack had disorganised the British forces as much as the Germans. Trucks and men were missing.

Captain Harry Sell
Officer Commanding, D Company, 8th Battalion, Durham Light Infantry

Told to do another breakout, so off we shot in our vehicles and we got through the Germans and into the desert. We went through the area that had been occupied by the 9th DLI. We knew that the Boche would be gone. We picked up some of the pay books from the dead DLI, and out into the desert, intending to hook right round. We were then recalled back to our old positions at Mersa Matruh. I don't know why. We managed to get back in.

Captain Michael Ferens
Acting Second-in-Command, 6th Battalion, Durham Light Infantry

Orders were received for the battalion to carry out a night attack in vehicles. By then I was acting 2IC of the battalion, and the CO gave me orders to act as whipper-in to the column. We formed up in four lines of vehicles with the carrier platoon on the outsides. The CO was in front, and I was at the rear. It was dark, and we set off in a southerly direction from Mersa Matruh. I was never told the object of the attack. It was a silent attack without an artillery barrage, and as we motored down into the desert, we came under fire from both sides of the column. The enemy were using tracer. And obviously the weapons they were using had five tracers in a clip, because we quickly learned that as the tracers came across the column, you counted five, and sped through, as the enemy were obviously firing on fixed lines. We lost a few vehicles and had a few casualties. We must have motored five or six miles into the desert and the column came to a halt. By then I discovered I had been wounded; one of these tracer bullets had hit a jerrycan behind my back. I was sitting in the front by my driver in the 15-hundredweight. The bullet exploded, it might have been an explosive Breda round. The first I knew I was sitting in a mess of blood. The column halted, I motored forward, found the MO, who stripped off my shirt, and put a field dressing on the wound. Orders were then given that the column was to turn round and retrace its steps back to Matruh. As we did this, again we passed through MG fire from both flanks, and again suffered more casualties. We merely motored south and motored back, which to me seemed a very stupid operation.

We arrived back below the escarpment at Mersa Matruh, about dawn. Some of the casualties had been brought back in the vehicles. I conducted a funeral service, and we buried them in a grave, which we dug.

Lieutenant Peter Lewis
Officer Commanding, 15 Platoon, C Company, 8th Battalion, Durham Light Infantry
Having knocked out German tanks attacking us, the German infantry attacks were broken up by machine-gun fire and artillery. At nightfall there was a lull.

Captain Harry Sell
Officer Commanding, D Company, 8th Battalion, Durham Light Infantry
The next night the grip had tightened round us. The same caper started that night. From my carrier I was watching Germans only ten yards off. We took a lot of German prisoners. The enemy probed, throwing grenades, and we threw grenades at them. That day we were issued with six-pounder anti-tank guns which nobody had seen before and didn't know how to fire. But one anti-tank gunner opened the breech of one of these guns, sighted the six-wheeled enemy armoured car through the barrel, loaded the gun and fired, and as he was only about a hundred yards or less away he blew it to smithereens. That was the way we learned to use the six-pounder. The Germans were outflanking us all the way. We learned of another breakout plan, the same as before. I was very tired, I'd had no sleep for days.

Captain Michael Ferens
Acting Second-in-Command, 6th Battalion, Durham Light Infantry

A conference was called at divisional HQ, the CO told me to go to it; there were reps from each battalion and the gunners. We were told that once again the division had been cut off, and it had been decided to breakout during the night and retire towards Fuka and Daba. Each battalion had to provide an officer to form the recce party, which was to find a position at Fuka. I went back to the battalion and passed on these instructions to the CO.

Sometime later, at dark, the recce party was formed up and the division began to move out. We were below the escarpment, so to get out and move further east we had to scale the escarpment. There were a few tracks and the vehicles had to climb these tracks on to the top of the escarpment. This was a major operation and took a long time but eventually – with difficulty – we managed to reach the top of the escarpment and set off south. We passed very close to groups of enemy vehicles. I assume the enemy were asleep; we were not fired on. We must have gone ten or fifteen miles south before turning east.

Lieutenant Peter Lewis
Officer Commanding, 15 Platoon, C Company, 8th Battalion, Durham Light Infantry

The battalion formed into two columns. Lieutenant Parker had recced the route over the escarpment, and at 9 pm the battalion was ready to move off, led by him. Using a rough track, and in the gathering darkness, the vehicles wound their way up the escarpment. As they entered a large wadi with steep sloping sides, enemy tanks could just be seen at the far end of the wadi across the battalion axis of advance. The CO and Parker tried to find a way to avoid the enemy armour. The Germans spotted the column and when about twenty vehicles breasted the slope at the top, the enemy opened fire. We had run into a trap. The order was shouted, 'Every man for himself.'

Dragging their anti-tank guns to the lip of the wadi, the Germans fired into the massed vehicles in the wadi, a pile-up of three-ton lorries and other soft-skinned vehicles; a potential disaster. A truck was stalled ahead of the others. Soldiers at last got the stuck vehicle moving and the others followed, only to be fired on as they moved on top. Every vehicle then motored off independently. The CO and adjutant acted as traffic policemen to get the trucks off in the right direction. Just below them, several riflemen took up positions and fired back at the Germans. In the wadi RSM Jennings and Private Fearon had quickly taken control of the situation by getting a Bren gun to fire back at the enemy, and a two-inch mortar to land bombs on Germans on top who were not dug in and therefore vulnerable to mortar bombs. Fearon kept on firing for about an hour. Jennings scored a direct hit on a German machine-gun post with the two-inch mortar, which eased the situation in the bed of the wadi, although trucks arriving on top still came under fire.

I got out of my truck and crawled up the slope and found myself face to face with a German, we both rolled back and away. Eventually the bed of the wadi was almost clear, except for wrecked trucks abandoned by their drivers and passengers. These men walked to the top of the wadi, walked and hitched lifts. Once there was nothing else to come out of the wadi, I hitched a lift with a passing truck. Most of my column got out, but those in the other column were trapped by the armour at the end and were taken prisoner. Those that climbed the sides mostly got out. Those that tried to get out at the end failed.

Once clear, except for D Company, the 8th Battalion – now broken into about a dozen small columns – drove across the desert at high speed, driving through Italian and German laagers. We kept going all night and just before dawn a thick mist descended on the desert, hiding us from marauding German armour until we reached Fuka and then Alamein.

Captain Michael Ferens
Acting Second-in-Command, 6th Battalion, Durham Light Infantry
Eventually we hit the Sidi Rahman track, turned north up the track, and reached the railway at Alamein station. Here we were told to move to a position some miles south of the railway. For the rest of the day other members of the battalion, brigade and division turned up. Some had been fired on during the night, some had motored, as I had, without any opposition back to Alamein. We were very disorganised. Ultimately the battalion moved further east, and here for the next couple of days or so we began to get organised again. I was still acting 2IC, and the CO was anxious to get some NAAFI stores for the battalion, and also some beer and comforts. With this in mind he told me and another officer to go into Alexandria and make some purchases. We took two trucks and drivers, found the NAAFI and made our purchases. Then, because we were tired and thirsty we went in and bought some beer. My back seized up at this point. Back at the battalion, the MO told me to go to bed. During the night I was violently sick, the MO decided

A German 88-mm anti-tank gun that was captured and restored to working condition by Australian troops, 3 November 1942.

An SAS jeep heavily loaded with jerrycans of fuel and water, and personal kit. The 'gunner' is manning the .50-inch Browning heavy machine gun, while the driver has a single Vickers 'K' gun in front, and a twin mounting behind.

I was to be evacuated to hospital. I was operated on the next day; I still had shrapnel in my back. The doctor who operated I knew well from peacetime; I used to go skiing with him. He gave me a local anaesthetic, and dug the shrapnel out of my back. Then he made a mistake, he sewed the wound up. In due course I was sent to a base hospital and was well looked after by QARANC nurses. But I complained to the colonel that there was a terrible smell. He told the nurse to take the dressings off my wound, and discovered that I had gangrene. I was operated on. To this day I have a hole in my back, because they didn't sew it up, but left it to heal.

Major General John Harding
Deputy Chief of the General Staff (Training & Equipment),
GHQ Middle East
The offensive by Rommel ended with the Eighth Army being driven back to the Alamein position. I was worried that the Alamein position had not been properly prepared. When Rommel began his second offensive, I had made a recommendation that the Alamein position be prepared for the final defence of the delta. It was the final defensive position that any one could hold before one was pushed back to the delta. Morale in good units of the Eighth Army was as good as it ever was. But the morale of the army as a whole was shattered because they were in a state of confusion and had been defeated.

Private Bill Loffman
D Company, 2/28th Battalion, 9th Australian Division
When we were sent from Syria back into the Western Desert, we were told to blacken our tan Australian boots, so we looked like Poms, to fool the enemy. I thought it was a bit comic. We were told, 'Rommel is heading for the Suez Canal, you blokes have got to stop him.' We all thought, 'That's no problem, we've stopped him before.' As the South Africans were retreating we met them and they said, 'Oh, you're going to get cleaned up.' They were disheartened and demoralised. They were gloom and doom. We were full of fight.

Captain Vernon Northwood
Officer Commanding, A Company, 2/28th Battalion,
9th Australian Division
We were told we were on a secret mission: blacken our brown boots, not wear Australian hats or insignia. We wondered what this was about, but

when we arrived in Egypt the kids ran alongside the train shouting, 'Aussie back, Aussie back.'

Corporal Ray Middleton
HQ Company, 2/28th Battalion, 9th Australian Division
We were told we were going to Alamein. We thought, 'Somebody's got to stop the bastards.' The 9th Division was required to fill the position in the Alamein position. Next door to us was a South African division, who were ashamed of what their 2nd Division had done in Tobruk, allowing it to be taken. The 9th Division was used to take some of the key observation points.

Private Bill Loffman
10 Platoon, D Company, 2/28th Battalion, 9th Australian Division
We were told that an OP officer had left his map in his knocked-out tank on some feature, and our company had to go out to retrieve it. We thought that was bloody silly. On that attack we lost an officer and several people were wounded. We didn't find the map case. That was the first patrol we went on at Alamein.

Company Sergeant Major Alan Potter
D Company, 2/28th Battalion, 9th Australian Division
On 17 July we did our first attack on Ruin Ridge, part of Miteiriya Ridge. That was with tanks, riding them to within two hundred yards of enemy, where we would get off, and the tanks would go ahead to the position; we would follow in. A couple of things went wrong there. First our company commander was held up at the conference before the attack, and we had to move before he could tell us what the plan was in detail. Instead of company HQ being put on tanks we had to walk; a good thing too. The tanks were from the 50th Royal Tank Regiment. They had never been in action. Once they got under fire, they didn't know what they were at.

We got to the objective, but the new OC 10 platoon was killed riding on the tank. His body was intact but picking him up was like lifting jelly, all his bones were broken. His platoon sergeant had both legs blown off; he died.

Private Bill Loffman
10 Platoon, D Company, 2/28th Battalion, 9th Australian Division
We had never liaised with armour before. Number 10 Platoon, thirty Diggers, had to sit on the Valentine tanks going into the attack. I said to the tank chap, 'Little guns you've got here.'

'Yes, two-pounders.'

'You know what you're up against,' says I.

'Yes, we know.'

These fellows were bloody heroes. They were going to take on the 88s and bigger tanks. Their tanks were still painted green. British armour was crap taken into action by heroes.

Our platoon commander was killed and the platoon sergeant had both legs blown off, and asked to be shot.

Company Sergeant Major Alan Potter
D Company, 2/28th Battalion, 9th Australian Division
Our CO, who had been 2IC of another battalion until recently, found it all a bit too much for him. We were ordered to retire about two thousand yards; we were badly sighted and positioned. My orderly-room corporal had the top of his head blown off. We had shared a tent in Syria, and every night he used to say to his wife's photo, 'Good night darling, keep your legs together until I see you.' He never saw her.

Private Bill Loffman
10 Platoon, D Company, 2/28th Battalion, 9th Australian Division
It was a cool night. As we waited on the start-line tape we came under shell-fire. We had one dead and one wounded before we crossed the Start Line. We had been told that we were to be supported by lots of guns. When the barrage started it gave you a good feeling. Our barrage went for about fifteen minutes and it rolled in front of us. We just walked behind it. In an attack you can't stop to look after wounded. If you do, eventually there isn't anyone left to take the objective.

Company Sergeant Major Alan Potter
D Company, 2/28th Battalion, 9th Australian Division
The next attack on Ruin Ridge was well planned to a degree. The battalion had to go forward for a couple of thousand yards. Our engineers had cleared a gap through the minefield and marked the gap with white tape. The battalion was to attack with two companies forward and two behind.

We crossed the Start Line at midnight. My company commander, a good soldier, was held up again at the battalion conference. But when we went forward it was copybook. The enemy artillery homed in on us pretty quickly, and we just had to keep moving. I called out constantly, 'Keep moving, keep

Private Bill Loffman.

moving.' When shells come over people have a tendency to go to ground and of course it becomes difficult to get them moving again.

Private Peter Salmon
C Company, 2/28th Battalion, 9th Australian Division
The Germans concentrated their fire but the chaps kept on going. The only people who stopped were people who picked up a rifle, stuck it in the ground by the bayonet, and put a helmet on top to mark where chaps were wounded, and walked on. Everybody is frightened, but you keep going to do the job. You don't need much egging on. In the attack I got hit in the hip and that took me out of the battle.

Company Sergeant Major Alan Potter
D Company, 2/28th Battalion, 9th Australian Division
The position was taken by the bayonet, and we consolidated. As CSM I had certain things to do, but I was also company 2IC; the 2IC was now company commander. I had to send out patrols by sending runners to each platoon with orders to send out a patrol. I was also responsible for resupply of ammunition and casualty reports. I also had to dig in, in very rocky ground. Just as well I am not six foot tall. All these things take time, and all the time there is a war going on around you. Prisoners had to be taken back under escort. But if you have only one or two prisoners do you lose a man to take them back? Or do you hang on to them? You have to decide.

We now waited for our support to come through. The Germans saw our line of vehicles coming in, and shelled them coming through the minefield gap; it was like Guy Fawkes night with exploding vehicles. Our fellows showed incredible bravery, because two trucks would come up, one would get hit, but the other would accelerate and get past him. So we did get a bit of stuff up, not much. We got a six-pounder up and one or two other things.

Corporal Ray Middleton
Pioneer Platoon, HQ Company, 2/28th Battalion,
9th Australian Division
We captured Ruin Ridge and started to dig in but the ground was hard and we had to build up sangars. We were told to wait for the tanks in the morning. We were told to hang on, the next battalion would be up soon, and our tanks. But unfortunately the tanks that got through had black crosses on them.

Captain Vernon Northwood
Officer Commanding, A Company, 2/28th Battalion, 9th Australian Division

It was moonlight, about one o'clock in the morning, and I saw a gun being pulled up on to the ridge. I thought that couldn't be one of ours, it was being brought up the wrong side of the ridge; it was about forty yards away. I watched, two truckloads of men came up, and I saw that it was an 88-mm gun. I turned my company to face them, and said we must go in with the bayonet. We could see men taking up positions to defend the gun; we had to act quickly. I got two platoons forward, I couldn't wait for my third platoon. I said, 'Into them.' It is difficult to get a bayonet charge going from a lying position. For a moment I was the only man on my feet, I thought I was the only one to go. I got a fright. I was shouting like a madman. You have to get yourself into a state of frenzy. You know that if the enemy are in a position to run they will, they won't face you, specially if they are lying in the open, not in a trench. I heard this noise behind me, all my men shouting and screaming, it was frightening. I only got a few paces, I took a bullet through the top of my steel helmet, above my forehead and scraped the top of my scalp, then one through the top of my arm. I thought I would lose it. It was like being kicked by a horse – I have been kicked by a horse. Then wham, one through my neck, a flesh wound. I was thrown down and dropped my rifle and bayonet. Somebody shouted, 'The skipper's been hit.' I said, 'I'm all right.' I didn't want them to stop. They got to where the gun had been, which had gone. I could see my men taking prisoners. Had the gun got into position it would have covered the rear of the ridge. I found I was able to walk, handed over to 8 Platoon commander, gave him my binoculars and compass. The company orderly came with me, I was feeling a bit groggy. I was worried about the vehicles not getting through. I said I would go and see why they were not coming up to reinforce us with anti-tank guns, ammunition, etc.

An orderly came with me. I went back towards the minefield and along the line of advance. I ran into a German army doctor who was a prisoner. He had a pistol and I took it. We went up to the minefield, and I could see eight vehicles blown up on the minefield. We stopped until an ambulance vehicle came up and took me out.

Company Sergeant Major Alan Potter
D Company, 2/28th Battalion, 9th Australian Division

We dug in and we didn't have a great deal of time. We had each carried up three sandbags, which we filled with sand. We did not have a great deal of

A field dressing station.

cover. With first light came the first German infantry in half-tracks who dismounted and advanced on us. This time we had enough ammunition to repel two attacks by the infantry. We were pretty confident of holding, although ammunition was becoming a problem. The battalion had advanced two thousand yards to take Ruin Ridge. It was planned that a tank regiment would come up on each side of us. A British brigade, the 69th, would come to cover our front and it looked easy. But because the enemy destroyed most of our support coming up through the minefield and we were running out of ammo, we had to rely on the tanks. These tanks started to advance to join us, but were driven off by 88s. All we saw of them on both flanks was some dust and then them retreating. So we didn't get the tank support. We were sitting out there like Aunt Sallys. The British brigade, which was to come across our front, ran into trouble and by the time they reached their objective the entire brigade had been annihilated. So we were still out there on our own. Then we saw help coming, tanks were coming from our right front, they appeared to be our tanks. We thought that something was happening in our favour. At this point, Jimmy Allen got the idea that he would take a vehicle and guide them into our position. He commandeered an anti-tank gun vehicle, and raced past and just beyond my sangar, about seventy-five yards out, a German shell landed on his vehicle and blew him out of the vehicle. He landed on his back, and I raced across to him to see what I could do. He was split right up through the body. He asked me to shoot him. I said, 'Don't worry, Jim.' I went back to my sangar. I didn't have enough shell dressings with me to bind up such a large wound. The German tanks were getting closer and closer, and firing. The company commander asked, 'What's happening?' I told him that Jim was badly hit, and wanted me to shoot him. But by now the tanks were getting really close.

Corporal Ray Middleton
Pioneer Platoon, HQ Company, 2/28th Battalion,
9th Australian Division
One of our own mortar trucks full of three-inch mortar bombs tried to drive past us, it was hit by an anti-tank shell: the truck started burning. At irregular intervals one or two of the mortar bombs went off. We kept our heads down waiting for the truck to burn out. Jack and I took cover in our sangar, and when the truck seemed burnt out, he stood up and swore. I stood up and there was a German half-track a few yards from me with a chap standing in it with a machine gun aimed at me, and all he said was, 'Come out Aussie.'

I surrendered right there. Anyone who made the mistake of bending down to pick up their weapon or equipment got shot at.

Private Bill Loffman
10 Platoon, D Company, 2/28th Battalion, 9th Australian Division
A German tank came up, it pointed its gun at me, and a fellow in the turret shouted, '*Raus*'. We came out and surrendered. We walked over the hill, and there was the battalion lined up in threes.

Company Sergeant Major Alan Potter
D Company, 2/28th Battalion, 9th Australian Division
The tank that came to my sangar had an officer in it with the top half of his body out of the turret shouting, '*Aus, Aus*.' I had with me a revolver and a sticky bomb, like a very large toffee apple and you pulled a pin on it, which released the cover, and you went up to the tank and planted it on the side of the tank, and raced away. But there was no way I could do that. I threw away a German compass I had, and my revolver. The German shouted, 'For you the war is over.' I took a risk and bent down and picked up my haversack. He didn't mind that. We were put in a column and marched away. As we started, our own artillery came down on us, and we had more casualties. One private jumped into a trench and a shell landed right on him. We got through the barrage, and then we were marched off, and taken in vehicles to our first POW cage. I had an OCTU [Officer Cadet Training Unit] coming up and wanted to escape. So I drifted back through the column and looked for an opportunity to escape. I had a total sense of frustration as a prisoner. I had never considered it as an option.

Private Peter Salmon
C Company, 2/28th Battalion, 9th Australian Division
A battalion is like your home. It's the only place where people know you. After Ruin Ridge it was pretty devastating, you didn't know what had happened to them. My brother was one of them. When I came back to C Company, there were only four men left of the originals.

Major General John Harding
Deputy Chief of the General Staff (Training & Equipment),
GHQ Middle East
Rumours started going round the place that Auchinleck was to be replaced. Alexander and Monty arrived and were knocking around GHQ. I didn't

know Alexander but knew Monty well; I had been taught by him at the staff college. One day I was sent for and told the C-in-C wanted to see me. I found Monty sitting in the C-in-C's chair and Alexander sitting on the desk. Monty said, 'Hello John, you haven't met General Alexander.'

'No, sir.'

Then he said, 'Sandy Galloway told me that you know all about the formations out here. I want you to tell me all about it, down to brigade level.'

I gave him my assessment of each of the formations in the Eighth Army down to brigade level. Then he said, 'Out of all this muckage, can you organise a corps of two armoured divisions and one mobile infantry division. I want to form a *corps de chasse* for a major offensive.'

I thought for a moment, and said, 'If you give me a little time and don't mind me putting it down in my own handwriting, I can do it.'

He said, 'General Alexander and I have got to go and see the ambassador, I'll be back in a couple of hours; I would like it then.'

I went back to my office, and sat down and locked the door and worked out what would be the best answer. That was the origin of X Corps. He took it and left to take command of Eighth Army.

Things began to get clearer at GHQ. Alexander took over as C-in-C, with Dick McCreery as his COS. Auchinleck and Dorman-Smith, his Chief of Staff, disappeared, and I was left as DCGS with responsibility for introducing Alexander to the desert for the next few weeks. He was a marvellous chap to work for. He may have been an enigma, and some people accuse him of being indecisive, but he could be decisive. I had the highest admiration and affection for him. Alexander operated by instinct. He had experience of the battlefield at every level. He liked to think that officers would do what was best; he operated by remote control. He was ready to leave responsibility to his subordinates. He was much more flexible than Monty. Alex gave Monty a free hand in training, planning, and stood between Monty and Churchill when he was under pressure to launch the Alamein offensive too early. Alex devoted himself to ensuring that Eighth Army was provided with every resource that they needed.

Dorman-Smith has claimed that the battle was fought on his plan. In my opinion it is difficult to pinpoint the responsibility for the conception of a battle plan, what really matters is the execution. Rommel was preparing for a further offensive. Monty put the armour in position on high ground overlooking the route Rommel had to take to get to the delta. Rommel had to take this ground first, and he failed. Monty's impact on the Eighth Army was tremendous. He made it clear that there was to be no further withdrawal. He went round, he saw everybody, and they saw him.

Lieutenant Martyn Highfield
Command Post Officer, 452 Battery, 74 Field Regiment,
Royal Horse Artillery

Eight weeks after having splinters taken out of my back, I was fit for duty and sent to the artillery base depot. After a couple of days I was with a group of officers standing around near the base HQ, when a truck drove up and I recognised the regimental number on it, and it was the CO's truck. Standing up in the truck was Collett-White who had been 2IC, but was now clearly the CO. I went up and spoke to him, and he said he would fix that I was to rejoin the regiment. I was relieved to be back in my regiment. In war you always want to fight alongside your friends.

I was posted as CPO of 452 Battery, and Bill Cheeseman was my battery commander. He was a TA officer, a very caring man with attention to detail. Major Collett-White was a regular, who had taken over as CO. His initials were HE, which also stands for High Explosive, and very appropriate. He was a very good colonel.

We were called forward from Meena and on this occasion didn't support the 50th Division: we supported 22nd Armoured Brigade. We moved forward in the dark and dug in on very rocky ground. Next day we went further forward and went into action on a sandy position where we could see in the distance the tanks of 15th Panzer Division several miles off. This was where Rommel's probing attacks had reached. There were some hillocks nearby and we were supporting an armoured unit, which was to join 22nd Armoured Brigade. They had come from Palestine and not been in action before. They had lost five tanks just joining up with 22nd Armoured Brigade.

Trooper John Lanes
Wireless Operator/Driver, The Nottinghamshire Yeomanry
(Sherwood Rangers)

We had been a regiment of horsed cavalry and converted to armour in Palestine. We had Crusaders; a fast tank, very low, but only a two-pounder gun with an effective range of eight hundred yards. We were really green at Alam Halfa. We formed a brigade with the Staffordshire Yeomanry, and the Greys.

We took the full brunt of the German attack that was trying to break through. We stopped them there. We knew where the Germans were coming and we had to meet them head on. You didn't move but stood there and shot it out with them. You moved a bit to find a good place to hide. It was a straight slug, and luckily we had brigades on the flanks as well that threatened them. I could see the enemy tanks quite plainly and see the infantry moving about as well – running and falling down. My job was wireless operator and loading the gun. You also needed to drive as a driver/operator, and fire the gun. I had headphones. When the commander was talking on the intercom to the driver he couldn't listen on the wireless, so you listened for him and kept him informed.

Lieutenant John Semken
Assistant Adjutant, The Nottinghamshire Yeomanry
(Sherwood Rangers)
The regiment was told to retake a position taken by the Germans. The result was disastrous: we lost about fifty per cent of the regimental strength in about ten minutes. We had always imagined that when tanks went into action they would close down, and everybody did close down. One chap got an MC for dashing round in a scout car and tearing open the turret lids in order to get people out before they blew up. Fortunately the brigadier, who was behind us watching, wanted us to withdraw. The colonel called for smoke from the artillery, and we were able to pull back with the remnants of the regiment. What was critical in this was that this message to withdraw was received in the tank I was in, the 2IC's tank. The theory was that in those days the command tanks communicated by the B set, which you switched over to and was a sort of house telephone system. Donnie Player, the 2IC, received this message from brigade, switched over to the B Set and conveyed it to the colonel who ordered the regiment to withdraw. But this is a crazy way to keep contact between a CO and brigade.

Every regiment has to learn the hard way. That is why a regiment has to acquire a 'fighting culture', learn to live on your tanks, what to do if you are hit.

Lieutenant Martyn Highfield
Command Post Officer, 452 Battery, 74 Field Regiment,
Royal Horse Artillery
This brigade had beaten off the German tanks. The action took place over three or four days. A contributory factor was the air: formations of our

medium bombers bombed the advancing armour of 15th Panzer Division. This was very heartening and we realised that, for the first time in the war, the balance of air power was changing.

Corporal Harold Wilmshurst
C Company, 5th Battalion, Royal Sussex, 44th Division
Our division was called forward to man positions on Alam el Halfa. We had just arrived in Egypt from England. You could see for miles around. It was very rocky and you couldn't get down very far. The Royal Engineers dug the trenches deep.

When the Germans attacked we stopped them. The first casualty was the OC's pickup truck, blown up. The German planes came over. They attacked us. We had three Bofors guns protecting us, and they put up a barrage to protect us. Over twenty planes were shot down that day, all round us. As the German aircrew came down on parachutes, a Polish tank regiment near us shot them as they descended, killing them. We lay low in our slit trenches.

Then C Company went forward with some tanks. They had been with us in Crowborough training. They were in 23rd Armoured Brigade. They took over the ground in daytime, and we took over at night, while they refuelled. The Germans retreated and we followed up. As they retreated, the RAF bombed them. We were attached to the West Kents, and they took a lot of casualties. We returned to our hill, and on the way we passed through our 4th Battalion, they had had a pasting. They cheered us as we went back.

Corporal James Sherwood
1st Special Boat Section
When the Germans reached the Alamein line, there was an air of defeatism all around. When everybody seemed to be pulling out, the SBS went in the opposite direction. Our officers hatched a number of operations against the Germans using MTBs. I went on one of these. Who selected the landing place I know not. It turned out to be a large German camp. The MTB crept in. We had one Folbot and an enormous blow-up RAF life raft, which held six men. In this contraption we gyrated our way gently towards the shore from the MTB, which unfortunately had been heard from the shore. Within minutes of landing, Very lights were fired, lighting up the whole area. A gun opened up on the MTB. We still went ahead and landed on the beach. We couldn't see anybody moving about. The Very lights went out, the gun stopped firing, perhaps thinking that what had been there had

Corporal James Sherwood (right) with Folboat at Kabrit.

sheered off. Our object was to place thermite bombs on the petrol tanks of any lorries we came across. We split into pairs. There was no plan. It was just, 'You go that way, you go there, you go there, and rendezvous on the beach at 0200.'

It was a moonless night. My colleague and I went up through some sand hills to the edge of a bluff overlooking the beach. We were about to scramble over the top when a giant figure approached, silhouetted against the sky. It was a German sentry, his rifle slung. He looked over the bluff while we crouched like a pair of rabbits in the sand with our pistols ready to drop this bloke should he spot us. He came on and stood about four feet away. He never saw us, turned, and walked away.

By now a great deal of time had passed, so we made our way back to where we had left the canoe and the raft. All but two of the blokes were there. They hadn't achieved anything. We discovered that the blow-up raft had a puncture. Fortunately it had a pump. It made a ghastly squeaking noise. We were certain someone would hear and investigate, but they didn't. We got the wretched thing inflated, and launched off. We left the canoe upside down, buried in the sand, in case the other two got away, and might be able to paddle along the coast to the British lines.

Afloat on the dark sea we worked the pump to keep the raft from deflating. We looked in vain for the MTB. We didn't have any binoculars, and were relying on spotting her silhouette against the starlit sky. But there was no sign of her. The raft had short wooden paddles, and we progressed in a series of whirls out to sea. We decided that if the worst came to the worst, we'd paddle on by night, land by day to lie up, and eventually get back to our own side of the lines. It was getting close to the rendezvous time with the MTB, when suddenly she started up. Immediately we pinpointed her. Why the Germans didn't open up again, I don't know. We got on board. The skipper said he'd hang about until just before first light in the hope the other two would turn up. He couldn't afford to stay after that, and even then he'd have to run back to Alexandria in daylight. They didn't come back. We got back to Alexandria. The raid didn't achieve anything.

Guardsman Bob Bennett
L Detachment, Special Air Service

David Stirling decided to get his own vehicles, and we stopped using the LRDG taxi service. We had armoured jeeps with twin Vickers aircraft machine guns on the back, which fired a thousand rounds a minute. They were terrific, loaded with one round of tracer, one of AP, one of ball and so on. On the front of the jeep we had a .5-inch Browning heavy machine gun.

Captain the Lord Jellicoe
L Detachment, Special Air Service
I went to attack the most easterly of the German airfields nearest to the Alamein lines. Because we had to leave in daylight to cover the distance, we were bounced by fighters. Robin Gurdon of the LRDG was killed. Two of our jeeps were destroyed by the first attack. I managed to hide my jeep in a wadi. We had to bring the whole party back in one jeep. The radiator was holed, so we stuffed it with plastic explosive and peed into the radiator to top it up. We eventually got back.

This was followed by a raid on Sidi Haneish led by David Stirling, with a force of seventeen jeeps. We approached under the cover of darkness, and formed up into two columns. Paddy Mayne was leading one and I the other. We broke our way on to the airfield shooting our way round it. They shot back. One chap was killed. We drove off after doing a lot of damage, about thirty to thirty-five aircraft. We lay up during the daytime, split into small groups. Unfortunately one of the French jeeps was spotted, shot up by aircraft, and a very fine officer killed.

We were well hidden and a German Fiesler Storch landed not more than six hundred yards from us. Two people got out and had a pee. We realised that, in our jeeps, we could get to the plane before they could and captured them. One was a German doctor, and as it turned out I had lunch with his parents in Bremen when I was driving in Germany with the son of the Crown Prince in 1936.

My days in the desert were drawing to an end because I had trouble with my ligament locking. It went again on this raid. Our doctor diagnosed one problem, the German doctor another. They were both right, because I had two problems. The German doctor eventually escaped with his companion. I was pleased. We went to look for them but couldn't find them.

I was evacuated in one of the three Bombay transport aircraft, which had flown out to take some of us back. I missed the great Benghazi raid.

Corporal James Sherwood
1st Special Boat Section
The SAS aspired to take over the SBS; we didn't want to join them, but in the end their greater influence prevailed and we were absorbed into the

SAS, while still known as the SBS. We were all told, 'Right, you'll all be doing a parachute jump.' We decided that we didn't want to do it. We asked for an interview with Major Kealey, our new OC, and said if we were told to do one we would ask to be RTU'd. He didn't call our bluff; luckily. We stayed, the only two who didn't make a jump. We felt we'd made a stand for the poor old SBS.

In August 1942 we were told that an operation was being mounted by the SAS in September in which the SBS would take part. This would involve a long drive south up the Nile valley to Assiut; from there we would strike west across the desert south of the Sand Sea for the oasis of Kufra, for an attack on Benghazi to divert the Germans and Italians from Alamein.

We set out. We had canoes on our trucks. The SAS went ahead. They hadn't given us any maps. The only instruction we had was to leave the Nile valley at Assiut, strike the desert track for the oasis at Kharga, take a westerly bearing, and follow that for some hundreds of miles, until we struck the Wadi Halfa–Kufra track. Here we would turn right, and we were told we would recognise it by the enormous number of vehicle tracks in the sand. The track could be miles wide depending on how many vehicles used it. If a vehicle stuck, the others would go round it to find firmer sand to drive on. We just followed this jumble of tracks for several days, until we struck another great conglomeration of tracks – we never did see how wide it was across – coming in from our left, which we rightly assumed, although with no great confidence at the time, must be the Wadi Halfa–Kufra track. In due course we got to Kufra. I suppose we couldn't have got lost anyway. If we had, someone from the SAS would have said, 'Isn't the SBS supposed to be with us? Perhaps we'd better send someone back to try to find them.'

At Kufra we had two or three days to gather our forces and get ourselves together. Here we discovered our role. While the SAS kept Benghazi occupied, we were to assemble our canoes on the side of Benghazi harbour, paddle out and sink the ships there with limpet mines. Nobody was enthusiastic about this, apart from the fact that we didn't want to be with the SAS anyway. A great deal of grumbling and moaning went on, quite amusing in retrospect, very irritating at the time. On 13 September 1942, we motored in trucks down the escarpment in the pitch dark towards Benghazi. We and the SAS were perched on our canoes in their bags in a three-ton lorry, with a whole lot of explosives under the canoes. We were half asleep, dozing on top of these canoes and explosives with the blokes grumbling at one another, 'Get your bloody boots out of the way,' sort of thing. When the truck stopped, one chap hopped over the side and had a crap at the side of the road, while the truck waited and the others went past. I can't remember any apprehension, just the coldness of the night, and everybody thoroughly out of sorts with one another.

Trooper Reg Seekings
L Detachment, Special Air Service
Our job was to tear round the streets and blast up the town. A big air raid had been laid on to keep Benghazi quiet until we got into town.

Corporal James Sherwood
1st Special Boat Section
The whole thing went wrong. We saw the raid from afar, and watched the fun and games, and fireworks and bombs, when we were still trundling down the escarpment, hopelessly late. For better or worse David Stirling decided the operation would be carried on. We went down the escarpment with headlights full on, Stirling hoped to bluff his way, on the basis that no enemy would be stupid enough to come down with their headlights on. We came on to a proper road. Ahead you could see a striped pole. David Stirling got out, and walked up to this pole just to see what was going on, all the headlights beamed away behind him. He was a very brave bloke. He quickly found out. Instead of Italians being there, the Germans were waiting for us. They knew all about it. They opened up with everything they'd got. The extraordinary thing was that they scored very few hits. Just as well, because sitting on our explosives we would have disappeared in a big bang.

Trooper Reg Seekings
L Detachment, Special Air Service
The first burst of fire hit another man in my jeep, and I threw myself down. The wounded man had been hit through the hips and had his penis and testicles blown off. I lifted him on to another jeep. I took the gun and Davey took the wheel, I poured fire into the enemy, I couldn't see them.

Corporal James Sherwood
1st Special Boat Section
We were told to get out of it, every man for himself, as best we could. There was a great deal of confusion, backing and filling of trucks trying to turn round, shot and stuff flying all over the place. One jeep was hit in the petrol

tank, which went up in flames, adding to the already illuminated scene. We headed out of it, having achieved nothing at all; a complete fiasco, the whole operation.

Trooper Reg Seekings
L Detachment, Special Air Service
My vehicle's sump had been pierced during the battle. On the way, I found the man who had been wounded in the hips, his vehicle had broken down too. I lifted him off the vehicle, he asked me to shoot him. I wrapped him in a blanket. I took his gun away. I told him I couldn't take him on my vehicle, as it was about to break down at any minute.

Corporal James Sherwood
1st Special Boat Section
At break of day we were all haring hell for leather across this big gravelly plain, trying to get to the Jebel area where there were ravines for conceal-ment before the planes got up to look for us. We weren't in time. They got the fighters up, strafing and bombing. I can remember lorries with great clouds of dust driving faster than they'd ever driven in their lives before, all trying to reach cover before the worst happened. None of us were hit. Some of us would bale out of the trucks, when we thought a plane was diving on us, and run like hell. But the plane wasn't diving on us, it was after another truck which it didn't catch. The driver of our truck would slow up so we could catch him, and we all jumped aboard, and off again. Eventually we gained the shelter of the Jebel, the planes having turned back, presumably to rearm and come after us again.

The first sight that greeted us when we got to a particularly deep ravine, was a group of SAS blokes with a fire going, cooking breakfast as though on a picnic. We didn't stop there. It was a daft place to be. We'd two officers with us, and we went up the ravine as far as we could. For the whole of the day we lay up under camouflage netting. Nothing spotted us. The rest of the force had a fearful dusting about a mile or two west of us, which went on all day, machine-gunning and bombing. How many were lost then I don't know; very few at the encounter at the border post, but a lot altogether.

We lay up all day. We'd received a message from Stirling, 'The operation all off. Head for Kufra as best you can.'

Lieutenant David Stirling in cap, with members of G Patrol SAS. Trooper Reg Seekings second from left in Arab head-dress.

Alamein

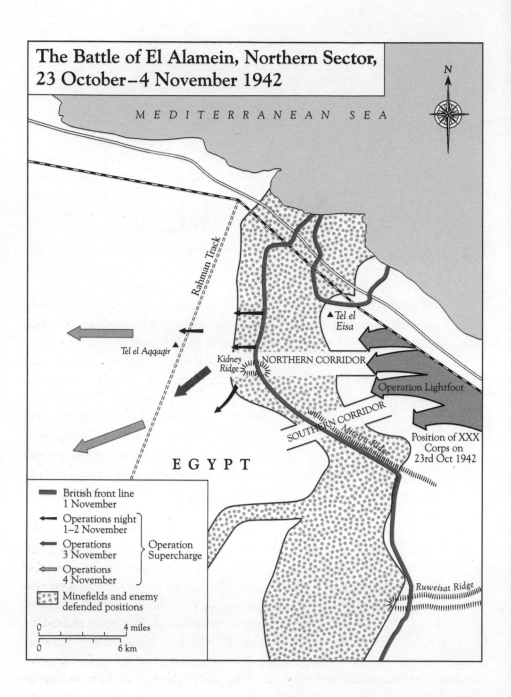

The Battle of El Alamein, Northern Sector, 23 October–4 November 1942

MEDITERRANEAN SEA

N

Rahman Track

▲ Tel el Eisa

Tel el Aqqaqir ▲

Kidney Ridge

NORTHERN CORRIDOR

Operation Lightfoot

SOUTHERN CORRIDOR

Miteiri Ridge

EGYPT

Position of XXX Corps on 23rd Oct 1942

Ruweisat Ridge

British front line 1 November

Operations night 1–2 November

Operations 3 November

Operations 4 November

Operation Supercharge

Minefields and enemy defended positions

0   4 miles

0   6 km

At 0105 the whistles blew, shells were screaming over us,
and off we went, accompanied by a crescendo of noise
that was to last for three hours.

After Rommel withdrew from Alam Halfa, both sides faced each other along a forty-mile long front that ran from the sea to the Qattara Depression. Both began to build strong defences of mines, booby traps and wire. Rommel knew that Montgomery would attack him, probably during the full moon period in the latter half of October. Rommel's defence layout included some 431,000 anti-tank mines, and 14,000 anti-personnel mines. Mines were laid in two belts, connected by other minefields to form boxes to restrict the British armour's room for manoeuvre. The front of each box was held by outposts; the rest was unoccupied, but sown with mines. The total width of the two minefield belts was some six thousand yards. Strengthened by both Italian and German reinforcements, the main line of defence for Rommel's Deutsch–Italienische Panzer Armee was behind the second mine belt, which was at least two thousand yards deep. German battalions were deployed throughout the position 'corseting' Italian units, to stiffen their morale.

Montgomery planned that the main attack at Alamein would be in the north, in Lieutenant General Sir Oliver Leese's XXX Corps sector. Here four divisions – 9th Australian, 51st Highland, 2nd New Zealand and 1st South African – would attack abreast on a ten-mile-wide front. The aim was to penetrate up to five miles in one night, thus reaching the rear of the enemy defences. Engineers were to follow, and clear two mine-free corridors to enable the three armoured divisions of Lieutenant General Herbert Lumsden's X Corps to breakout and seize the defensible ground astride the Rahman track near Tel el Aqqaqir, where they were to engage and destroy the enemy armour. As a diversion, a further breach was to be made by Lieutenant General Brian Horrocks's XIII Corps in the south. Here the 7th Armoured Division was to pass two armoured brigades through in order to 'fix' the enemy armour in this sector. Horrocks was told that the 7th Armoured Division was not to become mired in heavy fighting, but merely to fake a major attack. In addition, elaborate deception measures were concocted to try to persuade Rommel that the main thrust was to be in the south.

Eventually, Montgomery changed the detail for the operation in the north. Reports came in that the minefields were much thicker than originally estimated, and he realised that the standard of training in his army, especially among formations that had recently arrived in the desert, was not high enough for the task he expected them to perform. Now, his tanks, having passed through the minefield belt, would hold off the enemy, while his infantry destroyed the enemy infantry in a series of 'crumbling' attacks along axes parallel to the front, rather than through it, and attacking to the left and right of the main axis thus taking enemy positions in the flank.

At 9.40 pm on 23 October 1942, Operation Lightfoot began. Initially, the four assaulting divisions of XXX Corps made good progress, but were slowed by the final belts of mines known to the Germans as the 'Devil's Gardens'. By dawn the infantry was still almost a mile short of the objective as the minefields had taken longer to clear than was at first estimated. As the corridors were not clear, Lumsden was reluctant to launch his armour and charge through the last part of the minefield. Montgomery told Lumsden to fight his way out of the minefield, or be sacked, and ordered the 'crumbling' battles by Leese's infantry to begin at once. He hoped thereby to draw the German armour and anti-tank guns away from their positions guarding the breakout points, to defending their own infantry. Still Lumsden's armour failed to breakout. This was the crisis point of the battle. At this juncture, Rommel returned from one month's sick leave in Germany. He ordered a series of counter-attacks, which were beaten off without much difficulty.

Meanwhile, Montgomery devised a new plan, Operation Supercharge. While the Australians in the extreme north of the line held off the bulk of the German armour, two British infantry brigades attached to the New Zealand Division would punch a hole more than two miles wide through the enemy line just to the south of the Australians. Each brigade would have a regiment of Valentine tanks in support. Behind them, also

Montgomery with his corps commanders at Alamein: L–R, Lieutenant General Oliver Leese (XXX Corps), Lieutenant General Herbert Lumsden (X Corps), and on his left, Lieutenant General Brian Horrocks (XIII Corps).

under New Zealand command, would be the 9thArmoured Brigade, of three tank regiments. This brigade would extend the advance for just over a mile further, beyond the infantry brigades' objectives, and seize the area of the Rahman track. At this juncture, the 1st Armoured Division of X Corps, would move forward, cross the Rahman track, and engage the enemy's armour in the open. The 7th Armoured Division was brought up from the south to be ready to exploit the breakthrough and lead the pursuit of the retreating enemy. Meanwhile, XIII Corps, commanded by Lieutenant General Horrocks, were tasked with making every effort to keep the enemy busy on the south of the line by mounting a series of attacks.

Major General John Harding
General Officer Commanding, 7th Armoured Division
In early September I was sent for by Alex and told that Monty wanted me to command 7th Armoured Division. I was delighted. I had been up and down the desert, I had been staff officer to different generals. I had not had command since commanding the 1st Battalion Somerset Light Infantry. I was thrilled and apprehensive all the same; it was a terrific responsibility, I hadn't commanded a brigade. Not until we really got going in the pursuit did I feel confident. I had a brilliant G1: Mike Carver. I had an excellent staff, and a top-class armoured brigade commander, Pip Roberts: I had all the ingredients for success.

I spent all daylight hours going round talking to my division. The preparations for El Alamein were under way, although the details of the plan had to be worked out. The preparations included recce, patrolling, air recce, preparations for artillery bombardment, and building up of ammunition stocks, briefing commanders and staffs, and the deception plan.

Captain Hans-Otto Behrendt
Adjutant to Field Marshal Rommel,
Commander, Deutsch–Italienische Panzer Armee
Rommel's reaction to the failure at Alam Halfa was a cool realisation that he had lost the initiative for ever. He always called Montgomery 'the fox'. He thought he was very cautious. He told me at the end of September 1942, 'If I had been as strong as Montgomery is now, we wouldn't be here now.'

Pilot Officer Harry Hawker
208 *Squadron*, RAF

When I joined the squadron we were mainly doing visual reconnaissance over the Alamein line, at about four thousand feet, which was a bad height because you were shot at by light flak, and heavy flak from the 88s. Our job was to fly a number of recces a day. Each recce consisted of the pilot doing the recce and someone else weaving behind him to protect his tail. As you flew over the line, you didn't see much if they were well camouflaged. On a good day at four thousand feet you could see all the way from the Mediterranean down to Himeimat, thirty miles to the south; on a poor day, much less. What you were looking for was movement and the dust it caused. You had been briefed on what the last recces had seen, and the believed positions of the enemy; it was our job to point out any changes. You had to be quick at assessing numbers, so if you saw a bunch of trucks or tanks, you would have to say something like 'twenty-five plus'. You always flew with the hood open, because the visibility was so poor through the crazed Plexiglas. With a pencil, or just with your thumb, because you were sweating in the heat, you marked where the formation was on the map, so that when you were debriefed by very skilled air liaison officers, or ALOs – army officers who ran the operation – you could tell them what you saw and where; you were just their eyes. They were trusted by the aircrew and the army as well.

The German flak was accurate, but you weaved, so casualties were not high. Casualties from fighters were much higher. I was lucky only to have seen enemy fighters, but not to have been attacked by them, because they had about fifty per cent success against us. We were in the worst possible situation, at four thousand feet on a hot day, it was difficult to see enemy against a clear blue sky. The recce pilot was spending most of his time looking at the ground. The weaver, the less-experienced pilot, was supposed to be not only protecting the leader's and his own backside, but also understudying him to eventually enable him to do recce. Your result was compared with your leader's as a check.

The lead aircraft would tend to fly a fairly straight course, with just small adjustments of course and height. The weaver would position himself off to one side, and attempt to cover his stern, above and behind. The enemy 109 [a Messerschmitt 109] would get very high, go for us in a steep dive going very fast, so time to pick him up was short, and he would belt you with one short burst. If the weaver saw the attacker in time, he would call out, and turn into the attack, and if he could get round in time you had a good

189

chance of spoiling his afternoon. We lost twenty-one pilots in nineteen days on this activity over Alamein.

Recognition of equipment was vital. It was not always easy to distinguish between enemy and our own equipment. There were some clues: for example the British, Indians, New Zealanders and Australians all had their brew-up in the morning, and just after dawn there would be a myriad of little fires to show where our positions were. The Germans didn't do much low-level visual recce.

Pilot Officer Ian Smith
237 (Rhodesian) Squadron, RAF

We flew Hurricanes in support of the Eighth Army, attacking German ground troops, harassing their transport. All the squadron were Rhodesians. I crashed taking off in the middle of the night in a sandstorm. I thought I'd broken my back, but fortunately I didn't. Since then doctors always say, 'You've got a bloody awful spine, it's all buckled and bent.' They suggested that I be sent home, but I wanted to stay and fight. I stayed and rejoined the same squadron, and converted to Spitfires.

Lieutenant John Semken
Troop Leader, The Nottinghamshire Yeomanry (Sherwood Rangers)

After Alam Halfa we spent six weeks training, mainly on how to move by night – very difficult because of the appalling dust thrown up by tanks. All sorts of instructions were issued, for example, that no one, under any circumstances, was to go into a tank with bare arms or bare legs; however hot it was, you had to be properly covered. No one was to wear a lanyard on his pistol because when he bailed out it was certain to get caught on something. No one was ever to close down a turret lid in battle, the driver closed down, but not the commander, as you hadn't a hope of lifting that heavy lid once a tank caught fire. On the whole if a tank is hit, particularly Grants and Shermans, the fire didn't become extreme for about five seconds. This sounds a short time, but five seconds is quite long. You might lose one or two people, or have people badly burned, but you usually got some people out.

Lieutenant Emilio Pulini
Italian Folgore Parachute Division

We arrived in North Africa in good condition; we had tough training in Southern Italy over rough ground and in a hot climate. We were very fit, but unfortunately the conditions in the desert were not the same as in Italy. The weather was very hot as we arrived in the middle of July. We went immediately to the battle front which was a sudden change. There were things we did not like very much, like flies, and very hot sun, which was above us all day long. Being on the front line we had no means of providing shade. We had to spend the majority of the time lying in foxholes. These were the length of a man, may be ten to twenty inches deep. Sometimes they would take two people, but mainly for one. It was very uncomfortable to spend a whole day lying in these foxholes, from sunrise to sunset, just covered with flies, and doing very little.

Sergeant Herbert Holewa
2nd Battalion, Fallschirmjager Regiment, Ramcke Parachute Brigade
We landed in Tobruk, and moved forward to El Alamein by truck. Rommel divided our brigade; our battalion and the brigade staff went to the Qattara Depression. Rommel came and said in no circumstances can you go back. After a dogfight overhead a British pilot parachuted down into no-man's-land. We collected him. That was the first time I had seen condensed milk used on burns. He was flown out by a Fiesler Storch. Two hours later the doctor who tended him was killed by a shell splinter.

Bombardier Stephen Dawson
339 Battery, 104th (Essex Yeomanry) Field Regiment,
Royal Horse Artillery
I heard that the regiment was near Alamein, but got malaria and was sent to hospital. From there it was back to the base depot again; an awful place. You had good morale in the field, and bad morale there. One day we were on parade while people were being detailed off for fatigues, it went on for ages. An old regular from our regiment was beside me and he said, 'Let's bugger off.'

'What do you mean?'

'Just do as I say.'

We sprang to attention, turned right smartly, and marched off. We were not missed. The old regulars and their tricks always amazed me.

I wanted to go back to the battery. The Essex Yeomanry always tried to get their own men back. I wasn't the man I had been; I was tired all the time. We weren't in the front line. I was in charge of the battery captain's truck – Captain Adams, whom I liked and knew well. Then we moved to the rear of the Alamein line. We were told that we were not allowed to leave the position because we were told what was going to happen; for the first time ever we were told. We were the feint attack, the main attack would be in the north. The new CO gave us a briefing. He said, 'Before a rugger match I always tell the team, if the other team fight dirty, do the same, kick 'em in the balls. We've got a dirty opponent here, so treat 'em rough.'

We were given some words from Monty, that he had ordered should be spoken to everybody, he said, 'Trust in the Lord, God of battles.' We saw the preparations for the battle, for the first time it seemed organised. We saw rows of lorries made of plywood and canvas with tracks up to them. There was rows of posts with tins on them with pictures of symbols on them and a light inside to mark the way forward for the troops to their positions. If you had to speak on the wireless you just said, 'I am following the sun, or I'm on the way to the boat.' Which gave no clue to the enemy where you were.

We moved up into our position. We were in the division that was to fight our way in after the first day, so we were several miles back from the line. Going up through the Alamein area there was a huge hospital, all empty, and there were men outside digging graves. I felt so confident that I was all right, I shouted, 'I'm six foot three. Save one of those for me.'

Captain David Smiley
1st Household Cavalry Regiment

We were on the south end of the line at Alamein to begin with. An armoured car unit in the Western desert was a good unit to be in. You did get shot at sometimes. On one occasion I was attacked by our own fighters, mortared by our own infantry, shot at by Stukas and shelled by German artillery – all on the same day. We had no casualties, but we operated well forward in no-man's-land so there was sometimes a problem with identification. We were probably nearer to the German lines than our own.

Montgomery came and gave us a pep talk. We had confidence in him; he was a bit of a bullshitter, but that was part of his act, he had to publicise himself in competition with Rommel. He raised our morale, especially saying we wouldn't attack until we were ready. We had been fighting up to that stage in the war really at a disadvantage, so it seemed to us. We didn't have good tanks, and enough aircraft overhead. We all thought the world of Rommel. We had great confidence in people like Horrocks and Harding.

We did a big rehearsal for the battle. Well behind our lines they laid out minefields just like the ones in front of us, and we were used as umpires and enemy. We reported on the things that had gone wrong. People got lost and units got out of position in the rehearsal. One hopes that rehearsals will go wrong.

Trooper John Bolan
Tank Driver, 1 Troop, A Squadron, 6th Royal Tank Regiment
Back in Alexandria we worked on tanks that had been knocked out, taking the extra armour plates off. Out of curiosity we looked inside, and in some of the burnt-out tanks we found remains of the crew, like a leg; just bits, pretty gruesome. We asked the padre in the camp to bury them. He said, 'No, you bury them.' So we dug a hole in the sand and buried the parts. No tags or anything to tell who they were.

When I went back to the regiment they had formed the Montgomery protection squadron of four tanks. The main gun was taken out and room inside was made for maps, etc.

Sergeant Douglas Covill
Tank Commander, A Squadron, 10th Royal Hussars
Day after day our composite squadron went up to Ruweisat Ridge, motoring between dummy cardboard tanks to create dust and tracks for the enemy air reconnaissance. The Germans were about a thousand yards from us, and our two-pounder gun was no use over five hundred yards. Then we were issued with Sherman tanks with a 75-mm gun, which was the first time we had a tank with a gun as good as the Germans'.

Trooper E. Wainwright
47th Royal Tank Regiment
When we arrived in Egypt our tanks were on another vessel; this was fortunate, because we got the first Shermans. They were an improvement on any other tank we had before. We had some very interesting sessions with the American sergeant instructors who came and taught us how to use them. The great event was the arrival of Montgomery. Very quickly after his arrival a different feeling went through all the people who were there, they were all uplifted, and the whole tone changed from being 'mushy' to being keen-edged. Then Churchill came and in one of the papers I am just in the picture of a group talking with Churchill.

Lieutenant John Semken
Troop Leader, The Nottinghamshire Yeomanry (Sherwood Rangers)

We had leave in Cairo before Alamein, for about four days. I went with my great mate Ron Hill. On our last day we were going down the main street in a horse-drawn *gharry*, and Ron said to me, 'You wouldn't think that we are on the eve of one of the biggest battles in history. You are absolutely convinced that whatever happens to anyone else, it won't happen to you.' I said, 'That's right.' One of the chaps killed at Alam Halfa had a premonition of death, and I had no such premonition. With that thought we concluded our conversation on that topic.

Trooper Kenneth Ewing
Gunner/Operator, B Squadron, Nottinghamshire Yeomanry (Sherwood Rangers)

We lost a lot of men and learned a lot in our first action at Alam Halfa. We had a mixture of tanks, Lee/Grants, and some Stuarts, and some Crusader Mk IIs. As we set off, the Germans had Mk IVs on a ridge, covered by 88-mm anti-tank guns. We learned not to charge anti-tank guns. Out of the nine chaps that joined with me, I was the only one that survived Alam Halfa.

The problem with the Lee/Grant was that it had a side door, where the main gun was. If the tank caught on fire, you had a job getting the big square door open, plus the turret had to be in a certain position or the driver, co-driver and loader couldn't get out. So sections of the cage on the bottom of the turret was cut away, so nine times out of ten you could escape. Most tanks had an escape hatch on the floor on a pivot, so you could sometimes get out that way.

We were then sent to the left of the line and issued with canvas covers; these were to camouflage the tanks to look like lorries from the air. When we moved to a new area, and took the covers off, they replaced us with rubber blow-up tanks.

Major John Harris
Second-in-Command, 2nd Derbyshire Yeomanry

For the Battle of Alamein, initially we were down south with the 7th Armoured Division to make the Germans think that this was the main effort. One morning at daybreak, at stand-to, I was with the CO and he said, 'Look over there.' I saw a lot of our tanks moving behind us. He said, 'What's strange about those tanks?'

I replied, 'I don't know. Are they these new Shermans?'

He said, 'They make no noise, they've got no tracks, they are lorries with canvas over them made to look like tanks.'

There was a whole division of these phantom tanks. The phantom tanks were to deceive the enemy into believing that most of our tanks were down south; whereas the main attack was in the north.

Major General John Harding
General Officer Commanding, 7th Armoured Division

The minefields were very worrying. My division was on the left flank and the task I was given was to launch an attack between Himeimat and the north to hold 21st Panzer Division and prevent them from being able to move to attack our main attack further north. I had to keep 21st Panzer held down south by offensive action, but at the same time keep my division in being so that it could take part in a further offensive or pursuit later. This would be difficult. Himeimat was a big feature, well defended by the Germans and the approach was over a long, open stretch of heavy sand. This meant that it was difficult to get the artillery and support weapons forward quickly and slowed everything down. I had the Free French Brigade under command.

Piper Charles Miller
7th Battalion, Argyll & Sutherland Highlanders,
51st (Highland) Division

We used to go up the line at night, dig slit trenches, cover them with corrugated iron, put sand over them, and return to our original positions for the day. One night before the battle, we occupied these slit trenches, and stayed hidden in them all day, waiting for the order to come up.

Lieutenant 'Scotty' White
Officer Commanding, 11 Platoon, B Company, 9th Battalion,
Durham Light Infantry

One of Monty's qualities was the way he transmitted his intention to the army, to blokes like me right down at the lower end; the way he inspired confidence and that things went the way he said they would. Some couldn't care less what they heard, but allowing for that element, everybody was raring to go.

A posed photograph of Royal Engineers with a mine detector, and lifting a mine.

Captain Peter Lewis
Officer Commanding, B Company, 8th Battalion, Durham Light Infantry
On 19 October, our CO went for a briefing of all COs by Monty, and he passed it on to us. Monty said there would be a dogfight for ten days. He explained how the battle would be fought and was confident of the result. When we were told this on 22 October, when all leave was cancelled, there was a tremendous state of enthusiasm and morale was terrific. We had never had an army commander who gave us such a message. Our chaps were pretty good, and will do what they are told, and do it even better when they know what they are supposed to be doing.

OPERATION LIGHTFOOT – THE DOGFIGHT

Gunner Martin Ranft
220th Artillery Regiment, German 164th Light Division
On 23 October 1942, at nine o'clock in the evening, we thought the world was coming to an end. We had a terrible artillery bombardment from the British. I was in a hole, sheltering, and talking to a comrade about bygone days. The whole front line sky went red, and he said, 'Look at that.' When they came over it was horrible. I could hear the shells howling over me. It wasn't very nice. We thought that this was the end. But we survived. What we had was a hole about one and half foot deep, and when a shell came you knew when it was coming towards you. If it goes 'whheeeeee', that's good, it's gone past you. But if goes 'wheeeettt', it is coming near you. We sheltered all night long. They concentrated on certain areas. At times the barrage moved away from where we were. We had a quick look out and it looked like a ploughed field. There wasn't much left, and we said, 'How can anyone survive?' But we did. We had some casualties, but the infantry ahead of us had more, as far as I could tell. One of my friends had his foot blown off by a shell. He died the next day. One had a direct hit in a bunker, one shell went right in and blew his head off.

Piper Charles Miller
7th Battalion, Argyll & Sutherland Highlanders,
51st (Highland) Division
Then we came out of our slit trenches at ten o'clock: the battle started. Each line was marked with tape. Bofors fired to keep each unit in line as we

advanced. The barrage was loud, there was the smell of the cordite, the squeals and yells of the wounded. It was terrible. Our first casualty was shouting for his mum. He died. We had orders to keep on and ignore the wounded. They were left for people behind: the stretcher-bearers. It was a matter of not showing to your pals that you were frightened. There were some tanks dug in, firing, and we were to go on past them. Then there were the minefields; the engineers had cleared them and made a path through them. Some people trod on mines that hadn't been cleared. Pipers are very important to a Scottish regiment. We had to play the boys in; there were quite a lot of casualties among the pipers.

Pilot Officer Ron Dorey
Wellington Bomber Pilot, 148 Squadron, RAF
We were given a Bomb Line over Alamein, but didn't know that the battle was about to start. I have never seen anything like it – thirty miles of solid gunfire at night, from the coast nearly to the Qattara Depression. We said, 'Bloody hell what's going on?' We thought it was flak at first. As we got nearer we realised what it was, and we flew over the top; we'd been told not to fly below six thousand feet. They wanted us to fly up and down the Jerry front line and if we saw a flash, to bomb it – a bit ridiculous, at that height. So having tried this out, the air gunners started getting impatient, and wanted us to go lower so they could shoot at the enemy flashes. But we said that six thousand feet was to keep us above our own artillery shells. They said, 'Have a go,' so we went up to the coast and hurtled back down the line at about two hundred feet, and let them blaze away with their guns. I don't know if we hit anything. When we got back for debriefing, a wing commander walked up to another crew on the next table, going absolutely spare. They had done the same as us, machine-gunning, and unfortunately had got an artillery shell right through the fuselage – in one side and out the other. That was proof of the strength of the Wellington bomber. Luckily the shell didn't take the control rods with it, or explode on impact.

Sergeant Douglas Covill
Tank Commander, A Squadron, 10th Royal Hussars
We moved up, and into the battle. Our regiment was on star, moon and sun tracks. We set off at about ten o'clock that night. It was like daylight because the guns were firing the whole length of the front. Going through the minefield in the dark on the first night of Alamein, each regiment was

lined up one behind the other. At daylight we still hadn't got through. The colonel said 'disperse', but we couldn't because of the minefield. He said we were to do it rather than stay in line. We did; luckily it was a dummy mine-field. There were 88s on a ridge above us. The brigade commander ordered the regiment to go in. C Squadron started the attack. They went forward in line and suddenly five tanks were hit and brewed up. It was demoralising; we thought we had had a new tank and it was invulnerable. But the 88-mm shell could penetrate the Sherman. We were lucky, our squadron went to the left and managed to get in position behind a ridge and could see the enemy and destroyed many German tanks and vehicles. We had seven days of non-stop action here, and were then pulled back for three days, and were sent to south of Alamein Station.

Trooper John Lanes
Wireless Operator, Nottinghamshire Yeomanry (Sherwood Rangers)
We moved in front of the guns. It was dark and the mines had been lifted by the New Zealanders. The anti-tank shells had tracers in the base. There was a lot of dust, but you could still see the tracer on the 88-mm rounds flashing past. A lot of our tanks got hit. We got through but, without support, we had to turn back.

The second day we went back. We stopped to engage a German Mk IV with our two-pounder, and it just ricocheted off. We hit it eight times and did no damage. Why he didn't fire back I don't know. We then came across a screen of tanks around four 88-mms which were firing at aircraft, our light bombers. They bombed the 88s and got plumb right on them and there was a huge explosion.

The next day I was with Lieutenant Stockton and we were knocked out by an anti-tank gun. The squadron 2IC was knocked out by the same gun, but as they hit his tank, it rolled forward and ran over the gun. I got out first. I could see the track was broken on one side, the suspension torn off on the other side. We sheltered by the tank until evening, when we got picked up and taken to the laager. The next morning, before it got light, Sam Garrett claimed me as a wireless operator. I stayed with him for a long time.

Sergeant Harry Garrett
Anti-tank gun commander, 61st Anti-Tank Regiment, RA,
attached 51st (Highland) Division
On the third day of the battle we were held up by minefields and were counter-attacked by the Germans, and dived into the trench because things

were getting so hot. As the tanks approached we got out and fired at them, and back into the trench when the artillery came down. And my dear friend Frankie was in there with me. A shell landed right by the trench and I thought we were all dead – I heard singing and angels and all sorts of things. I thought this is the way we die. This wasn't the first time I had been knocked out, but this was different. I suddenly came to, and said, 'Frankie, what's the matter?' I heard him groaning, 'Help me, Harry, help me, I've got something in my back.' I looked at Frankie and the wound stretched from his neck right down his back. So I called for a groundsheet and I wrapped it round his body; the wound was too vast. I don't think he lasted long. I said put him on my back. I called the first-aid chap out and he took Frankie away. I crawled back and heard a scream from the other gun, and the sergeant on that gun had been shot in the head.

I had one reinforcement, a middle-weight boxing champion in Blackfriars. He was a bit of a bully, but in action he was a coward, and I had to send him back. I couldn't stand anybody like him. He was replaced by a man called Fincham: meek and mild. One day in action he was wounded, and he was very brave. He continued fighting. A piece of shrapnel went right through the top of his chest, missed the lungs, but he stayed with the gun until there was a lull, and I sent him back.

Bombardier Stephen Dawson
339 Battery, 104th (Essex Yeomanry) Field Regiment,
Royal Horse Artillery
In K Car, my truck, was Captain Adams, the driver Handy, and a new soldier, 'Blue', just out from England. In the evening we heard the barrage start. I went to sleep rolled up in a blanket; my feet were a few feet from the track. As the night wore on the track was like a busy main road with traffic moving forward.

I let Blue do all the wireless work. The battery went into action near the minefield, then we went on following a track and there were lots of rifles stuck in the sand by their bayonets with helmets on top marking the position of a dead soldier. There were white tapes marking each side of the lane through the minefield. We found a large shell hole, which we took cover in during the night, with a tarpaulin over the top and we could smoke under cover. A shell landed close to us, with a lot of clattering of shrapnel on the truck itself. Blue said, 'What was that?' and someone said, 'Nothing. Nothing.'

We were trying to protect him.

He got out, and said, 'That was a shell.'

'Was it?'

He replied, 'It has taken a man's head off about thirty yards away.'

He wasn't upset by it. After that we stopped trying to protect him. He was a very cool customer. The battle dragged on for days.

Major General John Harding
General Officer Commanding, 7th Armoured Division

The minefields in the northern part caused most trouble. If you are stuck in a minefield, tanks are a dead duck to anti-tank fire. The first night, the French got a foot on Himeimat but were driven back. Further north in the minefields we did get through the minefields but started to lose tanks, and because I had the restriction on me not to lose too many tanks, I decided to halt the attack and hold what I had. I told the French to try again in the morning. But they failed to capture Himeimat; we were stuck. This was the position for the next couple of days.

Lieutenant 'Scotty' White
Officer Commanding, 11 Platoon, B Company, 9th Battalion, Durham Light Infantry

To begin with at Alamein we were faced by the Italian Folgore Division; they were tough, all the things you hear about the Italians running away didn't apply to the Folgore. We respected them. After receiving our briefing about the general outline of the Alamein battle by the company commander, we were given the task of neutralising an isolated position held by the Folgore. On evening of the 23rd our company was to go to a taped Start Line, and part of the 7th Armoured Division were to advance to a place behind the strongpoint. Immediately they got behind the hill, the codeword Chicken would be passed over the wireless, and we on the Start Line would charge up the hill, through mines and wire and all. My platoon was to lead the charge. We walked out on to the tape and lay down. If the wire hadn't been cut by the artillery I was to fling myself on top of it and the rest of my platoon likewise and the supporting platoons were to run over the top of us. I thought that's a nice do. I had no sense of this being a foolhardy affair. Within minutes of getting there we got codeword Goose, which meant it was off, and we would go in on the night of the 24th. Down we go again, and now had more time to think about it, and hope it was worthwhile. Again, a few minutes before we expected to go, it was cancelled again.

Rifleman Douglas Waller
Anti-Tank Gunner, 2nd Battalion, The Rifle Brigade
We started the battle down in the south, opposite the Italian Folgore Division, which contrary to the general opinion of Italian troops were really tough nuts. We went in and got through the first minefield, and were in the gap when our portee got hit in the engine; probably a solid shot, because there wasn't a big explosion. We just heard a bang and something hit the front of the truck, and it folded up. We were then useless because we couldn't drag the anti-tank gun. We joined up with the infantry company and spent that first night attacking strong points. It was very hairy because they were well dug in. Some came out to surrender, and others would go on firing. We suffered quite a few casualties. Bill Ash was with me. We went in at platoon strength. Suddenly we came under mortar fire. Within five minutes Bill and I were the only ones left standing: all the others were either killed or wounded. Mortar fire is very frightening, you can't hear the bombs coming; you get rather large gaps appearing among the attacking troops.

The fighting went on through the night. The tops of the pits were covered with sandbags on top of corrugated tin or wood. You had to clear these. The machine-gun nests and mortar pits were the most difficult to clear. You ran in short bursts, covered by others in the platoon, and when you got near enough, and if the pit was open, you could toss in a grenade. Our barrage went on all night, it was tremendous. When this lot opened up the whole sky was lit up with flashes.

Eventually the Italians were subdued. By the next morning the battle was almost over except for mopping up, checking the slit trenches. Most of them were either dead, wounded or prisoners. The Germans had pinched their transport so they couldn't get away. They tried to retreat on foot but couldn't get far. We picked up souvenirs: you had to be careful because of booby traps. Mainly we picked up stuff that was scattered about. Don't pick up a nice-looking box. I picked up an Italian flag, and some postcards. Their food was even worse than ours, so you didn't touch that.

Lieutenant Emilio Pulini
Italian Folgore Parachute Division
Our division had very little transport, being paratroops. As far as I knew the Germans withdrew and left very little transport for us.

Trooper E. Wainwright
47th Royal Tank Regiment
It was unbelievable, the noise and stir and the advance through minefields marked by the sappers, marked by empty four-gallon diesel tins in which a pattern had been cut – ship, moon, star – and you followed from one to the next. If you hadn't been in it and seen it you couldn't imagine the confusion, and anxiety and strain of trying to get tanks through clouds of dust. And we were being shelled, although the German response was nothing compared with what our guns were dishing out.

We went in on Friday 23 October with two squadrons of Shermans, thirty-six Shermans, and the following Thursday I brought out one of six Shermans. We who were left were collected up and went up to Sidi Bishr, simply a piece of sand behind Alexandria, and there the 47th RTR disappeared and our rump became the 1st RTR C Squadron.

Trooper Geoffrey Bays
Tank Driver, 46th Royal Tank Regiment
We were supporting the Australians. I was driving the squadron leader's tank. I was lined up ready to attack and we were bracketed by heavy German artillery. We were told not to move. Then, a terrific bang; I heard a chap groaning and wondered who it was. I heard a voice outside the tank in a lull in the shellfire, 'Geoff, Geoff, are you all right?' I realised it was me groaning. I had red-hot pieces of shrapnel in my back. I tried to get out and couldn't, but this chap sat on top of the turret and helped me and the other chap out. How we survived I don't know. One of the engine covers was blown about a hundred yards, and the turret lifted out of its seating.

I was taken to the MO. And he said, 'Do you want to go to the CCS or shall I take the pieces out?' I said, 'Take them out.' So I lay face down and he took the pieces out of my back. The squadron leader took over another tank.

The CO sent me to recover a tank in no-man's-land. I was to drive it. At night a sapper came with me, and a couple of fitters. The fitters repaired the tank and we got it going. Some Australians shouted, 'You are in the middle of a minefield.' So we waited for first light. We *were* in the middle of a mine-field, so I and the two engineers cleared a path, prodding with our bayonets, and we finally got the tank out. We didn't realise that we were under observation by the Germans, until an Australian officer walking across to us got hit in the stomach by a bullet. After that we expedited our efforts to clear the minefield. When I got back to the regiment I found my squadron had been wiped out the night before.

The CO, whom I liked, told me I was now a tank commander. I went and collected a tank with a makeshift crew. That tank did smell. We scratched a bloke's brains off the driving seat, and found a finger in the turret.

Rifleman Fred Cooper
Mortar Section, attached C Company, 2nd Battalion,
The King's Royal Rifle Corps

Being in the battle was like being drugged or drunk; we were so tired and didn't know what was happening. We went back for a rest; our company commander, who was an Eton master, had a wound in his throat. Within two hours of going back into the battle he was dead. During the rest, the chaplain came round, and what he said put a morbid touch on things, saying we might all be dead tomorrow.

After the twenty-four-hour rest, at six o'clock in the morning the sun was shining as we went through the gun positions, firing in our support. When we looked back the sky was clear to the east, and looking to the west was like looking at a wall of sand, churned up by artillery fire and tanks. When we got near the objective we came across about three hundred German prisoners being marched along, they were unshaven and some were shaking. I thought that's another three hundred we haven't got to deal with. After a while I thought perhaps they are better off than we are. They have been taken from the carnage, and we are going back into it. We had a tough day, my mortar section of seven blokes had four casualties in fifteen minutes and the section was more or less non-operational. Our objective was a ridge not much higher than fifteen feet. We attacked with tanks and tried to make a wedge and drive in, but because we were in a wedge the Germans could fire on us from the sides and front. We got such a concentration of fire we pulled back. We went in again with such determination we got on to the objective. On top of the ridge were six Sherman tanks. One was white hot, glowing like a light bulb, the others various shades of red. At the end of that day we were relieved that the Germans had pulled back; but it was sad to see those tanks.

Rifleman Harry Suckling
B Company, 2nd Battalion, The Rifle Brigade

We was protecting the gap in the minefield. In the minefield gap we had good slit trenches because of the shelling. They sent for reinforcements, a big bloke come up, and being old soldiers we shouted, 'Get down in the slit trench.'

He said, 'What's the matter with you? Haven't you been in action before?'

We shouted, 'Get down!'

Just at that moment a shell landed, and he's got his leg blown off. I said, 'That'll teach you to do what I bloody well said.'

We was taking turns to have a brew-up. Every time a vehicle went through, even a bloody motorcycle, dust would go up, and we got shelled. Being an old soldier you could tell where they was going to land. Well, this time we had gone over to the section whose turn it was to brew up, and they had just got a brew on. All of a sudden a motorcycle went through with an MP riding it. No sooner was he past than they opened up and shelled us. The last shell landed right beside us, a lump of shrapnel went past me, didn't touch me arm, seared it, and hit a corporal, in his thigh. When you get a lump of shrapnel hitting you it makes a bigger hole coming out than going in, like a bullet does. He had a terrific wound, and I thought he'd lose his leg. But we got a couple of field dressings and patched him up. He came back a few months later. One lad I knew was wounded three times and came back each time. I asked him why he came back and he said that he missed the lads. The fourth time he was killed.

Lance Corporal Harold Wilmshurst
14 Platoon, C Company, 5th Battalion Royal Sussex
We didn't go in on the first night: we were in reserve. We went in on the 27th. They cleared the minefield, and on our way we passed the 51st Highland Division, and they said, 'You are lucky. There is nothing there now.'

We advanced and all hell was let loose. We went in with bayonets fixed and shooting from the hip. I was in 14 Platoon HQ and was told to report to battalion HQ as our runner was missing and I had to find him. I first went to company HQ. The enemy machine guns opened up and so did the mortars. My platoon was almost wiped out, but because I was at company HQ I escaped. I stayed with company HQ as they advanced. We eventually came on this anti-tank gun with Germans hiding behind it. We dealt with them, rifle and bayonet; wounding one, who begged us not to kill him. The CSM looked at me and said, 'Stay here.' There was a machine-gun nest on our left holding up 15 Platoon. The carrier officer came up with digging tools for us to dig in with. He tried to rally the troops on our left to attack the machine-gun nest. We saw them firing from the hip, with Bren guns, and just before they went in this officer was preparing to throw a grenade at the machine-

Lance Corporal Harold Wilmshurst.

gun nest, and he got shot through the shoulder. A chap called Brogden and myself patched him up as best we could with our first field dressings. As we finished, there was a single shot; he died. We lay beside this huge tank that was out of action, I couldn't see what it was. Then a corporal turned up with a Panzer Grenadier. He asked the CSM if I could take the prisoner out. The corporal had been wounded, and said he couldn't take him out by himself. I went with this chap. I had a tommy gun, which was jammed with dust. I took him back to the carriers, but on the way we had to take cover in a trench. At battalion HQ I had to stay to look after him. A little later an escort was sent from brigade HQ to take him away. Just as he left, battalion HQ got a direct hit from a shell, and two carriers were blown up and the men killed. I was told to report back to my company. I said it would be impossible to get back during the battle. So they said they would take me in a carrier the next morning. But no carrier came.

Eventually we saw some trucks coming up and asked if we could be lifted back to our company. We looked in the back of the trucks and they were full of dead men, they stank. Eventually we arrived at B Echelon, and the sergeant major tried to take us back to where the company was. As we approached, three Crusaders appeared; as we followed them up the hill, they brewed up.

Sergeant Joe Swann
Anti-Tank Platoon, 2nd Battalion, The Rifle Brigade

On 25 October we moved through the minefields on cleared tracks. On the 26th, we were given a briefing that we were going to attack that night, but that was delayed. On the 27th the attack went forward during the day. The rifle companies moved up in carriers, and took the position, and we were called forward with the anti-tank guns just as it got dark. We must have started moving at about ten o'clock at night. Major Tom Pearson led the dash up. The only thing about officers leading about a hundred vehicles in a jeep is that they can see the road, they are not having to deal with sand being flung up in front of them. I was about the last platoon, and I couldn't see anything. I finished up with just two guns.

I went and reported to Major Pearson. We were down to about two or three on each gun because of casualties. In the morning, there, in front of us, was a load of vehicles. We thought who the hell are they? And someone said, 'It's the enemy.' We opened up and caught a couple of armoured cars. If we'd had HE we'd have had a lot more. A solid shot just went straight through a truck. The tanks came out to deal with us. We sat there all day very short of water, fighting the tanks. Then a couple of Shermans came up and, boom, boom, they all went up. Meanwhile we were knocking out German tanks as they came in. Just before dark an infantry attack came in to our left. The first salvo from our own artillery, the first round, fell forward of us and the second shot right amongst us. I had one man killed, my corporal was badly wounded, and the other chap was unconscious. The other gun had sheared a bolt and wasn't firing, so I put the crew on my gun. I went forward; my head was spinning. I was sitting in a trench with a couple of chaps, and some tanks approached. I shouted across to Eddie Miles, on the gun fifty or sixty yards from me, to take them on. Somebody shouted out that he had been wounded.

I said, 'Let someone else fire the gun,' and they said, 'We can't.' I had to go and do it. I ran forward, and as I did, one of the chaps in the trench with me was shot. I got clear and could hear the machine-gun bullets hitting the ground behind me. I eventually got to Miles's gun and I swivelled it round and loaded it. A tank was about 150 yards away, and I took a bang at him and stopped him. The next shot I jammed his turret because it couldn't train round. The next shot I put in his side, and a couple of blokes jumped out. One bloke was trapped inside, screaming for help, for about eight hours. Then I went back, it was getting dark. And the infantry starting withdrawing, but the guns had to stay because the portees or trucks couldn't get forward.

At about ten o'clock they said dismantle the guns. So we took off the breechblocks and buried them. We walked back about three miles. Some jeeps came up and took the wounded, and left the dead. When we got back we had about an hour's sleep and then had to go back and pick up more guns. We went straight into another action.

Second Lieutenant John Campbell
B Company, 7th Battalion, Argyll & Sutherland Highlanders
I was sent up as a reinforcement in the middle of the battle. It was an extraordinary experience because it was like something I had never seen before, just slightly rolling desert, with scrub, and bangs going on all over the place. The platoon commander of the platoon I joined had been killed the day before. The platoon had been reduced from thirty to twenty-two, with one of the soldiers called 'Yorkie' still lying there, dead. When I arrived, we were static, doing nothing. But there were a lot of shells flying, generally solid shot – armour-piercing. I was sitting in a shallow trench and the man sitting

at right angles to me with his feet towards me asked for a light for his cigarette, and as I leant across, a solid shot blew the back of the trench out, where I had been leaning. Meanwhile, Lorne Campbell – the CO – stood up behind a carrier shaving, taking no notice of the bullets and shells flying about while we crouched down in our slit trenches.

Lorne Campbell was pleased to get hold of someone of the same clan, me. He said he had a good and exciting job for me to do. He wanted me to go out at night taking a telephone line to a ridge close to the German positions, and direct fire on the enemy positions. As my platoon went forward, a group of our Vickers machine guns was firing indirect fire on the Germans. The Germans retaliated by opening fire in the general direction of the Vickers. The bullets happened to land where we were. We were enveloped in a hail of bullets, and the chap who was reeling out the telephone line was hit plumb in the middle of his helmet and knocked out. A corporal, referring to me, said, 'He will get us all killed.' and turned and ran towards the main position, with the rest of the platoon. I wondered at the time should I shoot him? But couldn't bring myself to do it.

Major General John Harding
General Officer Commanding, 7th Armoured Division
I got orders to move further north to prepare for action in the northern part of the front, in reserve behind the front line where the main offensive was to take place, Operation Supercharge.

OPERATION SUPERCHARGE – BREAKTHROUGH

Lieutenant Colonel William Watson
Commanding Officer, 6th Battalion, Durham Light Infantry
On 28 October the battalion was taken out of reserve and warned for another role. At dusk, section by section, the battalion assembled and had a meal. In the early hours of 29 October we embussed in motor transport under the corps provost, and moved from the southern end of the Alamein line to the northern end. The whole route was marked with lights. At three in the morning we got to an area near the railway line and by the sea. We dossed down in the soft sand, and next day, we all got a bathe in the sea. We were told we would come under the New Zealand Division. We were told, 'No move until tomorrow,' and had yet another night sleeping in the soft

sand and having a bathe. But not knowing what is going to happen and what your fate is hangs heavily. It hung heavily on us all.

Lieutenant 'Scotty' White
Officer Commanding, 11 Platoon, B Company, 9th Battalion,
Durham Light Infantry
Then orders came we had to move up north. There had been no breakthrough up north.

We moved by truck right up to the sea, where we had a bathe. At this stage we had not been briefed yet. We said goodbye to our trucks and started marching forward. Once we got out of the trucks we seemed to be marching a long way.

Captain Peter Lewis
Officer Commanding, B Company, 8th Battalion,
Durham Light Infantry
From the Concentration Area, the CO took the company commanders to brigade HQ where we were told that the Germans had had such a severe battering for seven days it was now necessary to mount one heavy assault to punch a hole through the German lines. It was called Op Supercharge. It consisted of a Scottish brigade from 51st Highland Division on the left, the DLI Brigade on the right, and a battalion of Maoris on the right of the DLI Brigade.

Once we had punched a hole, the 8th and 9th Armoured Brigades, all of 1st Armoured Division and the whole of X Corps would pass through the gap we had made.

Lieutenant Bill Partridge
Platoon Commander, B Company, 9th Battalion,
Durham Light Infantry
We trucked our way north and the moment we arrived at a Concentration Area the preparations for a major attack took place. We were given food and water, more than we had previously had. We could send as many airmail cards as we wanted. All missing kit was replaced – the spare barrel of the Brens, for example. The MO came round and spoke to every single man. If he judged that a man was not fit to go into this big battle, he would take him out; not for the sake of the man, but for the sake of the other soldiers. He didn't take anybody out of my platoon. But every man

A Vickers machine-gun crew.

The commander of a Stuart tank by a knocked-out PzKpfw III tank scanning with his binoculars.

knew that everything that could be done had been. Pride in oneself was very important, not to let the side down. When you are in a group of men you are not going to let down the team. The RSM organised zeroing of weapons. We slept.

Lieutenant Colonel William Watson
Commanding Officer, 6th Battalion, Durham Light Infantry

The next day, 30 October, advance parties left in the middle of the afternoon. The brigadier unfolded his plan for Supercharge, which was to be supported by thirteen field regiments, and three medium regiments. The plan was to attack on a four thousand-yard front by the 151st Durham Brigade, and the 152nd Highland Brigade, the objective: the Rahman track, which ran all the way down from the sea to the Qattara Depression, with telephone poles along its length. Our arch-enemies, the German 90th Light Division, were in front of us. Our older guns were to fire well ahead of us, and the newer guns nearer to us. There were to be twenty-two lifts of the barrage until half time. The role of the 6th Battalion was to be in reserve. When we got to the line of seven dug-in enemy tanks or guns, we were to swing north. These guns had been marked on our maps so we could see where they should be. Then the artillery barrage would start up again. That was the plan.

Captain Peter Lewis
Officer Commanding, B Company, 8th Battalion,
Durham Light Infantry

During the night 30/31 October, the battalion moved in transport to an area originally held by 51 Highland Division. It was a noisy night as we passed a lot of artillery firing in support of an Australian attack. We arrived about 3.30 in the morning. There were plenty of slit trenches already dug for us to get into. The area was packed with transport, guns, tanks and limbers. One enemy plane, one only, came over and dropped one bomb and it hit the battalion HQ office truck, which caught fire and blew up, killing Julian Parker, the adjutant, who was sleeping beside the truck, not in a slit trench. The next morning a group of us, and the padre, gathered round and had a little service to bury him. It was difficult to find a little bit of desert to bury him in, the area was so packed.

Lieutenant 'Scotty' White
Officer Commanding, 11 Platoon, B Company, 9th Battalion,
Durham Light Infantry

All officers were briefed by the CO; we found out that this was to be the final attack, codename Supercharge. We had to break through so that the sappers could make two lanes through the minefield and get the tanks out, and 'tally ho' into the open beyond. At that time he gave us the scope of the attack – the whole brigade would take part, with the 8th battalion on our right, the 9th on the left of the 8th, and the 6th in reserve to watch the right flank. On the right flank of the attack there was a Maori battalion from the New Zealand Division as additional protection for us, and on our left flank we had a brigade of the 51st Highland Division. The Cheshires' machine guns would support us and there would be a massive artillery-timed barrage. The idea was that, to begin with, the artillery would fire on targets two thousand yards ahead of us, thereafter we would advance and keep as close as we could to the barrage as it crept forward. Bofors guns would fire tracer to show the limits of our flanks. When the barrage was going to lift, blue smoke would be fired. Every little detail was thought of. The attack was timed for the night 1/2 November – a delay of twenty-four hours.

Lieutenant Bill Partridge
Platoon Commander, B Company, 9th Battalion,
Durham Light Infantry

The day before the attack our supporting tanks arrived. Ours were the Warwickshire Yeomanry, Valentines. They came up to us so that each man could walk round the tank, talk to the crew, find out where the bell push at the back was to notify them that you wanted to speak to the commander; talk about the forthcoming battle. The tank crews knew that they would not come into action until we had gone through and the engineers had made a way for them. The fact that they were the Warwickshire Yeomanry was nice for me, being from Warwickshire, but to the company they were just tank men.

Lieutenant Colonel William Watson
Commanding Officer, 6th Battalion, Durham Light Infantry

During the afternoon I went forward with my intelligence officer to the Start Line, marked out with big oil drums. The Australians had been pulled out. The intelligence officers of all the battalions waited until dusk and taped out the Start Line and the route up to it. On the way back, some Stukas came over, rare birds by then, peeled off, and went for some gun positions nearby. One bomb dropped close by us, my driver swung off the road, and we all jumped into a ditch. An ambulance came by and stopped. The driver had all the skin flayed off his hands and arms by the shrapnel from this bomb, the chap beside him was dead, and a casualty sitting in the back had been wounded again. It was a terribly near squeak for us.

Captain Peter Lewis
Officer Commanding, B Company, 8th Battalion,
Durham Light Infantry
The company commanders went up into the Australian positions to meet our opposite numbers, the Australian company commanders, to look at the ground over which we would attack. While this was going on the British artillery was firing over our heads. On our way back to our jeeps an Aussie stuck his head out of his dugout and asked if we were the 'covies' who were going in tonight. And when we said we were, he said, pointing in the direction of a German machine-gun position that fired from time to time, 'Well, be sure and fix those bastards, they think they're there for the duration.' We found the Australians very rough and ready. A filthy-dirty bearded chap addressed our CO as 'Hey, mate'. We got back to the battalion to find that the attack had been postponed for twenty-four hours.

Captain Ian English
Officer Commanding, C Company, 8th Battalion,
Durham Light Infantry
This gave us more time to prepare. The next day the CO held his conference, and his plan was for the battalion to attack with two companies up, A right, B left, and C behind A on right rear. The Maori Battalion was to seize the strongpoint on the right, which was five hundred yards beyond the Start Line.

When we had reached the first objective, my company was to move up on the right of A Company, and we would continue the attack with three companies up. The first objective was codename Cherry, the 865 easting grid, 3,500 yards from the Start Line. We were to halt there for half an hour, and the barrage was to halt there too. We would then advance again to the next objective, five thousand yards on. The boundaries for battalions and brigades were marked by Bofors firing red tracer, firing every two minutes; very useful. The battalion had two troops of New Zealand anti-tank gunners

214

with six-pounders under command, and we also had a platoon of medium machine guns from the 2nd Cheshires. In support of the battalion was a squadron of the 50th RTR in Valentines.

Lieutenant Colonel William Watson
Commanding Officer, 6th Battalion, Durham Light Infantry

On 1 November, the next day, in the afternoon we moved to a concentration area very near Tel el Eisa station – the little hill of Jesus. Here we had a last meal. So the enemy would not gain information that might be of use to him, we had to hand in all our private letters and papers, and put them into sandbags to be kept by the QM, hopefully for our return. Just as the sun had set, at seven o'clock, we set off for our five-mile march to the Start Line. It was a sticky night, and as we passed Tel el Eisa station it would be about half-past seven. The track we were marching on was Diamond track. There were vehicles passing us the whole time. On our right I could see in the dark a minefield. There were some New Zealand gunners, stripped to the waist, pumping shells into the guns, so the noise was terrific. They were supporting a diversion near a place called Thompson's Post, which was held by the Australians. They were to make a diversion later in the night. It was a nasty, unpleasant march; there was a horrible smell of death from corpses lying on the minefield wire. Eventually we arrived at the FUP, at nine-thirty. We had to be there by ten o'clock, to allow the tanks, our own carriers and transport, including anti-tank guns, to get up to us and move in behind us in the FUP in readiness to pass through the gap. After we had done the attack, the New Zealand sappers behind us were to make the gap through the minefield. So that all these vehicles, tanks, anti-tank guns, carriers could come up. The tanks were to get out into the open, having passed through us.

Captain Ian English
Officer Commanding, C Company, 8th Battalion,
Durham Light Infantry

We left the Assembly Area at 1900, led by the 2IC, up Boomerang track, a journey of seven miles to the FUP. The track was at least ankle-deep in dust. And we got completely covered in dust and at the far end we missed the road, and there was some confusion before we found the FUP. The mood in the battalion was quiet. We realised we were going to be in a fight. We wore khaki drill shorts, shirt and pullovers; the night was cold and we got cold.

We carried an extra bandolier of ammo and full equipment. Every man had either a pick or shovel as well as an entrenching tool, but that wasn't very effective in the desert. We arrived in the FUP at 2330 hours, and had more than an hour lying there, trying to get some sleep and getting colder and colder. The FUP had been marked with white tape by the intelligence officer and his section.

Lieutenant Colonel William Watson
Commanding Officer, 6th Battalion, Durham Light Infantry
It was November; we were only in khaki drill and it was pretty chilly. The intelligence officer, Jerry Mansell, checked the compasses with the company commanders. He got in touch with the 8th and 9th Battalions. He had an intelligence sergeant who could speak German. Every man lay down, the noise of battle died away, it became quiet. Very occasionally you could hear the sound of machine-gun fire a long way off. Very occasionally a Very light went up. Otherwise it was absolutely silent. There was the taped Start Line, waiting for us to cross it. I did try to get some sleep but I couldn't. There is a certain responsibility resting on your shoulders as a CO. I always told any new chaps who had never been in battle before that we would be thinking about them going into battle. But the one thing they must do is to keep themselves occupied, don't sit and think. Do something. If you sit and think about it you will fail. All sorts of things went through my mind.

Captain Ian English
Officer Commanding, C Company, 8th Battalion, Durham Light Infantry
My plan was 14 Platoon right, 13 left and 15 in reserve between the two. I would be between the two leading platoons with my batman Private Crawley, to whom I gave the job of counting paces, which, advancing over five thousand yards at night while being shot at, is no mean job. I would be dashing about; he had to stay on his line, and keep counting. We also had Private Davis from the intelligence section, who kept a check on our direction. I had two runners with me. Company rear HQ was behind 15 platoon. We had a bit of a flap; the mortars and other support arrived late. The information about the enemy was that the positions were held by the German 90th Light Division on the north side, and the 164th Infantry Division further south in front of us, with elements of the Italian Trieste Infantry Division. Behind them was the counter-attack force of the 15th Panzer and Littorio Divisions. The Germans hadn't had time to fully develop their posi-

tions, and we didn't think we would run into anti-personnel mines, which was a relief.

Private William Knowles
Signaller, 8th Battalion, Durham Light Infantry
When we got to the FUP I was told to join a rifle company. We got to the Start Line and there was quite a bit of shouting, getting everybody sorted out. You had been briefed about the operation in general, but not the details. All you knew was the objective was a certain distance in front; the Rahman track. Cherry was the codename for the first objective, Brandy the second. We had been told how important it was to succeed. The first attack had not succeeded.

Lieutenant 'Scotty' White
Officer Commanding, 11 Platoon, B Company, 9th Battalion, Durham Light Infantry
I was the right-hand platoon of our company and the 8th Battalion was on our right. Teddy, our company commander, came along on the Start Line and told us to pair up and keep warm. We were in khaki drill shorts and jerseys. He told me to go forward and look at the wire, a single strand of concertina wire put up by the New Zealanders. I walked off with my batman, found the wire about two hundred yards in front of where we formed up. What would I do? Would cutting a gap be any use? Would I find the place again having returned to my platoon? So I snipped the wire, didn't pull it apart, and thirty yards along I snipped it again. Back we went. Two runners appeared with big Thermos containers of rum and hot cocoa. Then it was 'On your feet'. I drank lots of it. I'd never drunk rum before. We had five minutes to go and fixed bayonets. Then all of a sudden all hell was let loose. It had been so quiet. Most men had been very quiet too, it had been a time for thought, 'What happens if...?' Everybody seemed in good heart.

Lieutenant Colonel William Watson
Commanding Officer, 6th Battalion, Durham Light Infantry
At about 0015 a rum ration was issued. The empty HQ rum jar was left on top of one of the oil drums nearby. I wonder how long it stayed there. At 0040 everybody stood up and shuffled into their equipment. I loaded my revolver, and carried it throughout the advance. Another thing you heard was click, click, click, as the chaps fixed bayonets. At five minutes to one

we started to walk slowly forward through the minefield. I had one chap killed almost immediately. At five minutes past one every gun opened up, shells came screaming over our heads. The Bofors started to fire, to give us direction. I could hear the pipers from the Highlanders on our left. Twenty-five-pounder shells don't make a bang and a thud when they go over your head, they sound like a whiplash. It was nerve-racking to start with, but then the whole thing started to be like a song. The shells came over and exploded ahead of us.

Lieutenant 'Scotty' White
Officer Commanding, 11 Platoon, B Company, 9th Battalion,
Durham Light Infantry

We all turned round to see if we could see the gun flashes. Teddy blew his hunting horn, his secret weapon. There was a continuous wall of sound. What with the Maoris screaming on the right, Teddy blowing his horn in front of us, and the bagpipes squealing, it kept our minds off other things. I bumped into Teddy, he said, 'I've lost my bloody hunting horn.' Somebody found it.

Captain Ian English
Officer Commanding, C Company, 8th Battalion,
Durham Light Infantry

Promptly at 0105 hours we crossed the Start Line in formation with bayonets fixed. At that time it was pretty dark, and quiet with the occasional Very light going up from the Germans, and the odd gun firing. Ten minutes later the barrage started. We had been expecting a lot of noise. We heard the guns behind us and could see the flashes, and hear the whistle of the shells going over our heads and an enormous crash and clouds of dust in front of us. The barrage continued for the next two to three hours. The noise was tremendous, you had to go very close to someone to make them hear what you said. But nevertheless, the barrage was our protection. The barrage dwelt on the first position for twenty minutes, and while we closed up to it. This was the first attack we had done behind a barrage and it had been emphasised that we should always be no further than a hundred yards behind it, so that when it lifted we would be on the enemy position within a few moments of the barrage passing over. Inexperienced troops often think that they will advance into their own barrage. It is fortunate that the 25-pounder shell has a tendency to explode forwards, so the splinters go away from you.

Captain Peter Lewis
Officer Commanding, B Company, 8th Battalion,
Durham Light Infantry

At 0055 A and B Companies spread themselves out along the tapes. Bayonets were fixed. It seemed to go quiet. Then behind us the guns opened up, flashes and the sound of guns firing, the fantastic barrage. The troops sat down and looked behind them, the whole sky was pierced with hundreds of gun flashes. At 0105 the whistles blew, shells were screaming over us, and off we went, accompanied by a crescendo of noise that was to last for three hours. My company advanced two up and one back and I moved between the two leading platoons. I had a navigator from the intelligence section with me to count the paces. I had my batman and three platoon runners. Behind was main company HQ. A company occupied about 150 yards in width, men were about five yards apart. So gaps were quite big between companies, so some German positions were not cleared as we advanced. Supercharge was a First World War-style attack; walk forward, behind a barrage.

There were shouted commands as we closed up to the barrage until the smoke shells were fired, which indicated that the barrage was about to lift. The smoke shells caused more confusion than they were worth. Straight away we were into the smoke and dust and muck thrown up by the barrage. The air stank of HE, making the troops cough and splutter. In the distance I heard the sound of a hunting horn, one of the DLI company commanders in the neighbouring battalion always blew a hunting horn. German Very lights went up, calling for defensive fire, which came down, and some of our chaps were hit by machine guns firing on fixed lines; there wasn't much enemy artillery fire, as far as I could see.

Private William Knowles
Signaller, 8th Battalion, Durham Light Infantry

Then the advance started. We had quite some distance to walk. We had the wireless with us. We were on listening watch. My role was a signaller on the 18 Set, on the battalion net. There were three of us. I had my pack and shovel, ammunition in my pouches, Bren gun magazines, bandoliers of rifle ammunition. We operated in pairs: one carried the wireless set, the other operated it. If you could you would have three chaps on the wireless: two to operate it, and one to hop off and carry messages to the company commander. It was heavy. Even on flat ground it was a burden. The company commander was ahead of us, and we were with the company main

HQ, in rear with the company 2IC. It was dark except for the odd flare being fired by the Jerries. It was a very flat piece of desert, firm except where it had been churned up by vehicles. There was a hell of a lot of shouting, keeping people in line and together. Every now and then we would pause, and then go on again.

The enemy were firing machine guns on fixed lines, you could see the tracer. We passed people lying or crouching. Then the heavier stuff started coming down, and people started dropping. You couldn't stop for anyone who was wounded; you knew that. A person who was hit might be lucky and be picked up by the stretcher-bearers, but you could only receive first aid, and then it was back to the RAP. But the time taken to do this might not be quick. If there were a lot of wounded, the stretcher-bearers couldn't cope, the ambulances might be delayed. The wounded just lay about. A person who was badly wounded probably lapsed into unconsciousness.

Then we had trouble with the 18 Set and couldn't receive. The enemy fire got stronger. I went forward to the company commander to tell him that we were out of communication with battalion HQ and the other companies. Putting the wireless right in the dark was a problem. The company commander had a couple of runners to take messages. Things had hotted up, and it was a job getting back from the company commander because of mortar and artillery fire, and hoping that one of your own side didn't take a potshot at you. The acrid, bitter smell of cordite was very strong. Later you got the smell of blood and sweet smell of death.

Lieutenant Colonel William Watson
Commanding Officer, 6th Battalion, Durham Light Infantry
The whole atmosphere was full of smoke and sand, and then figures with their arms up came looming out of the fog, surrendering. After we'd done about 880 yards, we were fired at by enemy fire coming from our right across our front; we could see the tracer going past, about man height or a bit higher. We had to hold up a bit until it stopped. But in our keenness to get on we must have walked over lone enemy soldiers who lay doggo as we passed, and some of them killed my RSM Page and the MO who was tending him, as well as Sergeant Fairlie, who played cricket for the battalion, and young Second Lieutenant Vickers who had just joined the battalion. It was a great blow.

Lieutenant 'Scotty' White
Officer Commanding, 11 Platoon, B Company, 9th Battalion, Durham Light Infantry

The Germans were about two thousand yards from the Start Line, but when we hit them we were in a minefield. We just walked through it. Most were anti-tank mines, but we thought there would be anti-personnel mines too. It was the only way we could do it. You couldn't clear mines from the frontage of two brigades side by side, you had to accept there were mines there, some of them might be anti-personnel. Mines are nasty, but there is nothing more terrible than a machine gun stuttering across your front. Following us very closely were the sappers going forward with the anti-mining gear and digging the mines out, creating a gap.

There was sporadic fire coming our way, some machine-gun fire, artillery and mortar fire. I was concerned with keeping my platoon together, and keeping touch with the platoon on our left, and listening for Teddy's hunting horn. You think, 'If I come across a slit trench, what do you do?' If you see anybody you prod them out, if you don't see anybody you might fire a round into it. But there was no sign of the enemy at this stage as far as I could see. I could make myself heard with difficulty. It was dark so hand signals were no use. I relied on my platoon sergeant and sections commanders, who helped me keep control. They were extra pairs of eyes, spotting things I missed. My NCOs were inspirational people.

I wasn't shouting encouragement at this stage, but started when I sensed that I was coming up against actual people; you can't keep up shouting all the time when you are advancing some five thousand yards in total. When you are in amongst them it is different. In this attack, by the time we got to where they had been, most of them had disappeared. It is not always like this. As we advanced I thought, 'We will be meeting them any minute, is everyone up with me?' I was keeping a watch on how we were progressing. At this stage we hadn't lost anybody as far as I could tell. It was still dark and the air was full of dust thrown up by our barrage. The sound of the hunting horn was a great encouragement to me. It kept us together, 'That's our hunting horn.' It gave us a sense of identity. 'We'll show the buggers.'

Captain Peter Lewis
Officer Commanding, B Company, 8th Battalion, Durham Light Infantry

My company was hard hit in the vicinity of the Australian outer wire, and I lost my two leading platoon commanders, killed. The Bofors firing tracer helped us keep direction. A Spandau opened up to our front, but he was firing high with tracer, and some of my chaps ducked under the tracer and bayoneted the crew. We reached the single line of concertina wire marking the German positions. We could see the mass of shell holes, lots of German and Italian dead. We started taking prisoners of war, some of them in a daze and hysterical. They wandered about, and unfortunately some got shot, as it was sometimes difficult to tell if they were trying to surrender or making off for a slit trench.

We had to keep on going behind the barrage. By now the line was probably getting a bit ragged, as people paused to clear slit trenches. Some of the Germans put up quite a fight. One German came out of a dugout as if he had been shot out by a launcher, and came straight at me with a pistol. One of my section commanders got him with a tommy gun. But some of them were pretty tough, they were bloody good soldiers. One bloke waited until we had got beyond him, and chucked a stick grenade at us. One of my chaps went back and found him already dead; he had thrown it while actually about to die.

Captain Ian English
Officer Commanding, C Company, 8th Battalion,
Durham Light Infantry

We continued and came to a single strand of barbed wire and guessed this was the start of the German minefield, and we saw some mines lying about. We then came across a German lying in the open. He might have been part of a German mine-laying party. He got up and surrendered. As we went on it was obvious that the barrage was having a tremendous effect. The Germans and Italians we came across were pretty stunned, and didn't offer much resistance. But of course they were good troops and if they were missed by the barrage would fight their guns.

We could hear the Maori battalion fighting and shouting on our right but had no idea what was happening. A German machine gun on our right started firing tracer, and this scared some of the men, but we pointed out that the rounds were going over our heads. We could hear A and B Companies ahead carrying out their attack. I found that short halts were essential to keep everyone together and ensure there was no straggling, and useful also for Private Davis to check on direction, and Private McCauley to check his paces. We came across several dead Germans and Italians. We began to collect prisoners. It is extraordinary how inexperienced British soldiers tend to gather round and gawp at enemy prisoners as though they are men from Mars, instead of getting on with their job, and this had to be checked. There were two men in 13 Platoon who were wounded, I sent them back with the prisoners. Then we came across an Italian tank about fifty yards away. I tried to get 13 Platoon to attack it with their anti-tank grenades, but it fired at them and stopped them. Sergeant Martin, the platoon sergeant of 14 Platoon, fired a grenade which landed just in the rear of the tank. That was enough to persuade the tank to move off. I was a bit annoyed that we hadn't stopped it going.

Lieutenant 'Scotty' White
Officer Commanding, 11 Platoon, B Company, 9th Battalion,
Durham Light Infantry
We were doing well, and I was pressing on a bit because I felt we'd got a bit behind the barrage, and that, I knew, was fatal. Suddenly a string of something exploded across my front, four or five in line, and I went sailing backwards. I actually thought I saw this thing coming to hit me, probably my imagination, and tried to jump to avoid it. But it might have been me being blown on my back. About five went down with me. I didn't feel pain – yet. I felt a hurt to my pride and a numbness in my leg. I tried to stand up, but couldn't. I couldn't control my left leg. My sergeant had seen what had happened, and shouted for the wonderful young medical stretcher-bearer who came along. After a few minutes' conflab, a chat with my sergeant, to ask if he had any query about anything, off he went with the platoon, saying, 'See you some time, good luck.' The young stretcher-bearer looked at the wound below my knee, put on a first field dressing, and said they wouldn't have to take my leg off, that sort of cheery thing. I still couldn't get up. Eventually he stood me up. The sappers were coming along, and all sorts of vehicles, and I didn't want to be lying flat on the ground quite so near the main route of the supporting tanks; I wanted to be seen. I saw our CO coming past in a carrier, and we waved to each other; he shouted, 'There's a machine gun over there, get after it, Scotty.' Fortunately he passed before I could answer back. He was just as excited as I was.

Captain Peter Lewis
Officer Commanding, B Company, 8th Battalion,
Durham Light Infantry
We came to an area of HQ dugouts and vehicles. On our right Chris Beattie was setting fire to abandoned German tanks by firing a Very light into the

petrol tanks. It was still very smoky and dusty. Anything that moved and came out of the dust was usually shot. No quarter was asked or given. The battle became a series of small-scale fights. We lost people too. My pacer was still with me; I was still keeping direction.

At 0230, one hour and twenty-five minutes after the start, A and B Companies arrived on the first objective. We were able to take a rough count of who was still with us as we had a pause on the first objective, and of the combined strength of A and B Companies nearly a hundred men had been killed or wounded, and of the eight officers of the two companies, five had been killed or wounded. In A Company there was only the company commander and one platoon commander, and in my company there was only me. Very soon after that I collected a gunshot wound in the right thigh while attempting to reorganise the company. I couldn't see who had shot at me. You couldn't see more than forty yards. What had been quite a busy place suddenly became deserted as the company, under the CSM and NCOs, moved off. All I could tell them was to get the platoons ready to move forward. One of my chaps put a first field dressing on me.

Captain Ian English
Officer Commanding, C Company, 8th Battalion,
Durham Light Infantry
We were now getting into the area of the German HQ. There was more enemy transport about, and the moon had now risen, and it was easier to see. Out of one of these trucks a man ran away, and it was light enough for me to shoot him with a rifle, which I was carrying. We got more prisoners, some out of dugouts using our 36 grenades. We came across a Red Cross tent and a man came out who said he was a doctor. I ordered the troops to leave that alone and we passed on. Then at 0245 we reached what we took to be the first objective, Cherry. I put up a Very signal – Green, Red, Green.

The commander of 14 Platoon reported that two of his sections seemed to have disappeared, so I moved 15 Platoon up from reserve and brought them in to take over 14 Platoon's job. We must have arrived on the first objective late because of the incident with the tank, because we had only quarter of an hour there instead of half an hour, but we did contact A Company, the right-hand platoon of which was now on our left. Everyone was doing well, using their weapons well. I came to realise that we were having some casualties, but not many.

We set off again when the barrage moved forward. I am sure that halting occasionally paid off. C Company was the only company to arrive on the objective more or less intact, fighting our way forward with rifle, bayonet and grenade. Then a chap with a rifle came up whom I didn't know and said he was from A Company. He seemed an intelligent sort of chap. So I said, 'You come along with us.' He had about ten men with him. He turned out to be an officer who had arrived just recently. In the second phase of the attack we captured about fifty more prisoners, mostly Italians. They were taken back by walking wounded. We had also been joined by a Maori soldier who had got detached from his battalion, and carried on with us. He seemed quite happy, carrying a two-inch mortar. Eventually I sent him back with my walking wounded and prisoners.

Lieutenant Colonel William Watson
Commanding Officer, 6th Battalion, Durham Light Infantry
At the 'halfway' line, we expected to find a row of dug-in tanks. When we reached them, we were to right wheel and face northwards. It was almost too good to be true when we saw them. Practically every one of the crews was still inside. I walked up to one, and a corporal shouted out, 'I've put a sticky bomb on it.' It exploded and burst inwards, killing the crew. I saw A Company trying to set one tank alight. We did the wheel and got into position and it so happened we were absolutely in the right place. Then the guns opened up again for the 8th and 9th Battalions to complete their advance to the El Rahman track. Meanwhile we waited for dawn. Behind us the sappers were making the gap through the minefield through which we had just walked. The mines were mainly anti-tank mines. There may have been a few anti-personnel. It was fortunate we were able to walk through.

Lieutenant Bill Partridge
Platoon Commander, B Company, 9th Battalion,
Durham Light Infantry
We knew that we just had to keep going, so we did. We kept up a steady pace. We knew that we were walking through an intensive minefield. As far as we were concerned, our job was to get through to the other end. We had engineers with us. The enemy infantry at the end of the minefield, and beyond it, had to be cleared out; they didn't just give up. The enemy were either in large slit trenches or in sangars. Nobody stopped for casualties; nobody disobeyed the order not to stop. If everybody had stopped for casualties, we wouldn't have got there. We sent POWs back. We just pointed

and told them to start walking. We didn't care much about how they got back. If they wanted to wander off into a minefield, so be it.

Private William Knowles
Signaller, 8th Battalion, Durham Light Infantry
We got to the first objective. I was sent back with the radio to battalion HQ and a chap from the Royal Signals replaced the valve, which was faulty. It was getting light. You couldn't see much because of smoke and dust. I then went forward again. By now the tanks had moved forward, Shermans, and they were firing at the enemy in a great long line. I was stopped from moving any further forward. The tanks went forward a few yards, fired, then moved back and to the side, then did it again. It was a sight; a great arc of tanks, all firing. On the flanks, about a mile away, you could just see armoured cars and light tanks, just shimmering in the desert. The Shermans were slowly being picked off, it was a terrible thing to watch. If a tank was hit it burst into flames. I didn't see anyone get out. Some shells hit the tanks and ricocheted off, you could actually see the shell twisting over and over up into the air making a peculiar noise. Then it would come down making a whirring noise. Quite a lot ricocheted off like that. Others just bounced off. I couldn't do anything: just sit there.

Captain Ian English
Officer Commanding, C Company, 8th Battalion,
Durham Light Infantry
After we had gone about thirty minutes from the first objective, at 0340 hours, Crawley said we were just about on the second objective. So I said, 'We'll go on another two hundred yards to make sure we were in the right place.' We soon realised we must be because the barrage halted and we closed up to it. We started to consolidate the position. The barrage went on until 0400 hours. The silence when it stopped was amazing. We had got used to this deafening noise, then it stopped and you could see the stars, it was a different world.

We had work to do. I sent up the success signal for the final objective, Brandy, which was Red, Green, Red. I allotted platoon positions as best as I could in the dark. I told the men to dig as they had never dug before, to get down quickly. The 18 Set was not getting through to battalion, and we didn't know where everybody else was. I had two sensations: first that the fog of war was complete, and we were the only members of 8 DLI in the desert; second an intense desire to lie down and go to sleep. After the pent-up excitement of the attack, now the guns had stopped and we were in one place, and not having to move, we just wanted to sleep. But there was no time for that. Everybody realised that if there was going to be any chance of staying alive they had to get below ground. We still had a quite a number of Durham pitmen in the battalion and they knew how to dig. By dawn we were fairly well down. I sent out contact patrols from 13 Platoon and 15 Platoon to find people on our flanks. It was getting lighter and we saw a German half-track about a hundred yards away. We went across to investigate and a German came out and surrendered. Our patrols also came across quite a number of German prisoners lying in the desert with our escorts. They had been shot at going back, and one of the men escorting them said, 'We moved when things quietened, but then we were shot at again, so we stayed where we were.'

We began to hear the roar of tank engines, and this was heartening because there were so many of them. The tanks were on our left, and the leading tank was just moving forward fairly slowly, when 'Bang', it went up in flames, then three more. This was a ghastly sight. It was obvious there was still a screen of 88s out in front, and the tanks were silhouetted against the dawn. The Germans had marvellous targets. Within two or three hundred yards of my company about twenty tanks were hit, and not many men seemed to get out of the tanks. This was the 9th Armoured Brigade trying to push through.

Lieutenant Bill Partridge
Platoon Commander, B Company, 9th Battalion, Durham Light Infantry
Once we were on the objective, it was our job to give what support we could when the tanks came through and fanned out beyond us. We dug in at the far end of the breach in the minefield, sited our two-pounders, and the tanks came through. We used shell holes, or old enemy positions. We watched the ensuing tank battle. We had seen tanks knocked out before, so that was nothing new, but to see it on such a scale was new.

Sergeant Albert Davies
Anti-Tank Platoon, 6th Battalion, Durham Light Infantry
The worst thing is waiting for Zero Hour, everyone is tense, but once you got going, it was better; you still had butterflies in your stomach, but had to keep going. It was so dusty, with tanks and carriers churning up the dust, that you choked on it. It was difficult to see which were German tanks or ours. Often

we drove right over German trenches before you realised they had enemy in them. When you did, you jumped out of the truck and took them prisoner. Sometimes they didn't need an escort, just took themselves back. They had had enough with the barrage and all our tanks attacking them.

We had strict instructions, if anyone was wounded, you didn't stop. The more men who stayed to look after the wounded the fewer to take part in an attack. If a bloke was wounded, he was looked after by the first-aid lads following up. You could hear the wounded cry out, you wanted to go, but you had to carry out orders.

We got to our objective and set up our anti-tank guns, and the armour came through the gap and spread out in front of us. That was our job done. We lost a lot of chaps doing it. As long as you kept close to the barrage the enemy didn't have much fight in them, except the fanatics.

Lieutenant 'Scotty' White
Officer Commanding, 11 Platoon, B Company, 9th Battalion, Durham Light Infantry

By heaving and hauling we got the other wounded, fortunately none of them serious, to my little raised piece of ground, so I could keep an eye on them. Before the stretcher-bearer went off the meat wagon – the ambulance – came up. I was very angry, thinking, 'Three years of doing nothing and just training and then this happens.' It was that sort of feeling. I wasn't concerned about the wound. We were taken off to the RAP. From there to a place where we could be given treatment for the wound, including surgery. I am not sure exactly how far back this was. It seemed to me not far behind our Start Line. We lay on the sand on stretchers. The CO of the Maori battalion was there, in a dreadful state with a bullet wound in his mouth, his jaw was broken, and blood everywhere. He was stripped to the waist; he was magnificent. I thought, 'What a waste.' They took my pistol off me, and all the ammunition and grenades. I was beginning to feel my wound. They don't tell you anything, except 'You'll be all right, lad'. A South African female nurse lifted me up on to the operating stretcher; lovely girl, but built like a tank.

Lieutenant Colonel William Watson
Commanding Officer, 6th Battalion, Durham Light Infantry

At four o'clock the artillery stopped. Something like 150,000 shells had been fired. At dawn I could see all three companies clearly as I was only about three hundred yards behind the centre company. They were thin on the ground and we had a long line to hold. We got in touch with the 8th Battalion and they were on their objective. The Germans were in sangars about four hundred yards beyond my companies. It was not advisable to do a great deal of walking about, as the Germans were a bit jittery. But any movement they made, the New Zealanders opened up with their machine guns. They must have had their thumbs on the thumbpieces the whole time, because the slightest flicker of movement from the Germans brought a hail of bullets. We fired at them too with our Bren guns. We watched them and they couldn't move without drawing fire. Very early in the morning Morris Kirby, the 2IC, brought up the anti-tank guns. He also brought some beer for A Company too. During the course of the day an enemy wireless wagon came into view. One of our anti-tank guns, only two-pounders, took a potshot at it and knocked it out at nine hundred yards, which was far too far off in theory. Then the brigadier came up, the one and only time I ever saw him wear a tin hat.

Private William Knowles
Signaller, 8th Battalion, Durham Light Infantry

I got instructions to go back and collect our truck and bring it up through the gap. Some prisoners started trickling back in our sector, there might have been more elsewhere. As I approached the gap, I saw, scattered here and there, some troops; not Durhams, I don't know who they were, and they were milling about individually over a wide area. Away on the flank there were some light armoured vehicles, and some of them started yelling at the top of their voices, panic stricken, 'They're counter-attacking, they're counter-attacking.' I thought, 'They weren't – not with tanks in front of us.' I thought this was a load of rubbish, but there was blind panic among these people milling around the gap. I noticed that these light vehicles on the flanks had kicked up a lot of dust, and I thought they wouldn't be beetling back like that in a counter-attack, more likely they are coming back to refuel, and get fixed up. I got to the edge of the gap, and there was a little tent on the opposite side, and out strode this officer with all his rank badges on his shoulders, immaculately dressed, his cap had a red band. He used every expletive in the world as he shouted at these soldiers, 'You bloody cowards, get out of here, there's no bloody counter-attack.' Following him out of the tent comes another officer, and another. This bloke stalks into the middle of this mob. The panic stopped, and they drifted off. By now the battalion was on the final objective.

Captain Peter Lewis
Officer Commanding, B Company, 8th Battalion,
Durham Light Infantry

I was lying on the ground, with my revolver. I couldn't stand. About the time the barrage lifted I saw two British soldiers escorting a party of Germans to the rear, and I shouted to attract their attention. The only way they could get me back was for four of the Germans to carry me on their shoulders. I was hoisted on to these shoulders, and was higher than I wanted to be, as stray bullets were still flying about and I felt vulnerable. It was a remarkable two-mile journey. The crash of bursting shells grew fainter and fainter as the barrage moved away and we walked in the opposite direction. There was no one else in sight and we might have been walking on the moon. At last we reached the British lines from where we had started, we saw our tanks moving forward, and knew that the infantry had reached the objective. I eventually got back to 50 Division's field ambulance. I lay next to a young Italian officer who asked me for a cigarette, turned, and died.

Captain Ian English
Officer Commanding, C Company, 8th Battalion,
Durham Light Infantry

As it got lighter, our guns started shelling the 88s. As the 88 is an AA gun adapted to the anti-tank role, it is a great big gun that takes a lot of concealing. They probably hadn't had time to do that and so were big targets.

I could see the positions my company had taken up. They seemed all right. We could see the Sidi el Rahman track about 150 yards in front of us, and the mosque of Sidi el Rahman just to our right; probably a German OP. We saw a great big pile of sandbags concealing an 88, and fired a two-inch mortar at it, which drove the crew away from the gun. As they ran, we shot them. That was one less 88.

The German artillery started shelling us. Then a Sherman tank came up, firing its Besa [machine gun]. The tank got a tremendous crack from an 88 on our left, when it was only about twenty yards from our position. Only the driver managed to stagger out and collapse on the ground. Two or three of our chaps went out and brought him in, he was dreadfully burned.

We collected wounded at our company HQ. We didn't have trenches to put them in, and the poor chaps were in the open, and as the day wore on the flies got terrible and the heat was a major problem. About mid-morning about ten German tanks approached our positions, and got within about two

El Alamein 1942: general view of the British night artillery barrage which opened the second Battle of El Alamein. Infantry carriers and ambulances waiting to move up are silhouetted against the glare from the guns.

E 18465

hundred yards; MK IIIs, Mk IVs and one Mk IV special with an immensely long 75-mm gun. By that time Corporal Simpson got the 18 Set to battalion HQ working, and we reported this. We had no anti-tank guns, they hadn't got up to us, so the men got their 68 grenades ready. Fortunately the tanks never came within 150 yards of us; they fired quite a bit, but we were dug well down, and the British tanks behind us may have put them off approaching any nearer. In a bit of a lull I sent Private Davis, the intelligence man, back to battalion HQ with a message asking for some vehicles to evacuate the wounded, and adding that if we could have some anti-tank guns up, we would feel happier.

Lieutenant Colonel William Watson
Commanding Officer, 6th Battalion, Durham Light Infantry
The day wore on. The tanks came up and tried to get through, but were knocked back by the 88s. Some of them were burning in clouds of black smoke. At about four o'clock, some tanks came up behind us to try and break out northwards. Then all of a sudden – to our absolute joy – ninety men of the 21st Panzer Grenadier Regiment, including their CO, the equivalent of a brigadier, put their hands up. It was a wonderful sight, a row of German soldiers standing up out of their sangars and holes in the ground, putting their hands up, and marching in. Jimmy Chapman, one of my company commanders, brought them in. I went over to the company and saw them all there. Their CO was a great big man; typical Prussian, he had his greatcoat on. I asked him what his regiment was. He asked if I spoke German. I said, 'No.' He apologised for the dirty state his men were in, and that some of his men were badly wounded. I knew what regiment it was from our intelligence. I put the CO in a carrier and sent him to brigade HQ. Their wounded we also put in carriers. It bucked us up no end. But the 88-mm guns were still being a nuisance.

Private William Knowles
Signaller, 8th Battalion, Durham Light Infantry
We brought the truck up, and there was no activity, and you couldn't see many people. They were dug in. We came across a huge bunker, and we made straight for it; it had contained a big German mobile gun. The CSM seemed to know about it. We stopped the truck. As we were getting off the truck a Breda opened up, it had a distinctive sound, and the bullets whizzed over us; it fired a heavier bullet than the .303 inch our machine guns used.

We went down into the bunker, and somebody said, 'I could do with a cup of tea.' So Branagan said, 'Why not? Let's all have a cup of tea.'

We had to find something to boil the water in. We could use petrol and sand to make a fire. We looked round this bunker and in the corner was this huge round tin, very clean, the biggest tin I've ever seen, about a foot across. We cleaned it out, we didn't know what it had been used for, it might have been a pee can. We got a petrol fire going, put a bit of water in from each of our water bottles, got a brew going. We had some hard tack and bully beef in our rations. We had something to eat, and about half a cup of tea, it fortified us. Looking out of the side of my eye, I thought the driver, a big ginger-haired bloke, well known in the battalion, was asleep; he didn't have any tea. He sat propped up in the corner of the bunker. The batman was about to open his mouth and go across and speak to the driver, but Branagan grabbed him before he got a word out, held his finger up to his mouth, and glared at me doing the same. I looked at this bloke sitting in the corner; he was far away, his eyes were open, red, glaring, sitting all tense. I thought he must have shell shock. Branagan was well known in the battalion as a tartar. He was a devil for discipline, everything had to be just so-so for him. I thought what a humane person this hard man really was; he wasn't going to let anyone worry the driver.

Captain Ian English
Officer Commanding, C Company, 8th Battalion,
Durham Light Infantry
At about 1100 hours we had a demonstration by the RAF; Mitchells, Bostons, medium bombers, attacking the German positions, coming over about every forty minutes, bombing extremely accurately. After about three or four hours of this, lots of Germans got up and walked across the desert and gave themselves up. Things were improving; the company was in good spirits again after the terrible tank losses. Our gunners were shooting well. We were doing all right. I reckoned we had lost about twenty men.

There was a bit of a diversion when an 88, towed by a half-track, drove across our front. Everybody fired at it but it kept going. Eventually a shell hit the half-track so that gun wasn't going anywhere.

The men had been carrying a packet of biscuits and a tin of bully each so we weren't going hungry. But we were a bit short of ammunition, particularly grenades. Shortly after midday, Private Davis arrived back having had a scary trek from battalion HQ, with the message that C Company was to withdraw and confirm to 9 and 6 DLI. I thought we were well situated, and this withdrawal worried me as we had to go across open desert. I ordered 14 Platoon to go first followed by 13 and 15 Platoon, in open order, leaving their Bren guns to go last. I ordered Harry Welsh – 13 Platoon Commander – to take charge of the operation and tell the CO that it was imperative to get transport forward to evacuate the wounded. I decided to stay with the wounded and Private Crawley stayed with me. I counted the company, and there were fifty to sixty men, so we had lost about thirty-five. The withdrawal went off well, there was a bit of shelling but no casualties.

Crawley and I had what seemed to be an interminable wait, but about an hour and a half later, a carrier flying a Red Cross flag and a jeep came up. We loaded the men on to these vehicles. While we were doing this we were bombed by Stukas, which didn't improve things. In fact it was just a lot of dust and noise. But the men lying there were scared stiff, so were we.

We got back to battalion HQ, and I was shown my new area where the men were already well dug in. I learned about our casualties, including my 2IC Ian Turnbull, whom no one had seen since crossing the Start Line. He was reported missing. No one had seen him wounded. He disappeared off the face of the earth.

Lieutenant Colonel William Watson
Commanding Officer, 6th Battalion, Durham Light Infantry
Just at dusk, the company three-tonners came up with an evening meal and greatcoats. An 88 opened up and smashed two of them, killed the drivers and CQMS Robinson; a good chap. We buried them then and there. Some of the companies had to go without their greatcoats and evening meal.

Then darkness fell. The brigade major came and told me that we would be relieved by a New Zealand battalion that night. It was a long and dreary wait. At about midnight an 88 drove straight into C Company HQ, it had lost its way. C Company put some tracer into the petrol tank of the tow vehicle and set it alight. The crew were rather stupid and wouldn't get out at once. One did eventually escape, two were brought in and taken prisoner.

Captain Ian English
Officer Commanding, C Company, 8th Battalion,
Durham Light Infantry
We heard that a New Zealand brigade was to relieve the whole of 151 Brigade at midnight. I told the chaps they had done well in the attack. Just before

dark the tanks of 9th Armoured Brigade withdrew, and at the same time the German artillery laid down a heavy concentration of artillery fire on us for about half an hour. We had more casualties from that than in the whole battle. I went over to see 15 Platoon to talk to Rusty Roberts. The shelling started again, I leapt into a slit trench with the platoon sergeant, Appleby, and landed on top of him. After lying there for some time, I ran across to company HQ; the cry of 'stretcher-bearers' went up. Sergeant Appleby had been badly wounded by German shelling just after I left his trench.

Lieutenant Colonel William Watson
Commanding Officer, 6th Battalion, Durham Light Infantry

By 4 am the relief was effected by the New Zealanders. We marched back to Tel el Eisa station. I was very tired. We marched in column of threes; there was no air threat. It was one long brigade column. We knew that we had been successful. The Australians told us that it had been a huge success. They brought me a cup of tea. One chap fell out; he had been wounded through the shoulder and had marched back without telling his company commander. All the way back there were fearful signs of war: derelict vehicles, dead drivers. After thirty-six hours we got back to where we had started. Breakfast was ready, and eaten in silence. The brigadier came round later that morning. I was lying almost comatose, asleep. He congratulated all the company commanders having gathered them all together. He took me aside and said, 'When I came up and saw your battalion HQ, I knew all was well. Every single soldier was unperturbed.'

Trooper John Lanes
Wireless Operator, Nottinghamshire Yeomanry (Sherwood Rangers)

The 9th Armoured Brigade was ordered to break out, and it must have been a horrific battle because all contact with them had been lost, and the Sherwoods were ordered to get across to them and make contact. The squadron leader, Major Christopherson, a super man, went in his tank, and Lieutenant Bethell Fox in his, and Sam Garrett, commanding my tank – he didn't take the whole squadron. We were always very well supported by the 1st RHA and the OP officer was Lieutenant Tyrell. We formed up and out on the right was Lieutenant Bethell Fox, Major Christopherson in the centre, and Sam Garrett on the left. Further on the left was Lieutenant Tyrell in his Honey tank. We had no information. We set off at a fair old lick, and everybody was a bit worried; you couldn't see anything except desert. Lieutenant

Tyrell came up on the wireless – everyone was on the same frequency – and said, 'Urging caution.' He'd seen something moving. We slowed down, but still moving forward. The tank commanders looked, and could just make out four lines of lorries, even through the binoculars they just looked like squares. We crept up and it was decided that we would creep up on them, but just before we got there, Christopherson's tank broke down so we immediately picked him up. So we had four men in the turret of our tank. Sam, I, and Christopherson and somebody else were all standing looking in different directions. As we went down each side of the line of lorries, Bethell Fox was knocked out by an anti-tank gun. That left one Crusader and Tyrell's Honey. He had spotted the flash from the anti-tank gun, but didn't put down a stonk. As we stopped at the front of the column, we saw three Sherman tanks close, back-to-back, in a triangle, pointing their guns outwards, it looked as though they had fought to the last tank. The two gunners of the anti-tank gun that had knocked out Bethell Fox surrendered to him. His driver was wounded, so he sent him across to our tank. There we were in no-man's-land with two prisoners. So Christopherson said you had better take them back; I didn't want to do that. But I got out of the tank with my tommy gun. I could see lumps in the ground and it was Italians, dug in by the lorries. Tyrell was waving, he didn't want to take prisoners. And these Italians were coming out as close as a few yards. They didn't want to fight, made no effort. So I started off back with these prisoners. I went back following our tracks and came across the MO who was bringing up the RAP. He walked among the prisoners to see if anyone was wounded. He counted them. There were four hundred. You could still hear firing, so the 9th Armoured Brigade must still have been fighting somewhere nearby. I walked for a good hour back and saw dust and it was vehicles coming our way. They had come to take the prisoners back.

Rifleman Fred Cooper
Mortar Section, attached C Company, 2nd Battalion, The King's Royal Rifle Corps

We started the battle in the 1st Armoured Division, the 'Charging Rhino', then got transferred back to the 7th Armoured Division. At nine o'clock at night were told we were to attack the Rahman Track at three o'clock the next morning. Preparations were made, and as we lay on the side of the road a fleet of ambulances came up to deal with our casualties – not exactly a morale booster.

Eventually we were on the Rahman Track and we stopped the truck near the track. We heard voices and couldn't make out if they were English, Italian or German. Our officer crept closer and said, 'They're Italian.' They didn't realise we were so close. The officer gave the command, 'Fix swords.' It was the only bayonet charge I'd done. He said charge, and I was confronted with three Italians round a truck; I went for one of them with the bayonet, and he turned, and I hit the metal on the truck with my bayonet and it broke, leaving me with about an inch and a half of bayonet. The Italian stood there with a smile on his face with his hands up.

Trooper John Lanes
Wireless Operator, Nottinghamshire Yeomanry (Sherwood Rangers)
I walked back to the RAP. Just before I got there, I remembered that Christopherson's tank was somewhere near, broken down. I got it going and went to join the others. Just after I got there we heard over the wireless, 'We're through!' It was the 9th Armoured Brigade. They had lost a lot of tanks. We could hear whooping and hollering; it was a great day.

Major General John Harding
General Officer Commanding, 7th Armoured Division
I was told to go in pursuit. We went through the old German front, there was a lot of dust and smoke and confusion. We got out into the open, a tremendous feeling. We ran into an Italian armoured division, and drove them off.

Bombardier Stephen Dawson
339 Battery, 104th (Essex Yeomanry) Field Regiment,
Royal Horse Artillery
About ten German prisoners came through our lines under escort. They were much more dignified than the Italians. The German counter-battery fire was rather feeble.

At dawn the shelling stopped and our tanks came through, a splendid sight with their pennants fluttering as they lurched and swayed.

Captain David Smiley
1st Household Cavalry Regiment
When we went through the minefields, there were dead men in the slit trenches. We had some small battles with pockets of Germans. The Italians

surrendered in thousands. We just pointed in the direction of Cairo and said, 'March that way'. We found small groups of starving Italians out in the desert short of water; their officers, or the Germans, had taken their transport. We put them on our armoured cars and took them to the road. They were delighted their war was over.

Sergeant Eric Watts
1/12th Regiment, Royal Australian Artillery

After supporting an attack by the 2nd/43rd Battalion, we were ordered to take our guns well forward, and any German prisoners would be guarded by us until they were taken away. Some Germans were being run back in front of a carrier, and the plan was that having dumped them with us they would go back to collect another lot. They collapsed on the sand, and one, a young German officer, could speak English, and asked for a cigarette. We handed them round. One of our blokes said to this German, 'Why don't you realise that the tide of war has turned, don't you realise that? Hitler has led you up the garden path'.

The young German officer jumped to his feet and he was seething: 'If that's what you think about Hitler, I'll tell you this, I was educated at Eton, and I heard your King stutter his way through his coronation speech.'

Even in defeat this young German officer was not going to let us get away with saying anything against Hitler.

Second Lieutenant John Campbell
B Company, 7th Battalion, Argyll & Sutherland Highlanders

When it was all over, and the Germans had withdrawn, the pipe major went up on the skyline and played 'Flowers of the Forest'. Everybody wept.

Operation Torch

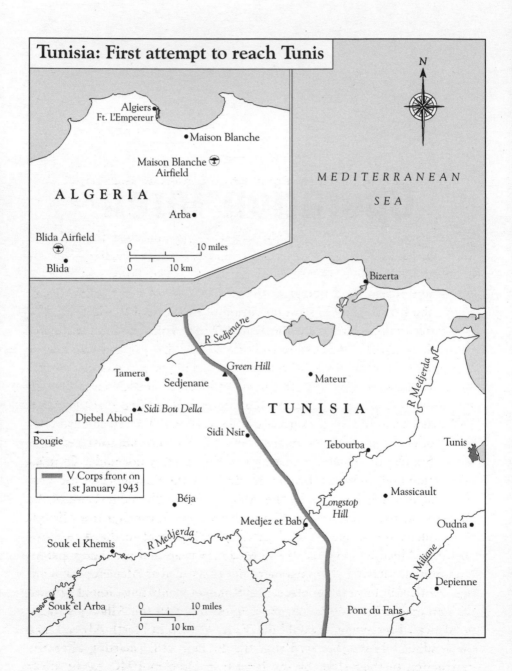

Tunisia: First attempt to reach Tunis

ALGERIA

Algiers
Ft. L'Empereur
• Maison Blanche
Maison Blanche
Airfield
Arba •
Blida Airfield
Blida

0   10 miles
0   10 km

N

MEDITERRANEAN
SEA

Bizerta

R Sedjenane

Green Hill

Mateur

R Medjerda

Tamera
Sedjenane

TUNISIA

•▲ Sidi Bou Della
Djebel Abiod

Sidi Nsir

Bougie

Tebourba

Tunis

V Corps front on
1st January 1943

Béja

Longstop
Hill

Massicault

Medjez et Bab

Oudna •

Souk el Khemis

R Medjerda

R Miliane

Souk el Arba

0   10 miles
0   10 km

Pont du Fahs

Depienne

None of us knew for sure what sort of reception we would get.

On 8 November 1942, as the Eighth Army pursued the defeated Germans and Italians westward from Alamein, the leading elements of another British army were landing in Algeria. This was part of Operation Torch, the landings at the western end of the North African shore; the first Anglo/US joint operation of the Second World War. The land forces taking part were the British First Army, under Lieutenant General K. A. N. Anderson, and the US II Corps, commanded by Lieutenant General Lloyd R. Fredendall. Overall command of all forces – land, sea and air – was in the hands of Lieutenant General Dwight Eisenhower, situated in Allied Force Headquarters (AFHQ) at Gibraltar.

At that time, Morocco, Algeria and Tunisia were French colonies, but were not occupied by the Germans. The colonies were administered from Vichy France: the name for that part of the country not under German occupation and, though officially 'neutral' for the remainder of the war, regarded as a 'puppet state' by the Allied powers. The Allies' aim in the landings, at the same time as Eighth Army was advancing from Egypt, was to deny the whole of the North African littoral to the Axis, thus ensuring Allied domination of the Mediterranean and providing a stepping stone to Italy. Had Montgomery not succeeded at Alamein, the landings would still have taken place, and Rommel would have found himself with an enemy behind him. A major question in all the Allied planners' minds was: how strongly would the Vichy French in North Africa resist the landings? It was believed that the French, still smarting after the destruction of their ships by the British in Oran in 1940, might allow feelings of outrage rather than common sense to dictate their actions if

241

they encountered British troops in the first assault waves. To reduce the possibility of the French impeding the landings, the leading troops to come ashore on all beaches would be Americans, even on those allocated to the British.

Three assault areas were selected and allocated as follows: Casablanca to American forces mounted from the United States direct; Oran to US forces mounted from the United Kingdom; and Algiers to a combined British/US force. Airborne operations were planned for Tunis, Sousse and other key airfields in Tunisia, but for lack of aircraft, only a battalion at a time, and then only after most of the parachute battalions had arrived by sea following the amphibious assault. In the event, most of the objectives for airborne operations were changed to reflect the progress of events immediately after the seaborne assault.

Fortunately there was only light opposition to the seaborne landings, allowing the Allies to land substantial bodies of troops in the first few days, because the German reaction to the operation was, as always, rapid. The Allies had hoped that following the surrender of all French forces in North Africa, the whole area from Casablanca to Tunis would come under Allied control. They hoped in vain. The Germans immediately flew troops into Tunis and Bizerta in an attempt to forestall the French defecting to the Allies. This move by the Germans transformed the campaign from virtually a picnic to a long, tough, six-month-long contest in the rain, mud and mountains of Tunisia.

To counter the Germans, it was decided to move the British 78th Division east into Tunisia with all speed. In support of this advance, General Anderson decided to open up the port of Bone. A landing by British commandos and a parachute battalion drop on the airfield took Bone without any trouble, forestalling a German parachute operation planned for the same day. To begin with – and until Allied fighters were deployed to airfields at Bone – the Germans, with plenty of airfields near Tunis, had a free run over that part of Tunisia, including bombing Bone and Bougie with impunity. The forward basing of Allied fighters had to await the landing of aviation fuel and ammunition, and also engineering work on the runway.

Although elements of British 78th Division, British 1st Parachute Brigade and the US II Corps got within sight of Tunis, they came up against increasing German resistance as the latter brought a flood of reinforcements to Tunis and Bizerta first by air, and soon after by sea. The

Lieutenant General Sir Kenneth Anderson, Commander First Army, in an Auster aircraft, at his Headquarters in Tunisia.

Germans reinforced their air force from Sicily, Sardinia and Italy. German and Italian infantry and armoured formations poured into Tunisia, including a complete panzer division, the 10th. To begin with these came from reinforcements held in Italy for Rommel's Deutsch–Italienische Panzerarmee.

In January and February, the Allies held the line in appalling weather in the mountains. German aircraft operated in support of their ground troops, in contrast to Allied soldiers who, fighting at the extreme range of their own air cover, were hard pressed to hold their positions with inadequate air support. The Allied air forces, operating from weather-bound strips, could not match the sortie rate achieved by the Germans using dry airfields on the Tunis Plain.

The Allied soldiers who landed in French North Africa were almost all inexperienced compared with their opposite numbers in the Eighth Army. The terrain was different and lessons learned in the Western Desert did not necessarily apply in Tunisia.

The Allied landings in North Africa were preceded by a remarkable clandestine operation. Eisenhower's deputy, the American Major General Mark Clark, was landed in North Africa by canoe to have discussions with the French Major General Charles Mast on the likely reaction of the Vichy government in France to the forthcoming invasion. At the time this meeting was deemed worth the risk that it could jeopardise the planned operation. Certainly, there were no surprises when the actual landings took place, so the gamble paid off.

The night before the landing on beaches in the Oran and Algiers sectors, Combined Operations Pilotage Parties, COPPs for short, and the SBS conducted reconnaissance and acted as beacons for the landing craft.

Lieutenant James Foot
Number 2, Special Boat Section
We were based on board HMS *Maidstone*, a submarine depot ship in Gibraltar. Captain 'Jumbo' Courtney, Lieutenant Livingstone and I were told to take four canoes and load them on board HMS *Seraph*, an S class submarine. We were not told what we were to do. In the evening, five Americans passed the mess we were using as our HQ, and shortly after we were called to the wardroom and introduced to the party. They were Major General Mark Clark, Brigadier General Lemnitzer, Colonel Hamlin,

Colonel Holmes, and Captain Wright of the US Navy. They told us we were to take them ashore in French North Africa, sixty miles west of Algiers.

We sailed shortly afterwards, at dusk, and proceeded on the surface into the Mediterranean. That evening we instructed the Americans in the use of canoes, inside the submarine, up on the casing, and paddled around close to the boat. Having satisfied ourselves that they knew how the paddles worked, we got back on board and went on our way. We sailed on the night of 19 October 1942, and arrived off the beach at about 0400 on 21 October. During the following day, while submerged, we carried out a periscope recce of the beach, including making a silhouette drawing to help with navigation.

The next evening we surfaced and waited for a light to appear as a guiding light from a house on the shore. At about midnight it appeared, the submarine proceeded towards the shore, and the canoes were launched. In the first was Lieutenant Livingstone with Colonel Holmes, I followed with Brigadier General Lemnitzer, followed by Captain Wright and Colonel Hamlin, and finally General Clark was going with Captain Courtney. Unfortunately Captain Courtney's canoe was damaged on launching. He had to call back Captain Wright and Colonel Hamlin, and he and Clark changed places with them. Livingstone led the party in. We kept in sight of each other and had no problems. On reaching the beach the recognition signal was exchanged with the shore party. We carried the canoes up the beach, through the woods and into a house where our canoes were locked up in a safe place. We went in, were given a drink, and were introduced to the members of the French party; not by name, I had no idea who they were. Then we were shown up to a room and had some sleep.

At dawn we were woken up with nice French breakfast and coffee. All the servants had been sent away. During the morning I was called down to check over the canoes for damage and to repair what I could. We carried small repair kits in the canoes. The rest of the day we slept, while the Americans and French were in conference. We were to leave as soon as possible after dark. We had just got the boats out into the courtyard, when a message arrived to say the police were on the way. We hurriedly put the boats back into the locked store. We were shown into a cellar. It was dark and we all sat round with our backs to the wall. The three of us providing protection for the Americans sat facing the trapdoor, with our Thompson sub-machine guns. If we were discovered, the Americans would try to bribe the police with gold – we carried about $2,000. Only as a last resort were we to shoot our way out.

We could hear the arguments going on upstairs. It seemed a long time. Courtney got a fit of coughing. General Mark Clark passed something to him and said, 'Here, Jumbo, suck this.' This seemed to do the trick. There was rather an ominous comment from the general, who was obviously playing with his carbine, 'How does this damn thing work?'

Courtney replied, 'For God's sake, just leave it to us.'

When we got out, Courtney asked what he had been given for his cough, and the general said, 'It's a bit of chewing gum that I've been chewing all day.' Courtney replied, 'I wondered why it didn't taste of anything.'

It was decided to get away as quickly as possible, as the police had said that they weren't satisfied and would be back. We carried the boats to the shore, and to our dismay we found that there was a lot of surf. This is not normally the case on this bit of coast. You get an onshore wind in the afternoon, but when the sun goes down, it tends to change round and blow off the land out to sea. Any sea kicked up by an onshore wind dies away. But on this particular evening it didn't happen. We decided we would have to get away anyway. We called up the submarine on the walkie-talkie, and explained the position, asking them to come in as close as they could. They came in so close, I could see *Seraph* with the naked eye from the shore.

Initially our getaway was not successful. I don't think a trained SBS crew would have had much difficulty. We would have swum the canoes out, and got in when we were beyond the surf line. You keep the canoe bows on to the waves. Once through, you climb on over the stem. The surf was too high to paddle a canoe through from the beach. First Courtney and Clark tried to launch from the beach. The surf overturned them. We had to go in and salvage the paddles: without the latter we wouldn't get away. I was told, 'Forget about the general, get the paddles.' We signalled the submarine and told them we would wait for a few minutes to see if the sea would subside. I was told to count the waves. You get a lull after a certain number of waves. Having established what we thought was a pattern, we decided to have another go. By now the French had come down to the beach, and we asked them to wade out with each canoe, to chest height, and hold it while the crew climbed in. We decided to put General Clark with Captain Wright in the first canoe, as they had the most knowledge of the forthcoming operation, and get them away first. We got them away safely by wading out, pushing the canoe as far as we could. I and Colonel Holmes got away after the second attempt, as did Courtney and Lemnitzer. Livingstone and

Hamlin got away at the first attempt. The sea was dropping all the time. The submarine was very close in, not more than four hundred yards off. We all got aboard quite easily. Except that most of the gold, and some papers, were sunk just off the beach when the first canoe capsized. A signal was sent to the American Embassy in Algiers to send someone to make sure nothing was washed up on the beach.

On the first morning after leaving North Africa, a Catalina came out from Gibraltar, landed alongside *Seraph*, which had surfaced, and picked up the American party. Clark was flown to Gibraltar and to London.

Major Bill Miskin
Officer Commanding, B Company, 6th Battalion,
Queen's Own Royal West Kent Regiment

We were part of the 78th Division, which was part of First Army commanded by General Anderson. To begin with, there was just the 78th Division. We sailed from Glasgow. The dockers were on strike so we had to load our ship ourselves. We duly assembled off the Clyde in an enormous convoy with a huge escort and set sail. We arrived off Gibraltar on 7 November, and sailed through the straits. There were no U-boats or enemy aircraft.

Sergeant Stan Weatherall
Number 2, Special Boat Section

I was taken in by the submarine *Ursula*, and dropped off in the Bay of Arzeu, east of Oran. I had a COPP navigator who sat behind me in the Folbot. He took us in on a compass bearing and we anchored about two hundred yards off the beach with a small kedge. The submarine went out about eight to ten miles to act as a beacon for the convoys carrying the troops. The first landing craft had one of our officers on board to guide them. Then we used a red Aldis lamp to guide them in. We began sending 'Z' in Morse from about midnight, as we were marking Z Beach. The craft should have arrived at one o'clock; they were about ten minutes late. Not too bad. We stayed there sending 'Z' so they didn't run into us. At daylight we landed.

Private John Gowan
C Squadron, 56th Battalion, Reconnaissance Regiment

Then we were told that we were to make a beach landing – just our squadron, C Squadron – at six o'clock in the morning on 8 November 1942. We went down scrambling nets on to pontoons. They didn't have doors at the front, we had to jump over the front. It is surprising how heavy the Bren gun is when you are jumping down from a height. The drivers were carrying the ammunition boxes with the spare magazines in. One of the officers was that keen that he jumped out before the boat hit the sand. He was drowned.

Second Lieutenant Mark Philips
Officer Commanding, 8 Platoon, Number 1 Company, 2nd Battalion, Coldstream Guards
When we left Gibraltar we got our briefing that we were to attack the Vichy French on White Beach. In fact there were very few Vichy French around. It was a straightforward landing. We took the town. We got a semi-friendly welcome by the inhabitants.

Second Lieutenant Henry Matthews
457 Light Battery, Royal Artillery
Ours was a six-gun battery of 3.7-inch howitzers operating in sections of two. I was right section gun position officer, or GPO. John Birtwhistle was my section commander, normally in the OP. The battery was embarked in a naval vessel with the guns in pieces on board and some ammunition. Our transport was in another ship. For the landing in North Africa we were attached to the American 168 Combat Team, and landed after them, on the Sidi Farouk beaches at about 8.30 am. The OP parties had landed with the Americans. We went over the side of the vessel down scramble nets into the LCM and our guns were hoisted over the side in pieces into the LCM. These we assembled in the LCM, but having no tractors we manhandled our guns ashore up the beach to clear the beach as quickly as possible. We had intended to manhandle the guns all the way to Algiers, but about half a mile along the road suddenly our tractors and carriers appeared, having landed on a separate beach. We hooked in, much to our relief, instead of pulling. And at about eleven o'clock I met a bunch of Americans marching towards us carrying the Stars and Stripes flag, shouting that there were tanks about. So I pulled my guns off the road, made ready in case there were tanks, and got on the wireless to my OP Officer, John Birtwhistle, telling him where I was and what I was doing. A few minutes after this, fire orders came over the wireless. I plotted the target on my map, and we prepared to fire. The first round was fired by B sub-section of my guns, the first artillery round fired by First Army in that campaign, at three minutes to twelve on 8 November 1942.

Just as I started to give out the fire orders, one of the gunners who had been taken short, appeared running, holding his trousers, shouting 'wait for me, wait for me'. We fired. The first ranging round landed somewhere near a petrol station. The second ranging round set fire to it. After two more ranging rounds, the order ceasefire was given, and we were told that the machine-gun post we were engaging had moved. A few minutes later we were told that the Fort l'Empereur, held by the French, had surrendered. So we drove straight into Algiers. There was no more fighting in Algiers, and we drove through to the airfield.

Private John Gowan
C *Squadron, 56th Battalion, Reconnaissance Regiment*
We walked up the road and were told to go to the back of the coastal guns. We had landed on the west side, and were supposed to take Blida aerodrome if necessary. We didn't have our vehicles at this stage and went marching along this road. This was the first time I had been further from home than Scarborough. We didn't know what was going on. Our vehicles were landed later and we met them in Algiers.

Squadron Leader 'Ras' Berry
Commanding Officer, 81 Squadron, RAF
We were taken by sea to Gibraltar and set off to Algiers on 8 November. We flew with external long-range fuel tanks. We had Spitfire Mk Vs with a snout to keep the sand out. It made the aircraft a bit slower than normal. After landing at Algiers, we were scrambled the first day, and patrolled, and on the second sortie we ran into Junkers 88s. I got one and shared a Heinkel with somebody else.

Sergeant Pilot Don Mitchard
72 Squadron, RAF
We were briefed at Gibraltar that we would be going to Algiers. Our Spitfires had been taken to Gib crated. We didn't have a chance to air test them. We took off on 8 November. We had 90-gallon long-range tanks on. We were told to fly very low, and under the radar coverage. None of us had flown from Gib before, I flew off as a number two, and thought 'Christ I'm not going to get off here', but it was OK. You flew on your long-range tank first, until it was empty. Then you had to switch your main tank on first before switching off the long-range tank, or you got an air lock. My long-range tank might not

have been quite full, the red light did not come on, and the engine stopped. I knew I had run out of fuel on my long-range tank. I thought 'Oh God, I'm in trouble'. I switched on my main tank and prayed, I started to lose height, and didn't have much to lose. I couldn't say anything on my RT because we had been told to keep strict RT silence. The Rolls-Royce Merlin – being a wonderful engine – suddenly kicked in. None of us knew for sure what sort of reception we would get. When we got there the airfield had been captured.

Major Bill Miskin
Officer Commanding, B Company, 6th Battalion,
Queen's Own Royal West Kent Regiment
We were landed in the course of the afternoon in landing craft in a bit of a swell. It was quite exciting to be in Africa. But by then they had sorted out the problem with the French, and we re-embarked.

Captain Vic Coxen
Second-in-Command, T Company, 1st Parachute Battalion
When we embarked we did not know where we were going. When we were at sea we opened sealed orders and were told that when we arrived in Algiers we would be put in aircraft and dropped on El Aouina airfield near Tunis. When we did get ashore at Algiers, we were told that the Germans had captured El Aouina. We marched one day's march out of Algiers, carrying all our stuff. In the night we were pulled into the side to some park-like place. In the morning I woke and saw a huge bunch of bananas over my head. I thought this is not bad, but it was the only bunch of bananas I saw in Africa. We were in the horticultural gardens.

Private John Gowan
C Squadron, 56th Battalion, Reconnaissance Regiment
Our squadron was to get to Tunis as quickly as possible, we had six hundred miles to go. It was the first time the new recce regiment organisation had been used by the British Army. We went along the coast road. Two-thirds of us were green; some had been at Dunkirk. Because some of the armoured cars had been lost, I was put in a carrier. We set off along the coast road.

At one place, we ran off the road completely. The rest went off, and we got the carrier back on the road eventually. I was standing outside the carrier with the sergeant and driver who had been at Dunkirk. I said, 'Look at these two Spitfires coming,' and as I said it, these two vanished. I wondered why.

I saw the bullets bouncing off the roads. The cannon shells went through the carrier and set the carrier alight. They were 109s. The petrol cans were set alight. I grabbed the Bren gun and moved away from the carrier. There was a lighthouse near the road. We ran into the lighthouse, and watched the two Messerschmitts circling and eventually fly away. The ammunition in the carrier exploded. 'Never trust an aircraft,' said the sergeant. 'You never know what they are.'

The carrier was pushed over the cliff to clear the road. I finished up on a soft-skin vehicle, a fitter's truck. I had lost all my gear, except my Bren gun, my pistol and what I stood up in.

Major Bill Miskin
Officer Commanding, B Company, 6th Battalion,
Queen's Own Royal West Kent Regiment
We sailed on to Bougie, held by the Vichy French who were opposing us. After all our landing exercises, this was to be an opposed landing. At two o'clock in the morning we got up and at four o'clock in the morning into our landing craft. We went in as dawn broke. There was a destroyer on either side of us, with their guns trained on the shore, it was a very eerie feeling, we duly landed, rushed up the beach and the only sign of anybody were two men in rubber swim suits. So we thought this can't be so bad after all.

We marched into Bougie and were made welcome by the local inhabitants. We all duly deployed out into the fields outside town. That evening the Italian and German air force came over and our five ships anchored off Bougie were sunk. All our transport, greatcoats and blankets and large packs were sunk. The nights were cold; it was very uncomfortable without our greatcoats.

Second Lieutenant Henry Matthews
457 Light Battery, Royal Artillery
The next day we returned to Algiers and were embarked in two assault ships, the *Princess Emma* and *Princess Beatrice*. I was on the *Emma*. We were rushed through the night to Bone, arriving early the next morning on a bright sunny day, eager to get ashore. We tied up in Bone harbour and were soon under air attack. We went over the side on scramble nets, lowering the guns over the side. The ammunition was in haversacks, two rounds and two charges in each bag. These we slid down a ladder sloping down from the ship's side to the dock, with a plank laid on top. Some rounds went into the water, but we

were anxious to leave because there was around forty tons of aviation fuel stacked on the deck of the ship.

While the gunners were assembling the guns, and getting the ammunition stacked up, I went looking for some French transport. I found a couple of charcoal burners, and immediately commandeered these; one with a little persuasion, having to draw my revolver on the owner. I took the vehicles back to the dockside, and loaded one gun in pieces with ammunition and the gunners on the flatbed of one, and the second gun we assembled and, using drag ropes, lashed to the back of the vehicle. We drove to Bone airfield just as the second wave of our parachutists arrived in Dakotas and started dropping. Fortunately there were no Germans; we had beaten them to it. We took up positions around the airfield, and stayed for about three days until our transport arrived by road.

Major Alastair Pearson
Second-in-Command, 1st Parachute Battalion
We were told we were to drop at Souk el Arba. The battalion took off and came back again. The reason was we had no air support. There was only one decent map. The map I had covered from the Atlantic to the Indian Ocean: not much use. We were sent again the next day.

Captain Vic Coxen
Second-in-Command, T Company, 1st Parachute Battalion
The second time they sent some aircraft ahead to pick a place to drop. During the flight, the door of the lavatory at the back in my aircraft opened, and the face of Colour Sergeant Cooke, the company quartermaster sergeant, appeared. He should have been back with the rear party. He had a parachute on. He was quite old. He had served in the French Foreign Legion before the war, and had two sons in the army. My company commander had been left behind, so I commanded the company.

Major Alastair Pearson
Second-in-Command, 1st Parachute Battalion
The CO, James Hill, led the first stick out. There was one casualty on the second drop. One man was tangled in his rigging lines and killed. At that time we had no idea what side the French would be on. The airfield was in the hands of the French, and they had some tanks with them. If they had turned nasty on us it would have been difficult. But actually they were friendly.

252

Major Alastair Pearson, the redoubtable Commanding Officer of the 1st Parachute Battalion in North Africa. Shown here while commanding the 8th Parachute Battalion before the invasion of Normandy.

The assistant adjutant and I went to the funeral of the chap who was killed. There were thousands of spectators. It was a very hot afternoon. We had to walk about two miles in all our equipment in the cortege. We rode back in the hearse. The next day the battalion moved to Beja on foot, I followed with the rear party by train.

We were getting a certain amount of intelligence from the French about where the Germans were. The French were holding the end of the railway at Sidi Nsir and there was a pass through the hills there to Mateur and on to Tunis. The Germans every day sent an armoured patrol from Mateur across to Sidi Nsir station. James Hill decided he would send a company out to ambush this patrol. They turned out to be half-tracks, and we captured one. We had a certain number of wounded, no killed. That was our first operation against the Germans.

Next James Hill decided to attack a position on a bridge held by a German company. I went too. Some engineers were taken on this operation. The first thing I heard was an explosion and I thought someone had stood on a mine. The engineers were carrying anti-tank grenades in a sack and they had very tricky fuses, and one of them had dropped the sack. The grenades all went off. That killed some of the engineers, including the squadron commander and his 2IC. James Hill was shot and badly wounded at point-blank range by an Italian tank. We won the battle. But I had to take over. We had no other casualties other than James, the adjutant and the engineers. We put James and the adjutant on a motorcycle and sidecar and took them to Beja.

Major Bill Miskin
Officer Commanding, B Company, 6th Battalion,
Queen's Own Royal West Kent Regiment
We only stayed a day at Bougie, and re-embarked; the four rifle companies on two destroyers, A and B on the destroyer called the *Wheatland*. We were due to advance to take Tunis and Bizerta, and land further up the coast. The following morning we came into Bone harbour. The Stukas arrived and we were dive-bombed as we came in and the captain brought his destroyer into Bone harbour without a pilot. He was a young lieutenant commander. Stukas are very frightening things and were to become the evil genies of the campaign. They had sirens on them making a screaming noise as they dived. The Germans were landing their aircraft on the airfields round Tunis and attacked us frequently. They visited us on our advance four or five times a day.

We managed to get ashore without losing anyone. The first time the Stukas came over, the guns on the *Wheatland* fired at them. The captain was furious because their gunnery was awful. The other destroyer had arrived with the other two rifle companies. We duly marched through Bone, and took up bivouac positions in a field, settled down and had breakfast. There weren't any Germans about. There were armoured cars of 56 Recce Regiment under Major Hart, ahead of us, called Hart Force. But we were about 150 miles ahead of the rest of First Army, and out on our own.

Private John Gowan
C *Squadron, 56th Battalion, Reconnaissance Regiment*

After the first two days, I got back into an armoured car. We were three troops of five cars each, and two of five carriers, but by then we had lost a few. The colonel came round and asked us not to wear our tin hats. We had brown berets. He said it would give the infantry confidence. We got our vehicles on the 12th, having landed on 8 November. By 20 December we had two armoured vehicles left and one Bren carrier, the rest damaged, mainly by aircraft. We still hadn't met much enemy. We covered six hundred miles in four days. We got within a few miles of Tunis before we hit the main body of the Germans. From then on we met increasing resistance.

Second Lieutenant Henry Matthews
457 *Light Battery, Royal Artillery*

It was decided that we would go to Sidi Nsir, and I was sent up the road to meet the Argylls and look for gun positions. I arrived at a pass in a carrier late in the evening. I decided that as I hadn't seen a soul, to stay there for the night, and wait for the Argylls. They appeared the next morning, marching up from Beja.

Mike Codner came up on a motorcycle, looking for battery positions for the CRA. He drove on over the ridge, we heard firing, and silence. Later when we went over the hill in a carrier with the Argylls, we found the motorcycle and the French farmer confirmed that there had been two German motorcycle patrols there all night. There had been a fight, Mike had been wounded, and they had moved off with him.

Private John Gowan.

Major Bill Miskin
Officer Commanding, B Company, 6th Battalion,
Queen's Own Royal West Kent Regiment
The CO sent for me and told me to take my company and D Company and head towards Bizerta and see if we could find the enemy. Ken Scott was in command of D Company. I asked about transport, and the CO said it had been arranged. The transport consisted of some antiquated lorries with 'Corona' written on them. They were fuelled by charcoal and driven by fierce-looking Arabs. We piled into these and off we went in the direction of Bizerta. At four o'clock in the afternoon we stopped because we had run out of charcoal. The whole advance came to a halt. When we got the English newspapers, weeks later, we were amused to see descriptions of First Army rushing across North Africa, when we had actually been waiting for more charcoal to enable us to continue our advance.

We found some more charcoal. When it got dark we had to stop, because the lorries had no lights. I borrowed a carrier from Hart Force and went ahead to see what was happening. I got to the Algerian/Tunisian frontier and there was an affable frontier guard and his wife, and his very pretty daughter sitting on the desk swinging her legs. I went in and asked, 'Have you seen any Germans?' They said, 'No, but we'll ring through to the town ahead to see if they've seen any.' In the meantime they gave us some red wine. We toasted each other, 'Vive la France. Vive les Anglais.' I thought this was a lot of fun, going to war.

Corporal Jack Vardy
Mortar Platoon, 2nd Battalion, Hampshire Regiment
I was an old soldier even when the war broke out. Our colonel was the adjutant when I joined the battalion in India in 1929 as a band boy.

We landed at Algiers, in the Guards Brigade. The landing was not too bad, as the fighting had been done before we arrived. We got on the road to make our way to Tunis.

Squadron Leader Charles Bartley
Commanding Officer, 111 Squadron, RAF
We came out on a huge convoy with our Spitfires in crates. We stopped at Gibraltar. Here our aeroplanes were taken off and assembled. Within four days I took my squadron flying with long-range petrol tanks to Algiers. That was the most horrific war, we flew all day, were bombed all day and night.

We had very little back-up. We leapfrogged from one airfield to the next. We flew off from one strip, which the engineers had built, and into the next strip. We lived in slit trenches, ate K rations, and fought all day.

Major Bill Miskin
Officer Commanding, B Company, 6th Battalion,
Queen's Own Royal West Kent Regiment

In the morning as we crossed the border, we were bombed by Stukas. All our transport was knocked out. Later in the morning the rest of the battalion caught us up. They had been in charcoal-powered buses, but were bombed by Stukas not long after crossing into Tunisia. Now we were all on our feet. We must have been about 150 to two hundred miles ahead of the nearest British troops and were out on our own. We pushed on and were bombed about every thirty minutes, but didn't have to do any fighting until about 15 or 16 November. We advanced on our feet to a little crossroads called Djebel Abiod. This was the first time the 6th Battalion had ever been in a serious action. By now we were down to three rifle companies because we had had to send one to the coast to guard our flank.

Djebel Abiod is a minute Arab settlement, but near an important road junction. One road crossed a river, and thereafter went south in one direction and north in another. We arrived there on Saturday night. We dug in. We had been told that a considerable German armoured column was advancing on us. A and C Companies dug in round the village and in the village. My company was up on a rise on the east side of Djebel Abiod. I had a good view of the village. I was taken up part of the way on the provost sergeant's motorbike because I had sprained my ankle.

We had our regular visitations by the Stukas. I had two anti-tank guns with me, sited in our position overlooking the approach road about four or five hundred yards away. We also had a battery from 138 Field Regiment, 25-pounders, in support of the battalion. One section of guns was sited in the village, the other further back along the road behind me.

At one o'clock the German armoured column arrived and attacked. The platoons in the village – greatly to their credit – put up a magnificent show fighting them. The 25-pounders were used as anti-tank guns. They knocked out five or six German tanks. The fighting went on all afternoon and into the next evening. We were just spectators, except for the anti-tank guns under the command of Sergeant Pooley. I watched him hitting the tanks and shells just bouncing off as if they were peashooters. They were the most

011086

Squadron Leader Charles Bartley, Commanding Officer of 111 Squadron, RAF, sitting in the cockpit of a Spitfire Mark VB, at Souk el Arba, Tunisia.

E12643

A 6-pounder anti-tank gun portee.

useless things produced by the army among a lot of useless weapons produced by the army. They were hopeless.

The following day the Germans withdrew. We resumed our advance. The battalion had done well. We marched on again towards Bizerta.

Second Lieutenant Mark Philips
Officer Commanding, 8 Platoon, Number 1 Company,
2nd Battalion, Coldstream Guards
We were told that the Germans were reinforcing Tunisia and seizing the hills overlooking the Medjez el Bab valley. We were sent forward. The 2nd Hampshires went about five days ahead of us.

Corporal Jack Vardy
Mortar Platoon, 2nd Battalion, Hampshire Regiment
We took over from the Northamptons about sixteen miles outside Tunis. We took over the positions forward of a place called Tebourba; we took on a brigade front, just a battalion. I was at HQ in reserve with my mortar.

After a day or so the attacks started all round us. I was in a copse, and there were hills all round the copse. The Germans were attacking. We hung on, but they were gradually overrunning us. I didn't do a lot of firing at that stage. We were getting shelled and mortared. I helped with the wounded at HQ. We saw some terrible sights. The MO ran out of morphia.

We had to move back because we couldn't hold the position. And then we were surrounded by tanks, being belted by Stukas, and attacked by infantry. Then I was called upon to bring down mortar fire. This lasted for another two days. That evening, the German tanks were laagered up around us, and the CO called what was left of us together. The remnants of the rifle companies fixed bayonets. I had a tommy gun, and we made a bayonet charge through the surrounding enemy. The Germans were smoking when we attacked, the boys in front were bayoneting them, and I fired at anything I saw. I don't know if I hit anything. There were cries, screams. I let go at anything that appeared in front of me. I think we took them by surprise. We had been told by the CO to make our way at night back to Medjez el Bab. We were told to keep away from bridges and the railway, which ran in the direction we were travelling in.

We tried to cross a river and at that stage in the darkness we were split up and I was on my own for bit. At times it was like a dream. We were told to move only at night, and I got under a thick bush to go to sleep, because I

Jack Vardy as a sergeant.

was so tired. I woke up because I heard voices. They were German voices. I smelt German tobacco smoke. I was frightened to move, my mouth was dry, my heart was beating. It was fear. I could just see two Germans with sub-machine guns. I just froze. I don't know how long I was there and eventually the voices moved away.

Eventually I met up with a couple more lads and the padre. There was no one else and we made our way back and got to Medjez el Bab where the remainder of the battalion was assembling. We remained there for a bit and then moved back to Beja. The battalion was demoralised and at sixes and sevens. It was a proper mess.

Second Lieutenant Henry Matthews
457 Light Battery, Royal Artillery
From Sidi Nsir the battery moved to Medjez el Bab and up the road towards Tebourba, and on the way my section was ordered into a gun position on the roadside to cover the gap between the road, the railway and the river. I was ordered to go forward to Tebourba itself. At that moment there was a tank alert. I rushed back to my guns. I gave out the orders to receive tanks. Just after midday some armoured cars of the Derbyshire Yeomanry withdrew back through the gun position.

The tanks appeared, in great clouds of dust. The lead tank stopped. I was looking through my binoculars, while standing on the railway line, and saw a very large gun swinging round to point at me. I screamed 'Fire!' at the guns, and they fired. At that moment part of the railway line near me seemed to disappear. I ducked down and ran over to one of my guns. We hit with the third round. I joined the other gun, which was out of view of the tank. One of the drivers stood on the crest and held up a stick to give the layer of the gun a direction in which to aim. We were able to use that gun to bring in-direct fire on the tank. For the next half an hour or so all hell was let loose: we were firing and the tanks were firing back at us. I climbed over the rail-way embankment and helped move Lance Bombardier Brown, the gun layer, who had been hit, and carry him to the rear of the gun. Lance Bombardier Green took his place, and was hit in the back by a round exploding by the railway embankment, showering us all with mud and stone. Lance Sergeant Ricketts climbed into the layer's seat and hit two tanks. We were replacing the gun wheel, which had been hit, with the wheel off the limber, when there was cry from the other gun that they were running out of ammunition. At that moment the tractor was hit and in forcing the door open to get the ammunition, I found the boxes of compo shattered and the whole of the inside was plastered with herrings in tomato sauce. I climbed over the embankment carrying with me some haversacks out of the tractor and telling my signallers and the 'ack' to do the same. After about half an hour, the cry went up, 'They're going.' I was delighted to see them go. They left six tanks behind. Three I claimed, and the others, which were partially hidden behind cactus bushes and folds in the ground, must have been hit by a troop of 25-pounders that had come into action on the hillside to my left, whose presence I was not aware of until the action started.

We started to clear up. One tractor had been hit and was out of action, the other had been hit but was workable. We took our casualties to the roadside to await the ambulance. Here we noticed a small cookhouse set up by the road and a hydro burner going with a meal, but no soldiers about. These were from an engineer unit that had harboured behind us. So here was a 'buckshee' hot meal, which we enjoyed. We were there for a couple of days and withdrawn back to Medjez. The night before we left there was a lot of noise on the other side of the river, indicating that the enemy were moving round that side. Survivors from the Hampshires and Northants walked back through the gun position back towards Medjez.

Company Sergeant Major Macleod Forsyth
A Company, 2nd Parachute Battalion
Our first drop was at Depienne, there was supposed to be an airfield there, but we couldn't find one, or aeroplanes. We were told that the army would come forward to us, but the bloody army didn't; we had to go back.

Private Mike Lewis
2nd Parachute Battalion
We were stationed at Maison Carrée. We were told we were to fly on our first operation to capture an airfield at Oudna, just outside Tunis. We would join up with tanks sent from Algiers. We took off during the day.

The German armoured cars came along, and there was a crackle of cannon fire. They surrounded us. We were sixty miles from any help. The Messerschmitts were swooping over us. I put my camouflage scarf over my face and looked up to see what was happening. About a hundred yards away an armoured car came over the hill. I was carrying the grenade launcher. I fired a grenade and it dropped just in front of us. I put in another grenade and fired, it exploded behind the armoured car and landed among the

Germans moving behind it. It had an immediate effect: they started to withdraw. I only had a limited number of grenades.

Someone came up with a Boys anti-tank rifle. My mate took it, fired, and missed. So he took aim again. The car was only about a hundred yards away; I could see the gun swinging round to point at us. I shouted at my mate to fire, but before he could, there was a tremendous explosion and my trouser legs were smoking, my flesh had been gouged, there were bits of him sticking to me, and he had been cleft from neck to leg. All the inside of him was lying there on and beside me. The officer, Crawley, shouted to me, 'Lewis, come back.' His face was covered with blood, and he was blinded.

The car did not come on. We ran back to company HQ in a shallow dip. Everyone was fighting isolated actions all over the hill. Night came and saved us. We bound Crawley's eyes up. My legs were beginning to stiffen. We hobbled down the very rough boulder-strewn hill, Crawley with a hand on someone's shoulder. We had run out of water. We found some water in a puddle; it was salty. We had no compass, no food. Fortunately the stars were brilliant, we found the pole star. We made our way north, not knowing what had happened to the others. During the day we slept among tussocks of rough grass.

Company Sergeant Major Macleod Forsyth
A Company, 2nd Parachute Battalion
Our CO used his hunting horn to rally us and give the signal to move off. We lost a lot of men simply through exhaustion. We didn't have a lot of water. I had hallucinations. I was marching along and I looked up in the sky and I could see this big bar and a man pulling pints of beer and they were foaming over.

We came to a river and most of us marched in and sat down and let the water run over us, and drank it. But it was very brackish and a lot of the boys were sick. It was hellish on the march; people were vomiting. We just carried on and each day the CO picked a spot where the battalion rested up for the day, and sentries were posted. The Germans were after us. In one place, a farm, two Germans drove up on a motorcycle and sidecar, and asked the farmer if he had seen us. And the farmer said, 'No.'

Private Mike Lewis
2nd Parachute Battalion
At nightfall the CSM had gone. The only fit man among all these walking wounded. Perhaps he thought he had a better chance on his own. We got

A 3-inch mortar crew in action, 31 January 1943.

back. I spent a short time in hospital. Those of us who were left were formed into one company.

Major Bill Miskin
Officer Commanding, B Company, 6th Battalion, Queen's Own Royal West Kent Regiment

Meanwhile we were advancing up to the north. We did some sporadic attacks where we were up against some Italian infantry who really weren't much good, and cleared out at speed when we arrived. We got on the road to Mateur, where the road went between two high hills about fifteen hundred feet high. The Germans were holding both these hills. We still had only three companies. It took us about two days to get deployed and dug in at the foot of the hills, and we were to attack the hills and the railway station behind. We did a night attack. It was disastrous. The battalion lost nine officers and 140 men. My company was in reserve. When the two leading companies had to withdraw, we attacked Bald Hill in order to cover them. We got up there and were then ordered to withdraw as best we could, which we duly did. Just before that we were shelled by our own guns; a bit unfortunate. When we got back the battery commander said, 'Terribly sorry, old boy, we just couldn't get the range right.'

We withdrew in reasonable order. My company had lost two officers and twenty men. Compared with the other companies we had got off quite lightly. One of the officers, Ronnie Palmer, disappeared, we don't know how. His body was never found.

After this attack we withdrew about half a mile and dug in; the beginning of the winter stagnation. The advance to Tunis came to a grinding halt.

Tunisia

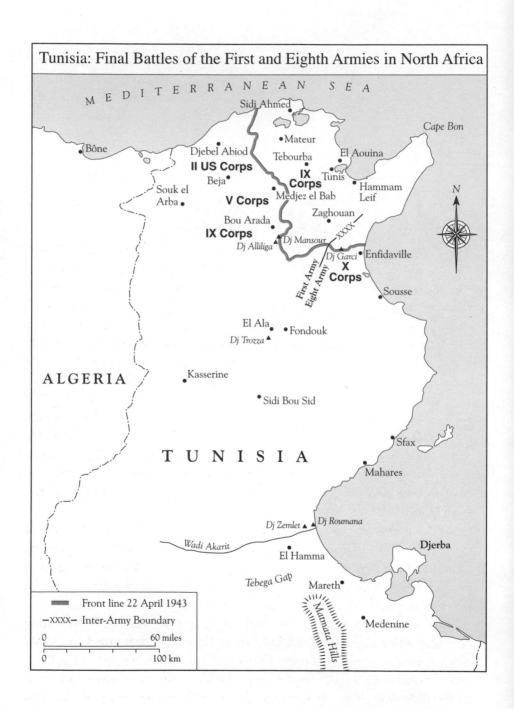

Tunisia: Final Battles of the First and Eighth Armies in North Africa

MEDITERRANEAN SEA

Bône

Sidi Ahmed

Cape Bon

Djebel Abiod

•Mateur

El Aouina

Tebourba

II US Corps

Beja•

IX Corps

Tunis

Souk el Arba•

Medjez el Bab

Hammam Leif

V Corps

Bou Arada•

Zaghouan

IX Corps

▲ Dj Mansour

Dj Alliliga

Enfidaville

Dj Garci•

X Corps

First Army
Eight Army

Sousse

El Ala•

•Fondouk

Dj Trozza ▲

ALGERIA

•Kasserine

•Sidi Bou Sid

TUNISIA

•Sfax

•Mahares

Dj Zemlet ▲ ▲ Dj Roumana

Djerba

Wadi Akarit

•El Hamma

Tebega Gap

Mareth•

Matmata Hills

•Medenine

| ▬▬ | Front line 22 April 1943 |
| —xxxx— | Inter-Army Boundary |

0 _____ 60 miles
0 _____ 100 km

N

It was a shambles. I don't know what happened in other places.
Nobody was ready for the attack.

When the attempt to reach Tunis failed, General Eisenhower ordered that the front should be held as far forward as possible. Although this stretched the Allied lines of communication, he did not want to concede any ground to the enemy that would have to be re-taken subsequently. Furthermore, the French, Tunisians and Algerians might construe an Allied withdrawal as weakness. It would certainly be highly unpopular with the United States and British governments. In order that the enemy would not be allowed to take the initiative on the weak southern flank of the Allied line in Tunisia, a plan was hatched for the US II Corps to launch an offensive in the direction of Sfax, on the Tunisian east coast. Sticking the Allied neck out so far would only be a viable proposition if done in conjunction with an attack by the Eighth Army. Montgomery heading north from Tripolitania was planning an attack on Mareth (see next chapter); this would be an ideal moment to launch the US II Corps.

In the meantime, the rest of First Army was not to be idle. Lieutenant General C. W. Allfrey's British V Corps was ordered to keep the enemy busy by limited attacks, while denying the key terrain to the enemy; ground which would eventually be important when the time came to renew the advance on Tunis.

The enemy, needless to say, had an agenda of his own: not sitting around waiting to be attacked, but hitting first. The first attack launched in mid-January 1943, codename *Eilbote* ('Express Messenger' in English), was uncharacteristically half-baked, lacking the customary German momentum and drive. It involved three battle groups each of infantry, armour and artillery, as well as elements of the 10th Panzer Division. *Eilbote* gained some ground of importance, and resisted most Allied attempts to take it back, but achieved nothing significant. The Allied air forces, flying some 11,000 sorties, played an important role fending off an enemy breakthrough.

On 3 February, Rommel estimated that two weeks might ensue before Eighth Army coming up from the south would launch a major attack. This would open a window of opportunity for inflicting a defeat on the Allies in Tunisia, aimed at putting them out of the game for several weeks, buying Rommel time to stop Montgomery in his tracks. Accordingly, on 14 and 22 February the 10th and 21st Panzer Divisions launched a smashing blow at the ill-prepared and badly led US II Corps at Kasserine and Sidi Bou Sid. The US II Corps suffered six thousand casualties, and in many places troops abandoned their equipment and fled. The debacle did nothing to raise the already low opinions the British had for American fighting ability; especially as British units were sent to shore up the II Corps line. It did not help that the commander of US II Corps, Lieutenant General Lloyd Fredendall, was virulently anti-British, as well as being, according to an eminent American historian, 'one of the most inept senior officers to hold high command in the Second World War'. He was relieved by Lieutenant General George Patton, who quickly turned the situation round. In the end Rommel gained very little from his offensive, other than giving the Allies a nasty surprise.

Not all British units in Tunisia were models of soldierly efficiency. Some were decidedly lacklustre compared with their German opponents, allowing themselves to be dominated by them. Others, such as Alastair Pearson's 1st Parachute Battalion, while admiring the Germans, were not in the least in awe of them, and outwitted and outfought them on more than one occasion. It all depended – as it always does in battle – on the quality of the leadership, irrespective of rank, from private soldiers all the way up to the top.

As the Eighth Army found at the other end of North Africa, the Germans in Tunisia were almost invariably formidable soldiers. They had one fault, noted by many who fought them in all theatres in the Second World War – they rarely engaged in major attacks at night. The Italians were, with few exceptions, uniformly second rate.

Squadron Leader 'Ras' Berry
Commanding Officer, 81 Squadron, RAF and Wing Commander,
322 Wing, RAF

On 13 November I moved the squadron to Bone, with thirteen aircraft, and I had just shot down my thirteenth aircraft. From then on it was very busy, patrolling Bone, and the enemy were attacking as often as possible, 109s and Macchis. The Germans had the aggression. The attacks were determined; JU 88s bombing all day. Some of them were very cocky, like the Ace of Spades Squadron from Abbeville. The Focke-Wulfe 190s were formidable. I got one on the 16 December. I was pleased about that. I out-turned the 190. They were very fast, and their pilots were very experienced; they were a bit sharper than the others. The Spitfire Mk V with its snout wasn't as fast as the 109, and even less so against the 190.

I became the wing leader when we lost our wing leader. We moved to Constantine and had a few days' rest. I had bellyached about the Spitfire V and it had some effect. We went to Gib to pick up some Spitfire IXs and we were the first squadron to have them outside the UK. From there we flew to our own airfield, to a place we called Tingli named after the engineer who built it. It was a nice strip with a hard top. Better than the muddy one at Bone.

The Spitfire IX was marvellous, it had a supercharger that cut in at twenty thousand feet. The Germans would attack in pairs, two up and two down. If you went down the two would get you, if you went up the other two would use their speed to catch you. The first time I got into combat with them flying a Mk IX. I shot down my first 109 on 21 January. The Germans had done the same, but we went after the two who had gone up, and they couldn't believe it. It was a delight to be able to out-fly them.

Second Lieutenant Mark Philips
Officer Commanding, 8 Platoon, Number 1 Company, 2nd Battalion,
Coldstream Guards

Then it was decided to attack Longstop Hill on 22 December. It was very difficult from our side of the hill to tell that there was another hill beyond, almost the same height as Longstop. That was to cause trouble. We in Number 1 Company moved through Number 4 Company, and attacked Longstop. We got nearly to the top of the hill when we came under heavy machine-gun fire and mortar fire. Immediately, my company commander, Paddy Chichester, ordered my platoon in. Number 7 Platoon gave us covering fire. We made a mistake throwing some grenades uphill, and they rolled back on us. We attacked their trenches. We killed some of them, but most of the Germans scarpered, although we managed to nab a couple of prisoners. We took Longstop with very little trouble. Our orders were to hand over to a combat team of the American army at 3 am.

The Germans shelled, mortared and machine-gunned us pretty well the most of the night, but we took good cover and returned the fire. It was then we began to realise that there was another feature about the same height as Longstop away to our left, and some of the fire was coming from there. A few guardsmen were wounded, and suddenly the machine-gun fire grew worse and our company commander was wounded by a bullet through the jugular vein. The CSM, Callaghan, a brave and fine man, crawled up to me and said, 'You'd better crawl back, sir, the company commander has been seriously wounded.' So back we crawled. They were raking the ground with machine-gun fire, but the worst was the mortars. As we crawled I was blown sideways by blast from a mortar bomb. I took about ten minutes to sort myself out and gather my wits, and crawled on to where Paddy was and obviously he had been badly wounded. To my horror he managed to croak out, 'It's all over to you, Mark.'

Those were almost his last words. He gave me a little grin and went into deep unconsciousness. I thought, 'Hells bells, how am I going to manage this?' In those days platoon commanders didn't have any training as company commanders. From commanding thirty-two men I found myself commanding over a hundred. I moved to company HQ, and we got Paddy back on a stretcher. They carried him two and a quarter miles and sadly he died two days later.

Suddenly the sergeant major crawled up to me and said, 'There is a bloody loud noise, what is going on?' It was an American combat team arriving, mess tins rattling, smoking cigars, a bit of a rabble, we thought. I went up to the commanding officer, a lieutenant colonel, a fairly jolly man, who said, 'This is the biggest thing since *Ben Hur*. This is good, we are going to kill those bastards.'

I said, 'Well they are pretty good actually, sir, I think you've got to be careful.'

By that time Sergeant Major Callaghan couldn't stand all the cigar smoking and roared out, 'Put those bloody cigars out! Stop rattling all that kit!'

I was very grateful to Sergeant Major Callaghan because all the cigars were immediately put out and I handed over the positions to the

The 2nd Battalion, Coldstream Guards on Longstop Hill.

An OP overlooking the enemy-held town of Mateur.

Americans. You couldn't dig in because of the rocks. It was very difficult to find enough cover.

I said to the American colonel, 'It's about time we went back. Are you satisfied with the positions?'

He replied, 'It's all right as long as it doesn't rain. You guys are lucky, you don't feel the cold like we do.'

Major Bill Miskin
Officer Commanding, B Company, 6th Battalion, Queen's Own Royal West Kent Regiment

We all dug slit trenches, about four feet deep. There we lived in the mud. It is very wet in Tunisia in the winter. There may be six inches of water in the bottom of the slit trench, and that is your home. All your personal needs have to be carried out within a short distance of your slit trench because if they start shelling you have to get back in quickly. You sleep there, you stay there in the day time. We were there for about six weeks. We all stank. We didn't have a change of clothing. We went out on patrol at night, got wet, stayed wet.

Dug in on our left we had a platoon of American Rangers. They were all very tall men, and carried enough weapons on them to equip a British battalion: knives, tommy guns, grenades. They had one problem. When the Germans shelled us they got out of their trenches and ran. This was stupid. I was told by my CO to go over and cope with them, and make sure they didn't leave their slit trenches when shelling started. Over I went, and asked, 'Where is your officer?'

'Oh, you mean Bud.'

'Well if that's his name, I'll talk to Bud.'

An enormous chap emerged from his trench and asked, 'What's your problem, major?'

'When the Germans start shelling your men get out of their slit trenches and run.'

'So?' he replied.

'It's a very bad thing to do. Because you are much safer in the trench and second, you give our positions away.'

'Oh,' he said.

'My colonel has told me to stop you doing it.'

'How do you propose doing that?' he said.

'Oh,' says I, 'very simple. If you look up to your right you will see two of my Bren guns trained on these trenches and if the Germans miss you, they won't.'

'You wouldn't fire,' he said.

'I am a very obedient officer, those are my orders; that's what I'll do.'

Fortunately it was never put to the test, because they were pulled out that night. The Americans in Tunisia were as green as grass.

Second Lieutenant Mark Philips
Officer Commanding, 8 Platoon, Number 1 Company, 2nd Battalion, Coldstream Guards

We returned to the battalion, which had gone back about five miles to what became called Grenadier Hill. I handed over the company to Captain Philip Kindersley. On Christmas Eve we were told that the stores were coming up from B Echelon and the whole battalion would all have Christmas dinner, out in the open. But on Christmas Eve we were informed that the Americans had lost the top of Longstop Hill and we had to go back and take it. Same procedure as before, we went through number 4 Company and attacked a position, now heavily reinforced by the enemy.

It was a hellish night, pouring with rain, and the German fire was very accurate. Somehow we managed to get back to the positions we had held two days before. I have to say in fairness to the Americans, their mortar team was brilliant and brave, and good at covering us in, and so was our own Royal Artillery with their 25-pounders. They were firing very close to us; we went about 150 yards behind their barrage to the top of the hill. Then the Germans came back in force. It was a swaying, swinging battle for most of the night. We lost at least three-quarters of the battalion's officers. The moon occasionally came through the clouds, and the machine-gun fire would intensify. We could hear German tanks behind the hill. We fought on, the guardsmen fought hugely bravely. Every man deserved a decoration.

While I was dashing forward I was hit, and couldn't walk. I managed to crawl back a bit. Colonel 'Bunty' Stewart Brown, a very brave man, came right up, some people say he should have stayed back. But he rallied us all. It was becoming a bloodbath. He was wounded. Phil Kindersley was wounded. The Germans began coming up, they passed within a few feet of where I was lying in a pool of blood. I kept very still and perhaps they thought I was dead. Phil Kindersley didn't keep still, so they nabbed him and took him prisoner. It was a nasty moment.

But we still stood our ground. The Germans swung round too far to the right flank. And we were able to fight on for a bit longer. Roddy Hill came up and took command of the battalion. They said they would try to get me back on a stretcher, but there were no more stretchers, they'd all been used up. Eventually Johnny Baxendale, the signals officer, came up with a message, because the wirelesses weren't working. He dragged, pulled and carried me down the hill to a carrier, driven by a cousin of mine, Bobby Philips, who lost his thumb that night.

They got me back to the farmhouse where the doctor, Elston Grey-Turner operated on me. I had lost a left testicle, and had hits all down the leg and stomach. He wished me a Happy Christmas. It was Christmas Day, 1942. All surgeons who operated on me since have all admired what he did intensely. There was very little anaesthetic left. The last man to get any was a black American Army truck driver. Elston Grey-Turner said, 'One thing I have got is a bit of whisky.' He was a great man with a sense of humour. He added, 'I am probably going to give you about half of this, and I'll probably have the last quarter.'

The Germans came close and fired on the ambulances. The padre and the doctor, although they were not supposed to fire weapons, kept the Germans at bay. The padre did great things, as did Elston Grey-Turner. We managed to get away in the ambulances. I came to thinking I was having a bad dream, with a German officer, who spoke very good English, standing looking down on me asking, 'Is there anything I can do to help?' I said, 'You speak very good English,' and he said that he had been at Oxford. He had been taken prisoner.

Lieutenant Tony Pawson
Platoon Commander, A Company, 10th Battalion, The Rifle Brigade
While at Bou Arada we patrolled a good deal. On one we liaised with some French Foreign Legionaries. They rode over on horses. They asked to join me. I had the whole platoon. We were ordered to see if a German armoured car was at a particular farm. I was worried by this clanking noise from sacks on the back of the Legionaries. I thought they must be Molotov cocktails. The dogs were barking. We got in a ditch about thirty yards from the farm. I asked the French officer if he was OK. He said, '*Un moment; le vin, le vin.*' The sacks were unloaded and we had to drink the revolting wine before moving up to the farm where, happily, there was no one except the farmer. He told us where the armoured car normally came in so I put down some Hawkins mines where it came in. Back we went.

A few days later my company commander, Dick Fyffe, thought the armoured car was bound to be back again, and took the whole company to

A Valentine tank crew relax after an action near Bou Arada, 13 January 1943.

nab it. In the dawn we spread out opposite the main entrance, which I had mined. Fyffe and a couple of chaps were on the roof of a cattle shed, and I was on the roof of the next one. At about ten in the morning the Germans did indeed advance down the road, but not an armoured car, a motorcyclist and sidecar, with three chaps: a driver and two others. It stopped, two got out, slung their sub-machine guns over their shoulders, while the driver turned his cycle round ready to get away quickly. They approached the farm chatting happily. Fyffe waved to us not to fire, but round the corner they came upon my platoon sergeant and a couple of riflemen brewing up tea. Panic all round. The Germans fled back to their cycle and the sergeant the other way. This time Dick Fyffe gave the order to fire. Dick Fyffe and the other two on the adjacent roof fired at the Germans with tommy guns but missed at ten yards range. I had a Bren gun. Instead of lying down and firing in short bursts, I was so excited I fired the whole magazine standing up from the hip. I planned to fire at the motorcycle to prevent it getting away, but missed. One of the Germans had a go at me. I was stupidly still standing up. Despite all my Bren gun training I couldn't understand why it wasn't firing – of course the maga-zine was empty and I hadn't got another magazine handy. One of the two halted and swung his sub-machine gun on to me, but luckily the other grabbed him and pulled him away and they all escaped. We decided to go home, having made a mess of it. I felt stupid, wondering what would happen next. How could three chaps with tommy guns miss at such short range? We were gathering together to return to base, when a German tank alerted by the noise came crawling down the road. Fortunately slowly, and then stopped, and that hurried our departure, but didn't fire at us, for some reason.

Major Bill Miskin
Officer Commanding, B Company, 6th Battalion,
Queen's Own Royal West Kent Regiment
We patrolled to try and get a prisoner. One night I was out on a fighting patrol with about twenty men and three Bren guns. We hid in a ditch about forty yards in front of the German position and the Bren gunners went out to a flank to cover us in. This took about quarter of an hour. Suddenly I felt my shoulder being shaken; I was asleep and snoring. The Germans had gone.

Every morning after stand-to, the first thing we did was to scrape the mud off ourselves using our clasp knives. We had a lot of people with battle fatigue. Every one has their limit, and it is merely a matter of luck at which point it afflicts you. I had two subalterns whom I had to pull along by their webbing.

Lieutenant Tony Pawson
Platoon Commander, A Company, 10th Battalion, The Rifle Brigade

My next patrol seemed a straightforward recce patrol. We hadn't seen any movement on the hill facing us. So I decided to take only a corporal and a rifleman so we could move silently. We weren't looking for a fight, but for information. The front of the hill was steep and pebbly so we couldn't avoid making a noise, but that didn't attract any attention. We saw nothing as we moved in bounds, in the moonlight. When we neared the crest we heard the sound of vehicles driving up the hill and the clatter of stores being unloaded. The dogs were barking. There were clearly troops moving up the hill on the other side. I sent the other two back to report this fact. I stayed on myself to see what developed, and climbed into a small olive tree to see better. I even read a letter from home in the bright moonlight. I checked the time, it was 3.30, and was thinking of returning. To my surprise I heard a thumping noise. I saw some Germans silhouetted on the skyline digging in. I climbed down the tree, trying to be as quiet as possible, but as I slid down the trunk the lanyard attached to my whistle in my breast pocket caught in a small branch. This left me suspended and twisting, with grenades dropping out of my battledress pocket. Finally the branch snapped and I landed with a thump, which fortunately did not disturb the diggers whose pickaxe noises covered my own. Soon I froze like a pointer dog, finding myself too close to a couple of Germans marking out a trench but with their backs to me. I crept away on my stomach to a nearby cactus square, easing in despite the numerous prickles, the five-foot high cactus compound was about fifteen yards long and ten feet wide. I tiptoed to the far side to make sure it was all clear there. No luck – a platoon had moved up and some of them were uncomfortably close to the cactus. I tiptoed across to the other side and they were setting up a heavy machine gun on the other side. My one hope of escape was the period of darkness just before the dawn. But as it got lighter and lighter I realised that this was illusory as far as this night was concerned. Then I began to think what it was like when *we* occupied a position at night. Clearly these were first-class troops from the quiet way they conducted themselves. But no one can avoid some confusion in these circumstances: you have no idea exactly where everybody else is, exactly where their positions are and whether they need to walk around for some reason. So I realised that no one was likely to worry about a shadowy figure walking out from *behind* them, and a challenge was unlikely when maintaining silence had clearly been a major feature of their orders. If I came out of the middle of the cactus those on either side might well think I'd come from the other side. So I removed my tell-tale side cap, shouldered my tommy gun, and with pulse racing walked slowly out as if inspecting the ground ahead. I nerved myself to walk slowly, although poised to break into a zigzag sprint should I be challenged. Only a hundred yards ahead there was a welcoming fold in the ground. As I disappeared from their line of sight, I did indeed sprint away. Fortunately there was no challenge, and no troops forward in the wadi.

Major Bill Miskin
Officer Commanding, B Company, 6th Battalion,
Queen's Own Royal West Kent Regiment
The Germans as soldiers were much better than we were. They were much more determined. When they got stopped, they immediately tried to find a way round, to keep pushing on; and in defence they were stubborn, much more so than the British soldier, of whom I was one. They were the first eleven. We were the second eleven. Not that we lacked training or lacked courage, but it was a difference in attitude.

Lieutenant Tony Pawson
Platoon Commander, A Company, 10th Battalion, The Rifle Brigade
When I reported, the company commander at once decided to take prisoners the following night to confirm who our opponents were. I volunteered without enthusiasm, realising that I was the person who knew the exact location to storm. However, it was decided another officer should go to get experience and I did my best to brief him as I pointed out the positions and the cactus square as we peered down from our positions. He took a section with him, and, as it seemed likely to me, it was the Germans who got the prisoners. There was a fierce exchange of fire and no one came back. That experience was frightening enough but there was worse to come before we could be classed as battle-hardened, although in my case never mentally hardened as much as I would have liked. It was the hope that I might survive that kept me sane and functioning. I had also to bear in mind that many orders of mine might put lives at risk. Until this patrol, it had all seemed a little farcical – playing at war, and not very well. These two days changed my whole attitude and suddenly the war was very near and very serious.

Corporal Dave Brooks
B Company, 2nd Parachute Battalion

The Parachute Brigade was used as a 'fire brigade' in Tunisia. It took me a long time to work out what we were trying to do. We stomped all over Tunisia.

Private Gordon Mitchell
11 Platoon, T Company, 1st Parachute Battalion

Where the line was threatened, or a breakthrough imminent, we were moved in.

Lieutenant Colonel Alastair Pearson
Commanding Officer, 1st Parachute Battalion

We were then moved very hurriedly by ship to Bone, then by road to the west of Pont du Fahs, to hold the right flank of First Army. I was ordered to take Djebel Mansour, and then go on to Djebel Alliliga. We were given forty-eight hours' notice. The night before I sent out a fighting patrol to find out what was at the top of Djebel Mansour, led by Vic Coxen and he took the IO. I wanted to find out where we should have a Start Line. The Germans were very good at setting up machine guns on fixed lines, but if you studied them, you could sometimes see a way through them. The Germans had a very good mountain regiment there.

Major Vic Coxen
Officer Commanding, T Company, 1st Parachute Battalion

The information on the terrain largely came from a French Foreign Legion officer attached to us. It was very rough country. I was leading the front section. I made the first contact when a voice said, '*Wer geht dort?*' I replied, 'Das is Willie Dumkopf.' The bugger threw a grenade at me, so my German obviously wasn't that good. My batman and I got some shrapnel in us, nothing to worry about. We moved out and took the position, including the chap who threw the grenade. It was obvious we couldn't stay up there, we were being shot at from several sides. So we went back. I said at the time that I didn't think that Mansour was tenable unless someone took Al Alligila, the hill on the right of it, because it completely dominated the whole way up and you would be enfiladed when you got up there. They took the advice and decided that the Guards should attack Alligila while we took Mansour. We had support from the French 75s and our mountain guns. The trouble with the 75s was that with a flat trajectory they had crest clearance problems.

We attacked, it was rough and we lost a lot of people. We moved up in the dark, it was not an easy approach, and the assault was at dawn. There was a lot of bravery, which was very expensive. When you attacked with the bayonet, sometimes the enemy would go on firing until you were about twenty yards away, and then put their hands up, to which the reaction was often, 'too bloody late. If you wanted to do that you should have done so earlier': you finished them off.

Lieutenant Colonel Alastair Pearson
Commanding Officer, 1st Parachute Battalion
We sent a patrol on to Alligila, which overlooked Mansour, and it was very strongly held. The next afternoon a company from 3rd Grenadier Guards was sent to capture Alligila; they should have sent a whole battalion. We saw them attack; all five officers were lost. The CSM led them out again. We sent a patrol to the top that night. I got permission to withdraw from Mansour, as it was overlooked by Alligila.

Private Gordon Mitchell
11 Platoon, T Company, 1st Parachute Battalion
The Germans were outstanding, and seemed to work much harder at their soldiering than we did. They not only had one alternative position, they seemed to achieve two. This meant that when you attacked them, the temptation was to get in their trenches. These were often booby-trapped, which we learned the hard way. Also, their first line of trenches was on a fixed line from machine guns so when you arrived they would hit you, you would dive for cover in a trench and get blown up.

In an attack or counter-attack, you go forward, get pinned down, lose some men, get pinned down again, lose more men, get up and go forward, and so on. Eventually you get on top of your objective, and having done all that, and lost a lot of friends, the German will then stand up in his mortar pit and say, '*Kamerad.*' There was a natural tendency not to be very kind at that stage. When your blood had cooled, you realised that here was a good soldier, his fears were the same as yours, and he was a human being. The next stage was to give him a cup of tea or a cigarette. The Italians were different, they were very poor soldiers. They didn't want to fight, their heart wasn't in it. I thought they were a pretty cowardly lot; they surrendered very quickly. We didn't abuse them. I remember sitting down twenty or thirty of them, and saying, 'We know you're no good at fighting, but we've heard you're good at singing, now bloody well sing.' And they did. They also carried wine in their water bottles. That became very welcome.

Lieutenant Colonel Alastair Pearson
Commanding Officer, 1st Parachute Battalion

In February we moved very suddenly right up to the north, to Tamera, where we took over from a Guards battalion. They were a full-strength battalion, we were down to just over three hundred. We held Tamera station and the cork forest above it. In that area there was no way that you really have a defensive position because if you sat still you would be bypassed. So we had flexible and mobile defence. The Germans did not like fighting at night; they would patrol, but not very well. I have never been attacked in strength by the Germans at night; last light, yes, and after first light, yes, but never in the middle of the night. So at night we patrolled as far as we could go, to keep them awake. But we didn't want to incur casualties on our side. It was a question of getting as close as possible and throwing grenades, but not closing with them. During the day we had standing patrols quite far out where we could watch for any movement.

Company Sergeant Major Macleod Forsyth
A Company, 2nd Parachute Battalion

We arrived during the night to take over from a company of another battalion. We went up into this wood on a hill. We couldn't find them. So here we were in the night shouting, 'Where are you?' Suddenly a little voice said, 'We thought you were Germans.' You should have heard the company commander. He cursed and swore, 'Get out of here, you.' What he called them was nobody's business. And he said to the company, 'Right, boys, spread out.' So we spread out in a circle, and he pointed out where the enemy were.

Just before dawn the Germans attacked. They thought they would find the other unit we had relieved, and got the surprise of their bloody life. We hadn't dug in; we were just lying there. They kept coming in. Suddenly an officer went past so bloody fast, and the company commander told me to go forward and see what was happening. I went forward and the Germans were hitting us hard and the boys were coming back. I shouted, 'The bastards are more afraid of you than you are of them.' We held them. That officer, if he had been a private, he would have been court-martialled and shot. Instead of that he was shunted sideways to another battalion. Mind you, he did well after that.

Lieutenant Colonel Alastair Pearson
Commanding Officer, 1st Parachute Battalion

Eric Down, who had been our first CO and then our brigade commander, visited. He was disappointed there wasn't a battle going on. I jokingly said that there would be one the next day. So he said he would stay another day. Sure enough, the enemy attacked in tremendous strength. Eric Down was at battalion HQ. I turned round to send a runner to Vic Coxen and said, 'That's for T Company.' The next thing I knew it had been picked up by Eric Down, and saw him running across to the company with a message in his hand. At one stage it looked as if battalion HQ was going to be overrun and the situation was saved by Sergeant Clements charging forward shouting, 'Whoa, Mohammed,' which had become the battle cry.

We then managed to get in behind the enemy and took two hundred prisoners. Every company had an area for which it was responsible. Every company commander had to recce routes forward to counter-attack enemy penetrations. We watched the enemy form up and use the road as an axis. We shifted one company right out on the flank. He very carefully held fire until the first two enemy companies were past him, and then opened up with all his Brens. The Germans attacked three times and were beaten off.

Company Sergeant Major Macleod Forsyth
A Company, 2nd Parachute Battalion

We were bombed, mortared, shelled. A mule train coming up with rations was hit by a bomb; what a mess. One poor chap had no arms and no legs. I collected some morphia tubes, and pumped him full of morphia and let him die. One of the boys got wounded, Hunt his name was, last I heard of him they were taking him down the railway that ran in the valley, and one of the stretcher-bearers stepped on a mine and blew the whole bloody lot up; just his luck. Get wounded, think you're lucky and got a 'Blighty one', and bang, you're dead. The fighting went on for days.

Lieutenant Tony Pawson
Platoon Commander, A Company, 10th Battalion, The Rifle Brigade

The war grew more serious. We were sent in a long move by road to support the Americans who had been driven back at the Kasserine pass. At the end of the long drive we were halted by our company commander some three miles behind the pass. Our CO, Lieutenant Colonel Adrian Gore, decided to go up and make contact with the Americans. Fortunately for him there was an ambulance driving about quarter of a mile ahead, which was suddenly ambushed. His driver had just time to spin round and drive back. But we had no chance now of linking up with the Americans. Obviously, troops had infiltrated behind us. So we set up a defensive position some three miles short of the pass, while our carrier platoon drove off with a small ambush group.

I had the upsetting experience of seeing a Valentine of the Lothian and Border Horse being shot up by our own anti-tank guns. I heard the sergeant in charge starting to give the order to fire, and immediately screamed at him not to do so. I was unable to stop him, and the Valentine was hit. We were then told to withdraw and join the rest of the battalion. The next night one of our positions was overrun by the Germans, who approached it with a captured Valentine tank with gun reversed. The defenders were overrun. I wondered if the sergeant was right, and if the Valentine we had hit was a ruse.

The following night we were ordered to withdraw. I took my platoon back, keeping well away from the road in case there was any follow-up by the German tanks. When I had joined the company I was pleased to see large numbers of Crusaders and Valentines ready to go into battle. We were told to go into reserve behind a strongly held position. We took our positions without any thought that we would soon be in action again with so much strength in front of us.

At first there were no problems, with firing away in the distance, but it got nearer and nearer. By nightfall we suddenly saw tracer bullets and shells crisscrossing the hill in front, and the sound of tanks coming nearer and the scene of tanks and trucks blazing. I was sent forward on my own to recce and see what was happening. I went up to the crest crawling or running in short bursts, passing a tank, which seemed to be very courageously motoring on although it was on fire. I soon realised that it was an illusion, it was merely the wind blowing the flames in streams and giving the impression that it was still moving. I went to the crest and looked down on a sight of total confusion, burning tanks, burning trucks, and a large number of prisoners. All we could do was to prepare for a massive attack the following day. One section situated by the road had a tank pass so close to their slit trenches that a corporal got up and blasted the commander who was well out of his turret. The tank was eventually knocked out by one of our 25-pounder guns close by.

I counted the remaining tanks on our side, drawn up close by, a mere seventeen Valentines and Crusaders. I was relieved during the day to see the anti-tank platoon drive up, with 17-pounders, which had just been delivered; the only anti-tank gun we had to match the German 88. The guns

The inside of a Valentine tank turret, gunner on the left and loader on the right, showing cramped conditions and the pitifully small two-pounder shell fired by this tank.

were sited in an oppressive silence, and waited for the expected onrush. Certainly the Germans could have overrun us without any trouble had it not been for the anti-tank guns. I was sent forward the next morning to find out what was happening as we had ceased to see any tanks. To my surprise I found the whole place deserted on the other side of the hill: just knocked-out tanks, knocked-out trucks, and general confusion. But of the Germans, there was no sign.

Private Patrick O'Sullivan
A Company, 2nd/5th Battalion, Sherwood Foresters
We stood-to one morning at Sedjenane, I was number two on the Bren with Corporal Barker. We thought the bloody war in Africa had finished because of the inactivity. We were all browned off. We were very lax. The Germans could see us better than we could see them. We had gone into the slit trench without a water bottle, because we thought it would be a normal stand-to and we would soon stand down. The CSM came round, 'How much ammunition have you got?'

'Just two magazines.' Here we were, on stand-to, with just two magazines for the Bren, that is how lax we had got. He threw us some more.

We asked, 'Can you get us some water?'

He got our water bottles and threw them at us, but they landed outside the trench, just out of reach. I looked at the water bottle, I was very thirsty, looked at this water bottle, and thought, 'Oh, bugger it.' I nipped out grabbed my water bottle, and 'P-I-I-I-NG', a German fired and missed.

Lieutenant Denys Crews
Platoon Commander, 2nd/5th Battalion, Sherwood Foresters
We had the 16th DLI in our brigade and the Leicesters. We were sitting on the top of the hill improving our sangars. It was a vast ridge, and I had put people out to the right and to the left, looking out on a deep valley out into the distance. We knew that there was a strong possibility of being attacked. Perhaps stupidly, I told my chaps they could stand down for lunch: biscuits and bully. Nothing seemed to be happening, when all of a sudden, advancing Germans in grey greatcoats covered the whole landscape. I thought to myself, 'Crews, you must wait until you can see the whites of their eyes.' I had never been in action before, I had been sitting on Green Hill for six weeks and never seen a German. It was an alarming sight, they seemed to be coming from everywhere.

I waited until they were 150 yards away before giving the order to fire. We let them have it. They all dropped to the ground; I thought they had disappeared. Then firing started, fire going over our heads most of it. I never reported the action to my company commander; I didn't know where he was. There was firing from left and right and I thought they were about to attack us from both sides. Were we to sit there? This started at midday, and the day seemed to be over when I thought we were surrounded. They were attacking all the other companies and had infiltrated up the wadis, between my platoon and the next platoon. Battalion HQ was surrounded. The firing got louder and louder, as we were on the extreme left of the battalion. I decided to move, I didn't want to be cut off here on my own. I stupidly blew my whistle to collect them together. I got my platoon together and got to where we could see the road and find out was going on. The enemy stopped advancing at this point. I couldn't find out what was going on. My wireless didn't work. We were all so spread out.

Private 'Wally' Binch
Anti-Tank Platoon, 2nd/5th Battalion, Sherwood Foresters
We dug in our two-pounder anti-tank gun on the bend in a road near a quarry where the whole carrier platoon was situated. They had their Brens with them. It was about two o'clock and we could hear an attack on the way, from the direction of Green Hill. Our own carriers had gone back. I'd left my rifle in my carrier. I went to the carrier platoon to borrow a rifle, but couldn't. So I went back to the gun, which was covering the road with a field of fire of perhaps a hundred yards or so. It was not dug in. We had no slit trenches.

Next, from the direction of the hill where I had been up to borrow a rifle from the carrier platoon came firing and it was Jerries, firing at us. We didn't know the carriers had been overrun; panic stations. Our gun is pointing the wrong way, 180 degrees. They were firing from above, from about 150 yards away, behind us. I had my greatcoat on. I took out the firing mechanism from the gun and put it in my greatcoat pocket. And Eddy Hallet and I ran forward and dived through a big concrete culvert under the road, and came out in a field on the other side. What happened to the other members of the crew I don't know. It was every man for himself. We ran across the field and could hear them shooting at us. As we ran, I said to Eddy, 'What colour is blood?' 'Yellow,' says he.

We ran to a road and along it. We saw Captain 'Johnny' Walker, our platoon commander, on an anti-tank gun belonging to someone else. As I ran up I saw a slit trench with a gun crew in the trench. I reported to him that we had lost our gun. We stayed there for a little, and as we were talking an officer shouted, 'Tanks coming, Johnny.' Captain Walker said, 'Man the gun.' I got in the loader's position, Johnny in the firer's position. The rest of the crew stayed in the trench. Round the corner came a German armoured car. Captain Walker fired, and it kept going, he fired again. He must have fired three shots, but didn't hit it. The tank disappeared, but didn't fire at us. We were sited near a cactus plant, and as the gun bounded back on each discharge I got stuck with cactus spikes. Captain Walker pulled out a flask of whisky from his back pocket and asked, 'Do you want a drink, Binch?' I said, 'No thank you, sir, I'd rather die sober.'

Sergeant Allan Orne
Platoon Sergeant, A Company, 2nd/5th Battalion, Sherwood Foresters
We could see people running about, didn't know if they were enemy or not. Suddenly realised they were Germans. I told my blokes not to start shooting yet. Behind us was company HQ, Captain Curly. Then someone in another platoon opened up with a rifle. That was the signal for everyone to open fire. The enemy went to ground. When they got up, we opened up again, and went on until they were about a hundred yards away. We started to run out of ammunition. I crawled back through the undergrowth, got back to Captain Curly, and told him, 'No ammunition.' He said, 'Get your men back here and we'll charge them.' But when I got back the Germans had taken my position.

I ran back to Captain Curly. He said, 'We'll soon have them off that. Fix bayonets.' There were only about six or so of us. So we fixed bayonets and went back up the hill. Captain Curly went up shooting his rifle, and was hit in the head. The Jerries came up and we had nothing to shoot with. Lieutenant Gilliver said, 'Go back.' I went back, the bullets were popping through the cactus. Four of us got back to a gully. And I said, 'If we can stay here till dark, we'll go east to our own men.'

Private Patrick O'Sullivan
A Company, 2nd/5th Battalion, Sherwood Foresters
We fired the Bren but couldn't really see the enemy. We abandoned the forward positions; we couldn't hit anything from there, and went back over the hill into the rear positions. The Germans took the top of the hill. Our company commander said we would charge up with bayonets. There was six

or seven of us: Rose, Lockwood, me, the company commander, a lieutenant, and one or two more. We fixed bayonets and we were going take the top of the hill back. We charged up the hill and covered about fifteen or twenty yards. The lieutenant threw a couple of grenades. A machine gun fired at us, killing or wounding four, including the company commander and the lieutenant, leaving me, 'Reggie' Rose and Lockwood. We turned and ran back. 'Reggie' Rose went straight into a cactus bush, and was caught up. All of a sudden they were all over us. The blokes who had taken the top of the hill came over the top of the hill, firing machine guns. The CSM put his arms up and that was it. I never saw anything of him until he put his hands up. The Germans said, 'For you the war is over'; some of them spoke good English. The first thing they did was take all the cigarettes and food, collected all the weapons. They didn't take any personal items off us. The Germans treated our wounded. There was no sign of our medics.

The Germans were marvellous and bloody fit. We had struggled up those hills, and they came up like gazelles. Their firepower was far superior to us. They had automatic weapons; we had bolt-action rifles. The Bren gun is OK, but their machine guns were better. Our Vickers was never fired, it was in a bad position firing on fixed lines. Our officer stood-to wearing a service dress cap, he was lax; we all were. It was a shambles. I don't know what happened in other places. Nobody was ready for the attack.

Sergeant James Drake
Platoon Sergeant, Machine-Gun Platoon, 16th Battalion,
Durham Light Infantry
I saw some troops walking towards Sedjenane and wondered who they were. While we were waiting for the runner to come back, some grenades started coming down on us from the top of the hill. So I swung the Vickers round on a swinging traverse. I silenced the first lot coming over, and shouted to everybody to get out. The lads all got out. Lieutenant Lacks says, 'I'm staying with you.' And I said, 'You'd better not,' and gave him some choice words. He wanted to stay, but I made him get out. Off he went. I stayed behind the gun and two or three came down throwing grenades, and I fired until the belt had gone through. The Germans were about ten yards away; they were that close I couldn't miss them. I had no ammunition left. So I whipped the lock out of the gun and rolled down the hill. It was fairly steep so I got a good roll on, and got to the bottom. I heard shots coming from behind me so I ran in a zigzag and dived into the riverbank. I hadn't got a scratch on me.

Private 'Wally' Binch
Anti-Tank Platoon, 2nd/5th Battalion, Sherwood Foresters

Along came a second armoured car and Captain Walker fired and hit it. We saw people getting out of it. It must have been about three or four hundred yards away. Another came along and we hit it. Captain Walker was firing as fast as I could ram the rounds in. By now it was starting to get darker.

Sergeant James Drake
Platoon Sergeant, Machine-Gun Platoon, 16th Battalion, Durham Light Infantry

I moved down the riverbank and caught up with the Bren gunner and one or two others. The Germans did not follow up. We waited there, keeping the Bren on top of the bank. As it grew dark I thought it was time to move out. We followed the river for a bit, and then got on top and walked back towards Sedjenane. On our way back, one or two Rifle Company men were wandering about and I told them to tag on behind us. I heard moaning in a bush. I went to investigate, and it was an officer from a rifle company. He'd been shot in the back. So I called over one of the lads and we carried him back. We went on picking up more people. I went into company HQ and pushed my face in and they all looked amazed, and I said, 'Sergeant Drake reporting back, and there's twenty-four fellers outside from different companies, waifs and strays I've brought back with me, and an injured officer.' They said, 'You've been reported dead.'

'Well,' I said, 'I'm here and I'm all in one piece.'

Private 'Wally' Binch
Anti-Tank Platoon, 2nd/5th Battalion, Sherwood Foresters

An officer from battalion HQ came up and asked Captain Walker to turn the gun round and fire at people coming over the hill behind us. But they were out of sight and we could not engage them. The rest of the crew sat in the trench. At dusk there was talk of pulling out. I had borrowed a pair of binos from someone and looking through them I could see Jerries. I passed them to Captain Walker and he lined us all up, and told us to fire ten rounds rapid at the silhouettes we could see on the skyline. Then we were to go down into a wadi. By then I had got a rifle and a couple of grenades from somewhere. There was no sign of the original crew. There was a bit of panic in the air. We were getting away. I was happy to be still alive. We were all a bit frightened. Sergeant Mackay had a tommy gun and he went in front. We were a party of about fifty gathered up by Captain Walker, all sorts: some from battalion HQ. The firing mechanism still in my pocket was weighing me down, so I flung it away. I was terribly thirsty, and saw a pool of water, I stopped for a drink and when I looked up everybody had gone, except for a sergeant. Eventually we made our way to join the rest of the battalion, I can't remember how we found them. It was towards Sedjenane.

Sergeant James Drake
Platoon Sergeant, Machine-Gun Platoon, 16th Battalion,
Durham Light Infantry

The people in the HQ were pretty quiet. All I could make out was that the battalion had had a nasty battering and were in a pretty bad way. When I came out of the HQ I heard that two of our carriers had been bogged in further up the hill. So I took some lads and a couple of drivers and some chains, and we got both carriers back. By now it was daybreak. We got orders, and twenty of us were told to defend the village so that the Germans did not attack the village from that end. They were moving down the road from Bizerta towards Sedjenane. The object was to prevent them taking Sedjenane because some of our tanks were being brought up by train.

Lieutenant Denys Crews
Platoon Commander, 2nd/5th Battalion, Sherwood Foresters

I was trying to keep my men together as a platoon, and get back and find out what was happening. It got dark, and when I got to the road, I met a lot of stragglers who said that lots of people had been cut off. I got to B Echelon with most of my platoon, and the stragglers. Here I heard that most of the battalion had been cut off. I was told that the CO was up with the carrier platoon trying to find out what was happening. We had done no recces taking over the position. It was totally disorganised. We had occupied the positions in the dark.

Sergeant James Drake
Platoon Sergeant, Machine-Gun Platoon, 16th Battalion,
Durham Light Infantry

There were two officers – Captain Valence, Lieutenant Lacks – Sergeants Dunn, Hitch, Walton, myself, and various ORs. We had to defend between Sedjenane and the hills. The colonel gave us our instructions. He announced that I was to be in charge of the operation, and did anyone have any objections. There were none. I said we would go down the riverbank, and walk back and forth from the riverbank as far as a small village of Arab huts surrounded by a cactus hedge. I knew that one of the companies had stored some ammunition in the village. For an hour or more we did nothing but walk from the riverbank to the little village, and back again. I knew Jerry would be in the hills watching, but wouldn't know how many was in the village. After this we assembled amongst the cactus, round the village, and dug slit trenches there. From the village we took as much ammunition as we could for riflemen and Bren gunners.

When the shelling and mortaring started, I reckoned there wasn't much chance of being hit as we were well down in slit trenches. I had put a Bren on each flank, about fifty yards apart, so they could fire across our front in a crossfire. I gave strict instructions that *nobody* must fire a shot until I said so. I had a couple behind a small haystack at the back with rifles. The shell and mortar fire stopped. We were in the best position. They had to come over open ground. We waited, we waited, we waited and – sure enough – they came. They stood up and walked towards us. I waited until they got within a hundred yards before I gave a fire order. I said, 'Right lads, fire!' Both the Brens started and we simply mowed them down. They all fell flat. The Brens kept going, and we were getting very little fire back. Some rounds splattering through the cactus trees. I says, 'Right, if you see any movement in anyone, put a bullet in him.'

Sergeant Dunn counted aloud as he fired, and got up to twenty-eight. I shouted to him, 'Stop counting, Dunny, just keep knocking them down.' I got a call from one of the lads from the haystack, they could see some coming from that side. There was a little mound obscuring their view and I told Sergeant Aitcheson to take a Bren in front of this mound. He said there was too much fire. So I grabbed the gun and took it forward and ripped one or two mags off; there was plenty to fire at. I shouted to Lance Corporal Gibson to bring me more ammunition. He came up with more mags, I stuck another in the gun, put him behind the gun, and went back to the others.

By now the light was fading. We'd been there since first thing that morning, and fired a lot of ammunition. There was a bit of a lull in the encounter. We had used more or less all the ammunition. On both the Brens the barrels were bent, including the two spares. I knew the Germans would patrol. As it got dark the Germans fired tracer, and set the thatch on the stone-walled huts alight. This was all right, because we were safe in the stone-walled buildings, but it lit up the scene for us, and on any German patrol approaching, whereas they could not see clearly through the cactus. I took some grenades, and walked to the edge of the cactus, and sure enough a patrol came along, and threw the grenades. Then I called up the next bloke. We used up all the grenades. We had nothing more to fight with. I sent them off in fours. I told them to go in different directions, telling them, 'You all know where to go. There is a good chance that some of you will get back to report.'

Private 'Wally' Binch
Anti-Tank Platoon, 2nd/5th Battalion, Sherwood Foresters
I heard that the MT platoon had left a lot of the transport in Sedjenane woods. They asked for volunteers to bring it back. I volunteered because my ukulele was in my carrier, even though I couldn't drive. I found my carrier, and the ukulele was OK. I saw a motorcycle. I could drive a motorcycle, and got on it. It ran out of petrol, so I made my way back to the battalion on foot.

Corporal Dave Brooks
B Company, 2nd Parachute Battalion
We fondly thought that we were going for a rest. But no, trouble had broken out in the Tamera Valley at Sedjenane. The whole brigade was put into this area. We occupied a hill called Cork Wood. They came at us.

Major Vic Coxen
Officer Commanding, T Company, 1st Parachute Battalion
The enemy got almost right into battalion HQ before we knocked them off. Alastair led the cooks in a counter-attack. We got about four hundred German prisoners. The enemy came marching down the road; they thought we had all gone. We watched and waited until they were all in sight. We had four Vickers on them. We had a troop of 25-pounders, two medium guns, some mountain guns, and our own mortars; more than we normally had.

Corporal Dave Brooks
B Company, 2nd Parachute Battalion
In the end, the brigade had to withdraw two or three miles from Cork Wood. To do the withdrawal you had to go along the bank of a river in flood; not a nice journey. A couple of days later we re-took Cork Wood. During the course of the battle, I was wounded by a Messerschmitt. It made several passes in my section, it killed Bill Bacon and Mick Miles, and

wounded Ron Moon and myself. It made a terrific noise. I was hit on the first pass; through the thigh, in and out the other side. Fred Martin came galloping up and put me over his shoulder and took me to a hollow where the MO was working. There were a dozen or more wounded in this hollow. One of them had both his legs blown off. He was just making little moaning noises. The doc said to me, 'Give us your morphia.' I thought he's going to give me a dose of morphia. I asked him, 'Aren't you going to give me that?'

'You don't need it, laddie, you're not bad enough.'

I could stand. The doc told me to take myself and a wounded German to battalion HQ. I said that I couldn't get down the steep hill. He said, 'You bloody well can, because nobody else is going to take you down there. Get yourself down there.'

Lieutenant Colonel Alastair Pearson
Commanding Officer, 1st Parachute Battalion
The 2nd and 3rd Battalions had tried, and failed, to take Sidi Bou Della. The corps commander, General Charles Allfrey, came up and asked, 'Are you all right to take that hill?' I told him that two battalions had had a go and I would not. I thought the BGS would have a fit. I said, 'I'll make a bargain with you, sir.' 'What's that?' he said.

I said, 'I'll take it but I won't hold it; I've the strength to take it, but not to hold it.' He agreed, saying, 'That's fair enough. The 3rd Battalion is sitting by the side of the road, they can hold it after you've taken it.'

He asked when I would do it, and I said, 'Tonight, just after midnight.'

We had to cross the River Oued el Medene to get at it; a stinking, sluggish North African river that smelt like a sewer. The engineers built a temporary bridge across.

Major Vic Coxen
Officer Commanding, T Company, 1st Parachute Battalion
One of my platoons was full of Irishmen from the RUR. I was to be the leading company, and spent the day looking at the objective from our side of the river Oued el Medene, and that night I swam the river and got right up close. Not even a patrol came down. We fixed a bridge over the river with the sappers. I moved up on to the ridge, a convex hill, so we were covered as we moved up, because the enemy field of fire was limited to about twenty yards. I went up with my leading platoons in line, and one in reserve. I told my platoons, 'When the firing starts, none of this fire and movement stuff,

295

they'll be only twenty yards away, get straight in at once, right in on top of the buggers.' I had arranged for the artillery to shell the top of the hill every hour on the hour, at seven o'clock, eight o'clock, nine o'clock and so on, and at twelve o'clock we would be behind it. I banked on the enemy would have their heads down, having got used to the hourly shelling. It worked.

I said I thought I could take it but not hold it. Alastair pushed two companies round to protect my flanks. I sent out a patrol to see how far the Germans had gone back. The patrol had been out for about half an hour and not returned, so I went out with my batman. He said to me, 'I think we are getting stalked, sir.' I took a chance on it being the patrol I had sent out, and called out, 'Who's that down there?' A voice said, 'Glory be to God, I was just about to throw a grenade at youse.' It was Sergeant Birmingham, one of the Irish platoon. I said, 'There is no point in going any further as we are running into our own artillery fire.' So we returned to the company. At the bottom of the hill there was a field of stubble and as we were crossing it, Birmingham said to me, 'What shall I do with this grenade sir?' I asked him what he meant. He said that he had pulled the pin out, and was still holding it. I told him, 'Don't bother me, just throw the fucking thing away somewhere.' He just turned and threw it. We were out in the open; I shouted, 'Down!' We all threw ourselves flat. The base plug whirred over me. For two pins I would have knocked his head off.

Lieutenant Colonel Alastair Pearson
Commanding Officer, 1st Parachute Battalion
I took my whole battalion down the minute I saw 3 PARA come up. They were badly mortared.

From Alamein
to Akarit

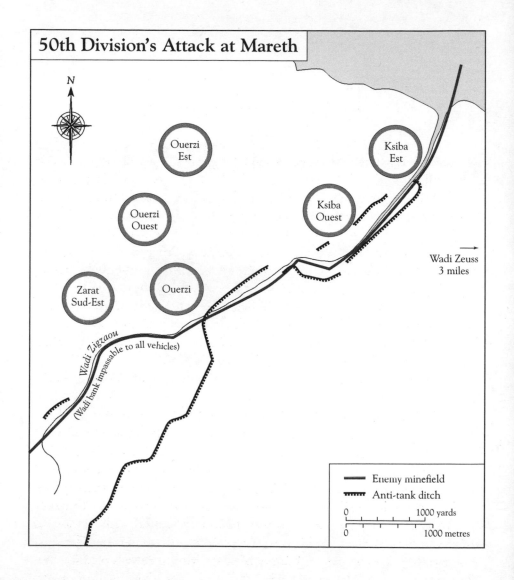

50th Division's Attack at Mareth

N

Ouerzi
Est

Ksiba
Est

Ouerzi
Ouest

Ksiba
Ouest

→
Wadi Zeuss
3 miles

Zarat
Sud-Est

Ouerzi

Wadi Zigzaou

(Wadi bank impassable to all vehicles)

—— Enemy minefield

⊓⊓⊓⊓ Anti-tank ditch

0   1000 yards

0   1000 metres

Typical of war, nothing went to plan.

After the Battle of Alamein, Rommel retreated west along the coast road, fighting a series of rearguard actions. Soon after Alamein, the Eighth Army's pursuit was badly hampered by heavy rain. Moreover, the logistic constraints that every commander in the desert war encountered when moving away from his base began to work against Montgomery, who was hauling his supplies over ever-increasing distances as he advanced into Tunisia all the way from his base in the Nile delta. Capturing Tobruk, Benghazi and Tripoli enabled supplies to be brought some of the way by sea, but they still had to be trucked forward from the port. Rommel had his problems too, chiefly having to look two ways: towards the Allied First Army in Tunisia, and Eighth Army advancing through Libya and eventually into southern Tunisia.

Rommel had been forced to retreat in the face of Montgomery's advance, and finally, because of ill health, he left North Africa on 6 March, being replaced by Colonel General Jurgen von Arnim. The rearguard battles fought by the Germans under both Rommel and von Arnim inflicted considerable casualties on men and materiel in the Eighth Army. Some historians – and some soldiers, notably Americans – have criticised Montgomery for being over-cautious and not dashing full tilt after Rommel, especially in the immediate aftermath of Alamein. Even in retreat the German army was a force to reckon with, one with which you took tactical liberties at your peril. Nowhere did the Germans demonstrate this more clearly than at Mareth. Montgomery's plan for the frontal assault on Mareth smacks of being less than well thought through. The attack eventually failed; not for lack of effort on the part of his soldiers. Only Montgomery's audacious plan to outflank the position through the Matmata Hills eventually saved the day.

The battle at Wadi Akarit could have been a repeat of Mareth, had it not been for the bold night infiltration tactics by the 4th Indian Division under the redoubtable Major General 'Gertie' Tuker.

One of the outstanding divisions in the Eighth Army was the 7th Armoured, whose formation sign was the desert rat, or jerboa – a secretive nocturnal mammal which survives in inhospitable desert, hiding by day in shallow burrows. Many people talk about the whole of Eighth Army as 'the Desert Rats'. Strictly speaking, the epithet applies only to the 7th Armoured Division. They had played a leading part in inflicting a crushing defeat on the Italians in 1940. Their commander at Alamein, and for the opening phases of the subsequent pursuit, was Major General John Harding, who had been BGS for Lieutenant General O'Connor in that campaign.

Major General John Harding
General Officer Commanding, 7th Armoured Division
We bypassed Tobruk and went straight across the desert, ran into the enemy rearguard at Agedabia, fought them, they withdrew. We pushed on again to El Agheila. We were held up at Agheila by a strong German defensive position. Reinforcements were sent up, and I got a brigade of the 51st Division under my command to break through. We did, and advanced to the south of Buerat in Tripolitania. There we halted to resupply. I wanted to continue on our own, when we were at the bottom of the Gulf of Sirte. But Monty said 'No'. He was determined not to allow what had happened on the two previous occasions, when a successful offensive had ended in being driven back.

Lieutenant John Semken
Troop Leader, The Nottinghamshire Yeomanry (Sherwood Rangers)
Our next move was on transporters to Benghazi. We had lost a hell of a lot of people. We thought that after Alamein we would be pulled out, lick our wounds and go back to Cairo for a bath and a good dinner. But in fact I didn't get a bath for five months. We re-equipped with two squadrons of Shermans, and one of Crusaders, and got rid of the Grants.

Trooper John Lanes
Wireless Operator, The Nottinghamshire Yeomanry (Sherwood Rangers)
Tripoli was our goal. As we were going up to Wadi Zemzem it was half light in the morning. Out on our left somebody was fighting, and we were sent across to investigate; it was the Scots Greys and the New Zealanders. I was

Trooper John Lanes.

with Lieutenant Stockton. We joined the rest of the squadron, and were hit there. Nobody was actually hurt by the explosion. Lieutenant Stockton was blown off the tank and for a few minutes he was stunned. We lay down, in the tracks made by our tank in the sand, until it got dark, then looked at the tank to see what needed doing; it had to be taken back for repair.

Lieutenant John Semken
Troop Leader, The Nottinghamshire Yeomanry (Sherwood Rangers)
At the Wadi Zemzem we lost eleven tanks in one hour. I lost some very good friends. A German tank destroyed my tank. I got a bit burnt. One of my crew was burnt to death, another died of his burns; the other two were in hospital for about four months. At the time I was knocked out my gun was out of action. The shell cases of the 75 mm were very thin. If dented, the round would jam when you tried to put it in the breech. Then, if you opened the breech, the claws pulled the round out at an angle, tearing the shell case away from the projectile. So you ended with a brass shell case in your hand, a scatter of propellant charge over the floor of the turret, and a round up the breech you couldn't get out, except by getting out of the tank, and pushing it out using a cleaning rod from the front end of the gun. It is very unpleasant meeting a German tank at short range when you haven't got a gun that works.

Major General John Harding
General Officer Commanding, 7th Armoured Division
Eventually we drove the Germans back and were fighting them at Tarhuna, which was the last rearguard position they could hold without evacuating Tripoli. We had covered about six hundred miles, so we hadn't done too badly.

I was in a hurry. For two and a half years I had been trying to get to Tripoli. My leading armoured brigade was held up by German anti-tank positions at Tarhuna. My plan was to outflank them in the south. It was pretty rough country – broken, hilly, with wadis and desert. The armoured brigade was fully engaged. The field artillery had deployed in action, and was being severely shelled by the German guns. Because of the difficult going, the medium regiment had difficulty getting forward at the same pace as the rest of the division, and was quite far back. I was anxious to get them up to start firing counter-battery and neutralise the impact of the German artillery, which were pinning my chaps down. So I went up in my Tac HQ, which consisted of a couple of cut-down Honey tanks. My forward control wireless was jamming my armoured brigade rear link, so I couldn't talk to them. So I left my two tanks and walked across and sat on the turret of the brigade commander's tank, which was just hull-down, in order to find out what was going on. As I was about to get off his tank I noticed a new German battery, which I hadn't seen before, open up just to my right. I put my binoculars up to see if I could spot exactly where it was, when 'crump crump crump', a 'stonk' fell just in front of us, one of the shells burst all over the tank. The brigade commander and brigade major dropped down inside the tank. I was left on the outside, and got plastered with shrapnel, across my legs and middle. I slid down and took cover by the tank. The others got the doctor up. I had on a new pair of cavalry twill trousers I was rather pleased with, and in order to get at the wounds they cut them off. I was rather annoyed. Then Mike Carver, my GSO1, got on to the RAF who sent in a light aircraft to pick me up. The doctor had told him that I wouldn't survive being evacuated by ambulance. So they cleared a strip and an aircraft came in under fighter cover. A mobile surgical team came in and they picked me up and took me back to the New Zealand field dressing station. I had a hole in my right knee, the thigh muscles in both legs were torn, and three fingers of my left hand blown off.

Lieutenant John Semken
Troop Leader, The Nottinghamshire Yeomanry (Sherwood Rangers)
After Zemzem we took Tripoli. By this time I was feeling low. You can only live on adrenalin for so long. I had lost most of my close friends. It looked as if it was going on and on and on like a dripping tap. I was sent back on a course to Cairo, because they had worked it out that I was the only officer in the regiment who hadn't been out of the fighting since we had begun.

Corporal Clifford Wrigglesworth
C Squadron, The Queen's Own Yorkshire Dragoons
I was sent on a recce patrol of two sections of 15-hundredweight trucks. It was bright moonlight; we must have been spotted and we were mortared. I was wounded; the others in my section were wounded or killed. I don't know where the other section went. Then a machine gun opened up. I was wounded in the knee. I didn't lose consciousness; I could hear one of the other fellows moaning. I sat there dazed. I could see blood running down my leg in the moonlight. I took my jacket and cardigan off, tore my shirt into strips and put a tourniquet on my leg. I sat there all night. Easing the tourniquet and tightening it up, I had put a field dressing on my wound but the dressing just disappeared inside the wound. It was rather a bad wound.

I sat there from about two o'clock in the morning to about ten o'clock, when four or five Italian soldiers came over the hill and cautiously approached. They had a conversation which I didn't understand, as I don't speak Italian. One of them disappeared and in due course appeared with a stretcher. They put me on it, carried me away and put me in a tent. I was in a pretty bad way. After a couple of hours two fellows, whom I assumed were doctors, came and had a look at me; shook their heads, and went away. Then a priest, who spoke English, came in and asked me my army number, which I gave him. He mumbled some prayers over me, and went out. The two doctors came in, I was carried to another tent, laid on a table, and they took my leg off. They didn't bother with anaesthetic, just took it off halfway between the knee and the groin. I think I was in such shock that I didn't feel much pain. The amputation was not as bad as the pain after. I was carried back into the other tent and left on a stretcher. I had various other wounds: shrapnel down the side of my face taking a lot of skin off, and several pieces in my throat. All I had on was my cardigan. I was there for about two days. They put me on a 15-hundredweight truck and took me with them as they retreated in front of the Allies. Why they didn't leave me behind I don't know. This went on for two weeks. I really suffered during these journeys, bouncing about in this truck. They dressed the stump about once a week. They never dressed the rest of my wounds, or even washed me. I arrived at Sfax, still on this stretcher, and was laid on the ground in the docks. After a while they laid the stretcher in the bottom of a lighter, and I was taken out to a hospital ship. The sea was rough, water came into the lighter and surged about in the bottom. I was glad to get to the ship, and put in a bunk. Someone washed me, the first time since being captured. Dressings were put on my face. In due course we arrived in Naples.

Captain Peter Lewis
Officer Commanding, B Company, 8th Battalion,
Durham Light Infantry
On 13 March the battalion arrived in a reserve area only a few miles behind the main body of Eighth Army. We had arrived at Mareth. It was a mini Maginot Line; the system of defences was unique in the North African war. Nobody had come up against anything like it before. It had originally been built by the French to protect Tunisia against attack by the Italians from Libya. It ran from the coast to the Matmata Hills. On the coastal sector, the defences were based on the Wadi Zigzaou, which we called the Wadi 'Zigzag'. It had been widened and deepened to form a colossal, natural, anti-tank ditch. The wadi was covered by enfilade fire along its entire length from concrete pillboxes, gun emplacements and blockhouses. These were all supported by a

deep trench system with dugouts. On the far side of the wadi, and before getting to the blockhouses, there was an anti-tank ditch twelve feet deep and fifteen wide, between the wadi and the main defence line. The whole area was heavily sown with Teller mines, the big German anti-vehicle mines, and AP mines and shrapnel mines. On 19 March we got a good briefing.

Captain Ian English
Officer Commanding, C Company, 8th Battalion,
Durham Light Infantry
The plan was for XXX Corps with 50 Division and 23rd Armoured Brigade under command to do a frontal attack on the coastal sector. The 69th Brigade was to seize the strongpoints on our side of the wadi. Our 151st Brigade, the Durhams, was to capture some strongpoints known as Zurat Sudest, Ouerzi, Ouerzi Ouest, Ouerzi Est and Ksiba Ouest. The sappers were to bridge the wadi and get the armour across.

Captain Peter Lewis
Officer Commanding, B Company, 8th Battalion,
Durham Light Infantry
We needed more information on the troops in the area and how best to get across the Wadi Zigzag. It had very steep banks on either side, almost unscaleable. Two patrols went out at night almost as far as the wadi, but not to the banks. Both reported that, as far as they could see, there was no minefield on our side of the wadi. They were able to recce the most suitable crossing places.

Lieutenant 'Scotty' White
Officer Commanding, 11 Platoon, B Company, 9th Battalion,
Durham Light Infantry
I went out on patrol the night before the attack on our side of the wadi to locate mines. We prodded with our bayonets, but didn't find any anti-personnel mines, only anti-tank mines. I was asked if I had got into the bed of the wadi, and I said 'No'.

Captain Peter Lewis
Officer Commanding, B Company, 8th Battalion,
Durham Light Infantry
The CO gave his orders on 19 March after the two recces. He told us that the 9th Battalion would be on the right flank of the brigade attack to capture one of the forts. The 8th, left of the 9th, had to take the Ouerzi Fort

and a strongpoint known as Little Ouerzi. When these had been gained, the Valentines would cross, followed by the 6th DLI, who would attack through the 8th and 9th to extend the depth of the bridgehead. We were told that, as usual, the Italians held most of the line, including Bersaglieri troops of the Young Fascist Division. The Germans were in the vital places. Our old adversaries of Gazala and Alamein, the 90th Light Division, were astride the main road in the area of the forts, and in reserve behind them was the whole of the 15th Panzer Division, an intimidating picture. The battalion plan was for C Company on the right to take Little Ouerzi and A Company on the left to take Ouerzi. My company was to be held in reserve to support A Company, when called forward. Both assault companies, A and C, had a Scorpion tank. This was the first time we had worked with Scorpions. They were flail tanks. They made such cloud of dust that they temporarily blinded themselves and anyone near. They moved at a walking pace when using their flails. These had to leave a cleared lane to the wadi to allow the infantry to get to the wadi. They couldn't cross the wadi until the sappers had bridged it. It was decided that the leading companies would advance behind the Scorpions in threes – highly unpopular. But it was considered the only safe thing to do. There was lot of moaning about it.

In his orders, Colonel Jackson came out with something that shook us all rigid. He said, 'We are going to want someone with a lantern to walk in front of the Scorpions to lead them when the barrage starts.' There was a dead silence. It was a suicide mission. The Scorpions were massive things and would draw the fire of everything within range. But the Scorpions wouldn't get to the wadi without a guide because they would blind themselves, and without them to clear the mines, the infantry might not get to the wadi. We company commanders weren't going to be picked for this. But there were quite a lot of others there from other parts of battalion who wondered who would be selected. After looking around, the CO said, 'This is a job for Lieutenant Douglas.' He was 2IC of the carrier platoon. He went white as a sheet. His face was a picture, and everybody laughed. We weren't laughing at Bill Douglas, but out of relief that we hadn't been chosen for this awful job.

Lieutenant Colonel William Watson
Commanding Officer, 6th Battalion, Durham Light Infantry
The 8th and 9th were told to take scaling ladders with them to help get in and out of the wadi, and also to descend into and climb out of the anti-tank ditch which was very deep, and only a matter of yards from the wadi itself. On the far side of the anti-tank ditch the ground rose appreciably. Just

A Scorpion flail tank.

opposite us was a very big fortified position, a labyrinth of trenches and pill-boxes. On the home side, our side, the ground rose again. You could not go and look into the Wadi Zigzaou unless you went right up to the rim, which was impossible because it was covered by enemy observation and fire. We had a French officer who described it as best he could; he had taken part in the building of the defences. There were one or two palm trees on the home side, and quite a sprinkling of palms on the other side, and on the top of the ridge, sufficient to hide a German counter-attack force.

Captain Peter Lewis
Officer Commanding, B Company, 8th Battalion,
Durham Light Infantry
The morning of 20 March was a lovely clear day. Just before midday, eighteen medium bombers flew over us. We could hear the intense German ack-ack. One of the bombers was hit. We watched the crew bale out; it wasn't far off. You watched with detached indifference. We felt sorry for the guys in the plane, but it wasn't happening to us.

In the afternoon the company commanders were taken up to have a closer look at the wadi and the enemy defences on the far side; not at the bit we were going to attack, but to give us an idea of what we would face in our sector. We had to crawl on our bellies to a 5th East Yorks section post a few hundred yards from the wadi. The East Yorks section commander was thoroughly fed up. He'd had the divisional commander up there, the brigade commander, the COs of each of the Durham battalions. As a result, his little post had been shelled several times, fortunately without causing any casualties. He said he didn't mind if people kept their heads down, but when the divisional commander and brigadier came up they bobbed about all over the place and didn't even take their red-banded hats off.

With our binos we could see the anti-tank ditch on the other side, the barbed wire, the concrete emplacements, the forts and the ground. The forts were underground, and apertures just above ground level, like a dug-in tank. The defence layout looked very difficult to clear properly and not guarantee that the enemy wouldn't keep coming back.

Captain Ian English
Officer Commanding, C Company, 8th Battalion,
Durham Light Infantry
We had a good view of the wadi, which was wider than we thought. The rains had swollen it, and we could see that it was about thirty feet wide and had

steep sides. We could see the strongpoints beyond. We had a French officer visit us that morning who went through some of the details with us. We also had a defence overprint map. This showed the gun emplacements. The main strongpoints like Ksiba Ouest and Ouerzi were extremely strong: concrete pillboxes, gun emplacements, and well-concealed communication trenches.

My company plan was to advance to the wadi in threes, with company Tac HQ consisting of myself, batman, a runner, and the sappers leading. Then would follow: 13, 14, and 15 platoons and the company rear HQ. My platoon commanders were Lieutenant Rory O'Connor 13 Platoon, he'd arrived after Alamein; Lieutenant Johnstone 14 platoon, who hadn't been with us very long; and Lieutenant Roberts of 15 platoon who had been with us for some time and had been at Alamein. Company 2IC was Harry Welsh, and I still had the redoubtable CSM Ransome who had won an MM at Alamein. After crossing the anti-tank ditch the company was to fan out with 14 Platoon right, 13 left and 15 in rear. H-Hour was 2230 hours on 20 March 1943.

Captain Peter Lewis
Officer Commanding, B Company, 8th Battalion,
Durham Light Infantry
Before any big show a number of officers and experienced troops were left out of battle or 'LOB', to form first-line reinforcements; this usually included the 2IC. Bob Lidwill, who had joined the battalion at Alamein, and had done extremely well, was by that time the 2IC of the 8th. He wouldn't stay back LOB, and came forward to keep himself in the picture.

Captain Ian English
Officer Commanding, C Company, 8th Battalion,
Durham Light Infantry
We left the Assembly Area, in the Wadi Zeuss, at about 1945 hours; the moon was coming up and we had good visibility. After the marching rifle companies came a convoy of jeeps, carrying two-inch mortars, wireless sets and canisters of hot cocoa. It was 2130 before we reached the FUP. This had been recced and marked with white tape by the IO. As we had some time before the attack started, people tried to get some sleep. This was rudely interrupted when an engineer three-ton lorry arrived at the FUP carrying scaling ladders, which we needed to cross the anti-tank ditch. It was a noisy vehicle attracting enemy harassing fire. One shell hit the truck, setting it alight. That brought down more fire on us. We hadn't dug slit trenches and people were lying on the ground in the open. Two men were wounded.

We were able to retrieve the scaling ladders from the truck and these were put on the Scorpions to be taken as far as the wadi. They were heavy, it took eight men to carry one. Time went on, there was still no sign of the jeeps. Soon it became clear that they weren't going to arrive, so no hot drink, no two-inch mortars and no wireless sets, but the 296 Battery commander, Major Guy Fawkes, came to the rescue and lent us some Number 18 sets, one to A Company and one to C. They were quickly netted in.

The barrage started at 2230, initially in support of the attack on our left. There was tremendous noise. We could also hear the rat-tat-tat of the 2nd Cheshires' machine guns shooting over our heads.

Lieutenant 'Scotty' White
Officer Commanding, 11 Platoon, B Company, 9th Battalion,
Durham Light Infantry

At H-Hour the attack started and we were shelled from the beginning. The Sappers in the truck with the Bangalore torpedoes were hit by a shell and blown up. Teddy led the attack. My platoon was behind him, moving in a double file within the confines of the path behind the Scorpion. We went up a slope, not a big one, and on the crest overlooking the wadi, Teddy was hit: a bullet through the fleshy part of his chest, very lucky. We got him patched up, and I asked him if he was going back. He said, 'No, I'm not missing this.' We went down into the wadi. Small-arms fire started coming in. We crossed at a fair lick. At the far side we formed a human pyramid, which we had rehearsed; it went like clockwork. Lifting Teddy up was a problem. He was fifteen stone, but a tough fellow, he didn't even whimper. Next we had to cross the anti-tank ditch. We made another human pyramid, got Teddy to the top. Now we encountered wire, the barrier to the fort itself. We took cover behind some rocks and a tree. We fired at the fort and anything we could see. A corporal cut the wire, and Teddy said, 'Come on.' We dropped into a communication trench and ran along it, throwing grenades at enemy we encountered. I had been hit below the ankle, only a minor wound. Teddy had put Bren guns on top of the trench firing at the fort.

The opposition was Italians, from the Young Fascist Division. They had no stomach for hand-to-hand fighting. They ran off in all directions. We came across some heavy steel doors built into the side of the communication trench. They weren't locked. I thumped on them, and shouted, 'Come out.' Masses came out and surrendered. We'd achieved our first objective. I said to Teddy, 'It's time for you to get back.' He didn't.

Lieutenant Colonel William Watson
Commanding Officer, 6th Battalion, Durham Light Infantry

It was a clear moonlit night, a full African moon. We set off in a snake-like formation to cross the mud flats, then to climb up through the gap in the minefields, up on to the ridge; turn left along the ridge to join up with our transport: mortar platoon, carriers, anti-tank guns and ambulances. These had gone round by the main road and up another track to join us.

As we climbed through the minefield, all hell was let loose as the 8th and 9th attacked. The enemy retaliated by shelling us on the ridge. The noise and dust was awful. We just lay where we were in this gap in the minefield. We couldn't get up on the ridge because of the shelling. One of my signallers was killed next to me. Another chap went berserk and had to be held down by the adjutant. It was appalling just lying there being shelled to hell. Finally as we lay there, the brigade IO said we had to stay there. We couldn't spread out on account of the minefield on either side of us. It was like a country lane it was so narrow and the whole battalion was in a long snake along the track and back to the mud flats.

Captain Ian English
Officer Commanding, C Company, 8th Battalion, Durham Light Infantry

Thirty-five minutes after the barrage started the companies moved off in threes towards the wadi following a white tape; through an olive grove, over a little crest and crossed the Start Line. The CO came up to me and said, 'These damn Scorpions are going too slowly, we're going to lose the barrage, there are no mines here anyway.' Just as he said that, there was big explosion in front of a Scorpion, which had set off a mine, so we decided to follow them after all.

As we got over a ridge we could see the wadi gleaming in the moonlight, the darker areas beyond, and the tracer from German positions behind all going over our heads and not causing us any bother. As we got to the wadi we took the scaling ladders off the Scorpions. At that moment, two shells landed very close to us, wounding three men and two platoon sergeants. Peter Wakeling, the FOO, reckoned a couple of our guns were dropping short throughout the barrage; there was nothing he could do about it. This shook the men up a bit and they lost faith in our barrage. It was quite a job to get them moving forward again.

We came to the wadi and found it deeper than we thought it would be, up to our knees wading, and also it seemed wider than we had been told. When we got to the other side we halted to check that everybody was there. We crossed the ground on the way to the anti-tank ditch. We knew this was mined, and the sappers began to swing their mine detectors. But it was hopeless because there was so much metal about from pieces of shells, and the noise of the barrage made it difficult to hear the sound in their earphones telling them that there was a possible mine ahead. We just had to go on. There was lot of enemy shelling, some of it landed among the sappers, killing the corporal and one of his men, as well as killing or wounding about six of the company. We reached the anti-tank ditch and flung a couple of ladders across, it was fifteen feet wide and twelve feet deep, and without the ladders we would not have been able to cross it. The ladders were long enough to bridge the gap. Once across, the barrage paused, and we shook out into a proper attacking formation. The change that came over the chaps was remarkable. Advancing in threes was so uncomfortable, and once they shook out, their attacking spirit returned and away we went. We could hear Bren-gun fire and small-arms fire on our right, which we judged to be the 9th attacking Ksiba Ouest.

There wasn't much opposition to us. After going about eight hundred yards we came to a road, and checked on my map that this was our objective, with Little Ouerzi just beyond it. At that moment a concentration of our own artillery came down, most uncomfortable. The only casualty was Harry Johnstone, a shell so concussed him he couldn't take any further part in the battle. We sent up the success signals using Very lights; the rockets we should have had didn't arrive. The signaller, Lance Corporal Simpson, confirmed success over the RT set, which was working well.

Captain Peter Lewis
Officer Commanding, B Company, 8th Battalion,
Durham Light Infantry
After the two leading companies and the CO went off ahead, no further orders came back. There was some machine-gun fire and shellfire. Most of it on the wadi, but one of my platoon commanders was killed by a burst of machine-gun fire. Just bad luck; it was obviously just a searching shoot. So before the battle started, that's one platoon commander gone. The CO was down in the wadi, missing. So I decided that, without being ordered to do so, I would carry out the original plan, take my company down, cross the Zigzaou and reinforce A Company. We didn't have a mine-detecting team with us. So I got the officers and NCOs together and told them we would have to run the gauntlet and take a chance with the mines; both on the far and near side of the Wadi. But the important thing was to get across without

delay and reinforce A Company on the far side. They accepted it, as British troops usually do. I led the company in single file with my leading platoon Doug Pinkney, who had only recently joined us.

I didn't know Doug Pinkney well, but he had said to me, after company orders, 'I'm not going to make it tonight. I won't come through.'

I said, 'Of course you will.'

He replied, 'Oh no, I'm not going to make it through the night.'

He definitely had a premonition. This was the only time I came across it, myself. By the time we got to the wadi, the enemy gunfire had slackened and the leading section waded through the muddy water to the far side. I knelt down to speak to Shepherd, an A Company platoon commander who had been wounded. He had managed to scrape out a shelter, but he had been wounded again. I bent right down and put my ear right next to his mouth, he was trying to give me some information about where A Company had gone. He hadn't said more than a few words before Pinkney, walking behind me, trod on a mine, killing him. The shrapnel wounded me, killed or wounded most of company Tac HQ, and attracted an immediate fierce concentration of mortar, artillery and machine-gun fire. The company 2IC, Foster Gedge, was wounded by artillery or mortar fire; he had come up from the rear of the company when he heard the mine explode, and was running up to me. My CSM crawled out to try and drag him into cover under the lip of the wadi but there was a hail of machine-gun fire so Branagan couldn't get to him. He tried again. He reached Gedge, dragged him to safety, and found he had died of his wounds. This left one officer, Jim Randall. While Branagan positioned the Bren guns, Randall came across to me, and I told him to take the company, cross the anti-tank ditch, and join A Company in Ouerzi. He and Branagan took the company forward and left the wounded in the wadi. There was very little cover. There followed several minutes of intense artillery and machine-gun fire enfilading the whole wadi. There was nothing you could do about it. When the firing finished there weren't many people left alive. I had collected quite a few pieces of shrapnel, including a piece about the size of a large coin embedded in my neck, and a piece behind my right ear. After talking to Branagan, the next thing I remember was Andrew Noble, the battalion MO, leaning over me in the RAP.

Lieutenant Colonel William Watson
Commanding Officer, 6th Battalion, Durham Light Infantry
Later, in a lull, we were able to move on to the ridge and turn right to go down to the wadi itself. Here we met the 9th Battalion transport trying hard

to get down into the wadi. So we had to stop there. Finally the brigade IO, Gerry Mansell, came up to me at about 0525 and said we were to return to our Assembly Area. Things had gone so stickily, there wasn't time for us to carry out our role. So we turned and marched the whole way back to the Wadi Zeuss. I had had twelve or fourteen killed or wounded without us firing a shot.

Captain Ian English
Officer Commanding, C Company, 8th Battalion,
Durham Light Infantry
At first light on 21 March, everything seemed to be pretty quiet. We could see, about five hundred yards to our front, an enemy strongpoint containing a 20-mm gun. It was obvious that 6th DLI had not come through as they should have done. We had most of our ammunition, and each man was carrying a tin of bully beef and a packet of biscuits so we were all right for at least a day. During the morning British bombers came over again and pounded the enemy rear areas. As things were pretty quiet I sent Captain Walsh back to battalion HQ taking walking wounded with him. I told him to report our position to the CO, and made a plea for anti-tank guns to be sent up and a mortar OP party if possible.

We were shelled by the 20-mm gun from time to time, but our Brens seemed to keep it quiet for most of the time. Meanwhile the crossing place over the wadi was being heavily shelled all day. Busty Roberts, commanding 15 Platoon, reported Italian infantry forming up for an attack. We stood-to, and informed battalion HQ over the wireless. Captain Wakeling, our FOO, made this a battery target for his guns. When his CO heard this, he made it a regimental target, and the fire of all thirty-six guns landed on these Italians who seemed to be in about battalion strength. They were caught in the open, hadn't advanced very far, and the artillery fire completely broke up the attack. About eighty prisoners were taken, some came into our positions, most into the 9 DLI position, C Company hadn't fired a shot. We wirelessed our thanks to the gunners.

In the evening Captain Welsh returned and brought with him food that was most welcome. But the news he brought wasn't. He told us that the CO, the IO, and Lieutenants Cantley and Bailey had been killed. The 2IC, who had taken over, had been wounded, as had two other company commanders, Chris Beattie and Peter Lewis. Major Lidwill, who had been LOB, much to his annoyance, but had crept into every conference he could – and a good thing too, because he was to take an active part in the battle – was acting as

CO. A and B Companies had been amalgamated. The 6th DLI was to attack that night at 2200 hours, and the 5th East Yorks were to attack Ksiba Ouest. Meanwhile, the Royal Engineers were to complete the crossing over the wadi, and the rest of 50th RTR was to cross. Only three tanks got across the first night. They were to be followed by the battalion support weapons, carriers, mortars and anti-tank guns. We were probably no more than five hundred yards in a direct line from the wadi, so the bridgehead was not deep.

Lieutenant Colonel William Watson
Commanding Officer, 6th Battalion, Durham Light Infantry

Next night we tried again. We went along the track up on to the ridge and down into the wadi. We weren't interfered with in any way. When I got to the wadi, Andrew Clarke, the CO of the 9th Battalion, came out of a hole in the ground and said, 'It's no good going across like that in formation, you've got to cross in dribs and drabs, because there are Germans hidden in all these slit trenches and holes in the ground on the far side, and they'll shoot you up.'

That delayed the operation considerably, as each company trickled across the wadi on to the far side. It was bright moonlight. There was a slight re-entrant leading up to the high ground and I sited battalion HQ in the bottom of this. It was beyond the anti-tank ditch, and beyond where the 8th and 9th Battalions were. We managed to get out there in fairly good form. But there were snipers all over the place. Andrew Wilmot got hit in the neck, and as his chaps were trying to get him out, he was killed by a second shot. The enemy were concealed everywhere. The RAP was in the wadi itself, up against the bank on our side, not in the water, there were the odd dry bits here and there. To add to our difficulties our wireless sets wouldn't work, and never did. The shelling cut any telephone cables we attempted to lay. Throughout the battle we had no communications to the rear. Added to this our gunners shelled us. The FOO of 74th Field Regiment went off his head and I had to send him back. His wireless set was knocked out.

Private Harry Wilkinson
13 Platoon, C Company, 6th Battalion, Durham Light Infantry

Mareth was my first battle. The word came to go forward and we advanced in extended line. We were two or three yards apart. Then in a bit of a dip to our left, somebody trod on a mine, there was a flash, screams; we couldn't see what happened to them. We shouted for stretcher-bearers, and went on. We had been told not to stop for wounded, and press on. What happened to them I don't know. One of the first men I actually saw wounded was coming back shouting for his mother, without one leg and hobbling along. It was grotesque. It affected me briefly, but I had to put it out of my mind. We came down the slope to the wadi itself and waded through the water, and a couple of tanks were crossing behind us on brushwood.

Lieutenant Colonel William Watson
Commanding Officer, 6th Battalion, Durham Light Infantry
Then next morning the tanks came down, each carrying a huge fascine made of palm branches and they dropped these into the wadi to make a causeway across it. Some tanks got across. They only had six-pounder guns and the Germans had Tigers. Within a short time our tanks were blown to hell. We were warned, about eleven o'clock, that German infantry and tanks were lining up for a counter-attack. That started at about one o'clock. The brigadier arrived at main battalion HQ and said, 'You've got to hold and fight to the last round.' But we were running short of ammunition. The tanks that did get across smashed the fascines, and one of my carriers, the first I tried to get across, tipped off the fascine causeway into the wadi, drowned the engine and soaked the load.

Private Harry Wilkinson
13 Platoon, C Company, 6th Battalion, Durham Light Infantry
We got across the other side, met the other wall, which was much steeper, and climbed it. I saw some chaps in a trench to our right, one was a Geordie called Purdy, who smoked a pipe upside down. They were absolutely still in the trench, killed by the blast of a shell. As we were going forward we dropped into a German trench; we set up the Bren gun on the lip. It was my turn on it. A mortar bomb dropped close and blew the gun over into the sand, so I had to scramble out to get it clean and working again, and I got back to the trench. The number one on the Bren was a Tynesider, called Chandler, and his number two was a chap called Spendlove, I was number three. I got back to Chandler to tell him what had happened, looked up and saw one of our tanks. It was about to pass straight over us. I shouted out, 'Down Chan,' and ducked down inside the trench, but Chandler threw himself forward on the parapet. The tank went over him, missed him, but halfway over, swung left, and ground him into the earth, squashed him. The tank chap looked down, saw what had happened, stopped, and shouted, 'Sorry mate, couldn't help it.' So that was that.

Lieutenant 'Scotty' White
Officer Commanding, 11 Platoon, B Company, 9th Battalion, Durham Light Infantry

We had to get forward to clear the ridge to take the pressure of the rest of the brigade. During the hours of daylight we could barely move. I lost my sergeant and two corporals to artillery fire, I suspect our artillery fire; our FOO was engaging a machine-gun post and I think he made a mistake.

That night we went in to attack the ridge. The firing was tremendous, so we dropped into some nearby trenches but the 6th Battalion was in them and they turfed us out. So we went forward, it wasn't bad, the fire was going over our heads. Suddenly I realised that a machine gun ahead of us was firing, but not at us. I led the attack through a gap in the wire. My ankle was beginning to hurt and it was quite difficult to move quickly, I moved at a fast hobble. A few yards inside the wire I saw a deep communication trench, jumped into it as I thought this would lead me to the gun. But in the dark I didn't realise how deep it was. I landed badly, and my ankle hurt excruciatingly. The gun seemed to have stopped firing, so I moved along the trench, it seemed to go on forever, probably fifty yards. I saw a recess in the wall of the trench. This was the back of the machine-gun position. I saw a bloke. I watched for a bit, and realised he must be dead. I looked, there were four men in there, all dead. The machine gun was on a tripod, and there was another piece of equipment, it might have been a range finder. I couldn't see how they had been killed. It was a dugout, but with only a tarpaulin as cover, not shell proof. Perhaps they were killed by an airburst.

Captain Ian English
Officer Commanding, C Company, 8th Battalion, Durham Light Infantry

The 6th DLI went in. We had no news of its success or otherwise, but at dawn we could see them out in positions in front of us. We also heard tanks moving, this was 50th RTR attempting to move out towards the enemy, but they were held up by anti-tank guns and mines. Captain Wakeling was ordered to leave us, and become an FOO for the tanks to try to help them move forward. Morale was pretty good because of the recent attacks, the enemy were pushed back a bit, and we could move about reasonably freely. Our company strength was four officers and sixty-five ORs. We had started the attack with ninety-three all ranks.

Lieutenant 'Scotty' White
Officer Commanding, 11 Platoon, B Company, 9th Battalion,
Durham Light Infantry

A lad had detached himself from my platoon and come with me, but then I lost him. I had a quick look round, and by now it was daylight, and we were getting thumped. I was making my way along the trench when I saw their tanks coming and some German infantry coming past my position. I decided to keep my head down and try to get back to the wadi under the cover of darkness. My thought was that I had cocked it up again. I had attacked a machine gun that had already been knocked out. I sat watching the German infantry. I had two rounds left. I threw a grenade at the tank. Round the corner came two Germans. They laughed. I must have looked a sight. They helped me out of the trench and took me to the aid post.

Captain Ian English
Officer Commanding, C Company, 8th Battalion,
Durham Light Infantry

At about midday, we heard over the wireless that air recce had spotted about seventy-five tanks with infantry moving up in the area of Zarat. This was plainly a counter-attack coming fairly soon. Again I requested anti-tank guns; I was confident that if we had well-sited anti-tank guns we could hold the position. A request for three-inch mortar targets to be registered came in. We did this. We made sure our Number 68 grenades were in order and waited for the counter-attack. At about 1330 the enemy shelling at the crossing place behind us increased considerably. This was very accurate, and lighter guns were firing on our positions very accurately. The Germans had obviously registered all these positions beforehand. We were not going to get any anti-tank guns. We could see enemy tanks and infantry about one mile away moving up, and reported this to battalion HQ. About 1400 the attack started in earnest. The Germans captured a strongpoint about half left of us, which had been held by the 6th DLI. We also heard that the 9th DLI had lost a position. About half an hour or so after this, three German tanks, two Mk IV Specials with a long 75-mm gun and a Mk III came into our company area, but outside grenade range. We had a number of casualties from this shelling. A big gun threw at us what the men called 'flying kit bags'. The only good thing about it was that its shells made such a noise coming that you could get down into your slit trench in good time.

The Germans concentrated first on the British tanks. The 50th RTR were totally outgunned by the German tanks and were knocked off one position after another. The tanks in our company area crept closer. Someone in 15 Platoon fired a 68 grenade at one of them and damaged the track of the Mk III; 14 Platoon were firing at the tank commanders with their Bren guns. But the tanks replied with long bursts from their machine guns, extremely rapid and rather frightening. We could do very little except sit it out. I asked for a concentration of artillery fire on the tanks and infantry behind. It was a pretty shattering experience for us because it was so close, but the Germans must have thought so too, because they pulled back a bit. The 15 Platoon commander sent his runner over to me telling me that he had fifteen casualties in his platoon and could they be evacuated. When he got up to return, I having told him that with enemy tanks sitting in our company area there was no way we could get wounded out, he was shot by a tank machine gun.

Lieutenant Colonel William Watson
Commanding Officer, 6th Battalion, Durham Light Infantry
During the course of the afternoon things got critical. Tank crews were coming back wounded, and some of my chaps as well. Then on the high ground on my right-hand side the 9th Battalion came back, out of ammunition. My chaps were coming back also out of ammunition. If I'd stayed put I'd have had the Germans looking down on top of me. So somewhere round about mid-afternoon, we pulled back. The 9th and I lined up along the anti-tank ditch and that was going to be our last stand until the end. The brigadier came along and we urged him to get us some ammunition, we said we couldn't fight without ammunition.

Captain Ian English
Officer Commanding, C Company, 8th Battalion,
Durham Light Infantry
About five o'clock the shelling increased considerably again and the tanks advanced, firing their machine guns almost continuously. Behind them we could see the Panzer grenadiers moving up to attack. We couldn't engage this infantry with our small arms because of the intensity of the tank machine-gun fire. One tank came right into 14 Platoon's position and started grinding in the slit trenches. At that point Sergeant Holborne and the eight men he had with him surrendered. CSM Ransome, with the company HQ Bren gun and a Bren gunner from 13 Platoon, fired at the tank commanders' heads and made them duck down inside the tank and also frightened the infantry. The tanks then turned to firing their 75-mm

guns at our slit trenches at close range. As CSM Ransome, in the same trench as I was, put his head up to fire again, he was shot straight through the forehead by a machine gun. So died a very gallant man.

It was getting dark. And I thought if we could hang on until dark, we could stop them. They didn't attack but started shouting out to us to surrender. We replied with rifle and Bren fire and threw grenades. B Company was off the air, and we were on a one-to-one wireless link with battalion HQ, giving a running commentary to the CO. Then a German tank with infantry riding on it came right up to the road. Private Lewis, who had taken over the company HQ Bren when Ransome was killed, fired at these infantry on the tank, and we threw grenades at them. The infantry retired and the tank soon after. A vicious artillery stonk came down on the company. It was pretty obvious that the end could not be far off. We only had .303 ammunition left and not a lot of that.

A shell landed between my trench and Corporal Simpson's, the 18 set went up in the air, that was the end of communications between us and battalion HQ. It was about seven o'clock and getting pretty dark, and the Germans seemed to pull back. Then a runner appeared from battalion HQ with orders for us to withdraw to the anti-tank ditch. I passed the order to platoons to bring out as many wounded as they could. Some could not be brought out and were taken prisoner. We began to withdraw. As we did so my batman was wounded. We collected in low ground behind the company position. I counted three officers and twenty-three ORs; we had been sixty-nine all ranks at midday.

Lieutenant Colonel William Watson
Commanding Officer, 6th Battalion, Durham Light Infantry
As the evening wore on and it began to get dark, we were all lining the anti-tank ditch like a trench in the First World War. Andrew Clarke and I were on the top of the ditch. How on earth we were not shot I don't know. During the night Dick Ovenden came from the company on the left to ask for some more ammunition, he walked along the top of the ditch and I said to him, 'There is the last box. I've nobody to take it to you. You'll have to take it yourself.' He was shot on the way back and killed.

Captain Ian English
Officer Commanding, C Company, 8th Battalion,
Durham Light Infantry
At the anti-tank ditch we were met by Major Liddell, the CO, and we were put on the left of the battalion positions which were aligned in and along the

Exhausted British troops sleep in a trench after fierce night fighting in the Mareth Line.

anti-tank ditch. It was a bad position. I was alongside Major Wood's company of the 6th DLI. There were a number of German attacks in the night and some got pretty close. Fortunately the 2nd Cheshire Vickers machine guns helped defeat the attacks. We were then told that the battalion was to attack Ouerzi as part of the brigade attack, to regain strong points we had lost. Fortunately this was cancelled.

Lieutenant Colonel William Watson
Commanding Officer, 6th Battalion, Durham Light Infantry

Ian Door, the mortar officer, did manage to carry three mortars and some ammunition across. When it got dark we fired the mortars into where we knew the Germans were forming up to attack us. You could see the Germans in the dark through the dust and smoke. The noise was terrific. The Germans were shelling the other side of the ditch behind us. Jackson, commanding HQ Company, was killed in the wadi. I had a machine-gunner of the 2nd Cheshires close to me who was pumping fire to prevent the Germans assembling and rushing us. He might have been on the ranges in England. He said to me, 'Last belt, sir.' And he fired his belt into the figures we could see in the dark, not far off. Then, 'Gun cleared.' I don't know how he got out.

We were all desperately tired. We could see the Germans forming up. I saw one preparing to throw a grenade. He was shot by one of my chaps. Just before dawn we managed to get two anti-tank guns across. OC S Company, Maurice Kirby, came in with the order that we were to get out in five minutes, and the 9th would follow. I lost my flask with whisky in it. Perhaps some German found it.

Captain Ian English
Officer Commanding, C Company, 8th Battalion,
Durham Light Infantry

An order came to retire to the other side of the anti-tank ditch. Unfortunately that order never reached my company. Soon after dawn I walked along the anti-tank ditch and was very surprised that there was no one on my right. I walked on and came across five Panzer grenadiers. I attempted to shoot them with my revolver, and managed to get one in the leg. But that was as far as I got; I fired all my rounds, and they came up and took away my revolver. They had automatic sub-machine guns. I was lucky not to have been shot.

Lieutenant Colonel William Watson
Commanding Officer, 6th Battalion, Durham Light Infantry
George Wood's company never got the message, but managed to get out the very last when the Germans were almost on top of him. I got out. Andrew said, 'I'll follow in five minutes.' I passed a palm tree that had been blown to smithereens, and a flail tank that had been knocked out as it had come down towards the wadi. I felt a German shell go past me; I suppose they must have thought the flail was a tank and still in action. A large Tiger tank came quite close, screened by some palm trees. I told Sergeant Scott to see if he could hit it with the Boys anti-tank rifle, the only time I ever ordered one to be used, they were useless. This was all in the dark in thick smoke, dust and noise. I passed the flail tank and on to the track along which we had come and was joined by Major Bill Robinson, the 2IC of the 9th Battalion, who was coming out. We had no ammunition left. That was the end of the battle.

Captain Peter Jones
Officer Commanding, D Company, 1st/9th Gurkha Rifles
My company was given the job of leading the battalion through the bridgehead established by 50 Div. It involved a seven-mile approach march. We set off and you could see the flashes of the guns and the noise was tremendous. We went through the gun lines. Then a message came saying that the bridgehead operation hadn't been successful, and telling us to return to base. So we marched the seven miles back. This took all night. When we got back it was chaotic. Because the right jab at Mareth hadn't been successful, the battalion was ordered to go through the Matmata Hills. Typical of war, nothing went to plan. We had recce parties going in three different directions. Orders were changed every few hours. Eventually the CO got it all sorted out.

Bombardier Cyril Mount
B Troop, 84 Battery, 111th Field Regiment, Royal Artillery
We fired a lot of ammunition at Mareth. We were supporting 50 Div and they got stuck. Then we had to move and were back with the 4th Indian Div, and were told to up sticks and go round the Matmata Hills to do a left hook with the New Zealand Div. There was terrific congestion on the roads. It was slow going along the mountain roads. I was with Captain Roach Brooke in the armoured OP vehicle for B Troop, driving slowly up a rough track on our way to the top of a hill from where to observe. Captain RB was standing in the front, I was on the wireless set and suddenly there was a loud

The aftermath of an attack by Stukas on vehicles on the Gabes road east of El Hamma.

thud and splintering of wooden floorboards. A 75-mm shell had landed in the vehicle but hadn't gone off. It was a miracle; if it had exploded we would have all been blown to kingdom come. We were shaking, and didn't touch the shell for a bit. We got to a high bit, and the driver, Walker, a real old sweat, North-West Frontier type, picked it up very gently, and threw it over a little precipice. It still didn't go off.

Trooper Kenneth Ewing
Gunner/Wireless Operator, B Squadron,
The Nottinghamshire Yeomanry (Sherwood Rangers)
Our biggest battle was the Tebaga Gap behind the Mareth line. Our task was to do a big left hook, go through a gap in the hills with the New Zealand Div, and through to El Hamma. There were three regiments in our brigade: 1 RTR, the Staffs Yeomanry, and Sherwood Rangers. The Shermans were spaced out at twenty-yard intervals right across the gap, and fifty yards behind them were the Crusader tanks, 170 tanks in all, Shermans and Crusaders. The Crusaders would carry the infantry on the back of the tanks. They were to advance behind a creeping barrage, and on top of that were fighter-bombers, Hurricane tank busters and Kittyhawks. The Hurricanes came over at fifteen-minute intervals. There was a dust storm and, what with the sand being thrown up by the barrage and smoke from the smoke shells, you couldn't see a thing. The Germans had positions with anti-tank guns and tanks. We were on the extreme right up against the hills where they had gun positions so we had some casualties. But we broke through the line. What helped was that 1st Armoured Division attacked at the same time from the south. At Tebaga Gap we were opposed by the 5th Regiment of the 21st Panzer Div.

Trooper John Lanes
Wireless Operator, The Nottinghamshire Yeomanry (Sherwood Rangers)
The Germans tried to bomb us with twin-engined aircraft, the bombs skidded along the hard ground and ended up among their own blokes. We had Hurricane fighters with a two-pounder gun in each wing. About twenty of them came over to attack German tanks, but attacked the Staffordshire Yeomanry and knocked out quite a few of their tanks.

At four o'clock in the afternoon we charged at El Hamma. We crossed the valley and advanced behind a creeping barrage of artillery. I don't know how many tanks we lost. I was the right-hand Crusader, and was warned that 88s that would hit us on the flank, but they had been taken out by our bombers.

On the back of each Crusader there were Maori infantry. They had been told to deal with any enemy infantry as we advanced. But as we started our advance the Germans fired their barrage over the top of the heavy tanks to catch the back-up troops, so the Maoris on my tank dismounted quickly. Then the rest of 1st Armoured Division came through us.

Lieutenant Colonel William Watson
Commanding Officer, 6th Battalion, Durham Light Infantry
After Mareth we were pulled out and within a short time the battalion was up and doing again; we had no time to brood on misfortunes. The first time you go into battle you are in splendid form. Gallantry and bravery is an expendable item, you lose a bit every time you go into battle. Most people find that their gallantry gets less and less.

The LOBs came up. The brigade commander came and said goodbye; he was sacked. The corps and divisional commanders came and said we had done our best. One of my officers took out a patrol early in the morning and discovered that the Germans were pulling out, covered by very heavy machine-gun fire, I assume to muffle the noise of their transport. Somehow we could feel that they'd had it. The Germans had to pull out because the New Zealanders came in at the back. This was a great boost to morale. Then at nine o'clock the next morning my IO, 'Tinker' Bell, took out a patrol and was killed on a mine. The sappers arrived soon after and started to clear the mines. One of them was killed.

On 3 April a warning order came to move. The next line of defence was the Wadi Akarit. The Wadi Akarit flowed into the sea like the Wadi Zigzou, but it was dry at this time. On the home side there was a very slight ridge, and on the far side two very clear features. On the right the Djebel Roumana, which ran down to the sea, and on the left the Djebel Zemlet el Beida. And in between the two was a gap of about 1,100 yards through which a road ran north-westwards. The Wadi Akarit was about twenty-five miles north of Mareth. I had been warned that I was to be the fourth battalion of 69 Brigade. I spent the night of 5/6 April at Div HQ while the attack was being prepared. The next day I took the battalion and moved just behind advanced brigade HQ while the attack was in progress. The Djebel Roumana was to be taken by Highland Div, and Jebel Djebel Zemlet el Beida by the 4th Indian Div, while 69 Brigade filled the gap in between the two. Towards the afternoon, the brigadier said to me, 'Take your battalion and fill the gap between the Roumana and el Beida feature.' The Green Howards, on the very edge of the Djebel Zemlet el Beida feature, which was to be on my left flank, were commanded by Colonel Lance. I took my party of company commanders, at teatime or thereabouts, up to join Lance so we could look down into the gap which we were to fill. It was being heavily shelled, so to do it in daylight would have been rather stupid. So I said to the brigadier, 'Can we move in after dark?' He agreed.

After dark, each company commander having seen where he was to go, came up and quietly got in, more or less in position. On the way in I ran over a bump in my Jeep. I asked my driver Parkinson what the hell he was doing. He replied, 'It's only a dead Italian I ran over.'

Bombardier Cyril Mount
B Troop, 84 Battery, 111th Field Regiment, Royal Artillery

We surveyed a new gun position so close to the wadi that we were under direct observation from German OPs on the hills, and were fired on, but managed to get the flags bashed in and we scooted off fast. We shot off down the back road to the battery. The digging party, followed by the guns, came up. I was driving a jeep with a new arrival, Lieutenant White, behind the battery commander's jeep. We trundled along this narrow tarmac road, and I had a feeling we had overshot the turn-off. The BC's vehicle stopped, and I jumped out and saw why; there was a burnt-out tank across the road. I said to the BC, O'Halloran, 'That wasn't there this morning. We've come too far.'

He 'pooh-poohed', saying to his driver, 'Right hand down, Walker.' He turned off the road and immediately went up on a mine. O'Halloran was lying there screaming about his legs. I went to lift him, and his legs were gone. He died in a few minutes. Walker moaned, 'I'm blind,' and died. The wireless operator had been blown off the vehicle and was all right. At this point White started yelling at me to take the vehicle back for the MO. I said, 'We don't need an MO, everybody is dead.'

He ordered me to take the vehicle back. We drove back to the column of gun towers and digging party in three-tonners. Everybody was standing about not knowing where to go. I said, 'We've come too far, the road is mined, turn around.' White kept screaming at me not to stop and not to tell the number ones of the guns this, and to keep driving. He threatened me, drew his .38 and said he would shoot me. He was in a blind panic. He got out at the rear of the column to find the MO. I decided to go back to the column. I found the spike and can marking the turn-off. The battery then started trundling into position. We found our position occupied by some other battery, so we had to find somewhere else. We couldn't dig, the ground was too hard, we had to build up, using sandbags filled with rocks.

Captain Peter Jones
Officer Commanding, D Company, 1st/9th Gurkha Rifles
This was the sort of country we loved, we were back on the North-West Frontier; it was mountain warfare again. Our men were very much at home in this terrain. Gurkhas are stocky, with strong legs, and travel across the hillside like goats. Our general, Tuker, was a 2nd Gurkha; decided this is the country for the Gurkha and Indian soldier, take advantage of the terrain. The beauty of an Indian Division was that in every brigade there was a Gurkha battalion, an Indian battalion and a British battalion. For a set-piece attack the British battalion would be better than anyone else. The Indian battalions and the Gurkhas take on the mountains.

Our sister Gurkha battalion, the 2nd Gurkhas, in the other brigade, 7 Brigade, was given the task of starting the attack on the enemy position by carrying out a silent attack before the main attack on the anti-tank line. So they did a silent attack through the mountains.

Captain Ronald Perkin
4th/16th Punjab Regiment, 7th Brigade, 4th Indian Division
We did a brigade silent attack, Gurkhas leading, then the Royal Sussex and then us in the pitch dark. After about half an hour or so they started sending back prisoners. The Gurkhas had done much slaughter with their kukris. The CO sent for me and said, 'See that hill over there?'

'Yes,' I said; it could have been a few yards off, or hundreds. He told me to take it. So I lined up the company, off we went, and the soldiers started yelling their battle cry. We took the hill. When dawn came, I saw some Italians about 150 yards off, lined up my chaps, fixed bayonets and charged the position. The Italians started to put their hands up, when we got there, except for a very smartly dressed young Fascist officer, I jabbed him with my sub-machine gun to persuade him to surrender. I thought of shooting him, but couldn't bring myself to do so.

Captain Peter Jones
Officer Commanding, D Company, 1st/9th Gurkha Rifles
The attack was very successful. By doing this we threatened the whole Wadi Akarit position from the left flank. My battalion in 5 Brigade followed up into the hilly mountainous area between the mountain on the left and the anti-tank defences.

Gurkhas advancing up a hill.

Lieutenant Colonel William Watson
Commanding Officer, 6th Battalion, Durham Light Infantry

The only opposition we had was about six random rounds of mortar fire. We heard motor transport moving in the distance and couldn't make out if they were pulling out or preparing a counter-attack. Suddenly a German despatch rider drove right into our position and told us that he had lost his way and his friends had gone. I sent out a patrol and they found the enemy positions empty. At first light I crawled out of my hole in the ground and talked to Morris Kirby; there was a solitary 'pinnnggg' close by, so there must have been a lone German or Italian about. We took cover. Then, almost at daybreak, the New Zealand armour started to come through our positions and along the track, chasing the Germans. In the morning it became a flood: hundreds of Italian prisoners coming in. About nine hundred passed through our IO's hands, mostly Italians, dirty, sullen and war-weary. There were a few Germans that weren't much better. We found four wounded Germans, all under twenty-one; one of them had been wounded in Russia before. Our MO, a German Jew, who spoke fluent German, worked like a tiger on all the wounded, no matter if they were our chaps or Germans.

The general came up and congratulated us on getting into position.

Capture of the Axis Bridgehead in Tunisia

Von Sponeck replied, 'We wanted to surrender to you, and not the Americans. We fought the Coldstream, the Grenadiers and the Scots Guards for many years in the desert, we wanted to surrender to you.'

The forcing of the Wadi Akarit position opened the way into the Tunisian plain for Eighth Army, which headed for Sfax and eventually for Sousse. At this stage a major reorganisation of the Allied armies took place. Eighth Army, now becoming funnelled into the narrowing gap between the spine-backed mountains of the Tunisian eastern dorsal and the coast, had only enough elbow-room to advance on a one-corps front, the Xth. Montgomery therefore suggested that First Army, moving on the high ground on the approaches to Tunis, should take on most of the weight of the final attacks. Meanwhile the Germans prepared to defend the Tunis bridgehead.

On 19 February 1943 General Alexander had handed over responsibility for Middle East Command to General 'Jumbo' Wilson, in order to take over as deputy to General Eisenhower, the Allied Commander-in-Chief, North African Theatre. Alexander was also appointed commander of the newly formed 18th Army Group, responsible for coordinating the operations of all the Allied armies in North Africa – British First and Eighth, the French, and the Americans. This was a sensible move. Alexander was a very experienced soldier, having commanded in battle at every level from platoon to army in two world wars. Eisenhower was thus left free to coordinate the activity of the Joint Allied Staffs, a job for which he was admirably suited. Eisenhower, for all his undoubted talents as a generalissimo, had never commanded so much as a platoon in action, and would have been out of his depth commanding in the field, as he was to demonstrate later in north-west Europe.

On 30 April 1943, in order to beef up the First Army for its task, Montgomery sent Lieutenant General Horrocks across to take over IX Corps from Lieutenant General Crocker, who had been wounded. Horrocks took with him the 7th Armoured Division, the 4th Indian Division and the 201st Guards Brigade. These were all very experienced soldiers who had been fighting in the desert since 1940.

First Army had recovered from the setbacks of the winter, and had made considerable progress during the month of April. While Eighth Army was fighting at the Wadi Akarit, IX Corps of First Army was attacking at Fondouk. The aim was that the two would eventually link up.

Lieutenant Tony Pawson
Company Second-in-Command, B Company, 10th Battalion,
The Rifle Brigade
We were told that the 6th Armoured was to attack as a complete division for the first time, with B Company providing the infantry for the 17th/21st Lancers regimental group. The enemy was holding Pichon, and the hills on each side of the Fondouk gap with five battalions of infantry, all German or Austrian. We were to move to a concentration area at El Ala that night, the attack to start at dawn. The hills on either side of the gap were to be stormed by British and American infantry, we were to pass through a huge minefield covering the gap, through into the plain, and drive through to the coast, cutting off Rommel's troops now in full retreat.

I went off with the other company 2ICs to recce our Assembly Area. The road to El Ala was terrible with bad surface, sharp turns, precipitous sides and makeshift crossings over the river. The whole division had to negotiate this in the dark without lights. Two Churchill tanks had already plunged over the sheer drop and lay drunkenly on their sides. The El Ala crossroads were being shelled as we turned off down a sandy track to our area, a cactus grove just by El Ala, right beneath Djebel Trozza. I tried to get some sleep, but a great blaze sprang up nearby as a truck caught fire; a rifleman tried to refuel it while smoking a cigarette. It was getting on for midnight as the division arrived, trucks bogged down, and the whole night was spent sorting them out and hiding them before dawn.

The attack was delayed by twenty-four hours: all tanks and guns were not up yet. At 0430 continuous flashes of gunfire lit the darkness. At dawn the barrage increased.

There was a jeep parked near us from the Phantom organisation, which monitors the battle. We gathered round their officer's map to watch the progress of the attack. On our left the Hampshires made wonderful progress. The American arrow had not started to move. The sun got higher, their arrow moved, and stopped near the gap at the foot of the hill. We were ordered to move up behind the Americans. We could get no information from the Americans, so we advanced by bounds. We neared the hills. Working between scattered clumps of bushes, odd parties of Americans appeared. The leading tanks reported coming under heavy fire. James Booth, my company commander, was called up to the nearest tank for orders and we followed. We went to the colonel's tank with its skull and crossbones 17th/21st Lancers pennant flying on its aerial. James gave out orders among a hail of shells; very distracting. As soon as it got dark I harboured the company in the midst of the tanks. Two of our officers took out patrols to locate the minefields and enemy outposts, since we couldn't get any information from the Americans.

At eleven o'clock the next morning a staff car came up, General Crocker got out, went to the CO of the 17th/21st and asked why he hadn't got on. The CO said that he had been told to wait for the Americans to capture the hills and clear the minefields. Crocker told him to charge the pass and force the gap whatever the cost. James was summoned for orders. He returned and gave us orders. The 17th/21st regimental group was to charge through the gap. The company would move in trucks in the middle of the regimental box. The company would debus to help clear a gap through the gap. We realised that this was as suicidal as the Charge of the Light Brigade. The gap was only seven hundred yards wide: even if the tanks got through, we would be easy meat in our trucks to the guns and mortars on either side. It was like hearing a death sentence. We struggled to find a cheering comment, but instead just wished each other luck. Before, we had been keeping low in our hastily dug slits. Now, we didn't care and sat on the edges dangling our legs. I found that I wasn't all that frightened but just wishing it was all over.

Waiting for the order to start was like being in a dentist's waiting room. I remembered a jar of rum in my vehicle and handed it out round the company. The long tense wait ended as the yellow flag went up, and I felt better with something to do. We all formed up behind the colonel's tank. A carrier received a direct hit. We went across to pull out the wounded. The tanks lumbered forward and we started to move behind them. Everything opened up on us. We tried to dodge the shells, peering through the slits of our command vehicle. In the confined space, near misses made a tremendous noise and concussion. Ahead I could see a tank on fire, still rolling forward. Shells and mortar bombs exploded, scared Americans waved us to go away. Over the wireless we heard the voice of the recce squadron commander, 'Five tanks knocked out; 88 mm I think. No, it's mines as well. Seven gone now. There doesn't seem any way through. Any further orders? Over.'

'Keep going.'

'Will do. Hell, I've hit a mine myself'.

As we edged up behind the tanks, our carriers were told to pick up crews from disabled tanks, many with tracks blown off by mines. James's vehicle was put out of action. He crammed into mine with his crew. We were told to withdraw five hundred yards. The other squadron of tanks was told to find a way through. As we withdrew we drew the attention of more guns. We stopped by the CSM's truck to give him orders. As we talked, a series of shattering explosions; so close the smoke drifted between us and the acrid stench hung in the air. The expression on the CSM's face changed from a fixed smile to shock and agony as he sank to the ground. All in the truck he had just left had been wounded or killed. A despatch rider I sent back for a truck to evacuate the wounded was hit and the rider killed. The next few minutes were a nightmare. More people were hit, and those going to their aid also hit. We worked feverishly, improvising bandages. Someone went berserk. James smacked him over the head and knocked him out, we put him on another truck to speed him to the dressing station. Having dealt with the wounded, we scraped holes. Only two or three of our trucks remained. We waited for orders. At last the tanks found a gap to go through, and others followed. The Guards were called up, and I watched the Welsh Guards go in. They advanced as though on parade. Ahead of us the tanks got stuck, and our A Company had to attack the anti-tank guns holding them up.

By now we had forty casualties in our company alone. We harboured for the night in a cactus grove with the tanks. At dawn the Americans put in a final attack on the by-now deserted hills. Thirty-seven tanks, most from the 17th/21st, were still lying in the minefields, mostly recoverable having only been damaged by mines. We advanced. We passed Fondouk, and the tanks formed up ahead. Now we were poised for the chase: before us stretched an endless vista of green corn. We advanced, turfing out small groups of demoralised Germans. It seemed like a triumphal procession. Suddenly there was the whine of shells coming in, and they crashed in among us. The explosions intensified. We harboured for the night in a cactus grove with the tanks. We were told that Germans were all over the place and not to make noise. We went about whispering. But the echelon came up with much shouting, and the noise of rearming and refuelling tanks.

Captain Peter Jones
Officer Commanding, D Company, 1st/9th Gurkha Rifles
From the Wadi Akarit, the enemy withdrew to Enfidaville, where we followed and that was our next battle at Djebel Garci. This Djebel was a large, bald feature; the start of the final lot of mountains south of Tunis. The armoured formations jabbed on the right by the coast, and were partially successful, while the infantry worked though the mountains. Djebel Garci was stony and you couldn't dig. Alongside Garci was a feature called Takrouna, allotted to the New Zealanders.

The 4th/6th Rajputana Rifles, the Indian battalion of our brigade, attacked Djebel Garci, gained a foothold, and we took over. The CO did the clever thing by changing the axis of the advance further to the right, to try to get round the German positions. He sent for me at about two o'clock in the morning and said, 'Right, get on to the mountain and take the highest feature you can find. I want the battalion established before daylight.' It was dark, but there was a moon, which helped. I sent off just a platoon. You could see the next feature silhouetted against the sky, and told the platoon commander that was his objective, 'Take it and when you have taken it, give covering fire to the next platoon.'

We started with a silent attack on the first feature and were able to take it without much trouble. But then the Germans realised what was happening and reinforced that flank in time to meet our next assault platoon. It was all hand-to-hand stuff. The Gurkhas drew their kukris and it was slaughter; occasionally a bayonet, but mostly kukri. I didn't use a kukri. The Bren gun crew with me were killed, and I took over the gun with quite good effect. I had been wounded in the neck a bit earlier, but not badly enough to stop me doing my job. My field of fire was limited, the enemy were never more than forty yards away. The Gurkhas would get amongst them, and the Germans would try to counter-attack, we would get round them and push on, the battle ebbed and flowed; all in the dark, with a slight moon lit by flashes from rifles and machine guns. Grenades were going off. You glimpsed people. If they were Germans you attacked them.

Sherman tanks advance past a knocked-out 88-mm anti-tank gun, 23 April 1943.

A Grant tank showing the side door, 75-mm main armament in the hull and 37-mm in the turret.

My leading platoon commander, having taken his position, went forward to do a recce. He came across a German section position. Their attention was focussed to their right, firing at the Rajputana Rifles, who were attacking up the main axis to our left. The platoon commander attacked them with his kukri and killed four, but the fourth made such a noise that more Germans were alerted and came after him. They got his kukri off him, and started to try and kill him with it. But they weren't very skilful, there was so much blood about that the kukri was slippery, and he evaded them. His head was in a frightful mess; he had lost his helmet. A few minutes later I appeared. He had been cut all over, and had lost a lot of blood. I sent him off with an escort.

As the battle went on we got short of ammunition. I got told my CSM to get some men and go to battalion HQ for more ammunition. But on the way he met the CSM of the next company, and said to him, 'I've just killed my first German, what about you?' And they set off to find more Germans. The next time I saw him I asked him if he had got more ammunition and he said, 'Yes, and I've also killed four more Germans.'

I said, 'That wasn't what I told you to do. I told you to get more ammunition.'

He said, 'I'm doing both: I am collecting ammunition, but also collecting heads with my friend in the next company.'

A Company came up on my left, and we fought shoulder to shoulder for the rest of the day. I was hit in the eye and in both thighs by splinters from grenades at about mid-morning. Although I could still carry on, I wasn't very mobile. I had a FOO with me who could see for miles and he just brought down artillery fire and broke up one enemy counter-attack after another. After a while I passed out, and my men carried me down on a stretcher to the RAP.

Rifleman Douglas Waller
Anti-Tank Gunner, 2nd Battalion, The Rifle Brigade

By now we were on about our fifth or sixth vehicle. Mines were a problem. On one occasion we were driving in the leading vehicle's tracks, thinking that it was safe, but the cunning Deutsches had mines that would allow five vehicles to go over it before it blew the sixth. Our water carrier was ahead of us, and the driver was in his mid-thirties and we called him 'Pop', because we were in our twenties, and he was actually married, with thinning hair. He drives over a mine and we all rush up and carry him out. We hadn't had any cigarettes sent up for a long time, and he asked, 'Anybody got a cigarette?' We gave him the last one. The MO came up, and said, 'You're all right,' and the chap who had given up his cigarette said, 'You cheeky bugger, give me back my cigarette.'

We joined up with First Army, who took a very poor view of us. Everything was chucked on, and we were in scruff order with dirty old cans, black with smoke, for brewing up hung on the vehicle. They were all trotting around in blancoed belts and gaiters, and they looked down their noses at us.

We began to come across Americans. When we laagered up they would come round asking us if we had any souvenirs, they wanted Berettas and Lügers and belts with *Gott Mit Uns* on them and would offer packs of cigarettes for them. They were the rear-echelon troops. We thought it a bit odd that they would give cigarettes for this stuff: we had masses of it.

Lieutenant Henry Matthews
457 Field Battery, Royal Artillery
We finished the campaign with 25-pounders still as an independent six-gun battery. We went into action in the follow-up of the enemy withdrawal at Sidi Nsir. I was battery leader, taking guns up the valley and ordered Ray Rissick into a gun position on the right of three small bridges which the engineers had built called 'Pip', 'Squeak' and 'Wilfred'. Rissick took his guns into position by one of the bridges. Left section came up through and joined right section well forward. Here we opened fire with 25-pounders for the first time.

We followed up from there by going round to get ready for the battle at Longstop. The battery went to Medjez and into a gun position for the Longstop battle. Being an extra battery and not having an RHQ, we were given the task of smoke battery. I was sent off to be FOO for the attack. We harboured for the night and at dawn went up Longstop. I was the OP on the right-hand side, with some tanks of the North Irish Horse. We got up on to the spur on the right with some tanks but the infantry had quite a battle getting up on to the main feature of Longstop.

Major Bill Miskin
Officer Commanding, B Company, 6th Battalion,
Queen's Own Royal West Kent Regiment
The day came for the attack on Longstop. The brigade was attacking and the Argylls went up first. The Argylls took two-thirds of the hill; they were

commanded by Jack Anderson. We followed up. Before we started I went across to find the tanks of the North Irish Horse who were supporting us. My CO, with whom I didn't get on, asked, 'How do we communicate with these tanks?'

I said I hadn't the faintest idea. So he went up to it and beat it with his walking stick. A chap popped his head out, and we agreed what we should do. The CO then tripped over a tripwire, and was lucky, because it only had a Bakelite grenade on it. He fell, saying he was wounded, and I turned him over, and his neck was lightly peppered with small pieces of Bakelite, nothing serious. But I said, 'My God, that is dreadful colonel. Now don't you move. I'll bind you up.'

I put on his field dressing, the medical corporal came past, I told him to take the CO back, which he did. That was the last we saw of this gentleman, much to our delight. We went on with the attack.

When I got up to the Argylls, Colonel Anderson was sitting up there by two dead men. He asked me if I had any water to drink. I offered him a flask of whisky. He drank it. The brigadier turned up, and asked me how many men I had got, and I said not many. I had started with three officers and about eighty men; I was down to one officer wandering about in a daze, and about twenty men. We still had part of the hill to attack. We were being shelled and mortared. Eventually the brigadier shouted at me to come back and that we would attack again in the morning. The North Irish Horse came up with their Churchill tanks and managed to take up defence positions; we used the German dugouts.

At 0800 the Buffs came and took the hill, but the Germans had withdrawn. When we got to the bottom of the hill, we were met by the brigadier. He sent me and one of the other company commanders off to Bone in a jeep, and told me not to come back for forty-eight hours. We went to the officers' club.

Lieutenant Henry Matthews
457 Field Battery, Royal Artillery

We went back to Medjez, crossed over the river, went into position for the final battle on Djebel Bou Aoukaz. Almost the last battle for Tunis. Tiny was FOO for the Guards going up the left side of Djebel Bou Aoukaz. I was with the Duke of Wellingtons down in the bottom of the hill, the reserve battalion ready to go up. Throughout the night the whole of First Army artillery pounded the enemy. The battery fired almost eight hundred rounds

The crew of a Valentine tank have a wash and shave in the Western Desert.

per gun that night. One gunner told me you could see the barrels glowing with the heat, and the oil in the recuperator was almost boiling.

The battle finished at about midday the following day with the capture of Djebel Bou Aoukaz and then 4th Indian, who had come over to join First Army, broke through and the race was on for Tunis. We hooked in and rushed with the others forward, everybody eager to get gun positions further forward than anyone else.

Major Bill Miskin
Officer Commanding, B Company, 6th Battalion,
Queen's Own Royal West Kent Regiment

It was time for the final attack on Tunis. We were told to secure the Start Line. We were given three minutes of artillery support; we had about six hundred guns supporting us. I looked back and it looked like Crystal Palace on fireworks night. We got to the Start Line and the attack moved through. The following morning I watched the armour coming through a valley full of standing corn, and it was a wonderful sight: two tank regiments deployed in battle formation. That was one day before Tunis fell.

Lieutenant Tony Pawson
Company Second-in-Command, B Company, 10th Battalion,
The Rifle Brigade

We were released to go for Tunis. We motored forward to the first objective, and were told to wait there as flank guard with some tanks. The whole area was in a haze, like a London fog, because of the dust thrown up by armour and shells. An enemy aircraft attack was beaten off by our planes. Our tanks went on and we could see the 7th Armoured Division attacking on the other side of the road into Tunis.

We drove through gaps in the minefields, watching the 7th Armoured on our right. We passed a sign saying 'Next stop Tunis'. We passed a dejected bunch of prisoners. We passed knocked-out Mk IV tanks on the side of the road. Our tanks attack 88s; crash on into Massicault. We passed German tanks and two Shermans burning. We couldn't believe we had broken through so quickly. The 17th/21st Lancers knocked out some Mk IVs and some anti-tank guns. We went so quickly that the Djebel on our left is to be ignored, much to my relief. Prisoners are saying that we have been too quick for them. They seemed bewildered. In one place we came across a bunch of Germans under an officer. Talking to them, they still seem to idolise Hitler

029484

Major Bill Miskin with the Duke of Kent.

and believe that Russia can be finished off quite quickly. This is the worst fighting they have experienced.

Lieutenant Henry Matthews
457 Field Battery, Royal Artillery
Eventually we ended up bypassing to the south of Tunis towards Cape Bon. It was obvious that the enemy was completely demoralised because there were crowds of them on the road. The gun position had Germans sitting around on the roadside. The bottom of Cape Bon was where the last resistance was being overcome.

Second Lieutenant Mark Philips
Officer Commanding, Pioneer Platoon, 2nd Battalion, Coldstream Guards
We had our final battle in Tunisia at Hammam Lif, where the Bey of Tunis's palace is. That was a crazy battle. The 3rd Battalion Welsh Guards went in by day, and suffered a lot of casualties. Our brigade took the three peaks dominating the town at Hammam Lif, and were held up by four 88s, well positioned, which held up our armour. So – typical cavalry officers – they decided to go along the beach and splashed along, led by the Lothian and Border Horse and destroyed the 88s. It was an extraordinary sight, seeing the tanks splashing along almost in the sea.

I thought that's that. I was sent for by the CO, who told me that the Pioneer Platoon was to take the palace and the harem, and seize the Bey and his guards prisoner. I thought this is a bit of a lark, and so did my chaps. We bashed our way in through the front door and we were fired at by the Bey's band from the top of the stairs. They put up a bit of resistance to protect their Bey. We had one casualty, but they weren't very good shots. So the next thing was to find the Bey. We found him in an upstairs room. He wasn't pleased to see us, he had supported the Germans. We were a little bit rough with him. But in a good-mannered way; we didn't handcuff him.

We rounded up the Bey's guards and the band, and went to the harem; an extraordinary sight. They were a pathetic lot, guarded by eunuchs, nasty fat smiley men, bowing to us. While we were interviewing a few of the French-speaking girls, a rather London sort of voice came from the corner of the room. It was a girl from Hackney Wick, and she had been put into the slave trade in about 1939, and had been in a brothel in Tunis for a time and then put in the harem. She was a very attractive, charming girl so we used her as an interpreter. It was an extraordinary day in the life of a soldier.

Rifleman Douglas Waller
Anti-Tank Gunner, 2nd Battalion, The Rifle Brigade

The Cherry Pickers – the 11th Hussars of our division – got in first. There was a little bit of odd sniping going on, but nothing much. But, before we got there, some Germans had surrendered to us. They tried to speak and tell us that one of their comrades had been wounded. We found him propped against a tree, so we got a door off a shed, put him on that and got him to the ambulance and they saw to him. I went back to check that we hadn't left any weapons around. His jacket was still there so I had a look at it. His wallet was full of Tunisian money, which I liberated. When we got into Tunis I said that we had better spend all this money. So Bill Ash and I bought some wine and drank it. The next day no one would take Tunisian money, because it had been forged by the Germans. No one had tumbled to it the first day. But we had managed to spend all ours.

Major Bill Miskin
Officer Commanding, B Company, 6th Battalion,
Queen's Own Royal West Kent Regiment

We all moved forward into Tunis itself. As 78 Div was the first into North Africa we led the way in. We marched in; there were garlands of flowers round our necks. I had a position in Tunis I was supposed to defend. Instead, we found a suitable flat on the first floor, and the platoons occupied equally nice flats. My sergeant major and others were sitting there being plied with drink by pretty girls, and everybody was telling us we were marvellous. Suddenly a door opened and, to my horror, round it came a cap with a red band. It was our brigadier who had been our CO when we landed, and promoted to brigadier at the beginning of the campaign. He looked at me and said, 'I want a word with you, Bill.'

I thought, 'I'm in trouble now.'

'You're losing your marbles, old chap.'

'Why, sir?'

'There are lots more prettier girls downstairs.'

That was the end of the Tunisian campaign as far as we were concerned.

The Scots Guards march past during the Victory Parade in Tunis. The 1st and 2nd Battalions fought in North Africa.

Captain Peter Child
FOO, 106 Field Regiment, Royal Horse Artillery
We attended the big Victory Parade. We were absolutely whacked, and late. But we had just time to clean one side of the vehicles and guns: the side that showed to the bigwigs on the saluting base.

Second Lieutenant Mark Philips
Officer Commanding, Pioneer Platoon, 2nd Battalion,
Coldstream Guards
On my twenty-first birthday, the officers sat down to dinner to eat together for the first time for months. That morning we had taken Lieutenant General Graf Theodor von Sponeck and his 90th Light Division prisoner. The general said, 'We've come round this way, which might surprise you, to surrender; we've got no more ammunition and no more food.'

Colonel Roddy asked him to come to dinner. The general and his ADC came and joined us. At dinner, Colonel Roddy said, 'I thought you came by a longer route than necessary to surrender, why was that?'

Von Sponeck replied, 'We wanted to surrender to you, and not the Americans. We fought the Coldstream, the Grenadiers and the Scots Guards for many years in the desert, we wanted to surrender to you.'

That was the end of the war in Tunisia

Final Words

I used to say my prayers. Of course when you're
in a tight spot, you promise all sorts of things.
Throughout the war I never expected to survive.

The Allies inflicted a massive defeat on the Axis in North Africa. The 238,243 prisoners taken and equipment losses in the final stages of the campaign in Tunisia alone were comparable to those lost by the Axis at Stalingrad. The German Red Cross estimates for Stalingrad losses are 200,000, plus around 30,000 wounded evacuated by air. In addition the Axis lost some 33,530 dead in the Tunisian and Western Desert campaigns. The Western Desert and Tunisian campaigns cost the British and Commonwealth 20,500 dead.

These campaigns were a necessary precursor to defeating the Germans in Europe. Had the British lost the Middle East, and especially the Persian Gulf oilfields, it is difficult to see how they could have continued the war against Germany. One could argue that Hitler missed an opportunity by not massively reinforcing Rommel and so, perhaps, enabling him to press on and seize those oilfields. Once Rommel had seized the British bases in the Nile delta, he could have advanced through Jordan into Iraq and the head of the Persian Gulf.

Rommel was a charismatic general, but also a bit of a gambler, as he demonstrated at Alam Halfa. The British took a long time to find someone to match him. In Montgomery they found the man, a consummate trainer of troops, and a resolute commander who cared for his men. Under his command the Eighth Army advanced some 1,850 miles from Alamein to Tunis in 201 days.

The British constantly lagged behind the Germans in tank design, and their tactics were often flawed, based on misconceived notions on the employment of armour. The main failure was not fighting an all-arms battle: an orchestration of armour, artillery, anti-tank guns and infantry. Instead, far too often, the armour on its own charged hull-down German tanks and anti-tank guns, with disastrous consequences.

In the end, when the strategy has been decided and the equipment provided, the outcome of any battle lies in the hands of human beings; from generals to private soldiers. Once the generals have decided on a plan, the final result will depend on how well trained, equipped and motivated are the soldiers and their leaders, from corporals to colonels.

In battle, soldiers fall into four categories: thrivers, stickers, survivors and failures. Which category you are in has nothing to do with rank, or what job you do. Thrivers are the tiny minority who blossom in battle, who find that their senses are so sharpened by the challenge of combat that they perform in overdrive, such as Sergeant Drake. They may be misfits or loners. Not all thrivers are necessarily good leaders though some, for example Alastair Pearson, were outstanding leaders. Vic Coxen said of him, 'He could read a battle like a good scrum-half can read a game of rugby.' The good leaders engendered an air of confidence in those they commanded. Gordon Mitchell, then a young private in Alastair's battalion, remembered, 'I always felt safer when Colonel Alastair was about.'

Stickers, again a small minority, but a larger group than the thrivers, are the natural leaders, and the backbone of any military organisation, providing the best soldiers, NCOs and officers.

Survivors make up the majority. If properly led and trained they will fight well, show fortitude under unpleasant conditions, and bravery in the face of danger. Failures, a tiny minority, will in all likelihood crumble under the strain of battle, or even before it starts.

Nobody knows which category they will fall into until they are subjected to actual combat. Just about everybody has a limit to the amount of time they can spend fighting before they become unfit to take any more.

The campaign in North Africa was, by the standards of others in the Second World War, for example Russia and Burma, a cleanly fought affair. There were no atrocities committed by either side. There were few civilians in the Western Desert, or in the Tunisian hills, and consequently few innocent victims of the conflict. The German army in North Africa did not include any SS units who in other theatres of war were mainly responsible for German atrocities, such as shooting prisoners and killing civilians. As is made plain by many of the voices in this book, the Germans were a formidable enemy; the Italians, largely for lack of leadership, poor soldiers.

The Americans began badly, thanks to poor training, a naïve approach to war, flawed tactics and a dearth of experienced senior commanders. They learned quickly, and although the fruits of their education at the hands of the Germans would not manifest itself until later campaigns, their best divisions became as good as anyone's. The best British units were as good as the Germans, but unlike the German army, the British were not uniformly good across the whole spectrum in every formation.

Lieutenant Paolo Colacicchi
Platoon Commander, Machine-Gun Battalion, Italian Tenth Army
Rommel became as much of a mythical figure to the Italians as the British. One regiment of Bersaglieri at Tobruk called themselves *Rommeletti* (little Rommels).

Captain Hans-Otto Behrendt
Adjutant to Lieutenant General Rommel
Rommel was much loved by the ordinary Italian soldier because he cared for them more than their own senior officers did. They called him 'Santa Rommel'. I have heard them say so.

Major General John Harding
General Officer Commanding, 7th Armoured Division
When I was still on my back and unable to walk, I got a message saying that Monty wanted to see me. I knew enough about what was going on to know that they were busy planning the invasion of Sicily. I thought he would just pass the time of day and that was all. But not a bit of it, he came up and pulled up a chair, and sat down beside my bed, sent his ADC off on some job or other and spent an hour or more telling me everything about what was going on and his plans for the future. I still have the letters he wrote me which told me that I could count on him for a good job. I always dispute the people who say that Monty lacked compassion. As far as I was concerned he showed great compassion.

Brigadier George Richards
Commander, 4th Armoured Brigade and 23rd Armoured Brigade
Monty was very easy to work with. But he allowed you to make only one mistake; that is all. He said, 'I am dealing with men's lives. I cannot afford to keep people who make more than one mistake.'

Sergeant Albert Davies
Anti-Tank Platoon, 6th Battalion, Durham Light Infantry
Before action, all your muscles were tight and you had a bad feeling in your stomach. Afterwards you got almost back to normal, almost because you knew it wasn't the end, there was more to come. Lots of lads cracked, cowered in trenches, and couldn't take it.

Bombardier Stephen Dawson
339 Battery, 104th (Essex Yeomanry) Field Regiment,
Royal Horse Artillery
I learned the value of comradeship and the strength of your mates. I am glad I was in the Yeomanry. When the war started I was offered a job in air-raid precautions in Southend, but refused it. I am glad I did not accept it.

Sergeant James Drake
Platoon Sergeant, Machine-Gun Platoon, 16th Battalion,
Durham Light Infantry
Always at the back of my mind was, 'If I kill twelve Germans before I'm killed I will have done my duty. If my name's on it, I'll get it. If it isn't, I won't.' I accepted that. It was a feeling in myself. In action I knew what I was doing. Some people lost their heads. I realised how important our training was.

Captain Ian English
Officer Commanding, C Company, 8th Battalion,
Durham Light Infantry
After being in action for some time, the reaction of men varies. Our first experience was a dive-bombing attack in France in 1940 and there had been no period of getting used to battle. NCOs and officers had a difficult job kicking people on to their feet. But after a couple more times of being bombed, you didn't take any notice of it. In the desert, some of the reinforcements after Gazala had a period in the forward area getting used to shelling, and that was useful. Everybody varies, some never get over it, and

are useless from then on; they are in a distinct minority. There are a few who grow into it and become bigger personalities, and if they have been frightened, as everybody is, and not shown it. There are the others who are shocked a bit but they get over it and become useful soldiers. But there is a definite limit that any human being can stand, and we had one or two cases: a most excellent Scots ex-KOSB soldier who became a CSM and got a DCM and MM and by Normandy he was doing everything to avoid risking himself. He should have been sent back to train others.

Company Sergeant Major Macleod Forsyth
A Company, 2nd Parachute Battalion

Officers were my downfall in the army: I opened my mouth too much. After the campaign finished and an officer took over my company we didn't get on. The first time we went on a training jump he was boozing away in the plane. I said to him, 'Look sir, in this battalion, we are heavy drinkers, but not when we are jumping.' He told me to mind my own business.

We went on three days' relaxation to the beach, and I got well and truly drunk and told him what I thought of him. I told him his backbone was the same colour as his shit: yellow. I was on a charge. I was given the option, court-martial or Return to Unit – RTU. I asked, 'RTU means my own unit, the Argylls?' Johnny Frost said, 'Yes, your own unit.' The way I looked at it was, tomorrow you could be dead. It was the only thing I was sorry about, leaving the Paras. If they had reduced me to private, I would have took it. This was after the campaign was over. I was awarded the MM for the Cork Wood action.

Company Sergeant Major Alan Potter
D Company, 2/28th Battalion, 9th Australian Division

Our impression of the Italians was that they were excitable and gutless. They didn't want to be in the war, they didn't feel they were defending their country. They were not by nature soldiers. The officers were like comic opera characters, strutting in their uniforms. Raids against Italians, especially the Bersaglieri, who wore feathers in their hats, was like going through a chicken run, with feathers on the ground. We didn't have much respect for the Italians. But they are lovely people. At one stage I was given the job of taking some POWs to prison in a truck. They were crying.

We had great respect for the Germans: trained, dedicated and tough. The British had some excellent soldiers, but some were not.

Sergeant Emilio Ponti
Tank Gunner, Italian Tenth Army
When asked why the Italians can't fight, my answer is that this was not our war.

Lieutenant Emilio Pulini
Italian Folgore Parachute Division
The war was a very important part of my life. I was eight years in the army, and this experience was worthwhile for me mainly because one gets a very good knowledge of people and one is wiser.

Company Sergeant Major Alan Potter
D Company, 2/28th Battalion, 9th Australian Division
In war, you expect casualties, and when it happens, you feel, 'I'm glad it isn't me.' You feel invincible. But when you have had a number of close calls, and you have to go back into battle, you get a cold feeling of dread in your stomach, and think, 'How much longer can I go on?' Some people were badly affected by war. They developed a nervousness and irritability, and some went very quiet.

Gunner Martin Ranft
220th Artillery Regiment, German 164th Light Division
There was no hatred between the two sides in North Africa. I have friends here in Great Britain who fought in North Africa, and we say how ever did we fight each other? We just spoke a different language. We didn't hate the English.

Private Kev Robinson
9th Australian Division
I think the six years I spent in the army were the most important part of my life. We finished the job, and a job that had to be done. The people's lives that were sacrificed were not wasted. The friendships I made were the most enduring of my life.

Private Thomas Thornthwaite
Carrier Platoon, 1st Battalion, Durham Light Infantry
I used to say my prayers. Of course when you are in a tight spot, you promise all sorts of things. Throughout the war I never expected to survive; you saw

how many people were lost, and you thought your turn was bound to come. The more action you saw, the more wary you became.

Major Denys Crews
Company Commander, 2nd/5th Battalion, Sherwood Foresters
Morale was very bad after Sedjenane. The soldiers couldn't have cared less. I took out the whole company on patrol with my 2IC, Tich Verity, to capture a German. We ran into the German positions, we lost Tich, but I got him back on my own. The rest of the company just ran off. I persuaded the CO to let me take them to a place where I could train them properly.

Private Tom Fitzpatrick
9th Australian Division
I don't regret being in the war. I satisfied my childhood curiosity to see what it would be like to be in action. It was an important part of my life, it was a turning point in many ways. I was self-centred before the war, with ideas of my own importance, but my service in a junior rank made me realise I was just one of millions of men, whereas up to the war I thought that I was rather more exclusive. Perhaps it gave me a sense of humility.

The people who took part didn't gain anything material. Perhaps a few did, but a great many didn't, but I think that those of us who took part might have contributed to a longer peace than the bigger powers have known, freedom from a major war.

Rifleman Douglas Waller
Anti-Tank Gunner, 2nd Battalion, Rifle Brigade
Suddenly everything came to an end. Everybody thought we would go back to the delta for leave or go home. This didn't happen. We were all called out on parade. The majority went out with their weapons, you could hear the bolts clicking, and the brigadier said, 'Don't do anything stupid.' Everybody had had enough. He said, 'You've got to be patient. The army have set up a rest camp.' What they meant was that they would set up a canteen: that didn't impress us much. Then they opened a cinema, so we went along, and they showed *Desert Victory*, which didn't go down very well. The next night the lads went out with petrol cans and set light to the cinema. The film was all right, but having spent the last two and a half years in the desert the last thing you wanted for amusement was to see *Desert Victory*.

Glossary

Ack-ack – slang for anti-aircraft (**AA**) fire from the phonetic alphabet in which 'Ack' for 'A'. By early 1943 replaced by 'Able', and now 'Alpha'. **'Ack'** was also used as shorthand for 'assistant', usually by the Royal Artillery. For example the NCO who assisted the gun-position officer was referred to as his 'ack'.

Adjutant – the CO's personal staff officer in a battalion or regiment in the British Army. In the Second World War, and for several years thereafter, there was no operations officer at this level, so the adjutant was responsible for all operational staff work as well as discipline and all other personnel matters.

AP – armour piercing (ammunition) – see **HE**.

Assembly Area – where infantry and armour about to attack marry up with each other and their other supporting arms: artillery, engineers and so forth. From here they will move to the **FUP**.

Bangalore torpedo – a metal tube packed with explosive, designed to be pushed into barbed-wire entanglements or other obstacles to blow a narrow gap.

BGS – Brigadier General Staff.

Bir – Arabic for a well.

Blighty one – a wound of sufficient severity that will probably result in you being evacuated back to the UK. The word Blighty comes from the Hindi word *bilayati*, meaning foreign. Used by the British in India as far back as the mid-1800s; for example, soda water was commonly called *bilayati pani*, or foreign water. *Blighty* was the British soldier's corruption of it. The word only came into common use as a term for Britain at the beginning of the First World War in France, in about 1915. It turns up in popular songs, such as: *Take me back to dear old Blighty, put me on the train for London town.*

Bofors – a quick-firing 40-mm anti-aircraft gun of Swedish design.

Bombardier – the Royal Artillery equivalent of a corporal.

Boys Anti-tank Rifle – a .55-inch anti-tank rifle that could penetrate 21 mm of armour at three hundred yards. Obsolete in 1939.

Bren – the British light machine gun of the Second World War and until the late 1950s. Fired a standard .303-inch round from a thirty-round magazine (usually loaded with twenty-eight rounds).

Brigade – a formation of two or more infantry battalions or armoured regiments, commanded by a brigadier.

Brigade Major (BM) – the senior operations officer of a brigade, *de facto* chief of staff.

Buckshee – free, costing nothing. From Arabic *baksheesh*, meaning a tip or gratuity, used by British Army in India from late 1800s on.

Carrier – a lightly armoured tracked vehicle, often called a Bren-gun carrier, although it was also used to carry the Vickers medium machine gun, and many other tasks.

CCS – Casualty Clearing Station.

C-in-C – Commander-in-Chief.

Concentration Area – where all the elements of an attacking force concentrate, having perhaps been moved in from locations many miles apart, or from a long distance away. From here they will move to an assembly area (see **Assembly Area**). In a Concentration Area, equipment may be refurbished or replaced, reinforcements received, and even some training carried out.

CO – Commanding Officer.

COPP – Combined Operations Pilotage Party; specialist swimmers who carried out beach reconnaissance and terminal guidance of landing craft. Usually taken to a point off the beach by submarine, and completed the last part of the journey by canoe and/or by swimming. The landings in North Africa in November 1942 were the first occasion COPPs were used on a major operation.

Corps – a formation of at least two divisions, commanded by a lieutenant general. Also a generic term for arms and services except armour, artillery and infantry, hence corps of Royal Engineers, Royal Signals, Royal Army Service Corps, Indian Army Service Corps, Royal Army Medical Corps, Indian Army Medical Corps and so on.

CSM – Company Sergeant Major.

DF – Defensive Fire, mortar, artillery, or machine-gun fire by troops in defensive positions against attacking troops or patrols. Usually pre-registered on a number of key places, and numbered, so a particular DF can be called down quickly by reference to its number. Guns and mortars will be laid on the DF SOS when not engaged on other tasks. As its name implies, the DF SOS is the target deemed to be the most dangerous to the defenders.

Direct Fire – weapons that have to be aimed directly at the target as opposed to indirect fire weapons such as mortars and artillery.

Division – a formation of two or more brigades, commanded by a major general.

Djebel – Tunisian for Jebel.

DSO – Distinguished Service Order instituted in 1886. Until the awards system was changed in 1994, it was a dual-role decoration, recognising gallantry at a level just below that qualifying for the VC by junior officers, and exceptional leadership in battle by senior officers. Officers of all three services were and are eligible.

Enfilade (fire) – fire from a flank, along a line of trenches, wire, minefields or attacking troops.

Erks – RAF slang for aircraftmen.

Fascines – bundles of brushwood, which could be dropped into a ditch to provide a quick means of bridging a gap; suitable only for tracked vehicles.

Flak – German slang for anti-aircraft fire; from the German for anti-aircraft gun *fliegerabwehrkanone*.

FOO – Forward Observation Officer, an artillery officer who directs artillery fire. Normally one with each forward rifle company and provided by artillery battery supporting the infantry battalion.

Folbot – originally a two-man, collapsible canoe built for recreational purposes by the Folbot Company. During the course of the Second World War, some eight marks of canoe were designed and built by the British to improve on the original design.

FUP – Forming Up Position, where the attacking units shake out into attacking formation before crossing the Start Line (see **Start Line**). The FUP will normally be right behind the Start Line.

G1 – short for GSO1, see **GSO** below.

GOC – General Officer Commanding.

GPO – Gun Position Officer.

GSO – General Staff Officer, a staff officer who dealt with General (G) Staff matters (operations, intelligence, planning and staff duties), as opposed to personnel (A short for Adjutant General's Staff), or logistic matters (Q short for Quartermaster General's Staff). The grades were GSO 1 (Lieutenant Colonel), GSO 2 (Major) and GSO 3 (Captain). The GSO 1 in a division was the senior operations staff officer, effectively the chief of staff. The AAG, or Assistant Adjutant General in a division was the senior personnel staff officer, and the AQMG, or Assistant Quartermaster General, in a division was the senior logistics staff officer.

HE – High Explosive.

H-Hour – the time that the leading troops cross the Start Line.

Honey tanks – M-3 Stuart tanks.

Hull-down – positioning a tank behind a hill or fold in the ground so that only its turret is visible to the enemy. It can fire its main gun (with the exception of a Grant) and the commander can see, without exposing the main part of the tank – the hull.

Hydro burner – a petrol-fuelled cooker.

In threes – a column of soldiers three abreast.

IO – Intelligence Officer.

Jebel – hill, mountain, or high piece of terrain (in Tunisia, Djebel).

Lead Pencil Delay fuse – a metal tube containing a strong spring pulled out to its full extent. When the retaining pin was removed, the spring was held in tension by a lead wire. A combination of the thickness of the wire and the outside temperature determined how long it took for the lead wire to snap, thus allowing the spring to drive a firing pin on to the detonator which set off the primer and the explosive. The warmer the temperature, the more malleable the lead wire, and the quicker it would break. Provided one could accurately forecast the temperature at the target, one could select the timer with the necessary thickness of lead wire to achieve the delay required.

LCM – Landing Craft Mechanised, depending on the mark, weighed between 37 and 42 tons, and capable of carrying between 16 and 30 tons.

Limber – two-wheeled wagon for carrying gun ammunition which, hooked to the gun, is towed by the gun tractor, vehicle, or horses.

Lysander – the high wing monoplane single-engine Westland Lysander came into service in 1938 as an Army co-operation aircraft. Maximum speed 211 mph, it was used as a transport for senior officers, and most famously for flying agents in behind enemy lines.

M&B tablets – named for the manufacturer, May & Baker. These would have been one of the sulphonamides, an early form of antibiotic.

Machine-Gun battalions – each infantry division had a machine gun battalion to provide fire support from thirty-six Vickers Medium Machine guns. These were converted from 'normal' infantry battalions, such as the 2nd Cheshires.

MC – Military Cross, instituted in 1914, and awarded to army officers of the rank of Major and below, and Warrant Officers, for gallantry in action. Now all ranks are eligible.

Mitchell – B-25, twin-engine, American medium bomber with crew of five. Good at attacking ground targets in support of ground troops.

MM – Military Medal, instituted in 1916, and awarded to army NCOs and soldiers for gallantry in action. Now discontinued, see **MC**.

MMG – Medium Machine Gun (see **Vickers**).

MO – medical officer.

Monitor – a shore bombardment vessel.

MTB – Motor Torpedo Boat, a small, fast vessel mainly armed with torpedoes.

NCO – Non-commissioned officer; from lance corporal to colour or staff sergeant. See also **Warrant Officer**.

Netting in – a time-consuming and laborious wireless procedure, necessary in the Second World War and for several years afterwards, and carried out after tuning the set, to ensure that all stations on the net can hear each other (everyone on the same frequency belongs to a net)

OC – Officer Commanding, applicable to commander of sub-units below battalion/regimental level: companies, batteries, squadrons, platoons, etc.

O Group – short for Orders Group, the group to which orders are given at any level of command from platoon to army. For example at platoon level, the platoon commander briefing his section commanders; the battalion CO briefing his company commanders; and at brigade level, the brigade commander briefing his battalion and supporting arms COs, and other people who need to know the plan.

OP – observation post.

Portee – both the two-pounder and six-pounder British anti-tank guns could be carried on the back of a truck, and fired from this position. This was known as a portee.

RA – Royal Artillery.

RAF – Royal Air Force.

RAP – Regimental Aid Post, the place where the medical officer (MO) of a battalion, or equivalent-size unit, set up his aid post. Usually the requirement here was to administer 'sophisticated first aid' to stabilise the casualty sufficiently to enable him to survive the next stage of evacuation.

Regiment (British and Indian Army) – originally of horse, dragoons or foot; raised by command of the king, and later parliament, and named after its colonel, originally a royal appointee. The regiment became the basic organisation of the British Army, for armour, artillery, engineers, signals and logistic units equivalent to battalions of those arms in other armies. In the case of the infantry, the battalion belongs to a regiment, of which there may be one or more battalions, and who may not serve together in the same area, or even in the same theatre of operations. In 1923 many British cavalry regiments were amalgamated, retaining both their old numbers, hence the 17th/21st Lancers was a combination of the 17th and 21st Lancers, not the 17th Battalion of the 21st Lancers. In typical idiosyncratic British fashion, this rule did not apply to infantry battalions, so that the 2nd/5th Sherwood Foresters was the 2nd of the 5th (TA) Battalion of the Sherwood Foresters Regiment. See **Territorial Army**. To add to the confusion, the Rifle Brigade was not a brigade, and the King's Royal Rifle Corps (KRRC) was not a corps; both were regiments of British infantry. The pre-independence Indian army was different again, so the 1st/9th Gurkha Rifles was the 1st Battalion of the 9th Gurkha Rifle Regiment, and the 4th/6th Rajputana Rifles was the 4th Battalion of the 6th Rajputana Rifle Regiment.

Regiment (German and Italian) – a formation of three infantry battalions, usually stronger than a British brigade.

Regimental Sergeant Major (RSM) – in the British Army, infantry battalions and regiments (artillery and armoured) all have a Warrant Officer Class 1 called the Regimental Sergeant Major. He is the commanding officer's right-hand man and adviser on many aspects of battalion/regiment daily life, especially matters involving the soldiers and NCOs. The CO and the RSM have very likely known each other since the former was a second lieutenant and the latter a young private or equivalent.

RT – radio telephone, another name for the wireless.

RTU – Returned to Unit, back to your parent unit, from an all-volunteer unit like the commandos, paratroops, SAS/SBS.

RV – rendezvous.

Sangar – a protective wall built of stones constructed in ground too hard to dig.

Sapper(s) – the equivalent of private in the Royal Engineers, or a name for all engineers.

SBS – there were two organisations with the acronym SBS in the Second World War. The first was founded as a Folbot Section in 1940 and was known as the Special Boat Section (SBS). The sections were numbered, and Number 2 SBS appears in this book. This was entirely separate from the Special Boat Squadron (also SBS) formed from a squadron of the Special Air Service in the Middle East after the North African campaign was over.

Scorpion Tank – a tank fitted with chain flails in front rotated by an auxiliary Ford engine. As the tank moves forward, the flails beat the ground to detonate mines and clear a path for armour following behind. In this campaign, rotor and flails were mounted on a Matilda Mk II.

Section – in the infantry, about eight to ten men commanded by a corporal. In the artillery, two guns.

Start Line – a line in the ground, usually a natural feature, wadi, bank, or fence, preferably at ninety degrees to the axis of advance, which marks the Start Line for the attack and is crossed at **H-Hour** in attack formation. Can be marked by tape if there is no natural feature which lends itself to being used as a Start Line.

Stick – an aircraft load of paratroops due to drop on one drop zone in one run over it.

Stonk – British army slang for a concentration of mortar or artillery fire.

Tac HQ – Tactical Headquarters, a small group including the CO, or brigade, divisional, corps, or army commander, forward of the main HQ.

Tank Types – see table at end of Glossary.

Territorial Army (TA) – part-time soldiers who are mobilised in war. The pre-1939 TA was a large organisation consisting of regiments and battalions of all arms; armour, artillery, engineers, signals, infantry, service corps, etc.

VC – Victoria Cross, the highest British award for bravery in the face of the enemy. To date, in the 145 years since its inception by Queen Victoria during the Crimean War of 1854–55, only 1,358 VCs have been awarded, including a handful of double VCs, and the one presented to the American Unknown Warrior at Arlington. This figure includes the many awarded to Imperial, Commonwealth and Dominion servicemen.

Very pistol – a smooth-bore pistol for firing green, white or red Very signal cartridges. Hence Very lights.

Vickers Medium Machine Gun – First World War vintage, belt-fed, water-cooled machine gun, rate of fire five hundred rounds per minute. Maximum range with Mark VIII Z ammunition, 4,500 yards. Last fired in action in 1962.

Wadi – Arabic for valley, or riverbed; in French North Africa sometimes Oued.

Wagon Lines – the artillery name for the area in which the transport waited while the guns were in action.

Yeomanry – British volunteer cavalry, formed in 1794 by William Pitt to provide cavalry to assist in the defence of Britain in the event of invasion by the French. In 1921, some Yeomanry regiments (by now part of the Territorial Army) were converted to artillery or signals. In 1939 some Yeomanry, with their horses, were sent to Palestine as part of the 1st Cavalry Division. These mounted units were converted to armour in 1941 and were often supported by Yeomanry artillery regiments such as the South Notts Hussars.

TANKS

The main types of tank used by both sides, as the campaign progressed between 1940 and May 1943, are listed in the table below:

British

Type	Main Armament	Thickest Armour	Remarks
Cruiser A 13	One two-pounder	30-mm	
Crusader Mk II	One two-pounder	49-mm	Unreliable and thin-skinned
Crusader Mk III	One six-pounder	49-mm	Still as unsatisfactory as the Mk II despite bigger gun
Matilda Mk II	One two-pounder	78-mm	Also called an Infantry or I tank
Valentine Mk II	One two-pounder	65-mm	An unsatisfactory tank
Valentine Mk IX	One six-pounder	65-mm	Still unsatisfactory tank
Stuart Mk I	One 37-mm	44-mm	American tank also known as the 'Honey'
Grant Mk I	One 75-mm M2 in sponson One 37-mm in turret	57-mm	Also known as Lee/Grant
Sherman Mk II & III	One 75-mm M3	57-mm sloped armour	Mk III had a diesel engine
Churchill Mk I and III	Two-pounder Six-pounder	102-mm	

German

Type (Panzer-kampfwagon) Pzkw	Main Armament	Thickest Armour	Remarks
Pzkw III	One 50-mm short	62-mm	
Pzkw III model J	One 50-mm long	50-mm	Gun equivalent to six-pounder
Pzkw III	One 75-mm short	50-mm	spaced armour
Pzkw IV Model E	One 75-mm short	60-mm	
Pzkw IV Model F2	One 75-mm long	50-mm	
Pzkw VI Tiger	One 88-mm long	102-mm	Only about 22 of these tanks – all in Tunisia

Italian

Type	Main Armament	Thickest Armour	Remarks
M13/40	One 47-mm	40-mm	
M14/41	One 47-mm	40-mm	Better engine than M13

Index of Contributors

Number in brackets denotes IWM Sound Archive catalogue number.
Page numbers in **bold** refer to photographs.

General Index

Entries in **bold** indicate photographs or maps.